PAINE AND JEFFERSON
in the Age of Revolutions

JEFFERSONIAN AMERICA

Jan Ellen Lewis, Peter S. Onuf, *and* Andrew O'Shaughnessy

Series Editors

PAINE *and* JEFFERSON
in the Age of Revolutions

EDITED BY

Simon P. Newman

AND

Peter S. Onuf

UNIVERSITY OF VIRGINIA PRESS
Charlottesville and London

University of Virginia Press
© 2013 by the Rector and Visitors of the University of Virginia
All rights reserved
Printed in the United States of America on acid-free paper

First published 2013

1 3 5 7 9 7 8 6 4 2

Library of Congress Cataloging-in-Publication Data
Paine and Jefferson in the age of revolutions /
edited by Simon P. Newman and Peter S. Onuf.
       pages   cm. — (Jeffersonian America)
Includes bibliographical references and index.
ISBN 978-0-8139-3476-1 (cloth : alk. paper) — ISBN 978-0-8139-3477-8 (e-book)
1. Paine, Thomas, 1737–1809—Philosophy. 2. Paine, Thomas, 1737–1809—Influence.
3. Jefferson, Thomas, 1743–1826—Philosophy. 4. Jefferson, Thomas, 1743–1826—Influence.
5. United States—History—Revolution, 1775–1783. 6. France—History—Revolution,
1789–1799. I. Newman, Simon P. (Simon Peter), 1960– author, editor of compilation.
II. Onuf, Peter S., editor of compilation.
JC177.A4P35 2013
321.8092′273—dc23   2013013750

MONTICELLO
Preparation of this volume has been supported by
the Thomas Jefferson Foundation

CONTENTS

Introduction   1
    Simon P. Newman and Peter S. Onuf

PART I. PAINE AND JEFFERSON: RADICALS AND DEMOCRATS

The Radicalism of Thomas Jefferson and Thomas Paine Considered   13
    Gordon S. Wood

"The Whole Object of the Present Controversy": The Early Constitutionalism of Paine and Jefferson   26
    Francis D. Cogliano

Thomas Paine's Early Radicalism, 1768-1783   49
    Jack Fruchtman Jr.

Paine, Jefferson, and Revolutionary Radicalism in Early National America   71
    Simon P. Newman

Paine, Jefferson, and the Modern Ideas of Democracy and the Nation   95
    Armin Mattes

PART II. JEFFERSON AND PAINE'S EUROPE: FRIENDS, AUDIENCE, RECEPTION, AND REPUTATION

Thomas Paine and Benjamin Franklin's French Circle   121
    Philipp Ziesche

Revolutionaries in Paris: Paine, Jefferson, and Democracy   137
    Mark Philp

CONTENTS

The Troubled Reception of Thomas Paine in France, Germany, the Netherlands, and Scandinavia — 161
Thomas Munck

PART III. COMMONALITIES AND DIFFERENCES: PAINE AND JEFFERSON, PAINE VERSUS JEFFERSON

Empire without Colonies: Paine, Jefferson, and the Nookta Crisis — 185
Edward G. Gray

Thomas Paine and Jeffersonian America — 209
Emma Macleod

Thomas Jefferson's Portrait of Thomas Paine — 229
Gaye Wilson

Two Paths from Revolution: Jefferson, Paine, and the Radicalization of Enlightenment Thought — 252
Michael Zuckert

Conclusion: Thomas Paine in the Atlantic Historical Imagination — 277
Seth Cotlar

Notes on Contributors — 297
Index — 301

PAINE AND JEFFERSON
in the Age of Revolutions

Introduction

SIMON P. NEWMAN and PETER S. ONUF

On March 4, 1809, Thomas Jefferson concluded his second term as president of the United States and retired from public life. Three months later, on June 8, Thomas Paine died in Greenwich Village, New York City. To mark the bicentennial of Paine's death, a small group of scholars gathered at the Reform Club in London under the auspices of the Robert H. Smith International Center for Jefferson Studies. For three days, we discussed Thomas Paine's place and significance in the Age of Revolution, often in direct comparison with his friend and fellow radical, Thomas Jefferson. This volume of essays is the result of that meeting in London's great monument to democratic reform. Remarkably, this is the first collection of scholarly essays on Paine to have been published by a major press, and the first to examine Paine and Jefferson in relation to one another.

Much can be learned by investigating Paine in this comparative light. Paine and Jefferson were both participants in the early and most radical phases of the American Revolution, and they remained steadfast defenders of the new republic throughout their lives. The two men defy easy categorization. Paine, in particular, does not sit easily in the pantheon of the founders, nor has he been fully integrated into any of the major historiographical schools of the American founding. Instead, historians have employed Paine to support a wide array of often conflicting interpretations, glossing over anything that he wrote or said that contradicts their arguments. Progressive historians portrayed Paine as the embodiment of a radical American Revolution, while ignoring his support of what they interpreted as a counter-revolutionary federal constitution. Charles and Mary Beard believed that "Paine's services to the Revolution were beyond calculation," and they lamented the absence of this "fiery radical" during the Constitutional Convention of 1787. Despite, or perhaps because of, Paine's support of the Constitution, he was not mentioned once in Charles Beard's epochal *An Economic Interpretation of the Constitution*.[1]

A generation later, Louis Hartz portrayed a consensual rather than a radical Paine whose anti-monarchism reflected the already existing liberal opinions of Americans. For Hartz, Paine was "a common sense philosopher . . . [who] had come to the most common sense country in the world." Hardly a radical, Hartz's Paine simply articulated the sentiments of liberal-minded colonists. Those historians who subsequently elaborated a "republican synthesis" in place of this liberal consensus acknowledged Paine's contribution to the American Revolutionary cause, but neglected radical ideas that did not fit their interpretive framework. In his great work on the ideology of the American Revolution, Bernard Bailyn wrote more about attacks on Paine's radicalism than on what Paine actually wrote and argued.[2]

It is not only academics who have selectively appropriated Paine to serve their interpretative purposes. In late 1963, for example, the National Emergency Civil Liberties Committee (NECLC) presented a newly created Tom Paine Award to Bob Dylan, which he received with a short speech lauding contemporary political activists such as the members of the Student Nonviolent Coordinating Committee. On the other side of the political spectrum from the NECLC, libertarian conservatives such as Ronald Reagan have approvingly quoted Paine's defense of individual liberty and his attacks on overly large and powerful government.[3]

Sophia Rosenfeld's recent *Common Sense: A Political History* has sought to place Paine along a well-traveled political continuum by demonstrating that throughout the eighteenth century, "common sense" was employed by both reactionaries and radicals to present their partisan ideals in the guise of uncontroversial truth. In this light, Paine appears less as an idealistic radical and more as a polemicist who brilliantly deployed popular language to mobilize patriotic resistance to the Crown. His *Common Sense* was purchased by tens of thousands, and read by many more, and it clearly reached a far larger audience than did any of the more conservative articulations of this Enlightenment philosophy.[4]

Seth Cotlar, in another recent volume, has argued that Paine helped inspire a radical democratic sensibility in the early American republic, with adherents favoring a participatory democratic nation. Cotlar suggests that newspapers and election rhetoric illustrate this wave of democratic enthusiasm, and like Rosenfeld, Cotlar is also careful to situate Paine and his beliefs in a transatlantic context.[5]

Yet despite this excellent recent work, Paine continues to appear as a far more one-dimensional historical figure than does Jefferson. It remains far easier to recount the narrative of his remarkable life than to comprehend the nature and significance of ideas and writings that have resonated so differently with so many different kinds of people in the two centuries since his death. Paine was born in 1737 in the Norfolk market town of Thetford, and he worked in various careers and locations in England before departing for the colony of Pennsylvania in 1774. As editor of the *Pennsylvania Magazine*, his literary reputation grew, culminating with the publication of *Common Sense* in January 1776—the most widely read and influential political pamphlet of the entire American Revolutionary struggle. During the early years of the war, he served with the Continental Army, and then with the Continental Congress, and wrote a series of essays known as *The American Crisis*, designed to rouse popular support for the patriot cause.

During the mid-1780s, Paine worked on his design for an iron bridge, which he took to Europe in 1787. The early stages of the French Revolution soon commanded his attention, and Paine was thrust into the second great revolution of his age, publishing *Rights of Man* in 1791 in response to Edmund Burke's highly critical *Reflections on the Revolution in France*. Although he spoke little French, Paine was elected as a deputy to the National Convention in late 1792. Soon he was mired in the internecine warfare of French Revolutionary politics, and after bravely arguing against the execution of Louis XVI, Paine rapidly lost ground. At the end of 1793, he was denounced, arrested, and imprisoned. Fortunate not to be executed, Paine was not released until November 1794.

Paine published the two-part *Age of Reason* between 1793 and 1795, and then in 1796 he published an acerbic open letter to his former comrade, George Washington, complaining that the president and his administration had done too little to protect Paine, an American citizen, during his imprisonment in Paris. In that same year, Paine published both *Agrarian Justice* and *Decline and Fall of the English System of Finance*.

Fearing capture by the British Royal Navy, Paine did not venture out of France until 1802, when a suspension in the Franco-British wars and an invitation from President Thomas Jefferson persuaded him to return to the United States. He continued to write and publish various essays, and to correspond with friends, but increasingly burdened by ill health, he stayed with friends and in rented accommodation, dying in Madame Bonneville's Greenwich Village house in June 1809. Refused interment in the Quaker burial grounds, Paine was laid to rest on his farm in New Rochelle.[6]

The essays collected in this volume examine the different contexts within which Paine pursued his eventful career, offering fresh insights into his controversial reputation on both sides of the Atlantic. Paine was a gifted polemicist, the master of a new political vernacular who effectively communicated with a broad new political public and thus earned the enmity of defenders of the old order; he was also a serious thinker who attempted to make sense of the revolutionary changes that he had helped unleash. There was no one quite like Paine, as these essays confirm. But that does not mean we cannot situate him better—in his British, American, and French contexts, and in relation to his Revolutionary friends and counter-Revolutionary foes.

The most illuminating comparison, we suggest, is with Thomas Jefferson, another iconic figure of the democratic Enlightenment. Generations of scholarship dealing with Jefferson has given historians a nuanced understanding of a complex and often contradictory man, and whether in the latest academic study of Jefferson, or in the tours given by Monticello guides, we are now familiar with the paradox of an elite planter with democratic sensibilities, a slave owner whose best-known words enshrined human equality as a natural right. In stark contrast, much of the work on Paine has focused on whatever aspect of his beliefs and actions most attracted or repelled the beholder, and he has often appeared as a one-dimensional hero (or villain) of left or right. This began during Paine's lifetime and has continued to the present, from attacks on him as a godless infidel to celebrations of his egalitarian rationalism.

This volume's juxtaposition of these two great democrats in different times and contexts gives us a more nuanced view of Paine. The ideological and philosophical affinities of the artisan and aristocrat testify to the extraordinary, epochal changes they witnessed; their subsequent careers suggest the fundamental diversity of the Revolutionary experience and divergent national histories in the post-Revolutionary age. Jefferson never forgot or neglected Paine, even as Paine's reputation waned and Jefferson ascended to the presidency in his "Revolution of 1800." The relationship between Paine and Jefferson provides a crucial and illuminating context for interpreting both men. By foregrounding these two great revolutionaries, we hope to enhance understanding of Paine's role and significance in the Age of Revolution, for this was as much the "Age of Paine" as it was, for Americans, the "Age of Jefferson."

Part I of the volume explores Paine's and Jefferson's radicalism. Gordon S. Wood's essay explores the Revolutionary enthusiasm shared by Paine and Jefferson. With their common faith in the innate moral goodness and common sense of their fellow man, Paine and Jefferson trusted the people more and government less than did most of their fellow Americans. While the assertion that all men were *created* equal was far from novel, a belief that all men *remained* equal throughout their lives was, Wood contends, at the heart of Painite and Jeffersonian radicalism. Both men accepted that virtue emanated from participation in a harmonious society, nurturing the affections and sensibilities that bound an enlightened people together. Republics depended upon the maintenance of a virtuous society for their very survival, and both Paine and Jefferson lauded civil society while decrying government, which, along with state-building, burgeoning public debts, and chronic warfare, was more likely to do ill than good. Wood suggests that the major difference between Paine and Jefferson was not in sentiment, but in the desire to publicly articulate personal belief. As a party leader and as president, Jefferson was cautious about publicizing opinions that Paine was eager to disseminate, and this, Wood believes, is one of the main reasons why Americans have treated the two men so differently.

Francis D. Cogliano points out that Paine's and Jefferson's earliest efforts as constitutional reformers in their respective states are much less well known than their contributions to the movement for national independence. The two men who were so influential in destroying monarchical government in America played significant roles in the construction of republican forms of government in Pennsylvania and in Virginia, and Cogliano explores the similarities and striking differences between their ideas about republican society and government. Paine's republicanism took shape in the towns of Georgian England and then crystallized in the social and political strife of Revolutionary Philadelphia, while Jefferson's was born in the plantation society of rural Virginia. These very different backgrounds nurtured some notable differences, such as Paine's support for unicameralism, in opposition to Jefferson's preference for bicameralism. However, Cogliano suggests that what is most striking was Paine's and Jefferson's shared objective of transforming Revolutionary America by means of an expanded franchise and a capacious republican definition of citizenship.

Jack Fruchtman Jr.'s essay centers on Paine's *Letter to the Abbé Raynal* (1782), suggesting that this lesser-known piece was the key link between Paine's justification of American independence in *Common Sense* and his espousal of international republican revolution in *Rights of Man*. In trying to correct what he saw as the abbé Raynal's errors in his history of the American Revolution, Paine articulated his own understanding of the event and its significance. He affirmed in the most striking terms yet that the American Revolution was a pivotal event in world history, initiating republican revolution far beyond America's own borders. Rejecting Raynal's contention that British taxes were the major cause of the Revolution, Paine employed universal language to describe the Revolutionary War as a struggle between tyranny and servitude on one hand, and republicanism and liberty on the other. Fruchtman suggests that Paine's letter to Raynal was the closest he came to completing his proposed history of the American Revolution, and that it required him to consider republicanism's universal significance. This pivotal document, Fruchtman contends, encouraged Paine to see himself as an international revolutionary, thinking and acting beyond the borders of the new American republic.

Paine's radicalism may have given him iconic status among the early supporters of Jefferson's nascent Republican Party, Simon Newman shows, but deteriorating Franco-American relations, the increasing radicalism of Paine's publications, and, most especially, his printed attack on Washington, massively eroded Paine's popularity. He became an easy target for Federalists, who were eager to associate Jefferson and his party with the bloody radicalism and alleged godlessness of Jacobin revolution. As a result, Jeffersonian Republicans strove to distance themselves from controversial radicals such as Paine, casting themselves instead as moderate nationalists. As enthusiasm for the transnational democratic movement waned in the late 1790s, Paine all but disappeared from the festive lexicon of the Jeffersonian Republicans, and toasts to Jefferson replaced those that had honored Paine.

For Paine and fellow cosmopolitan patriots, revolution promised to liberate the people from the shackles of Old Regime tyranny. Democracy and national self-determination were inextricably linked. In the concluding essay in the first section, Armin Mattes shows that optimistic faith was shattered. The French Revolution, Mattes contends, changed ideas about what constituted the nation, not only in France, but also in the United States. In France, there was a bloody clash between two irreconcilable visions of society—one based on equality and the other on hierarchy, or inequality—and in its wake, American politics featured a less bloody, yet ideologically fraught struggle over similar principles. Paine and Jefferson played a key role in both of these struggles, as they helped to chart the emergence of a modern conception of democracy and nationhood.

The essays in Part II explore Paine's presence and impact in Europe. As becomes clear in these essays, Jefferson was less well known and less influential than Paine. Philipp Ziesche illuminates the way in which Paine was able to

INTRODUCTION

integrate himself so quickly and so effectively into French society, and thus come to play such an active role in the early stages of the French Revolution. Benjamin Franklin was particularly important in this regard. When Paine decided in 1787 to take his design for an iron bridge to Paris, he knew virtually nobody in France other than Jefferson and the Marquis de Lafayette, and so turned to Franklin, who generously provided Paine with four warm recommendations. These were markedly different in style and tone from the formulaic letter of introduction Franklin had written for Paine when he traveled to America in 1774, or indeed from the many such letters Franklin had written for other Britons crossing the Atlantic. With these letters, and with eight more letters from Franklin to his French friends, Paine gained entrée into Franklin's circle of leading French politicians, scientists, and intellectuals. In many cases, these letters represented the first communication from Franklin since his return to America, and thus they helped ensure a warm welcome for Paine. Ziesche suggests that not only did Franklin give Paine's Revolutionary career in France an important boost, but also that Franklin's and Paine's experiences in Paris encouraged them to develop similar ideas about the dangers of hereditary privilege.

Mark Philp acknowledges that the American Revolution profoundly influenced Paine's and Jefferson's reactions to the French Revolution, but suggests that Paine's years in London and in Paris during the late 1780s and early 1790s reshaped his interpretation and understanding of both revolutions. When Jefferson and Paine were both in Europe during the two years preceding the fall of the Bastille, their interpretations of the changes wrought by revolution overlapped, as both emphasized the universality of the American experience. After Jefferson's return to the United States, the massive political and social upheaval of the Revolutionary age dramatically transformed Paine's political thought. Between 1787 and 1792, Paine's political vision broadened dramatically as he began to envision a revolutionary transformation of Europe along American lines, a process that led him to revise his understanding of what had happened in America. Rather than seeing Paine moving inevitably toward theories of government based on popular sovereignty and an ensuing espousal of the language of representative democracy, Philp underscores the radically contingent circumstances that shaped the development of Paine's thinking.

While Philp sheds light on the significance and the impact of Paine's ideas and publications in Britain and America, Thomas Munck explores the revolutionary's influence beyond France. Paine's *Rights of Man* would appear to have great relevance to many western Europeans, yet the revolutionary and his works were less well known and appear to have been far less influential in

Germany, the Netherlands, and Scandinavia. In part this was because English-language texts often remained untranslated and inaccessible to audiences beyond France. Yet Munck shows that Enlightenment thought often transcended language barriers and traveled across northern and northwestern Europe, with literary reviews summarizing and discussing key foreign-language books and articles. Paine did not fare well in many of these publications, and *Age of Reason* met as chilly a response in continental Europe as it did in Britain and America.

The four essays that make up Part III of this volume explore the commonalities and differences between Paine and Jefferson, with particular reference to the period after Paine's return to the United States in 1802. Edward G. Gray examines the little-known Nootka Sound Crisis of 1790, one of the first diplomatic incidents confronted by the American republic, and one which might conceivably have sparked another major war in North America. Both Jefferson and Paine were alarmed at the prospect, albeit for somewhat different reasons. Jefferson feared European conflict in and colonization of the lands between the western boundary of the United States and the Pacific Ocean, and the threat that this would pose to the future of the American republic. Paine, however, seems to have been more confident about American prospects and rather more alarmed by the thought that such a war might prompt the British government to crush an increasingly vocal reform movement at home and thus forestall the spread of revolutionary republicanism. Gray suggests, however, that Paine's position was closer to that of Jefferson's than historians might expect, with both men embracing elements of an eighteenth-century form of statecraft. Paine may have been more Jeffersonian than we have realized in his concern with the realities of state power politics. It may also be true, as Gray suggests, that Jefferson was more Painite than we have assumed, in his espousal of radical political ideas.

Emma Macleod notes that throughout his time in Europe Paine regularly referred to America as a successful republic, though he feared for its success during the Washington and Adams presidencies. Militant radical émigrés from Europe condemned Jefferson's moderate leadership, but Paine remained an enthusiastic supporter, confident in the new nation's bright future. Paine's public support for Jefferson was not reciprocated; Jefferson's friendship with his Revolutionary compatriot remained a private affair.

From his place as one of the best known of the early radical revolutionaries, and as a hero of the early Jeffersonian Republicans—one who had joined their leader in welcoming the French Revolution—Paine all but disappeared from the political culture of the Republicans. Only in private could Jefferson

INTRODUCTION

continue to maintain cordial relations with Paine, a relationship symbolized by the portrait of Paine owned by Jefferson. Gaye Wilson explores this piece and its place in Jefferson's gallery of American Revolutionary heroes. Using the history of the portrait and its place in Jefferson's collection, Wilson shows that while the president sought to avoid the commotion that would ensue from any public display of affection for Paine, he nonetheless regarded Paine as a comrade in arms and a leading figure of the Age of Revolution.

Michael Zuckert then explores the effects of the French Revolution on both Paine and Jefferson. Both were radicalized, yet while other scholars in this collection have emphasized their common ground, Zuckert sees striking differences. He compares Jefferson's development of a theory of ward republicanism and his calls for participatory republicanism, with Paine's shift from his early libertarianism to the "welfarism" of his later writings on economic rights. Paine's ideas were rooted in the European context of an ancien régime, while Jefferson's depended upon access to free land in the New World. Despite their differences, the French Revolution forced both men to confront the problems of social justice and property rights, and each in his distinctive way became increasingly radical.

The volume concludes with Seth Cotlar's analysis of the complicated and contradictory understandings of Paine that persist in both historical writing and modern politics. Cotlar observes that people with particular ideas and agendas tend to focus on only one element of Paine's corpus, or on one period in his prolific career. Though Paine, and many of his contemporaries, insisted that he remained consistent in his beliefs throughout his career, Cotlar notes that radically changing circumstances prompted Paine to pose enduring political questions with no easy solutions. Paine's complexity arises from his eager embrace of "open-ended and essentially unresolvable questions that lay at the heart of the political culture bequeathed to the Atlantic World by the eighteenth century's Age of Revolution."

Cotlar concludes that we should apply the more-nuanced readings of Jefferson that fill modern scholarship to Paine. If we "loosen our grip on Paine the symbol," Cotlar suggests, we can evaluate him "more sympathetically as a socially embedded thinker whose effectiveness derived not from the emblematic clarity and consistency of his thought, but from his ability to shift his ground as the world changed around him." Paine's Revolutionary experiences on both sides of the Atlantic led him to engage with radically different and rapidly changing circumstances and challenges. If Paine helped bring down the ancien régime, he also sought to work out the implications of his radically egalitarian democratic principles for the new, post-revolutionary world.

The result is writings and ideas that can appear, and perhaps are, inherently contradictory.

Taken together, the essays in this collection illuminate Paine as a man of sometimes contradictory ideas and attitudes. While he thought of himself, and was often portrayed, as a lifelong revolutionary, his beliefs and actions were as complicated as was his reputation during his lifetime. Paine was far more than a one-dimensional cipher, and like Jefferson, the more we learn about him, the more complex he becomes. Countering the caricatures of Paine that have dominated historical scholarship as well as partisan polemics, the authors of this volume have illuminated the full complexity of his Revolutionary legacy. In doing so, they restore Paine to the place he deserves—by Jefferson's side in the history of modern democracy.

NOTES

1. See Charles A. Beard and Mary R. Beard, *The Rise of American Civilization* (London: Jonathan Cape, 1930), 261, 311; and Charles A. Beard, *An Economic Interpretation of the Constitution of the United States* (New York: Macmillan, 1913).

2. Louis Hartz, *The Liberal Tradition in America: An Interpretation of American Political Thought since the Revolution* (1955; repr., New York: Harcourt, Brace, Jovanovich, 1983), 73; Bernard Bailyn, *The Ideological Origins of the American Revolution* (1967; repr., Cambridge: Belknap Press of Harvard University Press, 1982), 285–90.

3. Anthony DeCurtis, "Bob Dylan as Songwriter," in *The Cambridge Companion to Bob Dylan*, ed. Kevin J. H. Dettmar (Cambridge: Cambridge University Press, 2009), 49–51; John Patrick Diggins, *Ronald Reagan: Fate, Freedom, and the Making of History* (New York: Norton, 2007), xviii–xix, 15, 48–52.

4. Sophia Rosenfeld, *Common Sense: A Political History* (Cambridge, Mass.: Harvard University Press, 2011).

5. Seth Cotlar, *Tom Paine's America: The Rise and Fall of Transatlantic Radicalism in the Early Republic* (Charlottesville: University of Virginia Press, 2011).

6. Leading studies of Thomas Paine include Alfred Owen Aldridge, *Man of Reason: The Life of Thomas Paine* (London: Cresset Press, 1960); David Freeman Hawke, *Paine* (New York: Harper and Row, 1974); Eric Foner, *Tom Paine and Revolutionary America* (New York: Oxford University Press, 1976); Ian Dyck, *Citizen of the World: Essays on Thomas Paine* (New York: St. Martin's, 1988); John Keane, *Tom Paine: A Political Life* (London: Bloomsbury, 1995); Jack Fruchtman Jr., *Thomas Paine: Apostle of Freedom* (New York: Four Walls Eight Windows, 1994); Rosenfeld, *Common Sense;* and Cotlar, *Tom Paine's America*.

I

PAINE AND JEFFERSON
Radicals and Democrats

The Radicalism of Thomas Jefferson and Thomas Paine Considered

GORDON S. WOOD

THOMAS JEFFERSON and Thomas Paine could not have been more different in background and temperament. Jefferson was a wealthy slaveholding aristocrat from Virginia who was as well connected socially as anyone in America. His mother was a Randolph, perhaps the most prestigious family in all of Virginia, and positions in his society came easy to him. Personally, he was cool, reserved, and self-possessed. He disliked personal controversy and was always charming in face-to-face relations with both friends and enemies. Although he played at being casual, he was utterly civilized and genteel. He mastered several languages, including those of antiquity, and he spent his life trying to discover (and acquire) what was the best and most enlightened in the world of the eighteenth century. He prided himself on his manners and taste; indeed, he became an impresario for his countrymen, advising them on what was proper in everything from the arts to wine. There was almost nothing he did not know about. "Without having quitted his own country," this earnest autodidact with a voracious appetite for learning had become, as the French visitor Chevalier de Chastellux noted in the early 1780s, "an American who . . . is at once a Musician, a Draftsman, Surveyor, Astronomer, Natural Philosopher, Jurist, and Statesman."[1]

By contrast, Paine was a free-floating individual who, as critics said, lacked social connections of any kind. He came from the ranks of the middling sorts, and, unlike, say, Benjamin Franklin, he never really shed his obscure and lowly origins. He had some education but did not attend college, and he knew no languages except English. He spent the first half of his life jumping from one job to another, first as a stay-maker like his father, then as a teacher, next a failed businessman, then back to stay-making, followed by two failed attempts as an excise collector; he also tried running a tobacco shop. He was slovenly and lazy and was described as "coarse and uncouth in his manners."[2] His temperament was fiery and passionate, and he loved his liquor and confrontations of all sorts. He came to America at age thirty-seven full of anger at a world that had not recognized his talents.

Yet as dissimilar as Jefferson and Paine were from one another, they shared a common outlook on the world, an ideology that was as radical for the eighteenth century as Marxism would be for the nineteenth. As a British dinner partner observed in 1792, Jefferson in conversation was "a vigorous stickler for revolutions and for the downfall of an aristocracy. . . . In fact, like his friend T. Payne, he cannot live but in a revolution, and all events in Europe are only considered by him in the relation they bear to the probability of a revolution to be produced by them."[3]

Jefferson and Paine were good republicans who believed in the rights of man. They thought that all government should be derived from the people and that no one should hold office by hereditary right. No American trusted the people at large or outside of government more than did these two radicals, Jefferson and Paine.

This confidence flowed from their magnanimous view of human nature. Both men had an extraordinary faith in the moral capacity of ordinary people. Being one of the ordinary people, Paine had a natural tendency to trust them. But even Jefferson, the natural aristocrat, on most things trusted ordinary people far more than he trusted his aristocratic colleagues, who, he believed, were very apt to become wolves if they could. Unlike the elite, common people were not deceptive or deceitful; they wore their hearts on their sleeves and were sincere. An American republican world dominated by common folk would end the deceit and dissembling so characteristic of courtiers and monarchies. "Let those flatter who fear: it is not an American art," said Jefferson.[4]

Paine agreed that everyone shared a similar social or moral sense. Appeals to common sense, he said, were "appeals to those feelings without which we should be incapable of discharging the duties of life or enjoying the felicities of it."[5] Reason might be unevenly distributed throughout society, but everyone, even the most lowly of persons, had senses and could feel. In all of his writings, he said his "principal design is to form the disposition of the people to the measures which I am fully persuaded it is their interest and duty to adopt, and which need no other force to accomplish them than the force of being felt."[6]

But Paine and Jefferson went further in their trust in common people. By assuming that ordinary people had personal realities equal to their own, Paine and Jefferson helped to give birth to what perhaps is best described as the modern humanitarian sensibility—a powerful force that we of the twenty-first century have inherited and further expanded. They, like most other revolutionary leaders, shared the liberal premises of Lockean sensationalism: that all men were born equal and that only the environment working on their senses made them different. These premises were essential to the growing sense of sympathy for other human creatures felt by enlightened people in the eighteenth century. Once the liberally educated came to believe that they could control their environment and educate the vulgar and lowly to become something other than what the traditional society had presumed they were destined to be, then the enlightened few began to expand their sense of moral responsibility for the vice and ignorance they saw in others and to experience feelings of common humanity with them.

Thus, despite their acceptance of differences among people—differences created through the environment operating on people's senses—both Jefferson and Paine concluded that all men were basically alike, that they all partook of the same common nature. It was this commonality that linked people together in natural affection and made it possible for them to share each other's feelings. There was something in each human being—some sort of moral sense or sympathetic instinct—that made possible natural compassion and affection. Indeed, wrote Paine, "instinct in animals does not act with stronger impulse, than the principles of society and civilization operate in man." Even the lowliest of persons, even black slaves, Jefferson believed, had this sense of sympathy or moral feeling for others. All human beings, said Jefferson, rich and poor, white and black, had "implanted in their breasts" this "moral instinct," this "love of others." Everyone, whatever their differences of education, instinctively knew right from wrong. "State a moral case to a ploughman and a professor," said Jefferson; the ploughman will decide it as well, and often better than the professor, "because he has not been led astray by artificial rules."[7]

This belief in the equal moral worth and equal moral authority of every individual was the real source of both Jefferson's and Paine's democratic equality, an equality that was far more potent than merely the Lockean idea that everyone started at birth with the same blank sheet. The idea that all men were *created* equal had actually become a cliché among the enlightened in the late eighteenth century. To believe that all men *remained* equal throughout their adult lives was, however, another matter, and truly radical. Not that Jefferson or Paine denied the obvious differences among individuals that exist—that some individuals are taller, smarter, more handsome than others. But rather, both radicals posited that, at bottom, every single individual, man or woman, black or white, had a common moral or social sense that tied him or her to other individuals. None of the other leading founders believed what Jefferson believed—not Washington, not Hamilton, not Adams. And since no democracy can intelligibly exist without some such belief that at heart everyone is the same, Jefferson's position as the supreme apostle of American democracy seems not only legitimate, but necessary to the well-being of the nation. So Lincoln's claim of "all honor to Jefferson" still stands, and remains as a rebuke to modern critics of Jefferson's hypocrisy.

Jefferson's and Paine's assumption that people possessed an innate moral or social sense had other important implications. It lay behind their belief in the natural harmony of society and in their advocacy of minimal government. People, they claimed, had an inherent need to socialize with one another and were naturally benevolent and affable. This benevolence and sociability became a modern substitute for the ascetic and Spartan virtue of the ancient republics. This new modern virtue, as David Hume pointed out, was much more in accord with the growing commercialization and refinement of the enlightened and civilized eighteenth century than the austere and severe virtue of the ancients.

The classical virtue of antiquity had flowed from the citizen's participation in politics; government had been the source of the citizen's civic consciousness and public-spiritedness. But the modern virtue of Jefferson, Paine, and other eighteenth-century liberals flowed from the citizen's participation in society, not in government. Society, to eighteenth-century liberals, was harmonious and compassionate. We today may believe that society, with its class antagonisms, business and capitalist exploitation, and racial prejudices, by itself breeds the ills and cruelties that plague us. But for eighteenth-century radicals, society was benign; it created sympathy, affability, and the new domesticated virtue. By mingling in drawing rooms, clubs, and coffeehouses, by partaking in the innumerable interchanges of the daily comings and goings of modern life, people developed affection and fellow-feeling, which were all the adhesives really necessary to hold an enlightened people together. Some even argued that commerce, that traditional enemy of classical virtue, was in fact a source of modern virtue. Because it encouraged intercourse and confidence among people and nations, commerce actually contributed to benevolence and fellow-feeling.

The opening paragraph of Thomas Paine's *Common Sense* articulated brilliantly this distinction between society and government. Society and government were different things, said Paine, and they have different origins. "Society is produced by our wants and government by our wickedness." Society "promotes our happiness *positively* by uniting our affections"; government "*negatively* by restraining our vices. The one encourages intercourse, the other creates distinctions. . . . Society in every state was a blessing; but government even in its best state was but a necessary evil; in its worst state an intolerable one."[8] If only the natural tendencies of people to love and care for one another were allowed to flow freely, unclogged by the artificial interference of government, particularly monarchical government, the most devout republicans, like Paine and Jefferson, believed that society would prosper and hold itself together.

These liberal ideas that society was naturally autonomous and self-regulating and that everyone possessed a common moral and social sense were no utopian fantasies, but the conclusions of what many enlightened thinkers took to be the modern science of society. While most clergymen continued to urge Christian love and charity upon their ordinary parishioners, many other educated and enlightened people sought to secularize Christian love and find in human nature itself a scientific imperative for loving one's neighbor as oneself. There seemed to be a natural principle of attraction that pulled people together, a moral principle that was no different from the principles that operated in the physical world. "Just as the regular motions and harmony of the heavenly bodies depend upon their mutual gravitation towards each other," said the liberal Massachusetts preacher Jonathan Mayhew, so too did love and benevolence among people preserve "order and harmony" in the society.[9] Love between humans was the gravity of the moral world, and it could be studied and perhaps even manipulated more easily than the gravity of the physical world. Enlightened thinkers like Lord Shaftesbury, Francis Hutcheson, and Adam Smith thus sought to discover these hidden forces that moved and held people together in the moral world—forces, they believed, that could match the great eighteenth-century scientific discoveries of the hidden forces (gravity, magnetism, electricity, and energy) that operated in the physical world. Out of such dreams was born modern social science.

Their complete reliance on a "system of social affections" is what made Paine and Jefferson such natural republicans.[10] Republics demanded far more morally from their citizens than monarchies did of their subjects. In monarchies each man's desire to do what was right in his own eyes could be restrained by fear or force, by patronage or honor, by the distribution of offices and distinctions, and by professional standing armies. By contrast, republics could not use the traditional instruments of government to hold the society together; instead, they had to hold themselves together from the bottom up, ultimately, from their citizens' willingness to sacrifice their private desires for the sake of the public good—their virtue. This reliance on the moral virtue of their citizens, on their capacity for self-sacrifice and their innate sociability, was what made republican governments historically so fragile.

Jefferson and Paine had so much confidence in the natural harmony of society that they sometimes came close to denying any role for government at all in holding the society together. To believe that government contributed to social cohesion was a great mistake, said Paine. "Society performs for itself almost every thing which is ascribed to government." Government had little or nothing to do with civilized life. Instead of ordering society, government "divided it; it deprived it of its natural cohesion, and engendered discontents and disorder, which otherwise would not have existed."[11] Both Paine and Jefferson believed that all social abuses and deprivations—social distinctions, business contracts, monopolies and privileges of all sorts, even excessive property and wealth—anything and everything that interfered with people's natural social dispositions—seemed to flow from connections to government, in the end from connections to monarchical government. Everywhere in the Old World, said Paine, we "find the greedy hand of government thrusting itself into every corner and crevice of industry, and grasping the spoil of the multitude."[12]

Both Jefferson and Paine believed deeply in minimal government—not as nineteenth-century laissez-faire liberals trying to promote capitalism, but as eighteenth-century radicals who hated monarchy, which was the only kind of government they had known. Calling them believers in minimal government is perhaps too tame a way of describing their deep disdain for hereditary monarchical government. Monarchy for Paine was "a silly contemptible thing," whose fuss and formality, when once exposed, became laughable. Jefferson felt the same; when he was president, he went out of his way to mock the formalities and ceremonies of the Court life of the European kings. His scorn of the European monarchs knew no bounds. They were, he said, all fools or idiots. "They passed their lives in hunting, and dispatched two courtiers a week, one thousand miles, to let each other know what game they had killed the preceding days."[13]

But what really made Jefferson and Paine hate monarchy was its habitual promotion of war. As far as they were concerned, as Paine put it, "all the monarchical governments are military. War is their trade, plunder and revenue their objects."[14] Angry liberals everywhere in the Western world thought that monarchy and war were intimately related. Indeed, as the son of the Revolutionary War general Benjamin Lincoln declared, "Kings owe their origin to war."[15] This recent Harvard graduate, like Jefferson and Paine, spoke out of a widespread eighteenth-century liberal protest against developments that had been taking place in Europe over the previous three centuries.

From the sixteenth century through the eighteenth century, the European monarchies had been busy consolidating their power and marking out their authority within clearly designated boundaries, while at the same time protecting themselves from rival claimants to their power and territories. They erected ever-larger bureaucracies and military forces in order to wage war, which is what they did through most decades of these three centuries. This meant the building of ever more centralized governments and the creation of ever more elaborate means for extracting money and men from their subjects. These efforts in turn led to the growth of armies, the increase in public debts, the raising of taxes, and the strengthening of executive power.

Such monarchical state-building was bound to provoke opposition, especially among Englishmen, who had a long tradition of valuing their liberties and resisting Crown power. The Country–Whig opposition ideology that arose in England in the late seventeenth and early eighteenth centuries was directed against these kinds of monarchical state-building efforts taking place rather belatedly in England. When later eighteenth-century British radicals, including Thomas Paine, warned that the lamps of liberty were going out all over Europe and were being dimmed in Britain itself, it was these efforts at modern state-formation that they were talking about.

Liberals and republicans like Jefferson and Paine assumed that kings brought their countries into war so frequently because wars sustained monarchical power. The internal needs of monarchies—the requirements of their bloated bureaucracies, their standing armies, their marriage alliances, their restless dynastic ambitions—lay behind the prevalence of war. Eliminate monarchy and all its accoutrements, many Americans believed, and war itself would be eliminated. A world of republican states would encourage a different kind of diplomacy, a peace-loving diplomacy—one based not on the brutal struggle for power of conventional diplomacy, but on the natural concert of the commercial interests of the people of the various nations. "If commerce were permitted to act to the universal extent it is capable," said Paine, "it would extirpate the system of war, and produce a revolution in the uncivilized state of governments."[16] In other words, if the people of the various nations were left alone to exchange goods freely among themselves, without the corrupting interference of selfish monarchical courts, irrational dynastic rivalries, and the secret double-dealing diplomacy of the past—then,

Jefferson, Paine, and other radical liberals hoped, international politics would become republicanized, pacified, and ruled by commerce alone, and a universal peace might emerge. Old-fashioned political diplomats might not even be necessary in this new commercially linked world.

Both men naturally and enthusiastically supported the French Revolution; indeed, both of them were close to Lafayette and his liberal circle and participated in the early stages of the Revolution. They had no doubt that the republican ideals of the American Revolution were simply spreading eastward and would eventually republicanize all of Europe. Although Paine became a member of the French National Convention and participated in its affairs, he turned out to be somewhat less fanatical than Jefferson. Paine never said anything comparable to Jefferson's comment of January 1793, in which the American secretary of state declared that he "would have seen half the earth desolated" rather than have the Revolution in France fail. "Were there but an Adam and an Eve left in every country, and left free, it would be better than as it is now." Indeed, while Paine bravely argued in the National Convention that the life of King Louis XVI ought to be spared, Jefferson viewed the king's execution as "punishment like other criminals." He hoped that France's eventual triumph would "bring at length kings, nobles and priests to the scaffolds which they have been so long deluging with human blood."[17]

For hard-headed realists like Alexander Hamilton, these radical ideas of Jefferson and Paine were nothing but "pernicious dreams." By abandoning the main instruments by which eighteenth-century monarchical governments held their turbulent societies together and ruled—patronage, ceremonies and rituals, aristocratic titles, and force—dreamers like Jefferson and Paine, said a disgruntled Hamilton, were offering "the bewitching tenets of the illuminated doctrine, which promises men, ere long, an emancipation from the burdens and restraints of government." By the early 1790s, Hamilton was alarmed by the extraordinarily utopian idea coming out of the French Revolution that "but a small portion of power is requisite to Government." And some radicals believed that "even this is only temporarily necessary" and could be done away with once "the bad habits" of the ancien régime were eliminated. Unfortunately, said Hamilton, there were wishful thinkers in both France and America who assumed that, "as human nature shall refine and ameliorate by the operation of a more enlightened plan" based on a common moral sense and the spread of affection and benevolence, "government itself will become useless, and Society will subsist and flourish free from its shackles."[18]

With all the "mischiefs . . . inherent in such a wild and fatal a scheme," Hamilton had hoped that "votaries of this new philosophy" would not push it to its fullest. But the new Jefferson administration that took over the federal government in 1801 was trying to do just that. "No army, no navy, no *active* commerce—national defence, not by arms but by embargoes, prohibition of trade &c.—as little government as possible." These all added up, said Hamilton in 1802, to "a most visionary theory."[19] Consequently, Hamilton and the other opponents of the Jeffersonian administration never tired of ridiculing the president and his supporters as utopians who walked with their heads in the clouds trying to extract sunbeams from cucumbers. Jefferson, the quixotic president, may have been ideally suited to be a college professor, they declared, but he was not suited to be the leader of a great nation.

But like many college professors, both Jefferson and Paine were optimists, believing in the promise of the future rather than in the dead hand of the past. Both loved inventions, like Paine's iron bridge, that made life and commerce easier. Both detested primogeniture and other aristocratic inheritance laws that treated new generations of children unequally. They hated charters and corporations that gave the few monopoly privileges that were not shared by the many. They were, said Paine, "charters, not of rights, but of exclusion."[20] The idea that corporate charters were vested rights that were unalterable by subsequent popular legislatures was, said Jefferson, a doctrine inculcated by "our lawyers and priests" that supposed "that preceding generations held the earth more freely than we do; had a right to impose laws on us, unalterable by ourselves, and that we, in like manner, can make laws and impose burdens on future generations, which they will have no right to alter; in fine, that the earth belongs to the dead and not the living."[21] Neither Jefferson nor Paine, in other words, had any patience with the sophisticated defense of prescription set forth by Edmund Burke.

Even the two men's religious views were similar—as radical as the enlightened eighteenth century allowed. Jefferson never publicly attacked orthodox religion in the extreme way Paine did in his *Age of Reason* (1794), in which he declared, "Of all the systems of religion that ever were invented, there is none more derogatory to the Almighty, more unedifying to man, more repugnant to reason, and more contradictory in itself than this thing called Christianity." But Jefferson did privately share Paine's scorn for traditional Christianity. Members of the "priestcraft," he wrote to friends he could trust, had turned Christianity "into mystery and jargon unintelligible to all mankind and therefore the safer engine for their purposes." The Trinity was nothing but "Abracadabra" and "hocus-pocus . . . so incomprehensible to the human mind that no candid man can say he has any idea of it." Ridicule, Jefferson said, was the only weapon to be used against it. But because he had been badly burned by some indiscreet remarks about religion in his *Notes on the State of Virginia*, he had learned to share his religious thoughts with only those he could rely on. "I not only write nothing on religion," he told a friend in 1815, "but rarely permit myself to speak on it, and never but in a reasonable society."[22] Paine's outrageous statements about Christianity in his *Age of Reason* helped to destroy his reputation in America. These views, coupled with his vicious attack on George Washington, meant that when he returned from Europe to America in 1802, he had few friends left in the country. But Thomas Jefferson was one of them.

Jefferson was the president and a political figure, and that made all the difference between the two men. On nearly every point of political and religious belief, the two enlightened radicals were in agreement. Where they differed was in Paine's need to voice his ideas publicly and in Jefferson's need to confine them to private drawing rooms composed of reasonable people. Paine was America's first modern public intellectual, an unconnected social critic who knew, he said, "but one kind of life I am fit for, and that is a thinking one, and of course, a writing one."[23] By aggressively publishing his ideas, Paine aimed to turn the contemplative life into an active one. Jefferson could not do this. Since he had a political career that depended on popular elections, he could not afford to spell out his radical ideas in pamphlets and books in the forceful way Paine could. Yet if he had written out in any systematic manner what he believed about politics, it would have resembled Paine's *Rights of Man*. As a politician, Jefferson continually had to compromise his beliefs—on minimal government, on banks, on the debt, on patronage, and perhaps on slavery. When he was speaking with his liberal friends abroad, he certainly took the correct line in opposition to slavery. Yet the intensity with which Jefferson enforced his embargo—his grand experiment in "peaceful coercion" as an alternative to war—reveals just how dedicated a radical he could be on some issues.

Although Jefferson was certainly cosmopolitan in an enlightened eighteenth-century manner, he was at heart a Virginian and an American deeply attached to his country. Paine was different. By the time he left America to return to the Old World in 1787, he had emotionally cut loose from his adopted home and had turned into an intellectual progenitor of revolutions. "It was neither the place nor the people [of America], but the Cause itself that irresistibly engages me in its support," he told the president of the Continental Congress as early as 1779; "for I should have acted the same part in any other country could the same circumstance have arisen there which have happened here." He had come to see himself as little better than "a refugee, and that of the most extraordinary kind, a refugee from the Country I have befriended." In the end, he became a man without a home, without a country, and, literally, as he said, "a citizen of the world."[24]

Because Paine after 1787 became as eager to reform the Old World as he had the New, his writings eventually took on issues that he had not dealt with earlier. Thinking of England and its huge numbers of landless people and its extremes of wealth and poverty, in the second part of *Rights of Man* and in *Agrarian Justice* he proposed systems of public welfare and social insurance financed by progressive taxation. Jefferson, as the patriot who believed that agrarian America was already an egalitarian paradise, felt no such need to express such radical views publicly. Yet as early as 1785 he privately suggested various measures to ensure that property in a state not become too unequally divided. Indeed, he declared, so harmful was gross inequality of wealth that "legislators cannot invent too many devices for subdividing property." In addition to proposing that all children inherit property equally, he, like Paine, advocated the progressive taxation of the rich and the exemption of the poor from taxes. Even in America, he said, "it is not too soon to provide by every possible means that as few as possible shall be without a little portion of land. The small landholders are the most precious part of a state."[25]

In the end, Americans treated the two men who shared so many ideas very differently. Although Americans have erected a huge memorial to Jefferson in Washington, D.C., and celebrated him as the premier spokesman for democracy, they have scarcely noticed Thomas Paine. He died in obscurity in the United States in 1809, and ten years later William Cobbett took his bones away to England. Although Jefferson declared in 1801 that Paine had labored on behalf of liberty and the American Revolution "with as much effort as any man living," Paine still remains a much neglected founder.[26] Perhaps it is time for that to change.

NOTES

1. Marquis de Chastellux, *Travels in North America in the Years 1780, 1781, and 1782*, ed. Howard C. Rice, 2 vols. (Chapel Hill: University of North Carolina Press, 1963), 2:391.

2. John Keane, *Tom Paine: A Political Life* (Boston: Little, Brown, 1995), 211.

3. S. W. Jackman, "A Young Englishman Reports on the New Nation: Edward Thornton to James Bland Burges, 1791–1793," *William and Mary Quarterly*, 3rd ser., 18 (January 1961): 110.

4. Jefferson, *A Summary View of the Rights of British America* (1774), in *The Papers of Thomas Jefferson,* ed. Julian P. Boyd et al., 39 vols. to date (Princeton, N.J.: Princeton University Press, 1950–) [hereafter cited as *Jefferson Papers*], 1:134.

5. Paine, *Common Sense,* in *The Complete Writings of Thomas Paine,* ed. Philip S. Foner, 2 vols. (New York: Citadel Press, 1945) [hereafter cited as *Complete Writings*], 1:23.

6. Paine, *The Crisis Extraordinary,* 4 October 1780, ibid., 1:182.

7. Paine, *Rights of Man, Part Second,* ibid., 1:363; Thomas Jefferson [TJ] to T. Law, 13 June 1814, in *The Writings of Thomas Jefferson,* ed. Andrew A. Lipscomb and Albert Ellery Bergh, 20 vols. (Washington, D.C.: Thomas Jefferson Memorial Association, 1903–4) [hereafter cited as *Writings of Thomas Jefferson*], 14:141–42; TJ to Peter Carr, 12 August 1787, *Jefferson Papers,* 12:15.

8. Paine, *Common Sense,* in *Complete Writings,* 1:4.

9. Jonathan Mayhew, *Seven Sermons upon the Following Subjects; . . .* (Boston: Rogers and Fowle, 1749), 126.

10. Paine, *Rights of Man, Part Second,* in *Complete Writings,* 1:357.

11. Ibid., 1:359.

12. Ibid., 1:355.

13. Ibid., 1:373; TJ to Governor John Langdon, 5 March 1810, in Thomas Jefferson, *Writings,* ed. Merrill D. Peterson (New York: Library of America, 1984) [hereafter cited as *Jefferson Writings*], 1221.

14. Paine, *Rights of Man, Part Second,* in *Complete Writings,* 1:355–56.

15. [Benjamin Lincoln Jr.], "The Free Republican No. III," *Independent Chronicle* (Boston), 8 December 1785.

16. Paine, *Rights of Man, Part Second,* in *Complete Writings,* 1:400.

17. TJ to Joseph Fay, 18 March 1793, *Jefferson Papers,* 25:402; TJ to William Short, 3 January 1793, in *Jefferson Writings,* 1004; TJ to Tench Coxe, 1 May 1794, *Jefferson Papers,* 28:67.

18. Alexander Hamilton to Rufus King, 3 June 1802, in *Alexander Hamilton: Writings,* ed. Joanne B. Freeman (New York: Library of America, 2001), 993; Hamilton, "Views on the French Revolution (1794)," in *The Papers of Alexander Hamilton,* ed. Harold C. Syrett et al., 27 vols. (New York: Columbia University Press, 1961–87), 26:739–40.

19. Hamilton, "Views on the French Revolution (1794)," in *Papers of Alexander Hamilton,* 26:739–40; Hamilton to Rufus King, 3 June 1802, in *Alexander Hamilton: Writings,* 993.

20. Paine, *Rights of Man, Part Second,* in *Complete Writings,* 1:408.

21. TJ to William Plumer, 21 July 1816, in *Writings of Thomas Jefferson,* 15:46–47.

22. Paine, *The Age of Reason, Part One,* in *Thomas Paine: Collected Writings,* ed. Eric Foner (New York: Library of America, 1995) [hereafter cited as *Collected Writings*], 825; TJ to Horatio Spafford, 17 March 1814, in *The Founders on Religion: A Book of Quotations,* ed. James H. Hutson (Princeton, N.J.: Princeton University Press, 2005), 68; TJ to James

Smith, 8 December 1822, ibid., 218; TJ to Charles Clay, 29 January 1815, in *Writings of Thomas Jefferson,* 14:233.

23. Paine to Henry Laurens, 14 September 1779, in *Complete Writings,* 2:1178.

24. Ibid.; Paine to Robert Livingston, 19 May 1783, quoted in Keane, *Thomas Paine,* 242.

25. TJ to James Madison, 18 October 1785, in *Jefferson Writings,* 841–42.

26. TJ to Paine, 18 March 1801, *Jefferson Papers,* 33:359.

"The Whole Object of the Present Controversy"
The Early Constitutionalism of Paine and Jefferson

FRANCIS D. COGLIANO

IN 1776 THOMAS PAINE and Thomas Jefferson were in Philadelphia and each made his most notable contribution to the American Revolution—Paine publishing *Common Sense* and Jefferson drafting the Declaration of Independence.[1] As a consequence of these activities, Paine and Jefferson are, perhaps, more closely associated with the colonies' decision to declare independence than any other figures. The case for independence, persuasively made by Paine in *Common Sense* and fluently distilled by Jefferson in the Declaration of Independence, has somewhat obscured their attempts to grapple with fundamental constitutional questions. The creation of republican governments—for the individual states and the American confederacy generally—was a direct consequence of the decision to declare independence. Independence necessitated the framing of new constitutions, which raised fundamental questions about the nature of the republican government: Who should draft the constitutions? Who should wield power in the new republics? How should the new governments be structured? What should the relationship between the individual states and the Continental Congress be? How would individual rights be protected? What were the rights of minorities? These were fundamental questions that republican revolutionaries on both sides of the Atlantic confronted in the late eighteenth century. Though less well known than their contributions to the decision to declare independence, Paine and Jefferson each contributed significantly to constitution-making in Pennsylvania and Virginia, respectively. Their efforts reveal the diversity of republican theory and practice during the American Revolution.

THE EARLY CONSTITUTIONALISM OF PAINE AND JEFFERSON

In 1976 Eric Foner observed: "The ideology of republicanism became the common language of politics during the revolutionary era. Jeffersonian and Painite republicanism shared many perceptions and values, yet their differing conceptions of the nation's future illuminate the diversity of Americans' reactions to the profound changes which overtook their society in the late eighteenth century." According to Foner, Painite republicanism was urban and forward-looking; it embraced technology, manufacturing, and the emerging capitalist order. Jeffersonian republicanism, by contrast, was fundamentally agrarian, rural and backward-looking. "Agrarian republicanism," writes Foner, "was essentially nostalgic. It placed primary value on independence and equality, but believed that the only way these virtues could be preserved was by resisting economic growth and capitalist development. To Paine, the past was a burden, not a guide, and the present only a stopping point from which to propel society into the future."[2] This essay develops Foner's comparison by examining the efforts of Paine and Jefferson to develop and implement republican government in the immediate aftermath of Independence. Paine's urban republicanism was forged in the towns and cities of Georgian England and tempered in the political strife of Revolutionary Pennsylvania, which was dominated, in large part, by Philadelphia. Jefferson's republicanism, by contrast, was agrarian, because colonial and Revolutionary Virginia was a rural and agricultural society. The differences between them did not arise because Paine was a forward-looking optimist and Jefferson backward-looking, nostalgic, and pessimistic about the future. On the contrary, as their efforts at constitutional reform in the years after Independence show, they shared a common objective to transform and improve American society by seeking to broaden the franchise and to design republics based on a capacious definition of citizenship. They differed in the particular constitutional reforms they supported because the local contexts in which they operated were so different.

Thomas Paine was born in Thetford, Norfolk, on January 29, 1737. His father was a stay-maker and tenant farmer. Paine received a basic education in the local grammar school. During the Seven Years' War he signed on with the crew of a privateer before working as an apprentice stay-maker in London. In September 1759 he married Mary Lambert, who died in childbirth the following year. After the death of his wife, Paine gave up stay-making and sought a career as an excise collector. He received appointments in Lincolnshire before he was dismissed from the service in 1765 for issuing certificates without completing the required inspections. Although he was eventually reinstated to the excise service, he made ends meet in the interim by a return to stay-making and teaching school in London. He spent several years in the metropolis before accepting a post as the excise officer in Lewes, Sussex. In addition to his excise duties, he went into business in Lewes with his landlord, Samuel Ollive. Ollive died in 1769, and Paine opened a shop with Ollive's widow and married Ollive's daughter, Elizabeth, in 1771. In 1772, Paine journeyed to London to campaign for improved pay for excise collectors. As part of this campaign, he published his first political pamphlet, *The Case of the Officers of Excise*. The campaign failed, and Paine returned to Lewes in 1773. Within a year, his life was in shambles—he was dismissed from the excise service for a second time, and his business failed in April 1774. A month later, Paine and his wife formally separated. In October 1774, Paine, aged thirty-seven, boarded a ship bound for America.[3]

Paine arrived in Philadelphia on November 30, 1774. He came bearing a letter of introduction from Benjamin Franklin, the city's favorite son.[4] Paine encountered Franklin during his time as a teacher in London in the 1760s. He had spent the six years prior to his departure for America in London and Lewes. Both places were characterized by political radicalism and popular protest. In both places, Paine mixed in the taverns and coffeehouses with radicals, republicans, and freethinkers. He associated with artisans and tradesmen who resented the privileges and political power of the wealthy. He attended lectures, read—especially science and politics—and debated the issues of the day in clubs and voluntary associations. Foner writes:

> By 1774, Paine had lived for thirty-seven years in England. He had matured during a time of widespread economic distress and had spent much of his life in centers of political disaffection. He had moved among critics of English government and society and was possibly familiar with underground currents of republican thought and religious millennialism. A man of skill in a craft, knowledge of science and with enough intellectual ability to work as a teacher and tax collector, his experience had been largely one of disappointment and frustration.[5]

When he arrived in Philadelphia on the eve of the American Revolution, Paine found a city in ferment. The city, the most important port in British North America, was characterized by increasing social stratification. It was dominated by a conservative merchant elite whose authority was under threat from a growing population of artisans, tradesmen, and laborers who had been emboldened and empowered by a decade's worth of resistance and protest against British tax policies. It was an environment in which Paine flourished.[6]

Paine soon found work as the editor of the *Pennsylvania Magazine,* a new journal owned by Robert Aitken, a Philadelphia printer and bookseller. Paine wrote approximately twenty essays for the magazine in 1775 that commented on the rapidly deteriorating relationship between Britain and its colonies in North America. Paine's writing brought him to the attention of leading political radicals in Philadelphia opposed to British rule, as well as the members of the Second Continental Congress, which began sitting in the city in May 1775 to develop a coordinated colonial response to the outbreak of fighting between the colonists and British soldiers in New England the previous month.

During the autumn of 1775, Paine, at the urging of Benjamin Rush, began writing a pamphlet in favor of colonial independence. He consulted Rush, who suggested a title for the polemic, *Common Sense,* which appeared anonymously in January 1776. Paine wrote *Common Sense* in a forceful, direct style that was readily accessible to the common people among whom Paine had spent most of his life. He began *Common Sense* by stressing the Lockean theme that government is a contractual relationship made necessary by human selfishness. "For were the impulses of conscience clear," Paine wrote, "uniform and irresistibly obeyed, man would need no other lawgiver; but that not being the case, he finds it necessary to surrender up a part of his property to furnish means of protection of the rest."[7] Government being a necessary evil, Paine sought to demonstrate that the British constitution was deeply flawed. The House of Commons was the only republican element in the British system, and it had been corrupted and compromised by the monarchical and aristocratic elements embodied in the Crown and the House of Lords.

Since the colonists had made a long-standing case against Parliament's authority over them, Paine concentrated his attack on the British monarchy. He argued that the hereditary kingship and aristocratic titles were unjust. According to Paine: "Government by kings was first introduced into the world by the heathens, from whom the children of Israel copied the custom. It is the most prosperous invention the Devil ever set on foot for the promotion of idolatry."[8] Rather than fear independence, Paine demonstrated, Americans should welcome the opportunity to sever their ties with an oppressive, unequal system of government that had no basis in scripture or natural law.

Having demolished the basis for colonial loyalty to the British monarchy, Paine turned his attention to the situation in America. He based his comments on "simple facts, plain arguments and common sense."[9] He argued that free trade would make an independent America the friend of all nations, and that American agriculture "will always have a market while eating is the custom in Europe."[10] Freedom in economics would complement the political freedom Paine envisioned in an independent America. Rather than fear independence, common sense dictated that Americans should welcome it, for national independence would lead to increased prosperity and liberty.

Paine's purpose in writing *Common Sense* was to persuade Americans to support independence from Britain. However, in making his case for independence, Paine provided an insight into his constitutional thinking. Having offered a critique of the British constitution, Paine suggested that the Americans should establish republics based on a broad franchise, annually elected assemblies, and a rotating presidency. "Let the assemblies be annual, with a President only," he wrote. "The representation more equal. Their business wholly domestic, and subject to the authority of a Continental Congress."[11] With respect to Congress, Paine wanted the membership of that body to be vastly expanded and its president to be chosen by a combination of rotation, lottery, and balloting by its members. He proposed that a special conference be convened to draft a constitution for the United States—a "Continental Charter" which would stipulate the powers of Congress. The selection of delegates to the conference is instructive with respect to Paine's constitutional and political principles:

> A committee of twenty-six members of Congress, viz. two for each colony. Two members for each house of assembly or Provincial convention; and five representatives of the people at large, to be chosen in the capital city or town of each province, for, and in behalf of the whole province, by as many qualified voters as shall think proper to attend from all parts of the province for that purpose; or, if more convenient, the representatives may be chosen in two or three of the most populous parts thereof. In this conference thus assembled, will be united, the two grand principles of business, *knowledge* and *power*. The members of Congress, Assemblies, or Conventions, by having had experience in national concerns, will be able and useful counsellors, and the whole, being impowered by the people will have a truly legal authority.[12]

According to Paine's plan, popularly elected delegates from the most populous parts of each state would dominate the "Continental Conference." Paine believed that the post-Independence American republics should be broadly democratic. He had learned in the taverns, coffeehouses, and debating chambers of Lewes, London, and Philadelphia that common people could govern themselves, and he intended that, as a direct consequence of Independence, ordinary Americans would exercise power in the new republic. In Paine's adoptive home of Pennsylvania this principle was enacted to a greater extent than anywhere else in Revolutionary America.

"A government of our own is our natural right," Paine observed. "And when a man seriously reflects on the precariousness of human affairs, he will become convinced, that it is infinitely wiser and safer, to form a constitution of our own in a cool and deliberate manner, while we have it in our power, than to trust such an interesting event to time and chance."[13] Americans, however, did not have the luxury of adopting constitutions in a "cool and deliberate manner." They did so while waging a war that often divided them. In Pennsylvania, Quakers and Anglicans from Philadelphia who were at best lukewarm supporters of the Revolution dominated the pre-Revolutionary political and commercial elite. Unwilling to replace the provincial government or to support Independence, these conservatives were swept aside by the Revolution. In June 1776, the pro-Independence members of the Pennsylvania Assembly withdrew from the body, denying it a quorum and rendering it impotent. A convention of county committees of inspection was called by the Philadelphia Committee of Inspection, with the support of the Philadelphia militia, to govern in lieu of the assembly. The convention met for a week, endorsing Independence on June 24, and called elections for a special convention to meet and draft a new constitution for the state. Traditional property requirements for voting were waived. Voting, however, was limited to those who supported Independence. Under this formula, previously underrepresented areas and social groups, like the frontier counties and Philadelphia's artisans, were overrepresented in the constitutional convention. Thus, the convention to draft the Pennsylvania constitution represented some of the poorest, yet most radical supporters of the Revolution in the state.

The Pennsylvania constitutional convention consisted of ninety-six delegates, who sat from July 8 until September 28, 1776. The resulting frame of government vested legislative powers in a unicameral legislature that would be elected annually by all taxpayers over the age of twenty-one and the adult sons of taxpayers. Such a broad franchise (Pennsylvania's suffrage requirements were the most generous adopted by any state) and the creation of a large, annually elected, unicameral legislature constituted a sharp break with colonial practice. Whenever possible, legislation had to be held over from one legislative session to the next so that pending legislation could be published and receive public consideration before the assembly acted. Executive power was vested not in an individual governor, but in an elected twelve-member executive council. Although the council would elect a president, his powers were largely symbolic. Crucially, the executive would have no authority to veto legislation adopted by the assembly. Judges under the system were elected to serve seven-year terms. Every seven years, a council of censors would review the actions of the government to determine whether the constitution had been violated or amendments to the constitution were necessary. Appended to the constitution was a broad declaration of rights that enumerated the freedoms guaranteed to the people of Pennsylvania.[14]

Pennsylvania was one state during the Revolutionary era where the political elite largely absented themselves from constitution-making, at least in the first instance, and the result was the most radical and democratic constitution of the era. The Pennsylvania Constitution of 1776 might be described as a Painite frame of government. It was drafted by a convention especially elected for the task of the type Paine suggested in *Common Sense*. The delegates to the convention were chosen by and often drawn from the ranks of middling and poorer Pennsylvanians, particularly Philadelphians, who dominated the process. Years later, Paine observed that "the groundwork of that Constitution was good." It was truly revolutionary because it was not encumbered by tradition and inherited privilege. "The Pennsylvania Constitution of 1776 copied nothing from the English Government," wrote Paine. "It formed a Constitution on the basis of honesty."[15]

Although the 1776 Pennsylvania constitution seemed to epitomize the principles that Paine had outlined in *Common Sense*, Paine did not have a direct hand in drafting the document. During the summer of 1776, he joined Pennsylvania troops who marched to New York to oppose General William Howe's expeditionary force, which captured the city in August. Paine marched as a volunteer with Washington's troops during their demoralizing retreat across New Jersey during the autumn of 1776. "Just at the time the Convention first met I went to camp," he recalled, "and continued there till a few days before Christmas. I held no correspondence with either party, for, or against, the present constitution. I had no hand in forming any part of it, nor knew any thing of its contents till I saw it published."[16] Although Paine was not involved in the drafting of the constitution, he was broadly sympathetic to the document and knew well many of the men who drafted it. They were his friends and allies among Philadelphia's radicals.

Although he did not contribute to drafting the constitution, Paine played a direct role in defending it, resorting to his talent as a propagandist. Conservative opponents of the constitution, known as Republicans, agitated for its replacement or amendment. Throughout the late 1770s and 1780s, Republicans and the supporters of the document, known as Constitutionalists, waged a bitter partisan struggle in which Paine was one of the protagonists. He recalled in 1786: "In the winter of 1778, a very strong opposition was made to the *form* of the constitution. As the constitution was then on an experiment and the enemy in full force in the country, the opposition was injudicious." Owing to the strength of the Republican opposition to the constitution, "the persons then in office and power," wrote Paine, "applied very solicitously to me to help them. I did so, and the service was gratis."[17] In 1777 and 1778, he wrote a series of newspaper essays to defend and promote the constitution. The most important of these was a lengthy, incomplete essay, "A Serious Address to the People of Pennsylvania on the Present Situation of Their Affairs," which appeared over four consecutive issues in the *Pennsylvania Packet* in December 1778. The "Serious Address," though little remembered (and not attributed to Paine until 1945), should be placed alongside *Common Sense* and *The American Crisis* as one of Paine's most important writings from the era of the American Revolution.[18]

In the "Serious Address," Paine reviewed the history of the drafting of the constitution and rehearsed its features. He provided a detailed analysis and defence of the plural executive, the unicameral legislature, the frequent elections, and the elected judiciary as mandated by the constitution. Perhaps the most striking passages concern the role of property and property-holding in Pennsylvania's new republican order. Paine defended the relaxation of property requirements and the extension of the franchise in exchange for militia service. He wrote:

> Property alone cannot defend a country against invading enemies. Houses and land cannot fight; sheep and oxen cannot be taught the musket; therefore the defence must be personal, and that which equally unites all must be something equally the property of all, viz. an equal share of freedom, independent of the varieties of wealth, and which wealth, [n]or the want of it, can neither give or take away. To be telling men of their rights when we want their service, and of their poverty when the service is over, is a meanness which cannot be professed by a gentleman.[19]

Paine asserted the political value and rights of men with limited means. His frustrations and failures in business had taught him that there was no necessary correlation between wealth and ability. "The impossibility of knowing into whose hands a distinction of rights may fall, should make men afraid to establish them, lest in the revolution of fortune, common to a trading country, they should get into the hands of those who were intended to be excluded, and severely exercised over those who were designed to inherit them." Paine argued that rights of citizenship in the new Pennsylvania republic should be extended to all men who served in the militia. His personal experience had taught him how capricious fate could be and to reject inherited political privilege. Rights should not be contingent on wealth. Paine's experiences among the radicals in Lewes, London, and Philadelphia shaped his political outlook and led him to conclude that it was imperative to *"Leave Freedom free."*[20]

Thomas Jefferson was born on April 13, 1743, at Shadwell, in Albemarle County, Virginia. His father, Peter Jefferson, was a surveyor and large planter, and his mother, Jane Randolph, came from one of Virginia's leading families. As a child, Jefferson was educated by private tutors before attending the College of William and Mary. After studying at William and Mary, he spent three years reading law under the tutelage of George Wythe, the leading Virginia jurist. Soon after, he was admitted to the bar and began to practice law. In 1772, he married Martha Wayles Skelton, a widow whose father was a wealthy merchant and slave trader and whose first husband had been a planter. Jefferson was well connected and well educated. In 1769, he was elected by the voters of Albemarle to represent the county in the House of Burgesses, the colonial assembly.[21]

While in the House of Burgesses, Jefferson came to identify with the opponents of British taxation. In 1774, he wrote a pamphlet, *The Summary View of the Rights of British America,* that offered a critique of British policy and a defense of colonial rights. The *Summary View* established Jefferson's reputation as an articulate and radical proponent of American rights, and, as a consequence, he was elected to represent Virginia in the Second Continental Congress. Jefferson arrived in Philadelphia in June 1775. Like Paine, he made his reputation with his pen while in Philadelphia. As a member of Congress, Jefferson drafted the official response to Lord North's reconciliation plan in 1775, and he had contributed to its later "Declaration of the Causes and Necessity of Taking Up Arms."

While Jefferson was in Philadelphia, the Virginia Convention, meeting in Williamsburg, unanimously resolved on May 15, 1776, that the Continental Congress should declare independence, and pledged to support "whatever measures may be thought proper and necessary by the Congress for forming foreign alliances and a confederation of the colonies, at such time, and in the manner, as to them shall seem best: Provided that the power of forming government for, and the regulations of the internal concerns of each colony, be left to the respective colonial legislatures." The resolutions reached Philadelphia in late May, and on June 7 Richard Henry Lee introduced resolutions calling on Congress to declare independence, form foreign alliances, and to establish a formal confederation for the soon-to-be independent colonies. As a consequence of Lee's resolutions, Jefferson was appointed to the committee created to prepare a draft declaration of independence.[22]

The resolutions of the Virginia convention clearly stated that "the power of forming government for, and the regulations of the internal concerns of each colony, be left to the respective colonial legislatures." While Congress must declare independence on behalf of the colonies collectively, the authority and responsibility for drafting constitutions lay with the new states. Jefferson believed that this would be the most important aspect of the Revolution. "In truth," he wrote on May 16, "it is the whole object of the present controversy; for should a bad government be instituted for us in future it had been as well to have accepted at first the bad one offered to us from beyond the water without the risk and expense of contest."[23] Jefferson began working on a constitution for Virginia sometime in May 1776, producing three drafts before June 13, when his mentor, George Wythe, departed Philadelphia bearing Jefferson's plan to Virginia.

Wythe did not arrive in Williamsburg in time for Jefferson's draft to substantially affect the constitutional deliberations of the assembly. In late June 1776, the assembly adopted a constitution that was largely the handiwork of George Mason. This 1776 constitution vested considerable authority in Virginia's legislature. According to the new constitution, the royal governor would be replaced by a weak executive to be elected annually by the assembly. The governor would be assisted by a council of state to be elected by the assembly, which would have a popularly elected upper chamber. The bicameral assembly would appoint the members of the judiciary. Representation in the House of Delegates would replicate the existing arrangements, with two representatives per county. Crucially, the constitution retained strict property requirements for voting, leading Dumas Malone to characterize the settlement as creating "an aristocratic republic, bottomed on inheritance."[24]

Jefferson's proposed constitution bore some similarities to that adopted by the Virginia convention. It called for the creation of a bicameral legislature that would wield most of the power within the government—electing the governor, who would serve a one-year term and whose powers were limited. In what may be read as a moment of uncharacteristic irony, Jefferson noted that the governor (whom he termed the "Administrator") "shall possess the powers formerly held by the king," before stipulating a lengthy list of limitations on the governor's authority, all of which meant his powers would be considerably less than those exercised by the king or his representatives in Virginia.[25]

While the structure of the government proposed by Jefferson and that adopted by the Virginia convention were essentially similar, Jefferson's draft challenged the bases of political authority in Virginia in ways the 1776 state constitution did not. With respect to representation, the 1776 constitution allocated two representatives in the House of Delegates per county. Jefferson proposed that representatives be apportioned according to population. This would have redistributed power away from the dominant Tidewater counties to the relatively underrepresented Piedmont and western counties of the state. Even more significant were Jefferson's proposals regarding the right to vote. Under Jefferson's proposed constitution, the existing property requirements would be maintained. All adult male taxpayers possessing a quarter of an acre of land in town or 25 acres of land in the country would be eligible to vote. Crucially, Jefferson proposed that all adult males in the state "neither owning, nor having owned 50 acres of land, shall be entitled to an appropriation of 50 acres of land or to so much as shall make up what he owns or has owned 50 acres in absolute dominion." The land should be taken from territory formerly owned by the Crown, forfeited by loyalists, or purchased from Native Americans by the government. Although he retained property requirements for voting, by proposing the wholesale distribution of lands to taxpayers, Jefferson was making it possible for all adult male taxpayers in Virginia to vote.[26]

Jefferson's proposal to redistribute public and forfeited lands appeared in the fourth article of his proposed constitution, headed "Rights Private and Public." In addition to the right to public land, Jefferson enumerated other rights, including the abolition of the slave trade, the right of naturalization, freedom of religion, separation of church and state, and freedom of the press.[27] Jefferson's draft constitution for Virginia needs to be read alongside the Declaration of Independence to gain a thorough understanding of his republicanism in 1776. In the Declaration of Independence, Jefferson asserted universal equality grounded in natural rights. His proposed constitution for Virginia would have established the means to achieve the principles Jefferson articulated in the Declaration. In the spring and summer of 1776, Jefferson proposed to strike at the roots of gentry power in Virginia. In *Common Sense*, Thomas Paine inveighed against hereditary privilege. "For all men being originally equals, no one by birth could have a right to set up his own family in perpetual preference to all others forever," declared Paine, "and though himself might deserve some decent honors of his contemporaries, yet his descendants might be far too unworthy to inherit them."[28] Inherited privilege was the cornerstone of power in Virginia. Jefferson, who acquired land and slaves from his father and his wife, was a beneficiary of the system. Nonetheless, in 1776 he sought to curtail the authority of the gentry by striking at the sources of its power—inherited wealth and privilege.[29]

The Virginia convention ignored the key elements of Jefferson's constitutional program. George Wythe explained that by the time he had arrived in Williamsburg, "the plan of government had been committed to the whole house." The convention adjourned before Jefferson's plan could receive due consideration. Indeed, Wythe "was persuaded the revision of a subject the members seemed tired of would at that time have been unsuccessfully proposed." He concluded that "the system agreed to in my opinion requires reformation. In October I hope you will effect it."[30] Jefferson left the Continental Congress in September 1776 and returned to Virginia in order to salvage the key elements of his constitutional program. He took up his seat in the House of Delegates and served in the legislature from October 1776 until June 1779, when he was elected governor of the Commonwealth. During this period, he served as a member of the legislature's Committee of Revisors that undertook to rewrite Virginia's laws in light of the state's new constitution. Over the course of the decade from 1776 to 1786, the legislature enacted many of the revised laws proposed by the committee. Among the legislation Jefferson championed were successful bills to abolish primogeniture and entail, reform of the state's penal code, disestablish the Anglican Church, and the establishment of a system of state-supported education. Jefferson intended these measures to complete the republican revolution begun in Philadelphia with the adoption of the Declaration of Independence. He remembered in his autobiography: "I considered 4 of these bills, passed or reported, as forming a system by which every fibre would be eradicated of antient or future aristocracy; and a foundation laid for a government truly republican." Jefferson's effort to revise Virginia's laws was a second attempt to strike at the roots of gentry power in Virginia by attacking inherited wealth and privilege in the interest of individual rights and equality of opportunity.[31]

Land reform was a key element of Jefferson's program. He sponsored successful bills which abolished primogeniture and entail in the newly independent Commonwealth. In his autobiography, Jefferson drew a direct comparison between these bills and the power of the gentry: "The repeal of the laws of entail would prevent accumulation and perpetuation of wealth in select families, and preserve the soil of the country from being daily more & more absorbed in Mortmain. The abolition of primogeniture, and equal partition of inheritances removed the feudal and unnatural distinctions which made one member of every family rich, and all the rest poor, substituting equal partition, the best of all Agrarian laws."[32]

Jefferson advocated land reform because it would, he believed, limit the gentry's power. Jefferson's advocacy of land reform demonstrates that his republicanism, while agrarian, was not backward-looking and nostalgic. On the contrary, as an agronomist and a republican, Jefferson sought to reform and improve the lives of farmers. He experimented with new crops and sought to improve productivity. While serving as the American minister in France, he tinkered with the design of a moldboard plow, intended to make plowing more efficient, which he introduced at Monticello when he returned to the United States. Whether engaging in constitutional reform or agricultural experimentation, Jefferson's republicanism did not hearken back to a golden age in the remote past, but sought to hasten the arrival of a glorious future.[33]

Land reform, however, was only the beginning for Jefferson. Just as the power of the gentry needed to be curtailed, the opportunities of poorer Virginians needed to be expanded. Jefferson sought to achieve this through reforms that would disestablish the Anglican Church and improve the education system. The partial success of these proposals reflects the limitations of Jefferson's reforms.

When Jefferson entered the House of Delegates in the autumn of 1776, he was also named to its Committee on Religion. That committee was inundated with petitions from dissenting religious groups—mainly Baptists, Presbyterians, and Methodists—who petitioned for relief from taxes to support the Anglican establishment, equality in the exercise of religious belief, and the complete disestablishment of the Anglican Church.[34] In 1777 Jefferson drafted "A Bill for Establishing Religious Freedom." After a lengthy preamble in which he advanced the view that religious belief should derive from reason rather than state coercion, Jefferson's bill asserted that "no man shall be compelled to frequent or support any religious worship, place, or ministry whatsoever, nor shall be enforced, restrained, molested, or burthened in his body or goods, nor shall otherwise suffer on account of his religious opinions or belief; but that all shall in no wise diminish, enlarge or affect their civil capacities." Jefferson, fearing the actions of future legislatures, yet aware that they could not be bound, concluded, "The rights hereby asserted are of the natural rights of mankind, and that if any act shall be hereafter passed to repeal the present or to narrow its operation, such an act will be an infringement of natural right." Jefferson's bill was not presented to the House of Delegates until 1779. Initially, the bill was tabled. It was not adopted, and then in amended form, until January 1786, when James Madison ushered it through the legislature in Richmond while Jefferson represented the United States in Paris.³⁵

The statute for religious freedom completely severed the ties between church and state in Virginia and guaranteed freedom of conscience throughout the state. Through the bill, Jefferson sought to strike a blow to the power of the Virginia gentry. He wrote, "The restoration of the rights of conscience relieved the people from taxation for the support of a religion not theirs; for the establishment was truly of a religion of the rich, the dissenting sects being entirely composed of the less wealthy people."³⁶ He took great satisfaction in his authorship of the bill. When it became law, Jefferson distributed copies throughout Europe in the form of a short pamphlet, and when his *Notes on the State of Virginia* was published in English in 1787, he had the statute added to the text as an appendix.³⁷ He did so because he believed that the statute had significance far beyond the borders of his native state. In Jefferson's mind, political and religious tyrannies were closely allied. Historically, state churches—by fostering obedience and ignorance—had assisted unjust rulers in subverting the liberties to which all humanity was entitled as natural rights. The overthrow of religious oppression went hand in hand with the defeat of secular tyranny. As he wrote in *Notes on the State of Virginia:* "The legitimate powers of government extend to such acts only as are injurious to others. But it does me no injury for my neighbour to say there are twenty gods, or no god. It neither picks my pocket nor breaks my leg."³⁸

Agrarian reform and the separation of church and state were important elements of Jefferson's program to transform Virginia. Perhaps the most important aspect of his program was the reform of education. Jefferson hoped that "the less wealthy people" would benefit from his proposed education bill, and "be qualified to understand their rights, to maintain them, and to exercise with intelligence their parts in self-government."³⁹ In the autumn of 1778, Jefferson drafted a series of bills to reform education in Virginia. Of these, Jefferson considered the most important to be the "Bill for the More General Diffusion of Knowledge." Under its terms, Jefferson proposed that each county in the state would be subdivided into wards, or "hundreds," each of which would contain a primary school. According Jefferson's plan, "All the free children, male and female, resident within the respective hundred shall be entitled to receive tuition gratis for a term of three years, and as much longer, at their private expense, as their parents, guardians and friends, shall think proper." Promising male students could continue their education at one of twenty secondary schools to be created throughout the state. Among these would be a small number of well-qualified poor students who would be provided with their education at state expense. Other students would pay for their tuition at the secondary level. Among the scholarship students the most worthy would be provided with state funding to attend William and Mary College, the state's preeminent institution of higher education.[40]

Jefferson believed that his plan for state-funded education for all free Virginians was necessary to safeguard the achievements of the Revolution. Widespread education was not only a necessary weapon that allowed the citizens of a republic to guard their liberties, it was also essential if people were to govern themselves properly. Since the Declaration of Independence had placed equality at the center of the Revolutionary ideology, the best way to guarantee equality of opportunity, and good government, was through education. He stated in the Bill's preamble that

> people will be happiest whose laws are best, and are best administered, and that laws will be wisely formed, and honestly administered, in proportion as those who form and administer them are wise and honest; whence it becomes expedient for promoting the publick happiness that those persons, whom nature hath endowed with genius and virtue, should be rendered by liberal education worthy to receive, and able to guard the sacred deposit of rights and liberties of their fellow citizens, and that they should be called to that charge without regard to wealth, birth or other accidental condition or circumstance; but the indigence of the greater number disabling them from so educating, at their own expence, those of their children whom nature hath fitly formed and disposed to become useful instruments for the public, it is better that such should be sought for and educated at the common expence of all, than that the happiness of all should be confined to the weak or wicked.[41]

Providing free education for poor students of clear ability (and need) would allow for the cultivation of a natural aristocracy of talent that was the best way to insure good government and the survival of liberty in the United States. Jefferson never realized his ambition to create a comprehensive education system in Virginia. The House of Delegates, concerned at the cost of the measures, declined to enact Jefferson's educational proposals.[42] The failure of the education bill, which Jefferson described in 1786 as "by far the most important bill in our whole code," suggests that Jefferson's reform agenda was only partially successful.[43]

Jefferson's radicalism is more difficult to explain than Thomas Paine's.

Jefferson was a wealthy member of Virginia's social and political elite, yet he sought to undermine the bases of the gentry's power and authority, first through his proposed constitution and later through his revision of Virginia's legal code. Jefferson's radicalism was tempered by circumstances and his own caution. While he took significant steps to curtail the power and influence of the gentry—notably land reform and the disestablishment of the Anglican Church—he never took serious action against slavery, *the* cornerstone of gentry power in Virginia and across the slaveholding South. While he condemned the Atlantic slave trade in his draft of the Declaration of Independence and proposed its abolition in his draft constitution, he did not pursue this when he returned to Virginia. Later in life, he reconciled himself to slavery and could not bring himself to break with the Virginia gentry.[44]

Thomas Paine returned to Europe in 1787, arriving in Paris at the end of May before going to London in the autumn. By December he was back in Paris, and during the winter of 1787–88, he met with Jefferson and Lafayette and the three men discussed the proposed federal constitution that the Constitutional Convention in Philadelphia had drafted during the summer. Both Jefferson and Paine supported the ratification of the federal constitution, with reservations. Their responses to the federal constitution were consistent with the views they had expressed and developed since 1776.

Paine's support for the federal constitution was more fulsome than Jefferson's. Support for the federal constitution was strong among urban artisans, particularly in Philadelphia, and Paine's support for the document was consistent with the views of his former neighbors and allies. Paine believed that creating a strong national government that could promote commerce was in the best interests of the common people of the United States. Although he made Pennsylvania his home during his tenure in the United States, he did not have a parochial attachment to the state, and favored ratification of the proposal, which would create a strong national government at the expense of the states. In *Common Sense,* Paine had outlined a plan for a national government that would unite the newly independent colonies. He was concerned about the power of the president and the length of the term for senators, but ultimately supported the constitution because of "the absolute necessity of establishing some Federal authority." He believed that the federal government would be able to protect and promote the commercial interests of urban artisans. Many such artisans agreed with him and lent their support for the constitution.[45]

Jefferson's response to the federal constitution was more equivocal than Paine's. When he received a copy of the document from John Adams in November 1787, he wrote, by way of an initial response, "I confess there are things in it which stagger all my dispositions to subscribe to what such an Assembly has proposed." He was especially concerned that the constitution lacked a bill of rights and that the president "seems a bad edition of the Polish king," an elective monarch who could serve indefinitely. When he received another draft of the constitution complete with a lengthy explanation of its drafting and provisions, from James Madison in mid-December (prior to his discussions with Paine), Jefferson moderated his tone somewhat. "As to the Constitution," he confessed on December 21, "I find myself nearly neutral. There is a great mass of good in it, in a very desirable form: but there is also to me a bitter pill or two." The bitter pills remained the absence of a bill or rights and the strength of the executive. Eventually, Jefferson came to favor ratification, provided that the new government supported amendments to protect civil liberties. In order to achieve this, he argued that a minimum number of states should ratify the constitution so that it would become law, but that the rest should reject it in order to force change. "Were I in America," he wrote, "I would advocate it warmly until nine should have adopted and then as warmly take the other side to convince the remaining four that they ought not to come into it until a declaration of rights is annexed to it." While few went so far as to endorse Jefferson's Janus-faced approach to ratification, his position, ratification on the condition that a bill of rights be amended to the constitution, prevailed among moderate Federalists during the ratification debates in the spring of 1788. Jefferson's concern about excessive executive rights and protecting civil liberties was consistent with the constitutional position he had advocated since 1776.[46]

Beginning in 1776, Paine and Jefferson engaged with the profound constitutional questions arising from the decision to declare independence. The constitutional structures they supported—the 1776 Pennsylvania constitution defended by Paine and the Virginia constitution proposed by Jefferson—differed significantly. The Pennsylvania constitution had a unicameral legislature and a plural executive, whereas Jefferson proposed a bicameral legislature and an annually elected governor. Despite these differences, the plans shared much. Executive power was diffused and limited in both. Both plans vested power in the electorate through a broad franchise and annual elections, thus extending the category of citizenship in the new republics that made up the American confederacy. Paine supported the federal constitution more vigorously than Jefferson, though they shared a concern at the power of the proposed executive. Paine believed that the new government would benefit urban artisans; Jefferson feared that it did not provide enough safeguards for individual liberties. This comparison suggests that the republicanism of Paine and Jefferson, while very different in its means, shared a common end: the empowerment of common white men.

Both men enjoyed only limited success. The Philadelphia merchant elite reasserted its influence over Pennsylvania politics during the 1780s. The Pennsylvania Constitution of 1776 was overturned and replaced by a more conservative frame of government in 1790. Jefferson's proposed constitution was largely ignored. In subsequent years, he fought a rear-guard action to enact key provisions of his program while awaiting a more propitious moment for wholesale constitutional reform. His major successes were the abolition of primogeniture and entail and the separation of church and state. While these struck at the roots of gentry power, Jefferson's failure to even attempt meaningful action against slavery helped to ensure that the slaveholding gentry in Virginia, and beyond, retained power until the Civil War.

This comparison of the efforts of Paine and Jefferson to affect constitutional and legal reform in the aftermath of Independence is instructive on several levels. Eric Foner was correct in his judgment that Painite republicanism was urban-oriented and Jeffersonianism was rural. However, where Foner sees the two as different strands of a common ideology—one forward-looking, protocapitalist, and modern; the other backward-looking, agrarian, and nostalgic—it seems these differences are overstated. Both Paine and Jefferson shared a common republican vision, premised on the ability of common people to govern themselves. Each drew on his particular strengths—Paine as a propagandist and polemicist; Jefferson as a drafter of legislation—in order to achieve a lasting republican settlement that would realize the ideals they articulated in *Common Sense* and the Declaration of Independence, respectively. If we take the constitutional settlements they supported in Pennsylvania and Virginia respectively as expressions of their ideological outlook, then it seems they have much in common. The differences between those settlements and the positions they took are the differences of their own life experiences and local contexts. In other words, they are merely the differences between Revolutionary Pennsylvania and Virginia.

NOTES

1. It is likely that Paine met Jefferson for the first time in 1775 or 1776, as the latter was a member of the Virginia delegation to the Continental Congress. However, the earliest documented meeting between the two did not occur until late 1787 or early 1788, when the men met in Paris to discuss the federal constitution and their common interest in sci-

ence (see Dumas Malone, *Jefferson and the Rights of Man* [Boston: Little Brown, 1951], 143, 171; and Paine to Thomas Jefferson [TJ], n.d. [1788?], in *The Papers of Thomas Jefferson*, ed. Julian P. Boyd et al., 39 vols. to date [Princeton, N.J.: Princeton University Press, 1950–] [hereafter cited as *Jefferson Papers*], 13:222–24). The men had corresponded previously (see Paine to TJ, n.d. [believed to be February 1788], *Jefferson Papers*, 13:4–5).

2. Eric Foner, *Tom Paine and Revolutionary America* (New York: Oxford University Press, 1976), 98–106 (quotations, 100–101, 105).

3. Mark Philp, "Paine, Thomas (1737–1809)," *Oxford Dictionary of National Biography* (Oxford: Oxford University Press, 2004); John Keane, *Tom Paine: A Political Life* (London: Bloomsbury, 1995), chaps. 1–2; Foner, *Tom Paine and Revolutionary America*, chap. 1.

4. Benjamin Franklin to Richard Bache, 30 September 1774, in *The Papers of Benjamin Franklin*, ed. Leonard W. Labaree et al., 39 vols. to date (New Haven, Conn.: Yale University Press, 1959–), 21:325.

5. Foner, *Tom Paine and Revolutionary America*, 6–17 (quotation, 16). Also see Keane, *Tom Paine*, 58–72.

6. Gary B. Nash, *The Urban Crucible: Social Change, Political Consciousness, and the Origins of the American Revolution* (Cambridge, Mass.: Harvard University Press, 1979); Peter Thompson, *Rum Punch and Revolution: Taverngoing and Public Life in Eighteenth-Century Philadelphia* (Philadelphia: University of Pennsylvania Press, 1999); Richard Alan Ryerson, *The Revolution Is Now Begun: The Radical Committees of Philadelphia, 1765–1776* (Philadelphia: University of Pennsylvania Press, 1978); Steven Rosswurm, *Arms, Country, and Class: The Philadelphia Militia and the "Lower Sort" during the American Revolution* (New Brunswick, N.J.: Rutgers University Press, 1987); Ronald Schultz, *The Republic of Labor: Philadelphia Artisans and the Politics of Class, 1720–1830* (New York: Oxford University Press, 1993); Foner, *Tom Paine and Revolutionary America*, chap. 4.

7. Thomas Paine, *Common Sense*, ed. Isaac Kramnick (Harmondsworth: Penguin, 1976), quotation, 62. The original edition of *Common Sense* was published in Philadelphia by R. Bell in 1776; all quotations in this essay are from the Penguin edition cited above. My summary of *Common Sense* closely follows Francis D. Cogliano, *Revolutionary America, 1763–1815: A Political History*, 2nd ed. (London: Routledge, 2009), 88–90.

8. Ibid., 72.

9. Ibid., 78.

10. Ibid., 81.

11. Ibid., 96.

12. Ibid., 97.

13. Ibid., 98.

14. For the Pennsylvania constitution, see J. Paul Selsam, *The Pennsylvania Constitution of 1776: A Study in Revolutionary Democracy* (Philadelphia: University of Pennsylvania Press, 1936); Willi Paul Adams, *First American Constitutions: Republican Ideology and the Making of the State Constitutions in the Revolutionary Era* (Chapel Hill: University of

North Carolina Press, 1980); and Richard Alan Ryerson, "Republican Theory and Partisan Reality in Revolutionary Pennsylvania: Toward a New View of the Constitutionalist Party," in *Sovereign States in an Age of Uncertainty*, ed. Ronald Hoffman and Peter J. Albert (Charlottesville: University Press of Virginia, 1981), 95–133.

15. "To the Citizens of Pennsylvania on the Proposal for Calling a Convention," *Aurora* (Philadelphia), August 1805, in *The Complete Writings of Thomas Paine*, ed. Philip S. Foner, 2 vols. (New York: Citadel Press, 1945) [hereafter cited as *Complete Writings*], 2:992–1007 (quotations, 993, 1001).

16. "To the People," *Pennsylvania Packet* (Philadelphia), 12 March 1777, ibid., 2:269–72 (quotation, 270). For Paine's activities during the latter half of 1776, see Paine to Henry Laurens, 14 January 1779, ibid., 2:1163–4.

17. "To the Printers," *Pennsylvania Packet* (Philadelphia), 7 April 1786, ibid., 2:419–25 (quotation, 420).

18. "A Serious Address to the People of Pennsylvania on the Present Situation of their Affairs," *Pennsylvania Packet*, 1, 5, 10, 12 December 1778, ibid., 2:277–302. For Paine's other writings in defence of the constitution, see "To the People," *Pennsylvania Packet*, 12 March 1777, ibid., 2:269–72; "Candid and Critical Remarks on a Letter Signed Ludlow," *Pennsylvania Journal* (Philadelphia), 4 June 1777, ibid., 2:272–77; and "To the Public on Mr. Deane's Affair," *Pennsylvania Packet*, 31 December 1778, 2, 5, 7, 9 January 1779, ibid., 2:111–34.

19. "A Serious Address to the People of Pennsylvania on the Present Situation of their Affairs," *Pennsylvania Packet*, 1, 5, 10, 12 December 1778, ibid., 2:288.

20. Ibid., 2:289.

21. Dumas Malone, *Jefferson, The Virginian* (Boston: Little, Brown, 1948); R. B. Bernstein, *Thomas Jefferson* (New York: Oxford University Press, 2003); P. S. Onuf, "Jefferson, Thomas (1743–1826)," *Oxford Dictionary of National Biography* (Oxford: Oxford University Press, 2004).

22. "Resolutions of the Virginia Convention Calling for Independence," *Jefferson Papers*, 1:291; "Resolution of Independence," [7 June 1776], 1:298. Also see Pauline Maier, *American Scripture: Making the Declaration of Independence* (New York: Alfred A. Knopf, 1997); Michael A. McDonnell, *The Politics of War: Race, Class, and Conflict in Revolutionary Virginia* (Chapel Hill: University of North Carolina Press, 2007); and Emory G. Evans, "Executive Leadership in Virginia, 1776–1781: Henry, Jefferson, and Nelson," in *Sovereign States in an Age of Uncertainty*, ed. Ronald Hoffman and Peter J. Albert, 185–225.

23. TJ to Thomas Nelson, 16 May 1776, *Jefferson Papers*, 1:292. For the documents relating to Jefferson's draft constitution and the Virginia Constitution of 1776, see "The Virginia Constitution," *Jefferson Papers*, 1:329–86. Also see Malone, *Jefferson, the Virginian*, 235–40; David N. Mayer, *The Constitutional Thought of Thomas Jefferson* (Charlottesville: University Press of Virginia, 1994), chap. 3; and R. B. Bernstein, "Thomas Jefferson and Constitutionalism," in *A Companion to Thomas Jefferson*, ed. Francis D. Cogliano (Oxford: Wiley Blackwell, 2012), 419–38.

24. George Wythe to TJ, 27 July 1776, *Jefferson Papers*, 1:476–77; "The Constitution as Adopted by the Convention," [29 June 1776], ibid., 1:377–86; Malone, *Jefferson, the Virginian*, 239.

25. "Third Draft by Jefferson," [before 13 June 1776], *Jefferson Papers*, 1:356–65 (quotation, 360). Jefferson wrote that the Administrator should be "bound by acts of legislature tho' not expressly named," and that

> he shall have no negative on the bills of the Legislature;
>
> he shall be liable to action, tho' not to personal restraint for private duties or wrongs;
>
> he shall not possess the prerogatives
>
>> of dissolving, proroguing or adjourning either house of Assembly;
>>
>> of declaring war or concluding peace;
>>
>> of issuing letters of marque or reprisal;
>>
>> of raising or introducing armed forces, building armed vessels, forts or strong holds;
>>
>> of coining monies or regulating their value;
>>
>> of regulating weights and measures;
>>
>> of erecting courts, offices, boroughs, corporations, fairs, markets, ports, beacons, lighthouses, seamarks.
>>
>> of laying embargoes, or prohibiting the exportation of any commodity for a longer space than [40] days.
>>
>> of retaining or recalling a member of the state but by legal process pro delicto vel contractu.
>>
>> of making denizens;
>>
>> of creating dignities or granting rights of precedence

but that "these powers shall be exercised by the legislature alone" (360).

26. Ibid., 1:362. For a discussion of the issues of representation and suffrage, see Edmund Pendleton to TJ, 10 August 1776, *Papers*, 1:488–91; and TJ to Edmund Pendleton, 26 August 26, ibid., 1:503–7.

27. "Third Draft by Jefferson" [before 13 June 1776], *Jefferson Papers*, 1:362–64.

28. Paine, *Common Sense*, 76.

29. Dumas Malone, Jefferson's foremost biographer, argued: "Jefferson took little pride in his proposals to this convention, for these afterwards seemed conservative and he doubted if he himself had penetrated to the true republican principle at the time" (Malone, *Jefferson, the Virginian*, 239). By contrast, just two years later, Julian P. Boyd, the editor of Jefferson's papers, wrote that the draft constitution epitomized "most if not all of the leading principles to which Jefferson's entire career was dedicated" ("Editorial Note," in *Jefferson Papers*, 1:330).

30. George Wythe to TJ, 27 July 1776, *Jefferson Papers*, 1:476–77.

31. *Autobiography*, in Thomas Jefferson, *Writings*, ed. Merrill D. Peterson (New York:

Library of America, 1984) [hereafter cited as *Jefferson Writings*], 1–101 (quotation, 44). For Jefferson's contributions toward rewriting Virginia's laws, see Malone, *Jefferson, the Virginian*, 235–85; and "The Revisal of the Laws, 1776–1786," *Jefferson Papers*, 2:305–665, esp. the "Editorial Note," 305–24.

32. *Autobiography*, in *Jefferson Writings*, 44–45. See also Holly Brewer, "Entailing Aristocracy in Colonial Virginia: 'Ancient Feudal Restraints' and Revolutionary Reform," *William and Mary Quarterly*, 3rd ser., 54 (April 1997): 307–46.

33. For a discussion of the moldboard plow and agriculture generally, see TJ to Sir John Sinclair, 23 March 1798, *Jefferson Papers*, 30:197–207. Also see Lucia Stanton, "Thomas Jefferson: Planter and Farmer," in *A Companion to Thomas Jefferson*, ed. Francis D. Cogliano (Oxford: Wiley Blackwell, 2012), 253–70; Lucia Stanton, "Better Tools for a New and Better World: Jefferson Perfects the Plow," in *Old World, New World: America and Europe in the Age of Jefferson*, ed. Leonard J. Sadosky, Peter Nicolaisen, Peter S. Onuf, and Andrew J. O'Shaughnessy (Charlottesville: University of Virginia Press, 2010), 200–222; and Joyce O. Appleby, "The 'Agrarian Myth' in the Early Republic," in *Liberalism and Republicanism in the Historical Imagination*, ed. Joyce Appleby (Cambridge, Mass.: Harvard University Press, 1992), 253–76.

34. *Autobiography*, in *Jefferson Writings*, 44, 35. See also "Notes and Proceedings on Discontinuing the Establishment of the Church of England [11 October to 9 December 1776]," *Jefferson Papers*, 1:525–58.

35. "A Bill for Establishing Religious Freedom," *Jefferson Papers*, 2:545–53 (quotations, 544, 545). Jefferson's version of the bill appeared as a broadside, A BILL *for establishing* RELIGIOUS FREEDOM, *printed for the consideration of the* PEOPLE (Williamsburg, 1779). For the textual changes made to Jefferson's draft by the House of Delegates, see the textual notes in *Jefferson Papers*, 2:547–53. For the drafting and adoption of the bill, see Thomas E. Buckley, *Church and State in Revolutionary Virginia, 1776–1787* (Charlottesville: University Press of Virginia, 1977); William Lee Miller, *The First Liberty: Religion and the American Republic* (New York: Knopf, 1988), 1–75; Malone, *Jefferson, the Virginian*, 274–80; and Edwin S. Gaustad, *Sworn on the Altar of God: A Religious Biography of Thomas Jefferson* (Grand Rapids, Mich.: W. B. Eerdmans, 1996), 63–70.

36. *Autobiography*, in *Jefferson Writings*, 44–45.

37. Writing prior to the adoption of the bill in 1786, Jefferson included a lengthy statement on the benefits of freedom on conscience (see *Notes on the State of Virginia*, in *Jefferson Writings*, 283–87).

38. Ibid., 285.

39. *Autobiography*, in *Jefferson Writings*, 45.

40. "A Bill for the More General Diffusion of Knowledge," *Jefferson Papers*, 2:526–35; "A Bill for Amending the Constitution of the College of William and Mary, and Substituting More Certain Revenues for Its Support," ibid., 2:535–43; "A Bill for Establishing a Public Library," ibid., 2:544. These were Bills 79, 80, and 81, respectively, of the proposed

"Revisal of the Laws" submitted by the Committee of Revisors to the House of Delegates on 18 June 1779.

41. "Bill for the More General Diffusion of Knowledge," ibid., 2:526–27.

42. Ibid.; TJ to George Wythe, 13 August 1786, ibid., 10:244. Jefferson elaborated upon his Revolutionary-era educational ideas in Query XIV of his *Notes on the State of Virginia* (see *Jefferson Writings,* 272–75). For a concise yet thorough overview of the subject, see Jennings L. Wagoner Jr., *Jefferson and Education* (Charlottesville, Va.: Thomas Jefferson Foundation, 2004).

43. TJ to George Wythe, 13 August 1786, *Jefferson Papers,* 10:244.

44. Paul Finkelman, "Jefferson and Slavery: 'Treason against the Hopes of the World,'" in *Jeffersonian Legacies* ed. Peter S. Onuf (Charlottesville: University Press of Virginia, 1993), 181–221. The literature on Jefferson and slavery is vast. For a summary and analysis, see Francis D. Cogliano, *Thomas Jefferson: Reputation and Legacy* (Charlottesville: University of Virginia Press, 2006), chap. 7.

45. Paine to George Clymer, 29 December 1787, *Complete Writings,* 2:1266; Foner, *Tom Paine and Revolutionary America,* 203–5 (quotation, 205); Malone, *Jefferson and the Rights of Man,* 142–43, 171.

46. TJ to John Adams, 13 November 1787, *Jefferson Papers,* 12:350–51; TJ to Edward Carrington, 21 December 1787, ibid., 12:446; TJ to William Stephens Smith, 2 February 1788, ibid., 12:558. Also see James Madison to TJ, 24 October 1787, ibid., 12:270–86; R. B. Bernstein, "Thomas Jefferson and Constitutionalism"; Andrew Burstein and Nancy Isenberg, *Jefferson and Madison* (New York: Random House, 2010), chaps. 4–5; and Malone, *Jefferson and the Rights of Man,* chap. 9.

Thomas Paine's Early Radicalism, 1768–1783

JACK FRUCHTMAN JR.

Between 1768 and 1783, Thomas Paine's political radicalism and revolutionary enthusiasm developed in two phases: in his experiences in the small towns and hamlets throughout Midlands England and Sussex, and then in his first year in America after his arrival in Philadelphia in November 1774. Once in his new country, he cultivated a vision of how Americans could transform their country into a genuine democratic republic. He then embarked on a quest to ensure that European nations, including Britain, followed the Americans by creating their own republics. Paine was among the first radical writers to demonstrate that a political career could be devoted to revolutionary change and republican democracy. His life after 1776 displayed a fabric of political engagement that commentators and historians have often neglected because of the wide gulf they detect separating his sparkling and anonymously published *Common Sense* from his later support of the French Revolution in *Rights of Man*.

Much of what we know of Paine's early life derives from his first biographer, George Chalmers, writing in 1791 under the pseudonym "Francis Oldys."[1] The British Crown hired him to counter the argument and conclusions in *Rights of Man* by publishing a scurrilous personal attack on Paine. A Scot who worked for the Board of Trade, Chalmers was living in Maryland when the Americans declared their independence. On his return to Britain, he hated all things American and all men who supported the separation of the colonies from the Empire. His biography focused on Paine's wandering lifestyle, his failed marriages, his inability to hold a job, his poor personal habits, and his unsuccessful career as an excise-tax collector. The important point is that the British government so feared Paine in 1791 that it tried to undermine his radicalism by revealing him as an idle, miserable, and malodorous drunkard.

Contemporary commentators and biographers typically appreciate *Common Sense* as a precursor to the more radical *Rights of Man*. They argue that the subject of *Common Sense* was American independence, while the focus of *Rights of Man* was global revolution and change. Bernard Bailyn reminds us of the centrality of *Common Sense* as "a superbly rhetorical and iconoclastic pamphlet whose slashing attack upon the English monarchy—the one remaining link, in early 1776, between England and the colonies—and upon the concept of balance in the constitution made it an immediate sensation."[2] But still it was about America, even if its radicalism cannot be overstated, as Harvey Kaye argues: While "Americans . . . turned Thomas Paine into a radical, a patriot, and a writer, . . . Paine . . . turned Americans into revolutionaries." But even Kaye argues that *Common Sense* was merely a manifesto for "a democratic America," and nowhere else.[3]

Other contemporaries have made this distinction between the two works. Craig Nelson argues that *Rights of Man* made Paine responsible for "the birth of modern nations," while Eric Foner concludes that it made him "one of the creators of the secular language of revolution." John Keane tells us that as a result of his European exploits after 1789, the "democratic republican" Paine "made more noise in the world and excited more attention than . . . well-known European contemporaries." These contemporaries included some of the shining luminaries of the Enlightenment: Adam Smith, Jean-Jacques Rousseau, Voltaire, Immanuel Kant, Madame de Staël, Edmund Burke, and even the obscure Milanese political economist Pietro Verri. Meantime, Bernard Vincent sees Paine in the 1790s as the "prophet and crusader of the republic in a universe peopled by monarchs," while Jean Lessay terms him a "professor of revolutions" and Maurice Ezran finds him to have been a "fighter in two revolutions," with the second one in France being far more important. Mark Philp refers to Paine in the same period as "the first international revolutionary," which is undoubtedly correct, and Ian Dyck argues that Paine thought his radicalism in France was so universal that he was simply a "citizen of the world." Isaac Kramnick's formulation for Paine is that his revolutionary fervor, again while in France after 1789, made him a "radical liberal."[4] Some, like Gordon Wood, are skeptical of Paine's influence, arguing that he was "a man out of joint with his times, and he has remained so ever since." Wood nonetheless finds Paine to be "America's first modern intellectual, an unconnected social critic" who "spoke out of a tradition of radical republicanism that ran deeper and was more bitter yet more modern than the balanced and reasonable classical republicanism of most of the founders."[5] John Pocock, too, wonders about Paine's historical place, when he concludes that his ideological views fell into no known class of British political thought. According to Pocock, Paine

> remains difficult to fit into any kind of category. *Common Sense* breathes an extraordinary hatred of English governing institutions, but it does not consistently echo any established radical vocabulary; Paine had no real place in the club of Honest Whigs to which Franklin had introduced him in London, and his use of anti-Normanism to insist that Britain did not have a constitution but rather a tyranny does not permit us to think of him (as contemporaries might have) as a New Model soldier risen from the grave. Moreover, when the Revolutionary War was over Paine returned to live under the "the royal brute of Britain" as if nothing had happened, nor was he pursued by the authorities until the very different circumstances of 1791.[6]

Only Edward Larkin understands that Paine wanted to carry his Revolutionary goals to Britain and Europe while he was still in America. Unfortunately, he does not detect this in *Common Sense* and the *Crisis Papers,* but only after the end of the American Revolution.[7]

Surely, *Common Sense* was a powerful critique of monarchy and aristocracy that persuaded many Americans that the British colonies in America must separate from the Empire and establish an independent republic. But the pamphlet contains more than just an appeal for separation: a close reading demonstrates that Paine used language to embrace a call to arms for global revolution against hierarchy, rank, and privilege. Six years later, in 1782, Paine's *Letter to the Abbé Raynal* took up many of the themes in *Common Sense* to declare that the American Revolution presaged fundamental global change. The American success in overcoming British tyranny was "distinguished by opening a new system of extended civilization."[8] He looked beyond America for revolutionary change, to the world itself. The letter to Raynal is, then, the central link between *Common Sense* and the more extreme *Rights of Man,* which contains Paine's most familiar, memorable, and stirring phrases of universal transformation. "It is an age of revolution, in which every thing may be looked for." And, "To use a trite expression, the iron is becoming hot all over Europe. The insulted German and the enslaved Spaniard, the Russ and the

Pole are beginning to think. The present age will hereafter merit to be called the Age of Reason, and the present generation will appear to the future as the Adam of a new world." Even South America, like Europe, was destined to follow the lead of America and France. Paine foresaw "the independence of South America, and the opening those countries, of immense extent and wealth."[9]

Paine's radical and revolutionary activism appeared as early as the two decades prior to his setting foot in Philadelphia, beginning with his experiences in the town of Lewes, where he lived for six years from 1768 to 1774. There, he wrote his first major political tract, an appeal to Parliament concerning the harsh working conditions and low pay of his colleagues in the excise-tax service. His thinking became further radicalized during his first two years in America after the events at Lexington and Concord in April 1775, which were a result of the increasing tensions building between the Crown and the Americans. These two experiences shaped him into the political radical and fervent revolutionary that made *Common Sense* an appeal for global change.[10] Certainly, the pamphlet presented the most cogent argument for American independence from Britain, which was the goal of those in his immediate circle, like Benjamin Franklin, Samuel Adams, and Benjamin Rush, all of whom initially reviewed his draft and made suggestions to Paine before he published it. A close reading, however, demonstrates that he also provided arguments for the promotion of democratic republics worldwide long before the fall of the Bastille on July 14, 1789.

PAINE'S POLITICAL AWAKENING, 1768–1776

Paine's life in Thetford, his birthplace, and the small towns and villages in the Midlands and Sussex until 1774 shaped his ideas and contributed to his political education. In each location—Thetford, Dover, Sandwich, Margate, Grantham, Alford, Diss, and Lewes—he witnessed the gulf separating the rich from the poor and the owners of the great landholdings from those who possessed little or nothing. He saw the sufferings of those who lived impoverished lives while great magnates like the Grafton family, which controlled the politics of Thetford, made certain that there was always a Grafton elected to the Commons from the district. Paine twice lived in London, once in 1757 for about a year while working for a master stay-maker, and again in 1768 to teach at a private academy while awaiting reinstatement to the excise authority. Those two periods exposed him to the social and political inequities inherent in a large eighteenth-century urban area where the powerful rich lorded over the poor. These experiences were reflected in his personal life. By the time he departed for America in 1774 with a letter of introduction from Benjamin Franklin, the then Pennsylvania colonial agent, Paine, who was always poor, had already passed through at least four career changes, including several stints at stay-making, two attempts at teaching school, two attempts at collecting the excise (he was dismissed both times), and one attempt at retailing (his second wife owned a dry-goods store she had inherited from her father, but he ran it into bankruptcy).

With his second appointment to the excise service in 1768, this time in the Sussex town of Lewes, he made his first foray into politics, when he became a member of the Society of Twelve, an unelected, self-perpetuating oligarchic town council that oversaw town business. With four thousand residents and a long tradition of self-government, Lewes had a coffeehouse for discussion and debate, a theater that played comic opera and Shakespearean plays, a lending library, a sizeable Dissenting community, and a large tavern called the White Hart Inn, which was the center of the town's social and political life. It was both a drinking establishment and hotel. Paine and his colleagues in the Society of Twelve managed town affairs from the White Hart, ensuring that the streets were clean, that the stray dogs and cats, pigs and cows were picked up, and that the town's two constables, clerks of the market, and other appointed officials did their duty. The Twelve also discussed taxes, mortgages, and other financial and political matters.

Paine's participation in town affairs opened up new vistas for the lower-middle-class craftsman and failed businessman. It launched his career as a political writer and advocate.[11] In Lewes he wrote his first major essay in 1772, which turned out to be a futile attempt to persuade Parliament to increase the wages of the excise-tax collectors. Paine's colleagues in the service saw him as the man to undertake the task. They specifically chose him to present their arguments to Westminster, and even chipped in travel money for him to spend time there.

The Case of the Officers of Excise was a radical, though exceedingly polite work. It did not threaten a strike, but maintained a pleasant though pleading tone, filled with facts and figures of the meager working and living conditions of the tax collectors. As Paine put it in his subtitle, he *humbly* addressed Members of Parliament.[12] And yet, for its time, *The Case of the Officers of Excise* was extraordinarily radical. To demand that Parliament increase wages was in itself extreme. From their annual salary of £50, excisemen could barely pay for the basic necessities of life: from grooming, feeding, and housing their horses, to lodging and feeding their families, as well as paying for clothing and the moving expenses they incurred when they had to relocate. Even the tax collectors in urban areas, who had no need of a horse (the "footwalks" as opposed to the rural "outrides"), could barely meet their living expenses, because the cost of living in the cities was higher than in rural areas. Paine figured that the actual annual wage was just £32 after basic expenses, or, as he put it, "one shilling and ninepence farthing a day." It is no wonder that the excisemen were tempted by "*Corruption, Collusion, and Neglect*": some tax men accepted tips or bribes, others let batches of goods like tea, tobacco, or brandy pass through without payment, or perhaps only a partial one. "The temptations of downright poverty" made cheating and dishonesty rampant.[13]

Outriders relied on their friends and family to "keep their children from nakedness, supply them occasionally with perhaps half a hog, a load of wood, a chaldron [sic] of coals, or something or other which abates the severity of their distress." The £5 million a year the English excise collected for the Crown was surely enough for a modest increase in wages. The men deserved a living wage, an outrageous thought to those who believed that the differences between rich and poor were as natural as warmth and cold. Paine invited all Members of Parliament to "descend to the cold regions of want, the circle of polar poverty," to see for themselves. Once there, "they would find their opinions changing with the climate."[14]

The Case of the Officers of Excise was an astonishing performance, appearing long before twentieth-century-style labor unions organized into collective bargaining units that battled management for increased wages and better working conditions.[15] The job itself was inherently dangerous because the excisemen also had to guard against armed and dangerous smugglers. With only their writing instruments and paper, they rode alone throughout the countryside on lonely roads, in all kinds of weather, and sometimes at night. Smugglers knew that if they were caught they would be hanged, so they were certain to carry weapons and use them against the tax collectors. A wage increase would have a twofold impact: by saving excisemen and their families from "the temptations of poverty," and the service from "the evils of it; the cure would be as extensive as the complaint, and new health out-root the present corruptions."[16]

While the address was radical even to appeal for a wage increase, it was not revolutionary. Paine neither challenged British authority nor its structure and hierarchy. Instead, his language was a cry from the roiling seas of the excise to the safe harbor of Westminster. Although it was polite and deferential, it also displayed his ability to draft a powerfully vivid argument. It laid the groundwork for his later engagement in Revolutionary ideas when he immigrated to

America. For it was there that he began in earnest to write not only radical, but revolutionary, tracts. As Paine worked to create a democratic republic in the United States as a model for the world, and then later in France, he was certain he was doing providential work.

PAINE IN AMERICA

America, Paine tells us, presented him with the opportunity to remake and redefine himself in a quiet, private life. He found a position with Robert Aitken, who had just started a new journal, the *Pennsylvania Magazine,* and he soon became its editor.[17] Within three months of his arrival, Philadelphians, including Paine, learned of the violence and deaths that had taken place in Lexington and Concord on April 19, 1775. As Paine later put it, "All the plans or prospects of private life (for I am not by nature fond of, or fitted for a public one and feel all occasions of it where I must act personally, a burden) all these plans, I say, were immediately disconcerted, and I was at once involved in all the troubles of the country."[18] In fact, "the country set fire about my ears almost the moment I got into it."[19] Paine seemed genuinely surprised by the anger, and even hatred, that many Americans had for the British ministry, and even the king. Everyone, he said, "felt the shock, and all vibrated together."[20] But they were wary of declaring independence from the Empire. "Their attachment to Britain was obstinate," Paine noted, "and it was at that time a kind of treason to speak against it. They disliked the ministry, but they esteemed the nation. Their idea of grievance operated without resentment, and their single object was reconciliation."[21] This he would not stand for. Well known by the end of the summer of 1775 to Benjamin Rush, David Rittenhouse, Thomas Jefferson, Samuel and John Adams, and of course, Benjamin Franklin, who had just returned from London the previous May, Paine was in a good position to join them as their publicist. When Rush asked him to prepare a pamphlet giving the reasons for the separation of the colonies from the Empire, he grasped the opportunity. The result was *Common Sense.*[22]

As a work designed to inspire Americans to move from their hopeless goal of reconciliation, *Common Sense* contains a variety of Paine's rhetorical techniques, including his crude demonization of the king.[23] The king was variously "the royal brute of Britain" and "a worm, who in the midst of his splendor is crumbling into dust." George III displayed "the cruelty of the monster," and perhaps worst of all, he was no better than Saturn, the Roman god who devoured his own children ("even brutes do not devour their young").[24] Paine best summarized his feelings about the king when he wrote at the end of 1776, "I should suffer the misery of devils, were I to make a whore of my soul by swearing allegiance to the one whose character is that of a sottish, stupid, stubborn, worthless, brutish man."[25] As monarchy was linked to the ancients, beginning with the pagan world that had invented it, it soon extended to the Hebrews who adopted it. A system of government, which deprives the people of virtually all of their rights, is "an original in the history of civilized barbarism, and is truly British."[26]

Conforming to the convention of the time to cite the role of God in society and politics, Paine carried this theme onward to formulate an argument that Providence, who had given men free will at creation, was on the Americans' side. Was his resort to biblical passages and theological doctrine simply in conformity to the conventions of his age, or in fact did he believe some of what he wrote in *Common Sense* and in later works when he referred to a republican Providence? While there is no doubt that he never accepted scripture as having been inspired by God and he always debunked organized religion as false and mythological, as a Deist, he did emphasize his belief in Providence as a creator of the universe. That said, he confounded the matter when he wrote private letters that make it appear that he often relied on providential intervention. In a letter to General Nathanael Greene in 1780, for example, Paine seemed ambivalent about his beliefs. He attributed the capture of Major John André, a British spy later hanged, and the escape of Benedict Arnold, with whom André was working, to a providential hand. André could have escaped, he said: he was after all on horseback and his captors on foot. "But there again comes in the answer. *It was to be—and so be it.*" As he put it, he did not want to "attribute the whole of this discovery to Providence," but sometimes "I almost feel myself a Predestinarian."[27]

Paine used scripture to persuade his audience of the wickedness of monarchy, as if to suggest that Providence was a republican who despised monarchy, aristocracy, and every form of tyranny. He carefully devoted long passages in *Common Sense* to demonstrating that monarchy was among "the sins of the Jews," and that "in every instance" it is "the popery of government," a characteristic Protestant Reformation blast at Roman Catholicism. God created human beings to be "originally equals in the order of creation," so that "no *one* by *birth* could have a right to set up his own family in perpetual preference to all others for ever." Hereditary rule is not only absurd but against God's will, or as he put it, "The word of God bears testimony against [it]." This is why he concluded, and noted twice to emphasize the point, that "virtue is not hereditary" from the perspective of both God and man.[28]

Paine's argument that God had chosen the Americans to lead the world to a new day resonated with his readers. We may now see the energy in the most famous statements in his pamphlet. The phrase "We have it in our power to begin the world over again" indicates that the Americans were like demigods undertaking God's work on earth. "A situation, similar to the present, hath not happened since the days of Noah until now," for God has now chosen the Americans to transform the globe. "The birthday of a new world is at hand," because the American people now begin their own creation, like God who created the universe and all that is in it.[29] It appeared to Paine, "by the late providential turn of affairs, that God Almighty was visibly on our side," he wrote in *The American Crisis*.[30] He pointed out that "the will of God has parted us. . . . When she shall be a spot scarcely visible among the nations, America shall flourish the favorite of heaven." After all, "Providence has some nobler end to accomplish than the gratification of the petty elector of Hanover, or the ignorant and insignificant king of Britain."[31] With the intervention of Providence, "and her blessings on our endeavors," America will overpower Britain.[32] When victory loomed after Lord Cornwallis's surrender at Yorktown in 1781, Paine claimed that Providence, "in every stage of the conflict, has blest her [America] with success."[33]

PAINE'S AMERICAN REVOLUTIONARY RADICALISM, 1776–1781

Common Sense was a gigantic leap from his polite and reasoned appeal to Parliament on behalf of his excise colleagues.[34] It was indubitably a call to his fellow Americans to strive for independence. We see this theme especially when he intoned at the end of 1776, "Let it be told to the future world, that in the depth of winter, when nothing but hope and virtue could survive, that the city and the country, alarmed at one common danger, came forth to meet and to repulse it."[35] He later told Sir William Howe, the commander in chief of the British armies in America, that the Americans were engaged in a defensive war, not one of aggression: "If ever there was a *just* war since the world began it is this in which America is now engaged. She invaded no land of yours. She hired no mercenaries to burn your towns, nor Indians to massacre their inhabitants. She wanted nothing from you. . . . [H]er defence is honorable and her prosperity is certain." America, he said, "has bravely put herself between Tyranny and Freedom, between a curse and a blessing, determined to expel the one and protect the other."[36]

The pamphlet, however, also contained subtle calls for global change to create democracies everywhere, a theme he elaborated six years later in his *Letter to the Abbé Raynal*. Paine may well have added the most extreme statements in the pamphlet after Rush, Franklin, and Sam Adams reviewed a draft of the work before its publication, because many of these ideas appear in an appendix to the third edition. But even his "editors" may have missed the revolutionary implications of key phrases in the original draft when, for instance, Paine proclaimed that "the cause of America is in a great measure the cause of *all mankind*. Many circumstances hath, and will arise, which are not local, but *universal*" (emphasis added). This language emphasizes the threat that any regime—in America, Britain, Europe, or anywhere for that matter—that denied human beings their right to live a decent life was ripe for overthrow. Only the democratic republic ensured that the people controlled the government, and not the other way round. Why else do we "have it in our power to begin the world over again," or why else is "the birthday of a new world . . . at hand"? The responsibility that had fallen to the Americans was stunning: "The reflection is awful, and in this point of view, how trifling, how ridiculous, do the little paltry cavilings of a few weak or interested men appear, when weighed against the business of the world."[37]

This was why "freedom hath been hunted round the globe," including Europe, Asia, and Africa, but found "an asylum for mankind" only in America.[38] The Americans possessed the spirit and fortitude to grant a safe harbor to the refugee and to extend its benefits and virtues. Hereditary rule is as corrupt as it is ungodly. No people, no nation, would willingly choose to live under despotism. Paine's role, as he himself saw it, was to begin the work of global revolution, beginning with the independence of the colonies and their transformation into a true united democratic republic. From there, revolutionary change could be exported to Britain and Europe.

The loyalist William Smith, an Anglican minister and provost of the University of Pennsylvania, who wrote under the pen name of "Cato," was frightened by the depth of Revolutionary fervor that Paine imparted in his pamphlet. In a series of letters addressed to the citizens of Pennsylvania, he railed against Paine's ideas, arguing that "it is a mistake to think that . . . the abuse of power is proper only to monarchies. Other forms of government are liable to this as well."[39] Responding to Cato's attack in a series of essays collectively called "The Forester's Letters," Paine first focused on the impossibility of reconciliation with Britain. In his third letter, however, he let loose his revolutionary vision of European transformation. "Nature seems sometimes to laugh at mankind, by giving them so many fools for kings; at other times, she punishes their folly by giving them tyrants; but England must have offended highly to be cursed with both in one." With a reference to Jean-Jacques Rousseau's 1761 "Plan for Perpetual Peace," he noted that such a peace envisioned by the great Swiss philosophe would provide a foundation "for every European state . . . to form a General Council" to work out matters of peace and war. "This would be forming a kind of European Republic," which was what the world needed but could not have, because "the proud and plundering spirit of kings" maintains a death grip on their nations.[40]

After the announcement of the American Declaration of Independence in July 1776, Paine devoted his energy to rally his fellow citizens to the American cause in another series of essays known as *The American Crisis*. Once Britain launched the largest naval and ground assault in the history of warfare against America, it appeared unlikely that this small backwater country could possibly resist the fierce enormity of Britain's armed forces.[41] It was crucial, therefore, for the powerful opening lines of *Crisis I* to reverberate throughout America when General Washington ordered that it be read aloud in all military camps: "These are the times that try men's souls. The summer soldier and the sunshine patriot will, in this crisis, shrink from the service of their country; but he that stands it now, deserves the love and thanks of man and woman. Tyranny, like hell, is not easily conquered: yet we have this consolation with us, that the harder the conflict, the more glorious the triumph."[42]

Even in the *Crisis* essays, Paine planted a vision of global change to encourage other nations to engage in revolution. At first he advocated an enlightened international system in which the new United States could secure a prosperous independence working alongside the "European Republic" he had idealized in "The Forester Letters." He knew that America would need to ally itself in a hostile world and to form trade and commercial relationships, even with monarchies, at least for the time being. Thus, he wrote that America simply wished to be let alone: "Let Britain but leave America to herself and she asks no more. She has risen into greatness without the knowledge and against the will of England, and has a right to the unmolested enjoyment of her own created wealth."[43] Then at times he was explicit about a potential revolution in Britain. Once the Americans succeeded in breaking free from the Empire, he wrote in *Crisis II*, the British people might rise against their government, "for I, who know England and the disposition of the people well, am confident, that it is easier for us *to effect a revolution there*." He promised to send *Common Sense* and his other writings to London, because he knew that when he did, "though it may put one party on their guard, it will inform the other, and the nation in general, of our design to help them."[44] He directly addressed the people of Britain to convince them that their interests lay in joining America to establish a democracy on their shores. "You had better risk a revolution and call a Congress," he told them, "than be thus led on from madness to despair, and from despair to ruin. America has set you the example, and you may follow it and be free." He noted that he dedicated one of his essays to the English people with the hope of "making it a Crisis" for them and for the Crown.[45]

By war's end, Paine began to think that the people of Britain and Europe were ripe for political change. After all, Britain "has been treacherous, and we know it. Her character is gone, and we have seen the funeral."[46] That nation had already been through its death march and burial, and all it now needed was the overthrow of its monarchy. Revolution must be extended to and then beyond Britain because America's duty was "to see it in our power to make a world happy—to teach mankind the art of being so—to exhibit, on the theatre of the universe a character hitherto unknown—and to have, as it were, a new creation intrusted to our hands."[47] The American Revolution was now a model for the entire globe.

POST-REVOLUTIONARY PAINE, 1781–1783

Having set forth a vision of political transformation in *Common Sense* and the *Crisis* papers, Paine saw two tasks before him after Yorktown, one domestic, the other international. First, he wanted to help consolidate the gains in America by advocating a strong political union among the newly created states, and second, and more to the point of this essay, he began to consider ways to export revolution.[48] The second task was as important to him as the first, in that it would secure a new political order in America while stimulating Britons and Europeans to end their monarchical regimes. Part of his strategy involved the production of a history of the American Revolution to instruct the world on republican regime change. He did not want the input of any patron, because he thought that if he appeared to be impartial, it would make his loaded political agenda more compelling to his audience. When Congress voted to pay him to write the text, he declined the offer. Instead, he began his work independently of Congress, "to inform posterity [and] to confirm them in the true principles of freedom and civil government," and this included "Europe or the world."[49]

Paine may have first considered writing a history of the Revolution as early as December 1776. He reminded Franklin in June 1777 that the great polymath had offered to support him in this enterprise. "When I mentioned [this project] to you the winter before last you was so kind as to offer such materials in your possession as might be necessary for that purpose."[50] He told Congress, just as he told Franklin, that he hoped to receive several documents from them, but that he should never be considered a congressional historian.

"For Congress to reserve to themselves the least appearance of influence over an historian, by annexing thereto a yearly salary subject to their own control, will endanger the reputation of both of [sic] the historian and the history."[51]

Paine never wrote his history as such. He did, however, consider his response to a work by the French cleric, the abbé Guillaume-Thomas Raynal, an appropriate substitute for his projected narrative. Raynal had written his *Révolution d'Amérique* as a liberal supporter of the American cause. He proposed that the main reason the Americans wanted to separate from Britain was because of the severe tax burden suffered without their consent.[52] As Abbé Raynal put it, "The whole question was reduced to knowing whether the mother-country had, or had not, a right to lay, directly, or indirectly, a slight tax upon the colonies: for the accumulated grievances in the manifesto [the Declaration of Independence] were valid only in consequence of this leading grievance."[53]

Paine doggedly objected to this position. In his marvelously imaginative way, Paine argued that Raynal's writings "represent a beautiful wilderness without paths; in which the eye is diverted by everything without being particularly directed toward anything; and in which it is agreeable to be lost, and difficult to find the way out." He told General Washington that Raynal, "in several places . . . is mistaken, and in others injudicious and sometimes cynical." While he wanted to disabuse an American audience of Raynal's argument ("I believe I shall publish [my response] in America"), his more immediate goal was "to republish it in Europe both in French and English" as a universal attack on monarchy and aristocracy.[54] The result was Paine's powerful *Letter to the Abbé Raynal*.[55] Within a year, Paine's pamphlet was published in a French edition in Paris.[56]

Paine's strategy was clear in the opening paragraphs when he argued that the British Crown and Parliament never legitimately exercised unlimited authority over the American colonies. Paine thus demolished the claim of the Declaratory Act "to bind America in all cases whatsoever." It "took in with it the whole life of a man, or if I may so express it, an eternity of circumstances." While law conventionally demands obedience, it now requires "servitude; and the condition of an American, under the operation of it, was not that of a subject, but a vassal." Tyranny was usually established when the law is absent, but in the case of British-American relationships, tyranny "was established *by* law."[57]

America's war against Britain was more than a battle to establish a nation independent of the Empire and founded on democratic and republican principles. Again, using universal language, he said that the war also promised "numerous benefits" to "mankind" as "a continued good to all posterity." American success demonstrated to all people that they too could secure happiness and freedom. Paine's letter was designed to awaken the revolutionary spirit he thought lay dormant in Britain and Europe.[58] Now the world itself may be transformed, thanks to the Americans, and it is prepared for the new world order. "We see with other eyes; we hear with other ears; and think with other thoughts, than those we formerly used." Because "a total reformation is wanted in England," he was prepared to agitate for change until reformation occurred, so that "it must be something new and masterly that can succeed." The American Revolution began the process of political transformation. It was now time to crush the ancien régimes in order to open "a new system of extended civilization" based on liberty, equality, justice, and commercial prosperity for everyone. National borders were irrelevant. We have the opportunity to create "a universal civilization," he said, for he himself was "a citizen of the world."[59]

Paine was so convinced of the importance of his answer to Raynal that he paid for its publication and distribution. He personally gave away some five hundred copies in the hope that the work would spread to Europe, and it soon did. He wrote that he had "made a present of one hundred copies to be sent to France," and he believed that "the publication arriving in England . . . could have no ill effect, and probably a good one." He especially wanted Europeans to make the connection between the revolution in America and a way out of their servile condition. "The matters which united themselves in this Revolution are . . . so connected in the beginning with the politics of England, and in its progress with those of almost every country in Europe."[60] He was not wrong. Within a few months, an American in Europe wrote that "I have lately traveled much, and find him everywhere. His letter to the Abbé Raynal has sealed his fame. . . . Even those who are jealous of, and envy him, acknowledge that the point of his pen has been as formidable as the point of a sword in the field."[61]

Paine intended to act on his words. In February 1781, he accompanied the young Colonel John Laurens to France as an unofficial member of the American delegation. Congress had appointed Laurens to assist Franklin, the American minister in Paris, to procure additional funding, men, and materiel from the French government (the alliance between France and America had been consummated on February 6, 1778). Paine was delighted with his reception, commenting that "I find myself no stranger in France; people know me almost as generally here as in America."[62] When he returned to America in August 1781, he began to think of returning to Europe, but he wanted to wait for the right moment and for when he had the cash to pay for the voyage. He told a friend that "the Marquis de Lafayette is on the point of setting out for France, but as I am now safely on this side of the water again, I believe I shall postpone my second journey to France a little longer."[63] Four days later, he wrote Washington to inform him of his "design to get to Europe, either in France or Holland," where he might render America "considerable service . . . to see her character as fair as her cause."[64] America was indeed a light shining on the rest of the world. He told Robert Morris, "I have the honest pride of thinking and ranking myself among the founders of a new Independent World," and that he was ready to move on. While in France, he said, he intended to "write a pamphlet," though he did not reveal its contents, but undoubtedly it had to do with freedom and justice, especially of the American cause.[65]

Even before the end of hostilities between the Americans and the British, he told General Nathanael Greene, to whom he was attached as aide-de-camp during part of the war, about the secret pamphlet he wanted to publish in London. There, he would "get out a publication" so he "could open the eyes of the country with respect to the madness and stupidity of its government."[66] At one point, he actually booked passage to London. Greene, however, persuaded him that he would likely be hanged as soon as he set foot on British soil.[67] The Benedict Arnold treachery had just occurred, with the arrest, military trial, and execution of Major John André, who had acted as the go-between for Arnold and the British High Command. Greene told Paine he would suffer André's fate if he attempted to return to Britain to stir up revolution (Greene had actually presided over André's military tribunal). Paine later recalled that he was "certain, that if I could have executed [this plan], it would not have been altogether unsuccessful," but he offered no additional detail about what success might have looked like or what his pamphlet would actually say.[68] He even thought of moving to Holland, to plan a European revolution from there, but by the time he thought of it, he lacked the funds to pay for the journey.[69]

Still, Europe might make "a happier home to me," he told Elias Boudinot, the president of Congress, because he was not dependent on America. "As far as it lay in my power to promote her cause of freedom and the happiness of mankind," he wanted the world to know that "every service of mine has been freely done and genuinely given."[70] He might, therefore, "wish her well and say to her, Adieu."[71] If he could return to France or go to Britain, he would work on behalf of these principles. After 1785, when Paine developed the plans for his iron bridge without piers, he began to think about traveling to

London and Paris for endorsements and to carry out his political platform. Momentous changes were blowing in the wind, and tyranny might soon be threatened.

Paine remained in America until 1787 to help consolidate the new American republic into a united country. He worked hard on several problems that threatened to undermine the new nation: he advocated a stronger central government; he argued for the states to provide appropriate funding to that government; and he personally assisted in the creation and development of the new Bank of North America. He appealed to Congress and some of the state legislatures to compensate him for his literary support of the Revolution during the war. He needed the money if he were to return to Britain or go on to Europe to carry through his political and personal goals. After Congress granted him a gift of $3,000, a gesture followed by stipends from New York and Pennsylvania, he set sail for London in the spring of 1787 to develop and manufacture his innovative iron bridge. He eventually secured the endorsements of the Royal Society of London and the Royal Academy of Sciences in Paris.[72] Within a short time, he was caught up in the upheavals in Paris after the fall of the Bastille in July 1789, though with consequences that nearly led to his death.[73]

NOTES

1. [George Chalmers], *The Life of Thomas Pain, the Author of "Rights of Men"* [sic]. *With a Defence of His Writings. By Francis Oldys, A.M. of the University of Pennsylvania* (London, 1791).

2. Bernard Bailyn, ed., *Pamphlets of the American Revolution, 1750–1776,* vol. 1 (Cambridge, Mass.: Harvard University Press, 1965), 179.

3. Harvey J. Kaye, *Thomas Paine and the Promise of America* (New York: Hill and Wang, 2005), 258, 49.

4. Craig Nelson, *Thomas Paine: Enlightenment, Revolution, and the Birth of Modern Nations* (New York: Viking, 2006); Eric Foner, *Tom Paine and Revolutionary America* (1976; updated with a new preface, New York: Oxford University Press, 2005), xxxi; John Keane, *Tom Paine: A Political Life* (Boston: Little, Brown, 1995), xiv; John Keane, "Démocratie républicaine, nation, nationalisme: Repenser les *Droits de l'Homme* de Thomas Paine," in *Thomas Paine, ou, La république sans frontières,* ed. Bernard Vincent (Nancy: Presses Universitaires de Nancy, 1993), 137–58; Bernard Vincent, *Thomas Paine, ou, La religion de la liberté* (Paris: Aubier, 1987), 12; Jean Lessay, *L'Américain de la convention: Thomas Paine, professeur de révolutions* (Paris: Perrin, 1987); Maurice Ezran, *Thomas Paine: Le combatants des deux révolutions américaine et française* (Paris: Editions l'Harmattan, 2004); Mark Philp, *Paine* (Oxford: Oxford University Press, 1989), ix; Ian Dyck, ed., *Citizen of*

the World: Essays on Thomas Paine (New York: St. Martin's Press, 1988); Isaac Kramnick, "Tom Paine: Radical Liberal," in *Republicanism and Bourgeois Radicalism: Political Ideology in Late Eighteenth-Century England and America* (Ithaca, N.Y.: Cornell University Press, 1990), 133–60. I too have fallen prey to the trend by referring to Paine as an "apostle of freedom" in emphasizing his French Revolutionary years (see Jack Fruchtman Jr., *Thomas Paine: Apostle of Freedom* [New York: Four Walls Eight Windows, 1994]).

5. Gordon S. Wood, *Revolutionary Characters: What Made the Founders Different* (New York: Penguin Press, 2006), 222, 218, 220–21. Two additional works by Wood reiterate this theme; see his "Disturbing the Peace," *New York Review of Books*, 8 June 1995, 20; and *The Radicalism of the American Revolution: How a Revolution Transformed a Monarchical Society into a Democratic One Unlike Any That Had Ever Existed* (New York: Knopf, 1991).

6. J. G. A. Pocock, *Virtue, Commerce, and History: Essays on Political Thought and History, Chiefly in the Eighteenth Century* (Cambridge: Cambridge University Press, 1985), 276. See also J. G. A. Pocock, "Political Thought in the English-speaking Atlantic, 1760–1790: (i) The Imperial Crisis," in *The Varieties of British Political Thought, 1500–1800*, ed. J. G. A. Pocock, with the assistance of Gordon J. Schochet and Lois G. Schwoerer (Cambridge: Cambridge University Press, 1993), 279–80, 282. "Normanism" refers to the ancient myth of the English constitution, which held that when the Normans invaded from France they brought with them the outlines of a constitutional structure to ensure the balance of King, Lords, and Commons. "Anti-Normanism" debunks this construction. The New Model Army was the citizen armed force under Cromwell during the mid-seventeenth century English Civil War.

7. Edward Larkin, *Thomas Paine and the Literature of Revolution* (Cambridge: Cambridge University Press, 2006), 87–95.

8. Paine, *Letter to the Abbé Raynal*, in *The Complete Writings of Thomas Paine*, ed. Philip S. Foner, 2 vols. (New York: Citadel Press, 1945) [hereafter cited as *Complete Writings*], 2:256.

9. Paine, *Rights of Man, Part the First*, ibid., 1:344, 449, 448.

10. The conventional view that *Common Sense* and his later publications until he left for France in 1787 were only about America and its disintegrated relationship with Britain has recently been repeated by Seth Cotlar: "Where *Common Sense* had invited readers into a new community of 'Americans' battling against monarchical Britain, the *Rights of Man* ushered in the next stage of that struggle. This time the battle was of an international scope" (see Cotlar, *Tom Paine's America: The Rise and Fall of Transatlantic Radicalism in the Early Republic* [Charlottesville: University of Virginia Press, 2011], 44).

11. For additional details concerning this argument, see Jack Fruchtman Jr., *The Political Philosophy of Thomas Paine* (Baltimore: Johns Hopkins University Press, 2009), 16–21.

12. *The Case of the Officers of Excise, with Remarks on the Qualifications of Officers, and on the Numerous Evils Arising to the Revenue, from the Insufficiency of the Present Salary: Humbly Addressed to the Members of Both Houses of Parliament*, in *Complete Writings*, 2:3–15.

13. Ibid., 2:4, 12, 9.

14. Ibid., 2:5–6, 9.

15. Marxist historians may argue that Paine's support of the exploited worker living a bare subsistence wage makes him a proto-socialist (see Gregory Claeys, "The Origins of the Rights of Labor: Republicanism, Commerce, and the Construction of Modern Society Theory in Britain, 1796–1805," *Journal of Modern History* 66 [June 1994]: 249–90).

16. Paine, *The Case of the Officers of Excise* . . . , in *Complete Writings*, 2:15.

17. See Larkin, *Thomas Paine and the Literature of Revolution*, 32–35, for the background. Larkin indicates that it was probably Franklin's letter of introduction for Paine that secured him the position of editor, in that Aitken was the publisher of works produced by the American Philosophical Society, which Franklin had founded in 1743.

18. Paine to a Committee of the Continental Congress, October 1783, in *Complete Writings*, 2:1227.

19. Paine to Franklin, 16 May 1778, ibid., 2:1150–51. For the other times he used the "fire around the ears" imagery, see Paine to a Committee of the Continental Congress, October 1783, ibid., 2:1227; and Paine, *The American Crisis VII*, ibid., 1:143–44. Paine signed all of his *Crisis* papers by his moniker "Common Sense," or simply "C.S.," which will not be noted here.

20. Paine, *The American Crisis III*, ibid., 1:84. Paine repeated his view of the impact of Lexington and Concord in 1782 in his *Letter to the Abbé Raynal* (ibid., 2:243).

21. Paine, *The American Crisis VII*, ibid., 1:143. In this number, Paine outlined his reasons why he thought Britain was intent on conquest, which in his mind was the moral equivalent to slavery.

22. Rush also claimed credit for supplying the title (see *The Autobiography of Benjamin Rush*, ed. George W. Corner [Princeton, N.J.: Princeton University Press, 1948], 114).

23. The best analysis of Paine's demonization of the king may be that of Ronald M. Paulson in his *Representations of Revolution (1789–1820)* (New Haven, Conn.: Yale University Press, 1983); see esp. 73–79. See also Jack Fruchtman Jr., *Thomas Paine and the Religion of Nature* (Baltimore: Johns Hopkins University Press, 1993), esp. 25–30.

24. Paine, *Common Sense*, in *Complete Writings*, 1:29, 10, 19.

25. Paine, *The American Crisis I*, ibid., 1:56.

26. Paine, *A Supernumerary Crisis*, ibid., 1:210. Paine was specifically referring to an incident in which an innocent officer was about to be executed even though the British held the true perpetrator of the crime (a murder) in custody.

27. Paine to Nathanael Greene, 17 October 1780, in A. Owen Aldridge, *Thomas Paine's American Ideology* (Newark, Del.: University of Delaware Press, 1984), 104. Paine himself noted that his feelings were ambivalent: "Were I inclined to be superstitious, I should attribute the whole of this discovery to Providence." But then he adds, concerning Arnold, "Why, if Providence had the management of the whole did she let Arnold escape?" (ibid.).

28. Paine, *Common Sense*, in *Complete Writings*, 1:10, 12, 9, 13, 16, 38, 45.

29. Ibid., 1:45. American presidents, quoting Paine out of context, miss the radicalism of his point (see Isaac Kramnick, "Tom Paine, Radical Democrat," *Democracy* 1 [January 1981]: 127–38).

30. Paine, *The American Crisis II,* in *Complete Writings,* 1:66.

31. Paine, *The American Crisis V,* ibid., 1:118, 120–21. Paine variously referred to "God" as a masculine figure and "Providence" as having a feminine personality. He used the two terms interchangeably.

32. Paine, *The American Crisis VI,* ibid., 1:131.

33. Paine, *The American Crisis X,* ibid., 1:194. Those who argue that Paine was an agnostic or atheist fail to explain his personalization of the theme of divine intervention fifteen years later in *Rights of Man,* by which he was God's personal messenger on earth, the man providentially chosen to lead the world to democracy. This was no mere Deism. "Why may we not suppose," he told his readers, "that the great Father of all is pleased with variety of devotion; and that the great offence we can act, is that by which we seek to torment and render each other miserable" (1:452). He then made the extraordinary statement that God had intervened to "choose" him, Thomas Paine, to perform His acts in human affairs: "I am fully satisfied that what I am now doing, with an endeavour to conciliate mankind, to render their condition happy, to unite nations that have hitherto been enemies, and to extirpate the horrid practice of war, and break the chains of slavery and oppression, is acceptable in His sight, and being the best service I can perform, I act it cheerfully" (ibid.; see also Paine to Samuel Adams, 6 March 1795, ibid., 2:1375–77).

34. Bernard Vincent appreciates the global nature of Paine's agenda. See his edited collection of Paine's works, *Thomas Paine, ou, La république sans frontières,* although it would be closer to Paine's ideas to have said it was "the revolution"—not the republic—"without boundaries").

35. Paine, *The American Crisis I,* in *Complete Writings,* 1:55.

36. Paine, *The American Crisis V,* ibid., 1:120. See also one of the essays Paine wrote early on in America, "Thoughts on Defensive War," which appeared in the *Pennsylvania Magazine* in July 1775 (ibid., 2:52–55).

37. Paine, *Common Sense,* in *Complete Writings,* 1:3, 45. Paine repeated the theme of the birthday of a new world in *The American Crisis V,* ibid., 1:123.

38. *Common Sense,* 1:30–31.

39. "Cato" [William Smith], "Letters to the Citizens of Pennsylvania" (Letter VIII), *Pennsylvania Packet* (Philadelphia), 29 April 1776.

40. [Paine], "The Forester's Letters" (No. 3), in *Complete Writings,* 2:79. For Rousseau, see Jean-Jacques Rousseau, *The Plan for Perpetual Peace, On the Government of Poland, and Other Writings on History and Politics,* in *The Collected Writings of Rousseau,* ed. Christopher Kelly, 13 vols. (Hanover, N.H.: University of Press of New England, 2005), 11:53–76.

41. The standard work on the American Revolution is Robert Middlekauff, *The Glorious Cause: The American Revolution, 1763–1789* (New York: Oxford University Press, 1982),

but see Jack Rakove, *Revolutionaries: A New History of the Invention of America* (New York: Houghton Mifflin Harcourt, 2010); T. H. Breen, *American Insurgents, American Patriots: The Revolution of the People* (New York: Hill and Wang, 2010); and Gary B. Nash, *The Unknown American Revolution: The Unruly Birth of Democracy and the Struggle to Create America* (New York: Viking, 2005). For a lively account of the weeks leading up to the Declaration of Independence, see William Hogeland, *Declaration: The Nine Tumultuous Weeks When America Became Independent, May 1–July 4, 1776* (New York: Simon and Schuster, 2010).

42. Paine, *The American Crisis I*, in *Complete Writings*, 1:50.

43. Paine, *The American Crisis X*, ibid., 1:192.

44. Paine, *The American Crisis II*, ibid., 1:71–72 (emphasis added).

45. Paine, *The American Crisis VII*, ibid., 1:155–56.

46. Paine, *The American Crisis XII*, ibid., 1:227.

47. Paine, *The American Crisis XIII*, ibid., 1:231.

48. The first of these is not the subject of this essay. Paine tackled domestic issues for the next five years until he finally departed for France on 26 April 1787, and he wrote about them in *Six Letters to Rhode Island* (see *Complete Writings*, 2:333–66); in *Dissertations on Government; the Affairs of the Bank; and Paper Money* (ibid., 2:367–414); and in his letters on the Bank of North America (ibid., 2:414–39). See also Paine to Robert Morris, 20 November 1782, ibid., 2:1213–15.

49. Paine to a Committee of the Continental Congress, October 1783, ibid., 2:1240.

50. Paine to Franklin, 20 June 1777, ibid., 2:1133.

51. Paine to a Committee of the Continental Congress, October 1783, ibid., 2:1240.

52. Paine noted, "The Abbé's high profession [is] in favor of liberty" (see *Letter to the Abbé Raynal*, ibid., 2:245).

53. Abbé Guillaume-Thomas Raynal, *The Revolution in America* (London: Lockyer Davis, 1781), 127. Paine quoted part of this passage in his response (see Paine, *Letter to the Abbé Raynal*, in *Complete Writings*, 2:216).

54. Paine, *Letter to the Abbé Raynal*, in *Complete Writings*, 2:246–47; and Paine to George Washington, 30 November 1781, ibid., 2:1204.

55. Paine had come by a copy of Raynal's history thanks to Robert Morris, who in 1781 loaned him a copy (see Paine to Morris, 26 November 1781, ibid., 2:1201).

56. Paine to a Committee of the Continental Congress, October 1783, ibid., 2:1240. See also Paine to Robert Morris, 6 September 1782, ibid., 2:1211.

57. Paine, *Letter to the Abbé Raynal*, ibid., 2:217.

58. Ibid., 2:238. Paine was under no illusions about France's motivation in entering into an alliance with the American patriots. It was not out of an appreciation of democratic and republican ideas, but because of its own self-interest. As Paine said, "By lessening the power of an enemy . . . she gained an advantage" (ibid.).

59. Ibid., 2:243, 255, 256. For the "citizen of the world" remark, see Paine, *The Ameri-*

can Crisis VII, ibid., 1:146. On Paine's universalism, see Thomas C. Walker, "The Forgotten Prophet: Tom Paine's Cosmopolitanism and International Relations," *International Studies Quarterly* 44 (March 2000): 51–72, esp. 52; David M. Fitzsimons, "Tom Paine's New World Order: Idealistic Internationalism in the Ideology of Early American Foreign Relations," *Diplomatic History* 19 (September 1995): 569–82; Ian Dyck, "Local Attachments, National Identities, and World Citizenship in the Thought of Thomas Paine," *History Workshop Journal* 35 (Spring 1993): 117–35; and Philp, *Paine,* 68–70. For Paine's search for ways to broaden the Revolution, see Larkin, *Thomas Paine and the Literature of Revolution,* 97–98; and Keane, *Tom Paine,* 200–202.

60. Paine to a Committee of the Continental Congress, October 1783, in *Complete Writings,* 2:1236–37, 1239. Paine was incorrigible in his hatred of monarchy (and monarchs) and aristocracy (and aristocrats). He did, however, maintain a curious soft spot in his heart for Louis XVI, who gave so much help, despite the self-serving French interests, to the American cause (see Fruchtman, *Political Philosophy of Thomas Paine,* 100–102; and Keane, *Tom Paine,* 210).

61. Quoted in Frank Smith, *Tom Paine, Liberator* (New York: Frederick Stokes, 1938), 100.

62. Paine to James Hutchinson, 11 March 1781, in *Complete Writings,* 2:1195.

63. Paine to Jonathan Williams, 26 November 1781, ibid., 2:1201.

64. Paine to George Washington, 30 November 1781, ibid., 2:1204.

65. Paine to Robert Morris, 20 February 1782, ibid., 2:1207.

66. Paine to Nathanael Greene, 9 September 1780, ibid., 2:1189. See also Paine's recounting of his conversation with Greene, in *Rights of Man, Part the First,* ibid., 1:407n.

67. For his booking passage, see *Complete Writings,* 2:1233.

68. Paine, *Rights of Man, Part the First,* ibid., 1:407n. For additional reasons why Paine did not leave America until 1787 to provoke revolution in Europe, see note 45 above, where he claimed he wanted to help consolidate the states into a stronger union.

69. "I intended to ask some merchant or Captain of a vessel to give me a passage to Holland, where I was sure of being safe, and . . . I could not be insensible that I had abilities that could be useful" (Paine to a Committee of the Continental Congress, October 1783, in *Complete Writings,* 2:1235).

70. Paine to Elias Boudinot, 7 June 1783, ibid., 2:1218.

71. Paine to a Committee of the Continental Congress, October 1783, ibid., 2:1242.

72. He did not give up on his political goals, either, as his actions indicate, once the revolution in France succeeded two years later (see Larkin, *Thomas Paine and the Literature of Revolution,* 114–52).

73. Paine's relationships with the marquis de Condorcet, Jacques-Pierre Brissot, Nicolas de Bonneville, and other leaders of the Girondin faction attest to his Revolutionary credentials, especially when he and Condorcet, as early as July 1791, collaborated on "A Republican Manifesto" and established the Republican Society in Paris (see Keane, *Tom*

Paine, 316–19). Two years later, he was arrested, ironically charged with being a British spy, and confined for almost eleven months in the Luxembourg Prison. He claimed to have seen his death warrant, personally signed by Maximilien Robespierre (see Paine, *The Age of Reason,* in *Complete Writings,* 1:516; Paine to Samuel Adams, 6 March 1795, ibid., 2:1376; Paine, "Letter to George Washington," 30 July 1796, ibid., 2:699; and Paine, "To the Citizens of the United States" [Letter 3], published in the *National Intelligencer* [Washington, D.C.], 29 November 1802, ibid., 2:920).

Paine, Jefferson, and Revolutionary Radicalism in Early National America

SIMON P. NEWMAN

No more than twelve people attended the funeral of Thomas Paine on June 10, 1809, when he was buried on his farm in New Rochelle, New York. No political leaders attended, no eulogy was given, and the event was little reported and largely ignored. In stark contrast, when Thomas Jefferson died, on the fiftieth anniversary of American independence, the entire nation mourned.[1] Why were these two Revolutionary brothers in arms treated so differently? In 1776 they had been the heroes of the American patriots, embodying the radical promise and potential of the American Revolution. As the authors of *Common Sense* and the Declaration of Independence, Paine and Jefferson had written the two most popular documents of the founding era, and both of them came to represent the democratic and republican promise of the great American experiment.

However, during the decade following the ratification of the federal constitution, Jefferson was transformed by his supporters into the living embodiment of the values of the American Revolution. During those same years, Paine was effectively removed from the pantheon of Revolutionary heroes, and he has been largely absent ever since. Today Jefferson remains the most significant representative of the Revolutionary generation in American political discourse. From the mid-twentieth century on, American politicians and leaders have fashioned Jefferson into the most useful founder, the man whose revolutionary ideals best fit modern beliefs.[2] Despite occasional attacks on Jefferson, often by those who focus on his complicated relationship with race and slavery, Jefferson remains the timeless symbol par excellence of the ideological origins of the American republic. In quite striking contrast, during the 1790s the growing ranks of Thomas Paine's American opponents castigated him as a dangerously radical revolutionary—a threat to law, order, and religion—and unwelcome in the American republic he had helped found. Excluded from the ranks of the founders, Paine has remained in the shadows ever since. Paine's rhetoric infuses American political discourse, from the speeches of Franklin Roosevelt, to Ronald Reagan, to Barack Obama in his inaugural address, yet Paine himself is seldom mentioned by name.³

In this essay, I will discuss how and why Americans treated Paine and Jefferson so differently during the last decade of the eighteenth and the first decade of the nineteenth centuries, and how this has largely excised Paine from American political memory and culture. I shall pay particular attention to the toasts drunk by Republicans and Federalists all over the United States during the 1790s. Toasts provided ordinary American citizens with an effective way of articulating support of or opposition to political principles and policies. The conventions of toasting gave these statements of opinion a power and validity unsuspected by many modern historians, and quite literally tens of thousands of toasts were drunk, published, and then often republished in American newspapers during the 1790s and early 1800s. Toasts allowed male members of the polity to express political opinions in a structured fashion whose significance was well known to contemporaries. All-male groups regularly gathered together and concluded their meal by raising their glasses to a set of toasts, or "sentiments." A set number of toasts were drunk, usually a "federal" slate, with one for each state in the union, although often these were supplemented by one or more "volunteers." Toasting was an important social ritual that served to strengthen the ties between those who raised their glasses, making it vital that toasters avoid sentiments that might prove unacceptable to one or more of those present: if one person present disagreed with the sentiment expressed in a toast, he would refuse to raise his glass and drink, thereby shattering the sociability and unanimity of the occasion. Thus, the language of toasts allowed those participating in such feasts and festivals to articulate and publicize political and patriotic beliefs that those present all shared, providing us with a wealth of information about the political opinions of a wide range of early national Americans. Newspaper editors enthusiastically published entire slates of toasts, which they regarded as "criterions of sentiment and truth" that were "indicative of the public sentiment." In fact, when the editor of the *New-York Journal* presented the key arguments against and in support of slavery, he could think of no better or more recognizable formula than to present these in the form of rival slates of toasts. For this essay, I will make use of toasts from twenty-five newspapers published during the 1790s and early 1800s, from Portland, Maine, to Lexington, Kentucky, to Savannah, Georgia.[4]

Thomas Paine was an iconic figure for supporters of the Republican Party, which began to take shape in opposition to the policies of the Federalists during the first administration of President George Washington.[5] During the 1790s Republicans complained that the Federalist administrations of both Washington and John Adams were betraying the ideology of the American Revolution. They focused their attacks on Hamiltonian economic policies, the quasi-aristocratic tenor of the federal government, and the increasingly pro-British and anti-French foreign policies of the Federalists. For much of the decade, Paine served as a powerful symbol and potent weapon for the Republicans. As the author of *Common Sense,* Paine had published the best-selling pamphlet of the entire Revolutionary era, converting many Americans to the cause of Independence and radical republican government. Thereafter, as a servant of the Congress and in the Continental Army, Paine had published *The Crisis* papers, rallying support to the cause during "the times that try men's souls." These publications had confirmed Paine's status as a leading patriot. Following his return to Europe and his participation in a French Revolution that was initially hugely popular among Americans, Paine's publication of *Rights of Man* (1791–92) added yet another powerful weapon to the Republican arsenal. For Republican Party supporters, Paine's role in the early and more radical and democratic stages of the American Revolution was consolidated by his early participation in the French Revolution, and to many Americans he appeared to personify the abstract ideas of radical revolution and democratic republican government.

During the early 1790s, Paine was the toast of the Republican Party. He was utilized by Republicans, who sought not just to celebrate the spread of republican revolution to France but also to protect the heritage of the American Revolution against the conservative and pro-British policies of the Federalists. Thus, on Independence Day, 1791, some three hundred residents of Bladensburg, Maryland, gathered to feast and drink toasts in celebration. They raised their glasses to just two individuals, offering a somewhat perfunctory toast wishing "Long Life to George Washington," followed by a considerably more elaborate toast to "Thomas Paine—the Author of 'Common Sense' and 'The Rights of Man.'" In Schenectady, New York, in 1793, those celebrating the anniversary of American independence raised their glasses to the sentiment "Thomas Paine—May he open the eyes of the blind," while on Independence

Day, 1794, in Hackensack, New Jersey, militiamen drank a toast to "Citizen Thomas Paine."[6]

In that same year, members of Boston and Charlestown militia companies gathered to commemorate the anniversary of the Battle of Bunker Hill. After saluting the heroes of the War for Independence, those in attendance turned to contemporary politics, toasting "the Democratic Societies throughout the Union" and celebrating the local organizations of Republicans whose members were monitoring and often criticizing the policies of the Federalist government. The militiamen then raised their glasses to "The equal Rights of Man," thus identifying themselves with the emerging Republican Party and with Paine's celebration of revolutionary radicalism. Their partisanship was confirmed by a toast to "Madison and all the virtuous Republicans in Congress," while they were far more circumspect when they raised their glasses to President Washington's "energetic measures to secure the rights of his fellow-citizens in a constitutional manner." To these Massachusetts militiamen, their loyalty to Washington was conditional upon his respect for the rights for which they and their fathers had fought in the War for Independence, and on Washington distancing himself from Federalist policies that allowed British "robbery and insult abroad" while threatening "tyranny at home." A month later, Republicans in Freehold, New Jersey, gathered at Robert Laird's tavern to feast and drink toasts in honor of Independence Day. After saluting "The virtuous republicans in Congress" and "Our allies the citizens of the French republic," they raised their glasses to "The *Rights of Man*" and then to "The spirit of 1776."[7] In the minds of these Republicans, it was Thomas Paine, more than any other man, who represented the ideology that united the American and the French Revolutions.

Some of the feasts and festivals organized by the nascent Republican Party were more explicitly favorable to the French Revolution, such as the Bastille Day feast of a radical democratic group of Philadelphia militiamen at Ogden's Tavern in the summer of 1792. Here, the toasts began with a salute to the French Republic, followed by the sentiment, "The United States, may they sedulously guard their rights." Their toast to "Paine, and the friends of freedom throughout the world" was the only one that saluted a contemporary by name, for they assiduously avoided the traditional salute to George Washington. Thus, a celebration of the French Revolution was colored by American partisan politics, including their celebration of Thomas Paine as an American patriot deemed to represent the core radical ideals of both the American and French Revolutions. At a similar Bastille Day celebration in Carlisle, Paine was toasted in conjunction with "all writers in defence of Liberty and the Rights of Man," and in New York City, the Tammany Society toasted both "The Clarion of Freedom, Thomas Paine" and "That unanswerable and invulnurable bulwark of freedom, the Rights of Man." Republicans in Philadelphia celebrated the French victory at the Battle of Valmy by following a toast to Paine with some pointed sentiments regarding American political leaders and their policies. These included: "Congress, so long as they maintain the principles of the constitution, by protecting the rights of man"; "All who are governed by principles not by men"; and "The undisguised political principles of 1776." Paine and the French revolutionaries were lauded in such toasts as heroes against whom the potentially counter-revolutionary Federalists might be measured.[8]

For two or three years following Paine's publication of *Rights of Man* in 1791, the title of the book and all that it effectively summarized and symbolized played a clear and significant role in American political culture. The "rights of man" functioned as a rhetorical badge of allegiance to the radicalism of the early years of the American Revolution, and of support for the French revolutionaries in their struggle against Britain, Prussia, and other European monarchies. Between 1791 and 1795, Republicans toasted "Thomas Paine" and the "Rights of Man" as much as any other American with the exception of President Washington himself.[9] When Republicans in New York City included a toast to "The Rights of Man" in their Independence Day celebration in 1795, those present greeted the sentiment with three cheers, a typical response. Paine and the *Rights of Man* were regularly employed in ritual affirmations of commitment to the revolutionary ideals on which the American republic had been founded, and in negative judgment of American leaders found wanting.[10]

Republicans thus focused upon Paine and all that he and the "rights of man" symbolized in toasts given at events commemorating and celebrating both the French and the American Revolutions. In 1792, at a celebration of George Washington's birthday by the New City Dancing Assembly of Philadelphia, a toast to "The 4th of July, 1776" was immediately followed by one to "The rights of man." Later that same year, a Boston militia company commemorated the fifteenth anniversary of the defeat of General John Burgoyne's British army in 1777, drinking a slate of partisan toasts that included, "The Vice-President, Senate, and House of Representatives of the United States— May they be in FACT, and not in NAME only, the Representatives of a free people," as well as, "May all governments be those of Laws, and all Laws be those of the People." These words of caution for the Federalist administration and Congress were followed by a later toast that saluted "THOMAS PAINE, and the Rights of Man—May all nations have wisdom to understand, and spirit to assert them." At an event celebrating French military victories in 1795, Republicans in Newark, New Jersey, toasted the rights of man twice before raising their glasses to "Thomas Paine—may Americans never forget the debt of gratitude due to the author of *Common Sense.*"[11] Paine effectively linked the revolutionary founding of the American republic with other revolutions in a way that appeared to validate the ideology of the American Revolution, thus providing a template for Republicans who sought to assess and critique what they interpreted as the counter-revolutionary tendencies of the Federalists.

The increasingly radical and violent tenor of the French Revolution helped fuel partisan politicking in the mid-1790s. In Elizabethtown, New Jersey, a celebration of the recapture of Toulon included a toast to "The rights of man, may the citizens of France and America never want spirit to assert, or courage to defend them." The implicit assertion that American citizens needed to protect their rights against both foreign British and domestic Federalist enemies was echoed by a group of "friends to the equal *Rights of Man*" in Philadelphia, who both toasted and cheered the sentiment, "Perdition and contempt to the tongue of calumny and malice, that would divide at this period, the friends of liberty and the equal Rights of Man."[12] Federalist attempts to interpret American neutrality in a manner that would distance the United States from France while seeking a closer connection with counter-revolutionary Britain were clearly of deep concern to American Republicans.

From the mid-1790s on, however, many Republicans began to tone down their enthusiastic toasts to the French Revolution, to Paine, and to the union between American and French Revolutionary republicanism that he had embodied. The Jay Treaty between Britain and the United States in 1795 led to a deterioration of Franco-American relations, which was followed by the XYZ Affair and the Quasi-War, further souring relations between the two countries. As the French Republic declined in popularity in the United States, Republicans disavowed the French and their supporters. While continuing to celebrate the Revolutionary virtues of *American* republicanism, Republicans made fewer and fewer references to Thomas Paine and *French* republicanism. Paine's ready association with the increasingly unpopular French Republic helps explain this process, but it was Paine's newer writings that effectively destroyed his standing among American Republicans. Paine's alleged assault on organized Christianity in the first two volumes of *The Age of Reason* (1794–95), and his personal attack upon President George Washington, turned the revolutionary into an appealing—and a politically expedient—target for Federalist invective, thus transforming Paine from a boon to a bane for Republicans who had been toasting him just months earlier. Wounded by his perception that President George Washington and the Federalist minister to France, Gouverneur Morris, had failed to protect him as an American citizen, Paine had written an open letter to Washington criticizing his military record, his policies, and his character. This short piece did as much to ruin Paine's reputation in America as *Common Sense* and *Rights of Man* had done to establish it.

As relations with France deteriorated into diplomatic stalemate and an undeclared naval war, the Federalists moved quickly to consolidate their newfound popularity, enacting the Sedition Act of 1798 in order to suppress criticism of President John Adams's administration. In response, the Jeffersonian newspaper editor Benjamin Franklin Bache lampooned Federalist attacks on Paine and radical Republican ideology. Bache published a letter from the fictional Federalist "Timothy Tremulous" attacking the "bloody-minded hell hounds" who had gathered in Philadelphia to commemorate Bastille Day with toasts to "Thomas Jefferson," "The rights of man" and "Thomas Paine." However, while a small number of radical Republicans like Bache sought to hold their ground and to defend Painite ideals, most Republicans were more cautious. Many reacted to Federalist attacks by endeavoring to separate the "rights of man," which they continued to toast and celebrate as a cardinal American political virtue, from Thomas Paine himself, who they increasingly ignored. Republicans now began to focus on their putative leader, Thomas Jefferson, raising their glasses to him and to "the spirit of 1776" and omitting Paine from the pantheon of heroes of that formative year. While Jefferson was lauded as "the friend of the people," Paine was now excluded. In his place, it was the leading members of the Republican Party, not Paine, who were linked with the rights of man. Thus, Paine was now conspicuously omitted from these toasts, such as one to "Gallatin, Nicholas, Livingston, Randolph, Condit, Kitchell and all other members of Congress, who are friends to liberty and the rights of man."[13]

Republicans strove to protect themselves and their party from identification with the now unpopular French Revolution while simultaneously presenting themselves as the legitimate heirs and defenders of the American Revolution of 1776. At the same time, Republicans sought to represent the Federalists as pro-British traitors to the American republic. Thus, William Duane, newly established as editor of Philadelphia's *Aurora,* published a fictional account of an Independence Day celebration of "*staunch federalists.*" These men had always "held in detestation revolutionary principles," and they enjoyed an oration "upon the blessings" of monarchical government and standing armies. Having ceremonially burned the Declaration of Independence, Duane's imaginary Federalists toasted the traitor "General Arnold," wished "Confusion to all republics," and hailed the "inflexible loyalists of '76." With other toasts condemning Independence, the "rebels who were shot in the revolution," and the "Old Whigs," Duane was caricaturing the Federalists as enemies of everything that the Fourth of July represented to truly patriotic Americans.[14]

Duane quite deliberately employed a Fourth of July celebration for his parody. By the end of the 1790s, the Republicans had effectively made Independence Day their principal political festival, and more than twice as many Republican as Federalist slates of Independence Day toasts were published in American newspapers. (The Federalists had turned annual celebrations of Washington's birthday into their principal political festival.) At the July 4th festival in Centreville, Maryland, in 1799, for example, approximately four hundred self-styled "Republicans" enjoyed a reading of the Declaration of Independence, militia maneuvers, and an open-air feast. They shared enthusiastic toasts to the "virtuous, and enlightened citizen Thomas Jefferson," to the spirit of 1776, and to "virtuous Republicans." Thomas Paine—either as an American or as a French revolutionary—was not mentioned in a single one of their toasts. Indeed, all over the United States, Republicans no longer raised their glasses to their erstwhile hero.[15]

In Scott County, Kentucky, some "600 people convened" for Independence Day orations and a large barbecue. This constituted approximately 23 percent of the adult white population and almost 45 percent of the adult white male population of the entire county. With toasts to Jefferson "and the patriotic minority in congress," and celebrations of the freedom of speech and of the press, this day belonged to the community's self-proclaimed Republican "sons of liberty," and their toasts articulated the ways in which the party faithful were identifying themselves and their leader as the true representatives of the cause and the achievements of the American Revolution. From the "Republicans and sons of Freedom" who gathered in Carlisle, Pennsylvania, to the "real friends of America" in Paterson, New Jersey, to the fifty-odd "old fashioned citizens of 1776" who assembled at Frankford near Philadelphia, to the "lovers of Liberty, Equality, and the Rights of Man" in Newark, New Jersey, Republican opponents of the Federalist government celebrated Independence Day as their own.[16] Thomas Paine, however, was almost completely absent from the political culture and Revolutionary heritage of a party that he had helped form.

The Republicans' move away from Paine and the French Revolution was encouraged by Federalist attacks on their former hero. For while Paine had functioned as a Revolutionary standard-bearer for the Republicans during the early to mid–1790s, the Federalists had always viewed him as emblematic of all that they abhorred, both at home and abroad. Federalists, who feared social and political radicalism and favored a well-ordered and hierarchical society and government, had applauded the replacement of Pennsylvania's radical Constitution of 1776 with a more conservative document, and they had celebrated the ratification of the federal constitution and Washington's leadership of the first Federalist administration. They were appalled by the increasing radicalism of the French Revolution and the ways in which it fueled Republican opposition and threatened a revival of popular radicalism within the United States. One Federalist expressed these sentiments in the *Connecticut Courant*, suggesting that "WHEN we observe the beneficial effects of moral and religious principles among the people of the United States, and the happiness we have enjoyed with the new constitution of our government, it seems astonishing that any person should wish to exchange these advantages for the modern refinements of sceptics and Levellers."[17]

The author went on to suggest that Jefferson was "the avowed patron of scepticism in religion, and of the levelling system of Mr. Paine in politics," before going on to dismiss Paine, because "he has no political system, and the engines he employs for the downfall of tyranny, are equally calculated to destroy all subordination in government." Paine was, the author asserted, "formed both by nature and by habit, not to establish but to pull down empires. . . . Yet such is the man, around whose standard the leader of the antifederal party has called on all Americans to rally, in opposition to the political heresies of the day."[18]

Similar attacks on Paine had long featured in the Federalist press. An essay published in the *Gazette of the United States* late in 1791 had attacked "the abuses that have already been committed, under the pretext of equality" under the influence of *Rights of Man*. The author lampooned Paine's work as proposing the idea that

> I am a man, consequently I am free; no man is, or can be, my superior;—this world was created for me, and not being accountable to any one for my actions, I will do what I please: Having neither for-

tune nor industry, I address myself to the first rich man that I meet, and demand the half of his property . . . and if my neighbour has a pretty wife or daughter, I will possess myself of one or the other, or both, if I like it. There is nothing more reasonable, according to these new discovered Rights of Man.[19]

A few months later, another correspondent complained that "Liberty and Equality, [and] Paine and the Rights of Man, are all the rage at the Eastward," and he ridiculed the Painite rhetoric and imagery of his Republican opponents by suggesting that these sentiments had spread to the Southern states, where white Republicans' "sable fellow creatures are frequently addressed, 'Citizen Caesar,' or 'Citizen Pompey clean my boots, &c. &c.'—This may be well—but to hear the Auctioneer cry, 'twenty pounds for Citizen Alexander—who bids more?' seems to be carrying the joke too far in a free country."[20]

Federalists did not hesitate to associate Painite ideology with what they deemed illegitimate crowd actions and protests against the Federalist administrations of Washington and Adams. When Bostonians gathered to protest against the Jay Treaty in 1795, a Connecticut newspaper condemned the "inflammatory speeches" made in the Boston town meeting on "the treachery of Mr. Jay, the Rights of Man, the spirit of '75, and the necessity of rejecting the Treaty or becoming slaves." Along much the same lines, a Philadelphian complained that the "*Cause* of liberty, the *rights of man,* the *happiness* of the people, are *words,* and very clever words, to collect a mob."[21] William Cobbett went even further, rejecting not just Paine and what he represented in the 1790s, but even Paine's actions before and during the War for Independence, as those of a traitor. While Americans had rebelled because of their inability to secure redress of grievances, "a man like Paine, just landed in the country, could have no oppression to complain of, and, therefore, his hostility against his country admits of no defence. He was a traitor. . . . No good man, however zealous he might be in the revolution, ever respected Paine, of whom the coldness and neglect he experienced, as soon as order was re-established, is a certain proof."[22]

As relations between the United States and France worsened, and as Paine published *The Age of Reason* and his attack on Washington, it became easier for Federalists to attack the pro-French and pro-Painite sympathies of their Republican opponents, who "do not believe in the bible . . . and [have] substituted Tom Paine's 'reason.'" While Republicans had celebrated Paine and his ideals in their toasts during the first half of the 1790s, as the decade ended, it was the Federalists who raised their glasses to his name, but this time in order to attack and discredit rather than to honor him. At a Philadelphia celebration of Washington's Birthday in 1797, for example, those present followed toasts to Washington and Adams with the implicitly Francophobic and Anglophile sentiment, "*Pain* to our *sham* friends, *Champagne* to our real ones; and *Tom Paine* to the devil." In Stockbridge, Massachusetts, Washington's Birthday was celebrated with a joyful reference to the French prison in which Paine had been incarcerated and almost executed, with those present wishing "A Luxembourg to all Gallo-American 'patriots.'"[23]

Paine's perceived attack on Christianity in *The Age of Reason* broadened opposition to his political philosophy at exactly the time that the French Revolution was declining in popularity and relevance in the United States. Federalists delighted in referring to the strength of Protestantism in America as evidence "that the Religious devotion of our Countrymen is unshaken, though the French have deserted God, and TOM PAINE has attempted to write down the *Bible*." A "monster of impiety," Paine "affixes infidelity in full colours, to the very title pages of his works."[24]

It was, however, Paine's public letter to and attack on George Washington that fatally undermined his reputation in the United States. Federalists seized their opportunity to attack "the most extraordinary composition of abuse, petulance, falsehood and boyish vanity that ever came from Grub Street or a garret." Washington's heroic status enabled Federalists to denounce Paine and the Republicans who had celebrated him. Lauding Washington's "spotless character," William Cobbett published his response to Paine's letter, writing that Paine's "attempt to blacken this character was all that was wanted to crown his honour and your infamy."[25] To Federalists, Paine's letter to Washington was his greatest crime: "It did not satisfy him, I say, to view France precipitated by his principles into unutterable misery, and all Europe shaken to its centre; he, with a degree of audacity which beggars description, with a portion of profligacy almost inconceivable, assailed the holy character of Washington."[26]

By this point, Thomas Paine had relatively little political standing in the United States, and he was certainly not a political threat to the Federalists. But his associations, both ideological and social, with leading Republicans gave assaults on Paine a domestic political resonance. Commenting on Paine's letter to Washington, William Cobbett observed that "the vile democrats, nay even Franklin Bache, with whom you boast of being in close correspondence, can say not a word in its defence."[27]

By the late 1790s, Paine had been all but eliminated from Republican toasts. At the same time, in reaction against the Federalists' proscriptive Alien and Sedition Acts, Republicans hastened to soften Jefferson's Revolutionary credentials, instead heralding their leader as the staunch defender of liberties enshrined in the Constitution. Thus, on Independence Day, 1798, Republicans in Newburgh, New York, gathered under a banner with the inscription *"Liberty or Death, a Constitution inviolate."* They raised their glasses to salute Thomas Jefferson "and the virtuous defenders of Liberty in both houses of Congress," and to hail "The Constitution—May it be held sacred without violation." No longer were Paine and Jefferson jointly celebrated as the radical revolutionaries of 1776 who had supported the French Revolution. Instead, Paine was no longer mentioned, while Jefferson was revered as the party leader, imbued with "republican virtues," who would defend the Constitution. The Alien and Sedition Acts and the raising of a large standing army prompted Republicans to present themselves as defenders of "the People of the United States; free, sovereign, and independent," and to toast to "The Constitution of the United States; may it survive the attacks of *artificial* Federalists, and the deep laid schemes of aristocrats and tories."[28] In comparison with the early 1790s, Jefferson was far less frequently hailed as the man "who drafted our declaration of Independence"; instead, he was far more commonly commended in strikingly un-Revolutionary terms, as "the friend of the people," a "worthy Vice President," and as the "Guardian" of the "country's rights." Only rarely were the rights of man mentioned, and then in softened and explicitly domestic terms they were associated with Jefferson rather than Paine, as in the toasts of some New Jersey Republicans on Independence Day, 1800, who raised their glasses to "Thomas Jefferson, the firm supporter of the rights of man—May his virtues be rewarded at the next election, with the Presidential Chair, by the free suffrages of an enlightened People." Rather than the radical revolutionary of 1776 who had supported the French Revolution, Jefferson had become "the mild and enlightened statesman and philosopher, who penned the declaration of independence," a man who, his supporters hoped, would "take the helm of government, and steer it to the haven of peace and plenty."[29]

Paine's enduring association with the French Revolution, his publication of *The Age of Reason*, and his letter to Washington, coupled with the dramatic deterioration of Franco-American relations, had all combined to eliminate one of the leading figures of the Age of Revolution from the political culture of the party that celebrated the American Revolution. Paine remained useful to the Federalists primarily as a means of associating the Republicans with the bogeyman who embodied discredited radical ideology. Thus, Federalist newspaper editors delighted in attacking the apparently Painite toasts drunk by their Republican opponents as having been "culled from [the] garbage of old democratic, antifederal disorganizing clubs . . . [which] consequently resembled those of the *beer house*."[30] During the late 1790s, Jefferson was increasingly criticized for his Painite sympathies, as when "Ascanius" attacked him as "the Great *Leviathon* of Jacobinism," writing: "It is a *fact,* that Mr. JEFFERSON publicly advised Mr. BROWN, or some other printer, to print the Rights of Man written by the infamous Tom. Paine, and that he then declared in a billet published with the work, that he thought we were degenerated, and that it was time to rally again around the standard of *Common Sense*—In other words, to create another Revolution."[31]

All too aware that the French Revolution in general, and Thomas Paine in particular, could damage their growing popularity, the Republicans worked hard to eliminate Paine from their celebratory lexicon. In his absence, Jefferson stood alone as both party leader and representative of the ideals of the Declaration of Independence and the American Revolution as his supporters interpreted them. During the late 1790s, the Declaration of Independence played an ever more important role in Republican Independence Day festivities, and those present hailed Jefferson as both author and current defender of American rights and freedoms. The Declaration was read aloud at Newark and under a new liberty pole at Jefferson's Village in New Jersey, before several companies of militia in New London, Connecticut, before the Tammany and Mechanic Societies in New York City, and all around Philadelphia. In Lancaster, Pennsylvania, residents drank to the wish that "every American who loves not above all the Declaration of Independence" may "become the subject of a tyrant," and many men raised their glasses to the Declaration. The toast of the Republican Blues and the Republican Greens in Philadelphia, to the "author of the Declaration of Independence," was echoed by opponents of Adams's Federalist administration all around the nation.[32]

Toasts to the more radical expressions of liberty, equality, and the rights of man that had been common during the heady early years of the French Revolution all but disappeared from Republican July 4th festivities, as the day steadily evolved from a memorial of Revolutionary republicanism into a partisan celebration of the Republican Party and its leaders and policies. But the Federalist attack on political expression in the Sedition Act clearly worried the thousands of Americans who attended oppositional Independence Day celebrations in the final years of the decade. By focusing on the Declaration as the principal articulation of the values for which Americans had fought in the War for Independence, and by lauding Jefferson as its creator and embodiment, Republicans were able to unite their party firmly with the spirit of 1776.

Such sentiments were expressed in Independence Day toasts hoping for "a free elective representative, democratic government," and the wish that Jefferson might become "the next president."[33]

In Philadelphia, in 1798, the Southwark Light Infantry took part in that city's military parade and review, but at their feast later in the day, they toasted "Republican governments—May they be so not only in name but in the action of its genuine principles." This implicit criticism of Adams and his government was made explicit when the diners did not toast the president, preferring to salute Vice President Jefferson, hoping that "his republican virtues [would] ever be remembered with gratitude." The Republican Blues militia company settled down to an Independence Day feast in the ruins of a British redoubt, symbolically uniting themselves with the patriots who had fought Britain two decades earlier. After listening to the reading of the Declaration, they toasted the document, and then—with thirteen cheers—lauded Jefferson as "the friend of his country, the framer of the declaration of Independence."[34]

The Republicans succeeded brilliantly in distancing themselves from their earlier enthusiasm for Painite international revolution and republicanism, instead presenting themselves as the legitimate defenders of a uniquely American Revolutionary republic. By the turn of the nineteenth century, Republicans had claimed Independence Day as their own, rejoicing in Philadelphia newspapers that "there was no *federal* procession or parade" in the capital. The Fourth of July, 1800, "WAS CELEBRATED BY REPUBLICANS—AND BY THEM ONLY." Independence Day had become a thoroughly Republican event, and the party's supporters in Philadelphia reveled in the fact that, having recently won the governorship from the Federalists, they had secured almost complete control over the celebration of what they viewed as the most important festival in the American calendar. Church bells were silent because Federalists refused to ring them, and there was "no joy, seen among those who *call themselves* Federalists." The friends and supporters of the Republicans took part in the militia parade with "conviviality and gladness" as they celebrated "the happy return of the nation from the delusion under which it has so long labored."[35]

The preamble to the Declaration, far more than any other single document, encapsulated and symbolized the republican ideology that was at the core of Republican popularity. For many white male Americans, the preamble confirmed that the American Revolution had been fought on their behalf and to secure their political rights. A group of Pennsylvania Republicans, celebrating their successes in the state elections of 1799, effectively summarized this ideology in their toasts. Having drunk to "The sovereignty of the people—The foundation of democratic republics," they raised their glasses to the sentiment: "Thomas Jefferson . . . May the spirit which dictated the declaration of independence—preside in the union." A year later, following their party's success in the presidential election, Democratic Republicans in Easton, Pennsylvania, drank to the day of Jefferson's election: "The third of December 1800—the legitimate offspring of the Fourth of July, 1776," while, in Lancaster, others saluted Jefferson's inauguration with the toast: "The principles of the 4th July, 1776, confirmed the 4th March, 1801." To these citizens, Jefferson better represented the spirit of 1776 than any other man living, and his Declaration of Independence was their ideological manifesto.[36]

The news of both Jefferson's election and inauguration prompted a large number of Republican civic festivals all across the country. Jefferson and his vice president, Aaron Burr, were toasted countless times, yet rarely did participants forget the political principles that these men symbolized. When Jefferson was toasted, it was often as a faithful servant of the people who adhered to the Constitution and the spirit of '76. On New Year's Day, 1801, in Lancaster, Pennsylvania, "the democratic republicans of this state at the seat of government, celebrated the success of the republican cause," drinking toasts "in the true spirit of liberty." The first toast celebrated "The PEOPLE—and the Constitution, which *they* have ordained." When Jefferson and Burr were toasted, it was because they had been "placed by the *People* on the Pillars of the Constitution." In East Windsor, Connecticut, Democratic Republicans toasted the day and then stated their principles: "May monarchy nor aristocracy never prevail over the genuine principles of elective democracy in the United States of America." Jubilant Democratic Republicans in Murfreesboro, North Carolina, toasted "The 4th of July, 1776," and quite often the spirit of '76 and the day of celebration were explicitly united, as when the Republican Greens militia company of Philadelphia gave as their first toast, "The Day we celebrate, being the completion of the revolution of 1776, and the commencement of the happy æra of true liberty." An editorial in a Rhode Island newspaper shamelessly predicted that "THE FOURTH OF MARCH 1801, will become as celebrated in history as the 4th of July, 1776."[37]

Hailed as "the able statesman and philosopher of Monticello," "the wise and virtuous Philosopher and Statesman," and "the friend of science and virtue," Jefferson had evolved from the politically radical architect of the Declaration of Independence, supporter of the French Revolution, and radical critic of the Federalists, into a revered president and national leader. His inaugural address, with its plea for reconciliation and national harmony, showed the president toning down the radical image that had helped define his popularity during the last quarter of the eighteenth century. Federalist newspapers continued to complain about toasts that "were truly Jacobinical," but in fact the radicalism of a decade earlier had—like Thomas Paine—all but disappeared from most Republican celebrations of Jefferson and his election. In many toasts, Jefferson was linked as often to the Constitution as to the radical Declaration, as when New Jersey Republicans raised their glasses to "The Federal Constitution—and Thomas Jefferson," a toast that echoed hundreds of earlier toasts to Federalist presidents Washington and Adams and seemed a long way from the Republican sentiments of a decade earlier.[38] Thomas Paine, and the radical and revolutionary ideology and language of 1776, were all but forgotten in celebrations of electoral victory, power, and the deposing of a Federalist administration believed by Republicans to have betrayed the Constitution.

However, when Jefferson extended an invitation to Paine to return to the United States, the president's Federalist opponents seized their opportunity to attack the president and declare him guilty by association.[39] Many Republican newspapers initially denied the existence of such an invitation, indicating that even partisan Republicans considered Paine to now be beyond the pale of respectable politics, but the publication of Jefferson's letter forced Republicans onto the defensive. One Federalist correspondent in the *Gazette of the United States* noted that Republicans had denied the existence of the invitation "as a charge derogatory to his [Jefferson's] character." Upon learning that Jefferson had indeed invited Paine to return to the United States, the author continued, Republicans were now falling over themselves to "tell us of the worth of Thomas Paine, of his attachment to republican principles; and the immense debt of gratitude, we owe him for his services in our revolution. This we must think is a most unfortunate defence, as the people of this country will not be easily convinced that they are under many and strong obligations to Thomas Paine."[40]

As Federalists argued, by denying that the president had invited Paine to America, "the friends of Mr. Jefferson necessarily admit, that the character of Mr. Paine has become so debased and blasted, as to render it disgraceful to invite him to our country."[41] The Federalists revived their attacks on Paine, seizing their opportunity to tar Jefferson with the brush of dangerous and unpatriotic revolutionary sympathies. Readers of the *Gazette of the United States*, for example, were treated to a detailed attack on Paine, as a man

> who published in his own name, that the Bible would be more consistently called the word of a Demon than the word of God. . . . The same also, who, in his own name accused General WASHINGTON of

cowardice, ingratitude, intentional falsehood and *treachery*. The man who, at this moment, is an outlaw for treasonable practices against the government of his native country. . . . Such is the man whom the President of the United States has selected from the nations, for an affectionate friend and correspondent.[42]

Another Federalist writer made headway by quoting from Jefferson's letter inviting Paine to return to the United States, damning the president as a Jacobin radical in the Painite mold. "You will," Jefferson had written, "find us returned generally to sentiments worthy of former times. In these it will be your glory to have steadily labored and with as much effect as any man living." Paine's and Jefferson's patriotism, and their commitment to liberty and republican government in the United States during the 1770s, were ignored by Federalists, who sought to condemn both men for their alleged support of the infidelity and the bloody democratic leveling of the French Revolution. When Republican newspaper editors defended Jefferson for offering Paine sanctuary in the United States, Federalists responded by declaring the president and his defenders guilty by association with "that living opprobrium of humanity, TOM PAINE." The "two great leaders of Democracy and Deism, Paine and Jefferson," were roundly condemned in the Federalist press.[43]

Paine's *Age of Reason* and his alleged infidelity provided the most useful ammunition for Federalists, who were eager to discredit Jefferson. One correspondent recalled how when Jefferson was accused of Deism during the presidential election, "his infidel friends laughed at the accusation, and the Christians, who afforded him their support, denied its justice." Without skipping a beat, the author moved on to Paine, arguing:

> There is, probably, no man in the present world who has laboured more strenuously to oppose and destroy the religion of Christ, and there is, perhaps, no one whose exertions have been attended with more effect upon the ignorant and unlettered parts of mankind. . . . Thus arrayed in hostility to the cause of God, and to the temporal and eternal happiness of man, he comes to our country by the solicitation of the first magistrate, and with the assurance of his *best wishes for the success of his labours*.[44]

Federalist attacks on their Republican opponents paled in contrast with the vitriol they poured onto Paine, beginning with his return to the United States in 1802, and continuing until his death seven years later. In an "Anticipated Elegy," one Federalist satirized Paine with a damning obituary, written almost a decade before his actual death.

> Sedition was his *fort:*
> But *Common Sense* is fled forever,
> Since *Tom* is turned to dirt!!
> Yet shall poor *Tom* not be forgotten,
> For *Monticello's* Sage
> Shall rank him, though with tipplers rotting,
> The wisest of the age.[45]

Paine's achievements in helping mobilize popular support for an American declaration of independence, and then in the war to secure that independence, counted for nothing, and Federalists rejoiced in advance at his death, ridiculing Jefferson for his association with "the fam'd Sot." As "the idol of such puny infidels as the editors of the *Aurora,* the *American Citizen,* &c.," Paine was an effective lightning rod for Federalist attacks on Jefferson and the Republicans. Federalists alleged that there was an "intimate connection subsisting between Thomas Jefferson and Thomas Paine," hoping to blacken Jefferson's reputation as a friend of liberty and the Constitution by proving his association with Painite bloody and radical democratic revolution, Paine's attack on Washington, and Paine's undermining of Christianity itself.[46] At first, Republicans sought to combat the Federalist strategy by trying to reveal what their opponents were doing:

> Jefferson and Paine!—and Paine and Jefferson! are found eternally resounding in our ears, and by tory editors seem to have been rendered perfectly one and indivisible—they appear to form the countersign for rallying the shattered power of a distracted faction, who finding themselves unable to tarnish the resplendent lustre of Jefferson's fair fame . . . meanly and wickedly resort to auxiliary means, which have as little connection with him, or his character, as the authors thereof have to truth or decency.[47]

Crucially, however, these kinds of articles criticized Federalists' tactics and defended Jefferson's reputation, but they were almost silent on Paine himself. In private, Jefferson and Paine remained friendly, exchanging letters regularly up until Paine's death. In June 1805, for example, Jefferson wrote a letter to Paine discussing everything from Paine's farmhouse, to Venetian blinds, to Napoleon and the Haitian Revolution. Jefferson ended, however, with a reference to continued Federalist references to their correspondence: "That tory printers should think it advantageous to identify me with that paper, the Aurora, &c., in order to obtain ground for abusing me, is perhaps fair warfare. . . . With respect to the letter, I never hesitated to avow and to justify it in conversation."[48]

Jefferson ended his missive with "friendly salutations, & assurances of esteem & respect," yet there was a certain hollowness to private assurances that were no longer articulated publicly in the political realm. Defending "the most infamous infidel and revolutionist in the universe" was too politically costly to Jefferson and his supporters.[49] From the mid–1790s on, but most especially after Paine's return to America in 1802, Republicans distanced themselves from Paine and eliminated him from their pantheon of heroes. No longer did they raise their glasses to toast the revolutionary and his achievements, preferring to salute Jefferson alone.

This was seen most clearly in Republican celebrations of the national political festival they had made their own, Independence Day. In Philadelphia, in 1801, for example, bands played the Republican anthems *Yankee Doodle* and *Jefferson's March,* while people sang *Jefferson and Liberty* in the streets. A group of citizens dining at Francis's Hotel drank toasts to "Thomas Jefferson—The patriot chosen to maintain in 1801 the principles which he declared in 1776." Similarly, the Philadelphia Blues acknowledged the Fourth of July, 1776, as "the first jubilee in the calendar of liberty," but their next toast was to "*The Year* 1801—The Political Millennium—The most glorious of jubilees, destined to restore and perpetuate liberty, peace, and happiness."[50]

Throughout the nation, the story was much the same, with Republicans monopolizing commemoration of the Fourth immediately before and after Jefferson's election. Even in their New England strongholds, Federalists often retired from the festive scene and generally refused to mount celebrations of a day that they could no longer control. Virtually no Federalist rites, and only a handful of Federalist toasts, found their way into the newspapers of either party, but even though the Republicans controlled the Fourth of July, they continued to laud Jefferson while ignoring Paine. The day, and to a degree, Jefferson himself, had been somewhat de-radicalized, and celebration of the president, the Constitution, and legitimate republican government had replaced earlier celebrations of Paine and Jefferson as the Republicans' standard bearers of radical Revolutionary republicanism. Toasts to Jefferson could be heard everywhere. Many joined the men of the Artillery Company who feasted in an Augusta, Georgia, tavern in 1800 by exalting Jefferson as "the drafter of the declaration of our independence," while others echoed the "true republicans" in Mifflin-Town, Pennsylvania, who drank to the wish that the author of the Declaration of Independence would "be acknowledged and rewarded by the suffrages of all republicans at the next presidential election."[51]

As the new American republic expanded and sought to protect its interests in the midst of the great European wars of the 1790s and early 1800s, the great achievement of Thomas Jefferson—and his Republican Party supporters—was to represent their leader and his party as embodying the values of the American Revolution, individual liberty, and equality. At the same time, as the Republicans sought to win power, first at the state level and then in the national government, they promised stability and secure constitutional government. Thomas Paine did not—perhaps could not—fit this new, moderate Republican Party, representing as he did the everlasting fire of eternal revolution. Paine changed relatively little between 1776 and 1809, yet America changed a great deal, with the result that Paine came to appear too radical and too politically dangerous for even those Republicans who identified with many Painite ideals. Once the Republicans were in control of the national government, the more radical oppositional rhetoric that had characterized their popular festivals, celebrations, and toasts during the early to mid-1790s was quickly forgotten. Thomas Paine and the rights of man were virtually ignored, as were liberty and equality, as well as the once familiar rites involving the liberty pole and liberty cap. Assaulted by the more conservative Federalists and abandoned by the more radical Republicans, Paine had been marginalized and then forgotten by the party of Jefferson. He has been largely absent from American political culture ever since.

NOTES

1. For descriptions of Paine's death and funeral, see Alfred Owen Aldridge, *Man of Reason: The Life of Thomas Paine* (Philadelphia: Lippincott, 1959), 316; and Alfred F. Young, "The Celebration and Damnation of Thomas Paine," in *Liberty Tree: Ordinary People and the American Revolution*, ed. Alfred F. Young (New York: New York University Press, 2006), 265–67. The reactions to Jefferson's death are described in Merrill D. Peterson, *The Jeffersonian Image in the American Mind* (New York: Oxford University Press, 1960); and Andrew Burstein, *America's Jubilee: How in 1826 a Generation Remembered Fifty Years of Independence* (New York: Knopf, 2001).

2. This point is made by Francis D. Cogliano in the introduction to his excellent study, *Thomas Jefferson: Reputation and Legacy* (Edinburgh: Edinburgh University Press, 2006), 6.

3. Barack Obama Inaugural Address (20 January 2009), *New York Times,* 21 Janu-

ary 2009. Obama mentioned George Washington in his speech, but then quoted from Thomas Paine's *The American Crisis* (see Paine, *The American Crisis I*, in *The Complete Writings of Thomas Paine*, ed. Philip S. Foner, 2 vols. [New York: Citadel Press, 1945], 1:55).

4. See "Of Toasts," *Columbian Herald, or the Independent Courier of North-America* (Charleston, S.C.), 23 June 1791; "New-York," *Gazette of the United States*, 10 July 1795; and Anonymous, "The Pro and Con," *New-York Journal, and Weekly Register*, 25 November 1790. For discussion of the rituals and significance of toasting, see Peter Thompson, "The Friendly Glass: Drink and Gentility in Colonial Pennsylvania," *Pennsylvania Magazine of History and Biography* 113, no. 4 (1989): 549–73.

5. In comparison with the other leading figures of the American Revolution, and those of the 1790s, Paine has received rather less attention from historians. However, several younger scholars have recently addressed Paine's place in the political culture of the early republic. See, for example, Seth Cotlar, *Tom Paine's America: The Rise and Fall of Transatlantic Radicalism in the Early Republic* (Charlottesville: University of Virginia Press, 2011); Matthew Rainbow Hale, "On Their Tiptoes: Political Time and Newspapers during the Advent of the Radicalized French Revolution, circa 1792–1793," *Journal of the Early Republic* 29 (Summer 2009): 191–218; and Matthew Rainbow Hale, *The French Revolution and the Forging of American Democracy* (Charlottesville: University of Virginia Press, forthcoming). For studies of the political culture of the early republic, see Simon P. Newman, *Parades and the Politics of the Street: Festive Culture in the Early American Republic* (Philadelphia: University of Pennsylvania Press, 1997). And for analysis of the role of American newspapers in the dissemination of radical news and ideas during the era of the French Revolution, see James Tagg, *Benjamin Franklin Bache and the "Philadelphia Aurora"* (Philadelphia: University of Pennsylvania Press, 1991); and Jeffrey L. Pasley, *'The Tyranny of Printers': Newspaper Politics in the Early American Republic* (Charlottesville: University Press of Virginia, 2001). For more general works on the politics of the early republic, see James Roger Sharp, *American Politics in the Early Republic: The New Nation in Crisis* (New Haven, Conn.: Yale University Press, 1993); and Stanley M. Elkins and Eric L. McKitrick, *The Age of Federalism: The Early American Republic, 1788–1800* (New York: Columbia University Press, 1993).

6. "Extract of a Letter from Bladensburg, July 5," *Albany Gazette*, 28 July 1791; "From a Correspondent at Schenectady," *Albany Gazette*, 29 July 1793; "Bergen County, Hackensack, July 8, 1794," *New-Jersey Journal* (Elizabethtown), 23 July 1794.

7. "BOSTON, June 20," *Daily Advertiser* (New York), 26 June 1794; "From Monmouth, July 4," *The Guardian; or, New-Brunswick Advertiser*, 22 July 1794.

8. *General Advertiser* (Philadelphia), 17 July 1792 [renamed the *Aurora and General Advertiser*—or, simply, *Aurora*—after November 1794; subsequent citations here will reference the *Aurora*]; "CARLISLE, July 18," *Carlisle Gazette* (Pennsylvania), 18 July 1792; "Anniversary," *New-York Journal*, 18 July 1792; *Aurora*, 2 January 1793.

9. This toast was given by inhabitants of Ulster County, New York, to mark the elec-

tion of the Republican, Peter Van Gaasbeek, to the House of Representatives. The only other American named in the sixteen toasts was "the President of the United States" (see "CATSKILL, March 4," *Albany Gazette,* 25 March 1793).

10. "NEW-YORK, July 8," *American Minerva, and the New-York (Evening) Advertiser,* 8 July 1795; "CHESTERTOWN, JULY 9," *Aurora,* 13 July 1793.

11. *Aurora,* 24 February 1792; "BOSTON, October 18," *Aurora,* 26 October 1792; "NEWARK, APRIL 8," *Aurora,* 10 April 1795.

12. *New-Jersey Journal,* 19 March 1794; *Aurora,* 21 March 1794.

13. "TIMOTHY TREMULOUS, 'TO THE EDITOR OF THE AURORA," *Aurora,* 21 July 1798. The account of toasts given following erection of a liberty pole in Connecticut appeared in *The Bee* (New London, Conn.), 31 July 1798; and "NEWARK, June 17," *Kentucky Gazette* (Lexington), 10 July 1800.

14. *Aurora,* 18 July 1799.

15. *Aurora,* 9 July 1799.

16. *Kentucky Gazette,* 25 July 1799; *Return of the Whole Number of Persons within the Several Districts of the United States, according to 'An Act for the Second Census or Enumeration of the Inhabitants of the* UNITED STATES*'* (Washington, D.C., 1801), 2P; Riley Moffat, *Population History of Eastern U.S. Cities and Towns, 1790–1870* (Metuchen, N.J.: Scarecrow Press, 1992), 63; *Carlisle Gazette,* 10 July 1799; "PATERSON, JULY 4, 1799," *Aurora,* 11 July 1799; *Aurora,* 6 July 1799; "ANNIVERSARY FESTIVAL," *Aurora,* 11 July 1799.

17. "THE AMERICAN—No. II," *Connecticut Courant* (Hartford), 14 January 1793.

18. Ibid.

19. "An Illustration of the *Rights of Man,*" *Gazette of the United States,* 12 October 1791.

20. "For the Gazette of the United States," *Gazette of the United States,* 2 February 1793.

21. Another Citizen of Connecticut, "For the CONNECTICUT COURANT," *Connecticut Courant,* 17 July 1795; *Gazette of the United States,* 31 December 1796.

22. [William Cobbett], *The Life of Thomas Paine, Interspersed with Remarks and Reflections by Peter Porcupine* (Philadelphia, 1797), 30–31.

23. "The Times," *Massachusetts Mercury* (Boston), 20 January 1797; "PHILADELPHIA, February 27," *Gazette of the United States,* 27 February 1797; "GENERAL WASHINGTON'S BIRTHDAY," *Porcupine's Gazette* (Philadelphia), 8 March 1797.

24. "Thanksgiving," *Massachusetts Mercury,* 30 November 1798; Titus Manlius, "Thomas Paine—No. 1," *Ede's Kennebec Gazette* (Augusta, Me.), 9 December 1802.

25. "Of Paine's Letter to Washington," *Massachusetts Mercury,* 13 January 1797; William Cobbett, "A Letter to the Infamous Tom Paine, in Answer to His Letter to General Washington," *Porcupine's Political Censor, for December 1796* (Philadelphia, 1796), 18.

26. Manlius, "Thomas Paine," *Ede's Kennebec Gazette,* 9 December 1802.

27. William Cobbett, "A Letter to the Infamous Tom Paine," *Porcupine's Political Censor,* 18.

28. "NEWBURGH, (N.Y.)," *Aurora*, 3 September 1798; "From a Toast to Jefferson by Members of the Southwark Light Infantry Militia Company in Philadelphia, Independence Day, 1798," in *Aurora*, 7 July 1798; "TOASTS Drank by the New-York Democratic Society, July 4," *The Bee*, 18 July 1798.

29. "Anniversary Festival," *Aurora*, 11 July 1799; "FOURTH OF JULY ... Celebration on Sagharbour (N.Y.)," *Aurora*, 21 July 1798; "Celebration of the 4th of July ... Bushwick, King's County (L.I.)," *Aurora*, 11 July 1799; "WINSLOW CELEBRATION," *Kennebeck Intelligencer* (Augusta, Me.), 13 July 1798; "TOASTS: North-Farms," *Aurora*, 11 July 1800; "NATIONAL FESTIVAL, Germantown," *Aurora*, 12 July 1800; "FOURTH OF JULY, 1800, "Montgomery County," *Aurora*, 10 July 1800.

30. A TRUE ANTIGALLICAN, "FOR PORCUPINE'S GAZETTE," *Porcupine's Gazette*, 15 July 1797.

31. Ascanius, "The Pseudo Patriot, No. III," *Massachusetts Mercury*, 30 June 1797.

32. "ANNIVERSARY FESTIVAL," *Aurora*, 11 July 1799; "Jefferson's Village, July 4, 1799," *Aurora*, 11 July 1799; "NEW-LONDON, JULY 10. FROM THE BEE," *Aurora*, 16 July 1799; "CELEBRATION OF THE IVTH OF JULY," *New-York Weekly Museum*, 6 July 1799; *Aurora*, 6 July 1799; *Aurora*, 10 July 1799; *Aurora*, 6 July 1799.

33. "BLOOMFIELD, FOURTH OF JULY, 1799," *Aurora*, 11 July 1799; *Aurora*, 30 July 1799.

34. *Aurora*, 7 July 1798.

35. *Aurora*, 8 July 1799. This report listed the names and the commanders of each militia company, allowing a comparison with an account of the 26 December 1799 procession commemorating the death of Washington, which listed the party affiliations of most of Philadelphia's militia companies (see ibid., 27 December 1799; and ibid., 7 July 1800).

36. *Aurora*, 12 November 1799; "EASTON, January 24," *Aurora*, 7 February 1801; "LANCASTER REPUBLICAN FESTIVAL," *Aurora*, 11 March 1801. I have found the following to be particularly useful in a consideration of the ideology and role of the Declaration of Independence in American politics: Garry Wills, *Inventing America: Jefferson's Declaration of Independence* (New York: Doubleday, 1978); and Daniel T. Rodgers, *Contested Truths: Keywords in American Politics since Independence* (New York: Basic Books, 1987).

37. *Aurora*, 7 January 1801; *The Bee*, 8 April 1801; "MURFREESBOROUGH, March 5," *Aurora*, 15 April 1801; "TOASTS," *Aurora*, 9 March 1801; *The Guardian of Liberty* (Newport, R.I.), 3 January 1801.

38. "Chester, Del.," *Aurora*, 13 March 1801; "GERMANTOWN CELEBRATION OF THE ELECTION OF A REPUBLICAN PRESIDENT & VICE PRESIDENT, OF THE UNITED STATES," *Aurora*, 16 March 1801; "Republican Celebrations," *The Bee*, 18 March 1801; *Gazette of the United States*, 9 March 1801; *Augusta Chronicle and Gazette of the State* (Augusta, Ga.), 7 March 1801.

39. Thomas Jefferson [TJ] to Thomas Paine, 18 March 1801, in *The Papers of Thomas Jefferson*, ed. Julian P. Boyd et al., 39 vols. to date (Princeton, N.J.: Princeton University Press, 1950–) [hereafter cited as *Jefferson Papers*], 33:358–59.

40. "Mr. Jefferson," *Gazette of the United States,* 11 June 1802.

41. *Gazette of the United States,* 11 May 1802.

42. "TOM PAINE, INVITED TO THIS COUNTRY BY HIS RIGHT WORTHY AND AFFECTIONATE FRIEND, T. JEFFERSON," *Gazette of the United States,* 9 November 1802.

43. TJ to Paine, 18 March 1801, *Jefferson Papers,* 33:359. Extracts of the letter were gleefully reprinted by Federalist editors: see, for example, Manlius, "Thomas Paine," *Ede's Kennebec Gazette,* 9 December 1802.; "Thomas Jefferson & Thomas Paine," *New-York Herald,* 11 August 1802; "Thomas Jefferson & Thomas Paine," *Washington Federalist* (Washington, D.C.), 16 August 1802; "Thomas Jefferson & Thomas Paine," *Windham Herald* (Windham, Conn.), 19 August 1802; Anonymous, "Tom Paine and Pat Duane," *Gazette of the United States,* 21 July 1801; and Anonymous, "Monticello, October 6, 99," *Gazette of the United States,* 9 October 1802.

44. *Gazette of the United States,* 11 May 1802.

45. Stanley, "Anticipated Elegy," *New-York Commercial Advertiser,* 1 June 1804. (This poem first appeared in the *Newburyport Herald* in 1801).

46. Stanley, "Anticipated Elegy," *New-York Commercial Advertiser,* 1 June 1804; Anonymous, "Monticello, October 6, 99," *Gazette of the United States,* 9 October 1802; Anonymous, "Paine and Jefferson," *Boston Gazette,* 16 December 1802.

47. Anonymous, "Jefferson and Paine," *South Carolina Gazette,* 30 December 1802.

48. TJ to Paine, 5 June 1805, in *The Works of Thomas Jefferson,* ed. Paul Leicester Ford, 12 vols. (New York: G. P. Putnam's Sons, 1904–5), 151.

49. Anonymous, "Mazzei, Callender, Paine, and Jefferson," *Jenks' Portland Gazette* (Portland, Me.), 6 December 1802.

50. *Aurora,* 7 July 1800; "FESTIVITIES, ON THE FOURTH OF JULY, 1801," *Aurora,* 10 July 1801.

51. "AUGUSTA, July 5," *Augusta Chronicle,* 5 July 1800; "MIFFLIN-TOWN, July 9," *Carlisle Gazette,* 16 July 1800.

Paine, Jefferson, and the Modern Ideas of Democracy and the Nation

ARMIN MATTES

D EMOCRACY AND THE IDEA of the nation are two concepts that over the course of the last two hundred and fifty years have significantly shaped the development of the modern world. As a result, historians and scholars of other disciplines have paid a great deal of attention to the history of these key concepts. Often, however, scholars concentrate on the empirical "realities" of democracy and the nation and neglect the conceptual changes that were essential to the rise of the modern forms of these two concepts.[1] To a degree, this neglect has shrouded the nature of their development and relationship. For example, many scholars agree that both democracy and the idea of the nation emerged in a recognizably modern form in the Age of Revolution in the last quarter of the eighteenth century. Quite a few have also recognized that the rise of the two concepts was in some way connected. But opinions differ considerably about the exact relationship between the modern idea of democracy and the modern idea of the nation.[2]

This essay addresses the origins and the relationship between the modern forms of the two concepts. The central argument is threefold. First, in their origin these two concepts were indistinguishable because they both arose from a common revolutionary impulse directed against the prevailing political and social order of the time, which was in essence hierarchical. Second, this revolutionary impulse that resulted in the reconceptualization of "democracy" and the "nation" received its decisive form in the French Revolution. Third, although the French Revolution was instrumental in generating the changes in the meanings of "democracy" and the "nation," these changes were neither confined to France nor did the new meanings of the two concepts merely radiate from France to other countries.

The French Revolution served as a catalyst for subsequent developments in both Europe and America because it caused the emergence of the binary of revolution and counter-revolution that in turn generated changes in the meanings of "democracy" and the "nation." The outbreak of the French Revolution and its ensuing radicalization raised the question of the nature of human relationships in a much more radical way than ever before. Assaults on noble privileges in the French Revolution called into question not only the legally defined privileges themselves but also their theoretical basis: the belief in natural inequality among men. This, in turn, set in motion a process of a dialectical reconceptualization of the terms "aristocracy" and "democracy," from narrowly defined political terms to broadly conceived social concepts evolving around the core ideas of equality and inequality. Thomas Paine's thoughts about democracy nicely illustrate this process.

The same revolutionary dynamic that resulted in the transformation of the meaning of "democracy" also led to the formation of a modern idea of the nation. "Nation," in its revolutionary context, meant the people—conceived as one indivisible body, in opposition to the traditional structure of society as a hierarchy of several corporate bodies. The fundamental and irreconcilable principle separating these two concepts was, again, the question of the equality or inequality of human beings. As a result, the same dynamism driving the reconceptualization of "democracy" also led to the reinterpretation of the meaning of the "nation." The development of Thomas Jefferson's understanding of what constitutes a nation during the early phase of the French Revolution demonstrates the original congruence of the modern concepts of democracy and the nation in the form of the revolutionary antithesis to the traditional order of society.

Finally, Jefferson's interpretation of the party struggles of the 1790s in America provides an example of how people all over the Atlantic World in the aftermath of the French Revolution began to perceive their internal struggles as tied into a larger, transnational, revolutionary movement. Consequently, they reinterpreted their specific, local political and social situations in the light of the broad framework of revolution and counter-revolution that had emerged in France. Jefferson's application of the revolutionary dichotomy to the American situation thus shows that the conceptual changes occurred simultaneously on both sides of the Atlantic and that they happened within the context of specific local circumstances.

THE MODERN IDEAS OF DEMOCRACY AND THE NATION

An analysis of Thomas Paine's works is especially suited to illuminating the origins of the modern concept of democracy. Most Paine scholars agree on one point—that Thomas Paine was both a democrat and "a symbol of the struggle for democracy."[3] This near consensus rests on excellent research demonstrating the ways in which Paine's position was "democratic" and how his actions and writings contributed to the breakthrough of what we call "democracy."[4] Building on Paine's own assertion that the principles of his later works were "the same as those in *Common Sense*," most scholars characterize his political writings as "democratic."[5]

Yet, before he wrote the second part of *Rights of Man*, Paine himself rarely used the terms "democracy" or "democratic"—and in the few cases he did, it was in a different sense than historians now understand and apply the term.[6] As a result of the broad characterization of his work as "democratic," Paine's relationship to the actual development of the concept of democracy has received too little attention. It is therefore my aim in the first part of this essay to examine more closely Paine's role in the development of the concept of democracy, from its traditional, narrow understanding—the rule of all in a polity—toward its much broader, modern meaning as a social and political concept.

Of course, Paine's contribution to the changing meaning of democracy has not gone unnoticed. In order to explain his systematic disquisition on democracy in the second part of *Rights of Man,* some scholars, rejecting Paine's claim to consistency, have argued that his political convictions changed fundamentally after the French Revolution.[7] Others, accepting Paine's invariance, contend that his "optimistic view of human nature" enabled him to disregard the classical stigma attached to democracy—its proneness to anarchy and mob rule—and thus to make it the basis of his ideal of a representative system.[8] The problem with the former argument is that the collected body of Paine's writings does not reveal a fundamental change in his principles. The latter position is valid with respect to Paine's anthropology, but cannot adequately explain why Paine only began to use and reinterpret the term "democracy" in the second part of *Rights of Man*. If one assumes a basic consistency in Paine's political principles, why did he suddenly invoke the concept of democracy in the second part of *Rights of Man* and not in *Common Sense*?

This essay offers an answer to this question within the larger interpretive framework of a universal democratic revolution, as developed in the 1950s by the historian Robert R. Palmer.[9] In his magisterial work, *The Age of the Democratic Revolution,* Palmer argued that during the last decades of the eighteenth century the entire Atlantic World had been swept by one great movement against a social order that was structured hierarchically into distinct social classes, with one or a few monopolizing political and social power. According to Palmer, this universal impulse toward a more egalitarian society assumed varying forms in different countries because it emerged out of specific, local causes.[10] But in all cases, the French Revolution led to an ideological polarization into two antagonistic camps: one side adhered to a hierarchical order founded upon the belief in a fundamental inequality of human nature, and the other to a conception of society founded on the principle of basic human equality.

The issue of equality, therefore, lay at the heart of the transatlantic revolutionary agitation. "Equality" in the late eighteenth century, however, was not a clearly defined notion that was applied in the same way by different persons and at different times.[11] Thomas Paine and Edmund Burke are a case in point. Paine, on one hand, embraced a radical idea of the political and social equality of all individuals. Burke, on the other, applied the notion of equality primarily to the corporate level—for example, among estates or states. Focusing on the concept of equality in both Paine's and Burke's writings on the American and French Revolutions can explain their basic agreement during the Imperial Crisis of the 1770s and their radical disagreement over the French Revolution; it will also show why the change in the meaning of democracy occurred only after the latter event.

The French Revolution brought Paine's and Burke's different understandings of "equality" into sharp focus, thus placing the two men squarely into the antagonistic camps of Palmer's revolutionary dichotomy. The need to adapt the political language of the time to the needs of this binary generated a reconceptualization of the basic terms of political theory and thus can account for Paine's sudden interest in "democracy" in the second part of *Rights of Man*.

Claiming that the French Revolution brought Paine's and Burke's views on equality into conflict does not mean that their differing views did not exist before. In fact, they were—at least with the advantage of hindsight—already discernible at the time of the American Revolution. Burke from the outset perceived the Imperial Crisis in the 1760s and 1770s as a traditional power struggle within the British mixed, or balanced, constitution. In his opinion, the Crown had assumed too much power, and had thus upset the constitutional balance, both among the three great corporate bodies of the British constitution—the Court, the House of Lords, and the Commons—as well as within the Empire.[12] His proposed solution within Britain was to curb the power of the monarchy and thus restore the constitutional balance, or equality of power, among the corporate estates of the realm.

Similarly, Burke's recipe for solving the crisis with the American colonies was to restore—or rather to create—a rough equality on the corporate level within the British Empire. To be sure, he never abandoned the theory of the supremacy of Parliament over the colonial assemblies, as stated in the Declaratory Act of 1766, which he regarded as essential to preserve the unity of the Empire.[13] But starting with his first speech on colonial affairs in 1766 and continuing to his *Address to the British Colonists in North America* eleven years later, Burke's position evolved, from advocating Parliament's voluntary abstinence from interfering in internal colonial matters, to a guaranteed right of taxation in all cases, and, finally, to a plan for a "federal union." This plan would have guaranteed the colonies autonomy and therefore, with respect to internal matters, an equal station with Parliament within the British Empire.[14] Parliament's main purpose would henceforth merely have been to preserve a "just and fair equality" among the Empire's various corporate entities.[15] Burke applied his notion of equality only on the corporate level, however, within the structure of a mixed constitution balancing the one, the few, and the many. Accordingly, he emphatically warned the colonists to not separate themselves entirely from the mother country and "embark on untried forms of government," because he was convinced that Americans were "not now, nor for ages, likely to be, capable of that form of constitution in an independent state."[16]

Paine's idea of equality during the American Revolutionary era was clearly not on a corporate, but on an individual, level. The assumption that "mankind being originally equals in the order of creation"—as he expressed the sentiment in *Common Sense*—was so obvious for him that he did not think it necessary to enter into any elaborate discussion of the subject.[17] Nevertheless, this notion of fundamental individual equality constituted the basis of his political thought in that pamphlet. Building on this premise, Paine attacked what he regarded as the "popery of government": monarchy.[18] "All men being originally equals," he could discern no "truly natural or religious reason" for "the distinction of men into kings and subjects."[19] On the same grounds, Paine also rejected the hereditary principle of succession as "an insult and an imposition on posterity."[20] Paine's notion of equality thus extended not only to the individual but also to any generation at any time. Although in *Common Sense* Paine did not deal extensively with "aristocracy," the same reasoning led him to summarily dismiss the British House of Lords as "the remains of aristocratical tyranny."[21] In short, the difference between Paine's radical individualist notion of equality and Burke's application of this notion to the corporate level was already apparent at the time of the American Revolution.

But this difference did not yet generate an animosity between Paine and

Burke, who became acquainted with each other in 1787 and remained on speaking terms until early 1790, nor did it provoke Burke, in *Reflections on the Revolution in America,* to lament the breakdown of a hierarchical social order.[22] That Burke refused to address the notion of individual equality directly, because, as he asserted time and again, he regarded it as dangerous to base one's political position on "abstract ideas" and "metaphysical speculations," certainly helped to conceal their differences.[23] But the cardinal reason why their different views on equality in the 1770s were not yet conspicuous lay in the peculiar character of American mobilization against the imperial authority. In Burke's opinion, the colonial assemblies constituted the "aristocratic" part within a balanced constitution between the monarch—or, in the case of the British Empire, the King-in-Parliament—and the populace at large. In their effort to resist British encroachments on their privileges, however, the colonial assemblies did not stress specific "aristocratic" privileges—which, due to the lack of a formal aristocracy, would have been difficult in any case—but rather extended their claims to liberty to the population as a whole, thus enabling a broad cross-class mobilization against British tyranny while at the same time avoiding social conflict at home.[24] As a result, during the time of the American Revolution, Paine's and Burke's applications of equality to the corporate and individual level were not obviously antagonistic, but could be seen as complementary in a struggle against a monarchy displaying despotic tendencies.

This does not mean that the two notions of equality did not come into conflict at this time. The debates over the Pennsylvania state constitution, as well as John Adams's apprehensions about the implications of Paine's ideas for the new state governments, show that they indeed did lead to disputes. But because of the peculiar cross-class mobilization during the American Revolution, they still appeared as linked together in a power struggle within the traditional conceptual framework of the mixed constitution. Figuratively speaking, Paine's and Burke's understandings of equality constituted rather the ends of a "republican continuum"—marked by endeavors to create a republican government—than two antagonistic opposites.

This situation changed with the onset of the French Revolution. The existence of an entrenched aristocracy fighting to preserve its privileges in the Revolution's early phase set Burke's and Paine's notions of equality on a collision course: any provision for equality on the corporate level within a mixed-constitution framework in France would inevitably mean the perpetuation of inequality on the individual level. These circumstances made the issue of equality central to the Revolutionary struggle, with one side advocating a social order based on the fundamental political and social equality of individual human beings, and the other adhering to a corporate concept of society based on individual inequality.

The centrality of equality is apparent in Burke's *Reflections on the Revolution in France,* where it is the key theme in his discussion of the French Revolution.[25] Applying "equality" exactly as he had done during the American Revolution to the corporate level, Burke contended that France might have followed the British example and created a mixed constitution. This approach, he asserted, would have resulted in a "free constitution" by balancing the various corporate entities, namely, "a potent monarchy, a disciplined army, a reformed and venerated clergy, a mitigated but spirited nobility," and a "liberal order of commons."[26] Only in such a mixed constitution could "the true moral equality of mankind" exist, with everybody in his or her proper place according to his or her natural abilities and eminence.[27] All other notions of equality, that is, individual political and social equality, Burke rejected as a "monstrous fiction" and an attempt to "pervert the natural order of things."[28]

In the first part of *Rights of Man,* Paine also felt the need to clarify his understanding of equality as the basis of his political thought. While in *Common Sense* he had more or less taken it for granted that "all men [were] originally equals," in *Rights of Man* he carefully deduced his assumption from his theological conviction that all human beings are made by the "Creator" and each one of them equally, "in the image of God."[29] Not only were "all men born equal," they were also—by virtue of this fact—endowed with "equal natural rights."[30] In Paine's opinion, these natural rights in turn were "the foundation of all his civil rights," because it made no sense to assume that man would "enter into society to become *worse* than he was before."[31] Any political system based on the inequality of individuals, such as Burke's favored mixed constitution, was therefore anathema to Paine.

Burke's *Reflections* and the first part of Paine's *Rights of Man* epitomize the emergence of a revolutionary dichotomy pivoting on the decisive question of equality. In the conclusion of the first part of *Rights of Man,* Paine recognized this dichotomy. In contrast to classical theory, he asserted that there were only two "distinct and opposite . . . modes of government": one "generally known by the name of republic," the other "by that of monarchy and aristocracy." One was based on "election and representation," the other on "hereditary succession"—which is to say, the one on equality, and the other on inequality.[32]

This reordering of the political landscape into two broad, antagonistic sides had far-reaching consequences. Most importantly, in the opinion of revolutionaries like Paine, it made irrelevant the hitherto dominant traditional political theory based on Aristotle's six forms of government, as well as the mixed constitution theory that had been regarded in the eighteenth century as the best way to combine the three good forms of government. Paine accordingly argued that "in a well-constituted republic" based on a fundamental notion of equality, "monarchy, aristocracy, and democracy" as distinct estates or orders of human beings were "but creatures of imagination."[33] The emerging revolutionary binary, therefore, generated a reconceptualization of the most basic concepts of political theory.

The most significant of these reconceptualizations concerned the question of how to describe the two sides of the dichotomy. In the first part of *Rights of Man*, Paine termed the egalitarian side a "republic." But as he soon recognized in the second part, a republic "is not any particular form of government" and could very well be aristocratic in nature.[34] According to traditional political theory, however, equality had long been regarded as "the essential principle of democracy."[35] Because of this association, "democracy" now began to lose its traditional, narrow meaning of the direct rule of all and to acquire a new, broader, and essentially modern meaning as the denominator for the egalitarian side of the revolutionary dichotomy. The emergence of a modern concept of democracy is thus reflected in both Paine's and Burke's writings: positively in Paine's, which were based on the new principle of equality, and negatively in Burke's, which were based upon its antonym, inequality.

But this change did not happen all at once. On the contrary, "democracy" acquired its new meaning step by step over the course of the last decade of the eighteenth and the first decades of the nineteenth century as it evolved in contradistinction to its counter-revolutionary opposite; that is, it evolved in a dialectical manner. Interpreted in this light, it is clear why Paine only dealt with the concept of democracy in a systematic way in the second part of *Rights of Man:* because it was one of the very first steps in this dialectical reconceptualization.

After determining that a republic is no form of government, Paine in the second part of *Rights of Man* argued that four forms of government thus far had been known: "the democratical, the aristocratical, the monarchical, and [as a new one] what is now called the representative."[36] But consistent with his stance within the revolutionary binary, he at once dismissed monarchy and aristocracy, or any mixture of the various forms, as nonsensical, and therefore proclaimed "democracy as the ground" upon which to build his preferred political system.[37] But democracy itself, according to its traditional definition, was too "unwieldy and impracticable" for a large country.[38] Paine's solution,

THE MODERN IDEAS OF DEMOCRACY AND THE NATION

as he famously described it, was to "ingraft representation upon democracy," thus arriving at what we would nowadays call a representative democracy.[39] But it is important to keep in mind that for Paine and many of his contemporaries, these were still two distinct forms of government. For years to come, intellectuals on both sides of the Atlantic would grapple with the exact relation of representation and democracy, until this new system would finally find its classic expression in Alexis de Tocqueville's *Democracy in America*. Nevertheless, this new idea received the first impetus for its development around the core principle of equality in the early stage of the French Revolution. The juxtaposition of Paine's and Burke's writings in that period can therefore illuminate the emergence of a modern concept of democracy.

The dialectical evolution of the new conception of democracy in the wake of the French Revolution is of prime importance because it also marks the emergence of the modern idea of the nation. The formation of the two concepts was not only simultaneous, it was also synonymous: "democracy appeared in the world contained in the idea of the nation as a butterfly in a cocoon."[40] The change in the meaning of the "nation" during the early phase of the French Revolution, and its relation to the new concept of democracy, is nicely captured in Thomas Jefferson's developing thought.

During the crucial years leading to the commencement of the French Revolution, Jefferson resided in Paris as the American minister to France. He did not, as he claimed, simply observe this development "as an uninterested spectator, with no other bias than a love for mankind."[41] His thinking about the "nation," traceable in his letters from 1787 to 1789, changed as the idea evolved in France in conjunction with the democratic part of the emerging revolutionary dichotomy.

Jefferson had left the United States in mid-1784 to join John Adams and Benjamin Franklin in Europe as minister plenipotentiary to negotiate commercial treaties with the European powers.[42] In March 1785, he had been appointed the successor of the latter as minister to France. During these early years in France, Jefferson still used the term "nation" as he had during the time of the American Revolution, in a relatively non-political way, to refer to the entire (white) population of a distinct territory. For example, when in 1786 he collaborated with the French essayist Jean Nicholas Démeunier on the article on the United States for the *Encyclopédie Methodique*, he wrote about possible "broils" among the "nations" that had formed the United States.[43]

With the onset of the French Revolution, this slowly began to change. Initially, Jefferson advocated gradual reform and advised French friends like the Marquis de Lafayette to "keep the good model of your neighboring country [England] before your eyes, [and] you may get on, step by step, towards a good constitution."[44] The obstacle for the attainment of a "good constitution" for France during this time was, in Jefferson's eyes, the absolutist monarchy. Accordingly, anybody who had "a very jealous eye [on] a court whose principles are the most absolute despotism" had his favor.[45] At this stage, Jefferson thus supported the demands of the aristocratic corporate bodies [*parlements*] and their patriotic movement for a greater participation in the affairs of France, and proposed as a goal a government modeled after the mixed constitution of Great Britain. His hope was that the "establishment of the Provincial assemblies [*parlements*]" would "be the instrument for circumscribing the power of the crown and raising the people into consideration."[46] Jefferson was optimistic this would actually happen, reporting in August 1787 "that in the course of three months the royal authority has lost, and the rights of the nation gained, as much ground . . . as England gained in all her civil wars under the Stuarts."[47] At this time, Jefferson defined the "nation" as the population of France, comprising nobles and commoners, in contrast to and implicitly excluding an absolutist, and thus despotic, monarchy.

One year later, despotism was still the foremost obstacle to real reform in France. Yet Jefferson's perception of what constituted despotism had changed. By August 1788 he no longer regarded the *parlements* as champions for the liberty of the nation in general.[48] On the contrary, he saw the struggle in France as "a contest between the monarchical and aristocratical parts of government, for a monopoly of despotism over the people."[49] Jefferson still hoped that events would turn out favorably, emphasizing that the nobility was "divided partly between the parliamentary and the despotic party, and partly united with the real patriots, who are endeavoring to gain for the nation what they can, both from the parliamentary and the single despotism."[50]

Jefferson's analysis of a rift in the aristocracy between a despotic and a "patriotic" part is crucial because it signals the emergence of the revolutionary dichotomy between an "aristocratic" and a "democratic" side. "Democratic," in this context, did not mean belonging to a clearly defined democratic class, nor did it merely mean the people in the form of the third estate. Rather, "democratic" came to denote a person who adhered to a democratic concept of society based on the principle of equality.[51] Hence, it could include liberal-minded nobles, like Lafayette, who were "real patriots" and who advocated an egalitarian social system. As Jefferson's comments mark the starting point of the "democratic" side of the revolutionary dichotomy, so they suggest that not only the king but also those parts of the aristocracy who supported a "parliamentary [or] single despotism" had moved outside the nation.

The development of the revolutionary dichotomy, however, was still embryonic in mid–1788, and Jefferson did not yet advocate a clear-cut opposition between the "aristocratic" and "democratic/national" sides. One reason for this was that he was not sure if the large mass of the French people, after centuries of living under a "despotic" monarchy, were ready for a thorough reform of the political system. It was a "misfortune that they [the French people] are not yet ripe for the blessings to which they are entitled."[52] He also feared that demands for radical reform would induce the Crown to use force. He therefore advised his friends to be "prudent . . . , lest they should shock the disposition of the court."[53] To avoid the estrangement of the king, Jefferson proposed that the patriotic party seek an alliance with him to gain the right of equal representation and the vote by heads in the Estates General, which had been scheduled to convene in May 1789. Jefferson, therefore, in early 1789 still thought that securing rights for the third estate within a mixed constitution would be all that could be realistically hoped for.

As the Revolution proceeded in early 1789, positions on all sides hardened; and in the wake of the opening session of the Estates General on May 4, the contours of the revolutionary dichotomy became much clearer. Writing to John Jay on May 9, Jefferson expressed this development and foreshadowed the further course of the Revolution: "The Tiers Etat, as constituting the nation, may propose to do the business of the nation, either with or without the minorities in the House of Clergy and Nobles, which side with them."[54] By now, the boundary of who belonged to the nation and who did not could be clearly drawn. The third estate together with the reform-minded part of the nobility and clergy alone constituted the nation; the absolute monarchy, traditionally minded nobles, and members of the clergy were outside the nation. The irreconcilable opposition was thus outlined and, in Jefferson's opinion, the balance between these two forces was held by the king.

Jefferson thought that Louis XVI was personally "honest, and wishes the good of his people," but he feared that "the expediency of an hereditary aristocracy is too difficult a question for him," and that the king therefore might support the latter.[55] This was indeed what happened, when on June 17, 1789, the third estate declared itself the National Assembly and announced that it would assume "the business of the nation." The king declared the actions of the National Assembly void and instead advanced his own program, which was similar to Jefferson's earlier proposals for a mixed constitution. But by mid-June 1789 the revolutionary dichotomy had been fully formed and the struggle was no longer about a right of representation for the third estate in the context of a mixed constitution (that is, Burke's corporate equality), but now focused on (Paine's radical) individual equality. As a result, Jefferson reported, "instead of being dismayed with what had passed, they [the people] seem to rise in their demands, and some of them to consider the erasing every vestige of a difference of order."[56] In other words, the Revolution had become a contest over the fundamental question of individual equality, juxtaposing two irreconcilable visions of how society should be ordered and pitting Burke's "aristocracy" against Paine's "democracy."[57] Simultaneously, as the development of Jefferson's thought demonstrates, the "democratic" part of this contest had become equated with the "nation."

With the king giving in and on June 27, 1789, ordering the other estates to join the National Assembly, Jefferson thought that "this great crisis [was] now over."[58] He could not have been more wrong. Yet, the subsequent radicalization of the Revolution, reflecting fears that "the despots around the throne [would have] recourse to violent measures" and attempt a counter-revolutionary strike, also completed the equation of the democratic side of the revolutionary binary with the nation.[59] By August 1789, Jefferson reported that the aristocrats "have been completely overthrown & the nation has made a total resumption of rights, which they had certainly never before ventured to think of."[60] As a result, the most intransigent nobles began to flee the country, leading Jefferson to rejoice that "seven princes of the house of Bourbon, and seven Ministers, fled into foreign countries, is a wonderful event indeed."[61] Over the following months and years, many more "aristocrats" would follow, but in Jefferson's thought these first emigrations marked the complete exclusion of aristocrats from the nation: they were now not only figuratively, but literally, outside the nation, and thus foreigners.

The transformation of the idea of the nation in conjunction with the emerging new conception of democracy was not confined to France or even Europe. Instead, the revolutionary dichotomy between "aristocracy" and "democracy" that emerged in France highlighted and exaggerated social divisions all over the Atlantic World and appeared to link them to the Revolutionary struggle in that country. As in France, the ensuing conflicts in the various countries comprising the Atlantic World triggered the reconceptualization of the key notions of democracy and the nation. The United States provides an excellent example of this process.

The peculiar mode of mobilization of American resistance against the British during the Imperial Crisis had combined the individual and corporate notions of "equality" as exemplified by Paine and Burke in a struggle against the danger of monarchical tyranny within the traditional framework of political theory. As a result, the question of what exactly "equality" meant did not have to be clearly defined and social tensions—which certainly existed in America as well—did not result in the emergence of the kind of ideological polarization that characterized France after 1789. Only with the outbreak of the French Revolution and growing recognition of its escalating violence did questions of the precise meaning of "equality" come to the fore. By thus forcing Americans to take a stand either for or against the Revolution, it became obvious in the early 1790s that many of the leaders of the American Revolution balked at the expansive new conception of individual equality. Equality for men like John Adams or Alexander Hamilton meant only an equality of opportunity, the chance for the naturally superior to rise to preeminence without being restricted by a formal, hereditary aristocracy. Their understanding of equality, therefore, did not include an "abolition of hierarchical ranks with a distinct and unitary elite at the pinnacle."[62]

For Jefferson, on the other hand, "equality" in both the corporate sense (state equality) and on the individual level had always been fundamental to his understanding of the American Revolution. Together they constituted his credo of "federal and republican principles."[63] Jefferson was thus predisposed to embrace the radical notion of equality at the basis of the radicalizing revolution in France. The French Revolution, therefore, revealed the differing meanings Americans had attached to "equality." By illuminating—and exaggerating—different conceptions of human nature and their implications for social order, the French Revolution ruptured the "republican consensus" among Americans and led to the realignment of the political and social situation along the revolutionary binary of "democracy" and "aristocracy."[64] As in France, moreover, this application of the revolutionary dichotomy between "aristocracy" and "democracy" resulted in the idea of the nation becoming confined to the democratic side (Republicans) as well, whereas "aristocrats" (Federalist leaders) were—at least figuratively—cast out of the nation as "foreigners."

Thomas Jefferson was one of the pivotal actors in this process. When he finally returned from Revolutionary France to the United States in late 1789 and assumed his new position as secretary of state, his thinking was deeply steeped in the framework of revolution and counter-revolution. As a result, Jefferson was one of the first to apply this dichotomy to the American situation, with all its consequences for the idea of the "nation." What first aroused Jefferson's suspicion about "aristocratic" tendencies in the United States was the elegant social life that he witnessed once he arrived in New York, then the seat of the federal government.[65] At a time when he just had witnessed the French people "erasing every vestige of a difference of order," the dinner parties of President Washington's cabinet members appeared to him as a deliberate attempt to re-create such "differences" in America. While attending those dinner parties, he learned to his dismay that this appearance accurately described the attitude of many members of Washington's cabinet, among whom, he observed, "a preference of kingly, over republican, government, was evidently the favorite sentiment," feeling himself to be almost "the only advocate on the republican side" among the nation's elite.[66]

Jefferson quickly identified the secretary of the treasury, Alexander Hamilton, as the mastermind pulling the strings behind the scene and setting the tone for the aristocratic faction. Suspicions of "aristocratical and monarchical" tendencies among leading politicians in New York and, from late 1790 on, in Philadelphia, became a certainty for Jefferson when Hamilton introduced his *Reports on the Public Credit* in 1790 and his *Report on Manufactures* in 1791. The "artificial creation . . . of a public debt" seemed to Jefferson an especially pernicious measure.[67] He regarded this policy of virtually inviting members of the legislative to participate in speculation in government bonds as a deliberate tool "to corrupt & manage the legislature."[68] For Jefferson, "the object" of Hamilton's various proposals "taken together" was obvious: Hamilton wanted to "subvert step by step the principles of the constitution," with the ultimate goal "to prepare the way for a change, from the present republican form of government, to that of a monarchy, of which the English constitution is to be the model."[69] Hamilton's preference for the English constitution and the creation of the public debt "for the avowed purpose of inviting it's transfer to foreign countries"—namely, Great Britain—meant for Jefferson the dual threat of changing the government toward the English model and bringing the United States back into dependency on Great Britain. These would be fateful steps toward reversing the two main achievements of the American Revolution: independence and self-government.[70]

The conclusion for Jefferson was that Hamilton and his supporters must be aristocratic counter-revolutionary tools of a foreign country, bent on destroying the United States. Thus, in his analysis of the situation in America, Jefferson applied the same revolutionary categories he had observed emerging in France at the commencement of its revolution. As the aristocrats in France were excluded from the "nation," so Jefferson began to imaginatively exclude the "monarchical Federalists" from the American nation by declaring them tools of a foreign country.⁷¹ This tendency was greatly increased after the outbreak of the French revolutionary wars, when Federalists advocated the support of Great Britain, which became the leader of the counter-revolutionary coalition of monarchies.

Jefferson's great hope throughout the 1790s was that this "sect" of "monocrats and aristocrats" would prove to be "preachers without followers, and that our people" would be "firm & constant in their republican purity."⁷² But the problem for Jefferson and his followers was that a great part of the people apparently did not see the threat the Federalists posed and accordingly kept voting them into office. Jefferson's cardinal task, therefore, was to open the people's eyes to the threat to their liberties and to enjoin them to fight to preserve the American Revolution's legacy. To do so, he had to expose the Federalists as what he was convinced they were: "foreign & false citizens" trying to subvert the republican independence of the United States.⁷³ But if he wanted to show that the Federalists' principles were "foreign" and Federalist politicians "foreign & false citizens," he first had to define clearly what real "American" principles were and what it meant to be "American." In other words, Jefferson had to make clear the line separating him (and thus the "democratic" side) and the Federalists (the "aristocrats"); and because the democratic side of the revolutionary binary, in Jefferson's thought, constituted the nation, this line simultaneously became the boundary of American nationhood.

The means to achieve his goals was the Republican Party. Because of the severity of the Federalist threat, Jefferson decided to take his opposition to Hamilton's policy out of the cabinet and into the public, thus creating a "republican party, [that] wishes to preserve the government in it's present form."⁷⁴ Preservation of the Revolution's legacy was the only cause that could have led Jefferson, who remained inimical to political parties throughout his life, to resort to partisan politics. But "when the principle of difference is as substantial, and as strongly pronounced as between the republicans and monocrats of our country, I hold it as honorable to take a firm and decided part, and as immoral to pursue a middle line."⁷⁵ The difference between Federalists and Republicans was thus no ordinary political difference. Rather, for Jefferson the contest was—as it had been in France—between "us" and "them," between "democratic" Americans and "aristocratic foreigners." In this way, adherence to the principles espoused by the Republican Party—Jefferson's "federal and republican principles"—became the litmus test of true American nationhood. In Jefferson's conception, the boundary of American nationhood thus was drawn around the Republican Party, and anybody who did not subscribe to the party's principles was at least imaginatively excluded from the nation. Jefferson himself clearly drew and propagated this conclusion, proclaiming that "the republicans are the *nation*."[76]

In the ideologically charged atmosphere of the 1790s, Republicans did not have a monopoly on regarding the opposition as tools of a foreign country and thus un-American. On the contrary, just as Republicans viewed Federalists as "aristocrats," so the latter treated Republicans as "Jacobins" and a "faction . . . disposed to overturn the government" in order to aid the cause of "the French Republic."[77] Moreover, just as Republicans sought to exclude those "foreigners" from the nation, so did the Federalists. The reality of the political situation in the late 1790s, however, resulted in diverging strategies to cope with the threat of those "foreign tools."

The Federalists, as the party in power, looked to the federal government as the focal point of the nation. Consequently, they regarded it as the duty of the government to protect the nation from "foreign" enemies within. The Federalist administration thus enacted the Alien and Sedition Acts in 1798 during the frenzy of the so-called Quasi-War with the French Republic from 1798 to 1800. Jefferson regarded the attempt to muzzle the Republican press through these acts as such a grave threat that he and his closest political collaborator, James Madison, set out to invoke the "spirit of 1776" and appeal to the corporate entities (the states) to secure their own and their citizens' liberty.[78] But in 1798, unlike 1776, most of the states did not rise to the challenge, failing to respond to the Virginia and Kentucky Resolutions.

As a consequence, Jefferson shifted his attention from the corporate to the individual level. The last hope for the defense of the principles of 1776, therefore, was now the "American" people at large. Jefferson remained optimistic, convinced that the "aristocratic" Federalist rule of the country was "not a natural one" and that "the body of our countrymen is substantially republican through every part of the Union."[79] Therefore, he argued that "time alone would bring round an order of things more correspondent to the sentiments of our constitution," and advised that all that was necessary would be "a little patience, and we shall see the reign of witches pass over . . . and the people . . . restore their government to it's true principles."[80]

Jefferson's prophecy proved correct. With the war hysteria subsiding, the Federalists' policies of repression of opposition newspapers, raising taxes, and creating a standing army backfired. In early 1799, Jefferson already observed that "time & truth have dissipated the delusion & opened their [the people's] eyes."[81] With their eyes thus opened, the American people realized the motives behind the Federalists' plans and that "they have been dupes of artful manoeuvres, & made for a moment to be willing instruments in forging chains for themselves."⁸² Once awakened from their slumber, however, Americans would not willingly submit to be chained, and would instead rally to the defense of the "principles of 1776." They would rally in defense of a union founded on the basis of equality on both the individual and corporate level.

The decisive event in this contest over the character of the nation was the election of 1800. With the rejection of the aristocratic pretensions of the Federalists, Jefferson believed, the American people had vindicated the legacy of the American Revolution by "restoring the government to its true principles."⁸³ But by doing so, the American people had done still more: they had also vindicated Jefferson's conception of an American nation. As Jefferson saw it, by upholding the "principles of 1776," the people had legitimated his equation of the Republicans with the "nation." The election of 1800, therefore, became a virtual plebiscite for him, and so in March 1801 he could argue in his First Inaugural Address that the contest of the 1790s had been "decided by the voice of the nation."⁸⁴

Jefferson's reference to the "nation" united by the principles of the Republican Party indicates that the struggles of the 1790s and their culmination in the election of 1800 had also resulted in the maturation of an idea of a single, united American people in his thought. The failure of the states to respond to the Virginia and Kentucky Resolutions in 1798 had proved to him that the union could only be preserved if all Americans shared a common commitment to fundamental republican principles. In other words, Americans must be self-conscious about what made them "American," and thus one single people, "united with one heart and one mind."⁸⁵ In this context, again, the influence of the idea of the nation as Jefferson came to understand it during the early phase of the French Revolution is apparent. Jefferson did not subscribe to the French Revolutionary ideal of "la nation, une et indivisible" in regard to the political structure of the union, but he did believe that Americans could only preserve their union and secure their Revolutionary legacy if they ideologically constituted a *nation* "une et indivisible."

This nation included the rank-and-file Federalists, who he thought had already come over to the Republican nation, or would soon do so now that the "reign of witches" had passed and their "spells dissolved."⁸⁶ He could include common Federalists because as the election of 1800 had shown, the majority of them, if presented with the choice of either supporting or rejecting the fundamental principles of 1776, would always come around and choose the right path: in the end, they were "brethren of the same principle."⁸⁷ This definition of who belonged to the nation, however, did not extend to leading Federalists, those "false & foreign citizens" who knowingly and on purpose had conspired to subvert both the "federal and republican principles" of the union. Under the influence of the transatlantic revolutionary dichotomy, therefore, Jefferson's conception of the nation had been transformed from a non-political, all-encompassing definition of a population in a specific territory, to a highly politicized, more exclusive meaning of that part of the population which supported the side that Thomas Paine at the same time was about to reconceptualize as "democratic."

Both France and the United States certainly were "nations" before 1789. Yet, in both cases, the idea of what constitutes the nation changed significantly as a result of the French Revolution. In the case of France, this change is more obvious. The overthrow first of an absolutist monarchy, and later the replacement of the monarchy itself with a republican regime, with its transfer of sovereignty from an individual to the people at large, as well as the abolition of aristocratic and regional privileges under the Revolutionary banners of equality and unity, clearly transformed the meaning of what constituted the French nation.

Although the partisan conflict of the 1790s in America and Jefferson's election to the presidency in 1800 did not result in such sweeping institutional changes, it was nevertheless in these years that the United States developed into a "nation" in the modern sense of the term.[88] It was during these tumultuous years that Jefferson and his republican followers defined exactly what it meant to be "American," thus endowing the young United States with "a strong moral and ideological foundation" in addition to political independence.[89] It was during these years also that Jefferson developed his conviction of the need for a self-consciously united, single American people. Together with the failure of other "republican experiments" in Europe, this idea of a—at least concerning ideological principles—single-minded, united American people, resulted in a growing sense of the peculiarity, or "exceptionalism," of the American nation in the modern world of nations.

These features of a modern nation did not—and perhaps could not—develop before 1789. The American Revolution, due to its cross-class mobilization, enabled the corporate and individual notions of equality to function in complementary ways within the traditional framework of a struggle against a potentially tyrannical monarchy. As a result, the American Revolution did not generate an ideologically polarized dichotomy and so did not precipitate the reconceptualization of basic terms of political theory. This happened only in the wake of the French Revolution, when two irreconcilable visions of how society should be structured—on the basis of equality or inequality—clashed.

THE MODERN IDEAS OF DEMOCRACY AND THE NATION

The ensuing dichotomy initiated the reconceptualization of the concepts of "democracy" and the "nation." Both concepts in their modern meaning, therefore, have their common origins in their revolutionary antithesis to the traditional order of society, whether in the form of legally privileged orders in France or in the aspirations of a "natural" aristocracy in America. It is in this sense that the modern concepts of democracy and the nation emerged and developed in conjunction on both sides of the Atlantic during the Age of Revolution.

NOTES

1. On the need for an integrated analysis of conceptual and political change, see Terence Ball, James Farr, and Russell L. Hanson, eds., *Political Innovation and Conceptual Change* (Cambridge: Cambridge University Press, 1989); and Terence Ball and J. G. A. Pocock, eds., *Conceptual Change and the Constitution* (Lawrence: University Press of Kansas, 1988).

2. See, for example, Liah Greenfeld, *Nationalism: Five Roads to Modernity* (Cambridge, Mass.: Harvard University Press, 1992), 10–14, who describes the connection between democracy and nationalism but traces the origins of their modern forms to sixteenth-century England. Eric Hobsbawm acknowledges the connection as well, although he emphasizes more the period from 1830 onward and does not address their relationship in detail (Eric Hobsbawm, *Nations and Nationalism since 1780: Programme, Myth, Reality* [Cambridge: Cambridge University Press, 1990], 18–23). Hans Kohn, in his major work *The Idea of Nationalism: A Study in Its Origins and Background* (New York: Macmillan, 1944), argues that the two concepts are related in the way that democracy gave common people a stake in society. For this point, see also David M. Potter, "The Historian's Use of Nationalism and Vice Versa," *American Historical Review* 67 (July 1962): 936. For a succinct survey on the idea of the nation, see Anthony D. Smith, *Nationalism: Theory, Ideology, History* (Malden, Mass.: Polity Press, 2001). For an overview on democracy, see John Dunn, *Democracy: A History* (New York: Atlantic Monthly Press, 2005).

3. For general information on Paine, see his two most recent biographies: Jack Fruchtman Jr., *Thomas Paine: Apostle of Freedom* (New York: Four Walls Eight Windows, 1994); and John Keane, *Tom Paine: A Political Life* (Boston: Little, Brown, 1995). The quotation is in Alfred O. Aldridge, *Man of Reason: The Life of Thomas Paine* (Philadelphia: J. B. Lippincott, 1959), 7.

4. See, for example, Howard Penniman, "Thomas Paine—Democrat," *American Political Science Review* 37 (April 1943): 244–62; and Eric Foner, *Tom Paine and Revolutionary America* (New York: Oxford University Press, 1976).

5. See, for example, Gregory Claeys, *Thomas Paine: Social and Political Thought* (Boston: Unwin Hyman, 1989), 1; and *The Complete Writings of Thomas Paine,* ed. Philip S.

Foner, 2 vols. (New York: Citadel Press 1945) [hereafter cited as *Complete Writings*], 2:910 (quotation).

6. In *Common Sense*, for example, the term "democracy" does not appear once.

7. Gary Kates, "From Liberalism to Radicalism: Tom Paine's Rights of Man," *Journal of the History of Ideas* 50 (October–December 1989): 569–87. Kates contends that Paine changed his position to such a degree that the first and second parts of *Rights of Man* contain "contradictory ideologies" (571).

8. Foner, *Tom Paine and Revolutionary America*, 90–91.

9. For the interpretive framework of a democratic revolution in the Atlantic World, see R. R. Palmer, *The Age of the Democratic Revolution: A Political History of Europe and America, 1760–1800*, 2 vols. (Princeton, N.J.: Princeton University Press, 1959–64).

10. Ibid., 1:1–24.

11. For a general overview of the notion of "equality," including its radical implications as well as its relation to hierarchy ("inequality"), see Jonathan Israel, *Enlightenment Contested: Philosophy, Modernity, and the Emancipation of Man, 1670–1752* (New York: Oxford University Press, 2006), 545–71. This essay concentrates on political and social equality. Although the question of economic equality did play a role in the controversy as well, it is neglected here because the former two notions are more central to the emergence of a new meaning of democracy.

12. Iain Hampsher-Monk, *The Political Philosophy of Edmund Burke* (New York: Longman, 1987), 22; Peter J. Stanlis, *Edmund Burke, the Enlightenment, and Revolution* (New Brunswick, N.J.: Transaction Publishers, 1991), 232–33.

13. This was especially so, since the Declaratory Act was enacted when his own party (the Rockingham Whigs) was in power (see Carl B. Cone, *Burke and the Nature of Politics: The Age of the American Revolution* [Lexington: University of Kentucky Press, 1957], 260–61).

14. For Burke's plan of a federal union, see especially his Second Speech on Conciliation, 22 March 1775, http://www.gutenberg.org/dirs/etext04/burke10.txt, and his speech in the House of Commons of 2 December 1777, in *The Parliamentary History of England from the Earliest Period to the Year 1803*, 36 vols. (London, 1806–20), 19:517. On Burke's move toward federalism in general, see Frank O'Gorman, *Edmund Burke: His Political Philosophy* (Bloomington: Indiana University Press, 1973), 70–72; and Peter J. Stanlis, "Edmund Burke and British Views of the American Revolution: A Conflict over Rights of Sovereignty," in *Edmund Burke: His Life and Legacy*, ed. Ian Crowe (Dublin: Four Courts Press, 1997), 30–38.

15. Edmund Burke, "Address to the British Colonists in North America," in *Edmund Burke: Selected Writings and Speeches on America*, ed. Thomas H. D. Mahoney (Indianapolis: Bobbs-Merrill, 1964), 239–42.

16. Ibid.

17. Paine, *Common Sense*, in *Thomas Paine: Collected Writings*, ed. Eric Foner (New York: Library of America, 1995) [hereafter cited as *Collected Writings*], 12.

18. Ibid., 15.
19. Ibid., 16, 12.
20. Ibid., 16.
21. Ibid., 9.
22. For an argument why Burke might have had reasons to write such a work in 1777, see J. C. D. Clark, "Edmund Burke's *Reflections on the Revolution in America* (1777); or, How Did the American Revolution Relate to the French?," in *An Imaginative Whig: Reassessing the Life and Thought of Edmund Burke*, ed. Ian Crowe (Columbia: University of Missouri Press, 2005), 71–75.
23. Edmund Burke, *Conciliation with the Colonies: The Speech by Edmund Burke*, ed. Archibald Freeman and Arthur W. Leonard (Honolulu: University Press of the Pacific, 2002), 48, 108.
24. Peter S. Onuf, "Democrazia, rivoluzione e storiografia del mondo contemporaneo," *Contemporanea: Rivista do storia dell'800 e del '900* 10, no. 1 (2007): 153–55.
25. Following a brief consideration of Richard Price and the Revolution Society. See Edmund Burke, *Reflections on the Revolution in France*, ed. J. G. A. Pocock (Indianapolis: Hackett, 1987), 31.
26. Ibid., 32.
27. Ibid.
28. Ibid., 32, 43.
29. Paine, *Rights of Man, Part One*, in *Collected Writings*, 463. On the theological roots of Paine's views on "equality," see Vikki J. Vickers, *"My Pen and My Soul Have Ever Gone Together": Thomas Paine and the American Revolution* (New York: Routledge, 2006), 105–26; for Burke, see R. R. Fennesy, *Burke, Paine, and the Rights of Man: A Difference in Political Opinion* (The Hague: M. Nijhoff, 1963), 52–60.
30. Paine, *Rights of Man, Part One*, in *Collected Writings*, 463.
31. Ibid., 464 (emphasis in original).
32. Ibid., 533.
33. Ibid., 536.
34. Paine, *Rights of Man, Part Two*, ibid., 565.
35. Israel, *Enlightenment Contested*, 561.
36. Paine, *Rights of Man, Part Two*, in *Collected Writings*, 565.
37. Ibid., 567.
38. Ibid., 564.
39. Ibid., 567.
40. I am appropriating here Greenfeld's apt phrase, although in her account the "nation" and "democracy" did not emerge in the wake of the French Revolution, but in England in the sixteenth and seventeenth centuries (see Greenfeld, *Nationalism*, 10).
41. Thomas Jefferson [TJ] to Richard Price, 8 January 1789, in Thomas Jefferson, *Writings*, ed. Merrill D. Peterson (New York: Library of America, 1984) [hereafter cited as *Jefferson Writings*], 936.

42. For a chronological narrative of Jefferson's actions during this time, see Dumas Malone, *Jefferson and the Rights of Man*, vol. 2 of *Jefferson and His Time*, 6 vols. (Boston: Little, Brown, 1948–81).

43. "Answers and Observations for Démeunier's Article on the United States in the Encyclopédie Methodique," 24 January 1786, *Jefferson Writings*, 578.

44. TJ to Lafayette, 28 February 1787, in *The Writings of Thomas Jefferson*, ed. Andrew A. Lipscomb and Albert Ellery Bergh, 20 vols. (Washington, D.C.: Thomas Jefferson Memorial Association, 1903–4) [hereafter cited as *Writings of Thomas Jefferson*], 6:101.

45. TJ to Edward Carrington, 16 January 1787, *Jefferson Writings*, 879.

46. TJ to John Adams, 30 August 1787, ibid., 906.

47. Ibid., 908.

48. For Jefferson's changing perception of the aristocratic resurgence, see also Merrill D. Peterson, *Thomas Jefferson and the New Nation: A Biography* (New York: Oxford University Press, 1970), 371–72.

49. TJ to St. John de Crèvecoeur, 9 August 1788, *Jefferson Writings*, 927.

50. Ibid., 928.

51. Palmer, *Age of the Democratic Revolution*, 1:15–17; the same also applies, vice versa, for "aristocracy."

52. TJ to James Madison, 18 November 1788, quoted in Malone, *Jefferson and the Rights of Man*, 195.

53. TJ to George Washington, 4 December 1788, *Jefferson Writings*, 932.

54. TJ to John Jay, 5 May 1789, ibid., 952.

55. TJ to John Jay, 17 June 1789, United States Department of State, *Diplomatic Correspondence of the United States: From the Signing of the Definitive Treaty of Peace, 10th September, 1783, to the Adoption of the Constitution, March 4, 1789 . . .* , 3 vols. (Washington, D.C.: Printed by Blair and Rives, 1837 [i.e. 1855]; published by John C. Rives, 1855), 2:292.

56. TJ to John Jay, 24 June 1789, ibid., 2:297–301.

57. Merrill D. Peterson describes Jefferson's recognition of the democratic nature of the revolution, but does not make the connection to the concept of the nation (see Peterson, *Jefferson and the New Nation*, 380).

58. TJ to John Jay, 29 June 1789, *Diplomatic Correspondence of the United States, 1783–1789*, 2:302.

59. TJ to Diodati, 3 August 1789, *Jefferson Writings*, 957.

60. Ibid.

61. TJ to William Carmichael, 9 August 1789, *Diplomatic Correspondence of the United States, 1783–1789*, 2:317.

62. Alan Taylor, "From Fathers to Friends of the People: Political Personas in the Early Republic," *Journal of the Early Republic* 11 (Winter 1991): 468.

63. First Inaugural Address, 4 March 1801, *Jefferson Writings*, 493–94.

64. On the rupturing of a republican "consensus," see Joyce Appleby, "John Adams

and the New Republican Synthesis," in her *Liberalism and Republicanism in the Historical Imagination* (Cambridge, Mass.: Harvard University Press, 1992), 203–4.

65. On Jefferson's reaction to the social life in New York after his return from France, see Joyce Appleby, *Thomas Jefferson* (New York: Times Books, 2003), 18.

66. Thomas Jefferson, "The Anas" (4 February 1818), in *Jefferson Writings,* 666.

67. TJ to George Washington, 23 May 1792, ibid., 985.

68. TJ to Washington, 9 September 1792, ibid., 992.

69. Ibid., 995. See also TJ to Washington, 23 May 1792, ibid., 987.

70. TJ to Washington, 23 May 1792, ibid., 986.

71. Ibid., 988.

72. TJ to Lafayette, 16 June 1792, ibid., 990.

73. TJ to Elbridge Gerry, 13 May 1797, ibid., 1043.

74. TJ to George Washington, 23 May 1792, ibid., 987.

75. TJ to William B. Giles, 31 December 1795, in *Writings of Thomas Jefferson,* 9:317.

76. TJ to Col. William Duane, 28 March 1811, ibid., 13:28–29.

77. John Page, *Address to the Freeholders of Gloucester County, at Their Election of a Member of Congress* (Richmond, 1799).

78. See TJ to Thomas Lomax, 12 March 1799, *Jefferson Writings,* 1062.

79. TJ to John Taylor, 4 June 1798, ibid., 1049.

80. Ibid., 1049–50.

81. TJ to Thomas Lomax, 12 March 1799, ibid., 1062–63.

82. Ibid., 1062.

83. TJ to John Taylor, 4 June 1798, ibid., 1049–50.

84. First Inaugural Address, 4 March 1801, ibid., 492.

85. Ibid., 493.

86. TJ to John Taylor, 4 June 1798, ibid., 1050.

87. First Inaugural Address, 4 March 1801, ibid., 493.

88. For definitions of a "modern" nation, see Smith, *Nationalism,* 9–20.

89. Kohn, *Idea of Nationalism,* 295.

II

JEFFERSON AND PAINE'S EUROPE
Friends, Audience, Reception, and Reputation

Thomas Paine and Benjamin Franklin's French Circle

PHILIPP ZIESCHE

AMONG THE INNUMERABLE BOOKS written about either Benjamin Franklin or Thomas Paine, none fails to mention the long-lasting friendship between the two revolutionaries. Paine's biographers are particularly fond of quoting Franklin's description of Paine as his "adopted political Son," without acknowledging that its source is none other than Paine himself.[1] The two men were close, but Franklin's role as a mentor has been misunderstood due to a narrow focus on Paine's early days in America. Less well known is Franklin's profound impact on Paine's later life through his introduction of the younger man to his circle of noble friends in Paris. The two Americans' interactions with this circle are reflected in their writings on aristocracy.

The letter that Franklin wrote about Paine to his son-in-law Richard Bache in September 1774 is one of the most famous introductions in American history. Franklin, then a colonial agent in London, explained that the thirty-seven-year-old Paine had been recommended to him as "an ingenious, worthy young man," and asked Bache to help Paine find employment in Philadelphia as "a clerk, or assistant tutor in a school, or assistant surveyor, (of all which I think him very capable)."[2] This letter is commonly depicted as the starting point of Paine's American career, putting Paine on the path to *Common Sense* and the colonies on the path to independence.

As if this was not already enough weight to bear for one quite ordinary letter of introduction, historians have speculated freely on what it reveals about the personal relationship between Franklin and Paine. It must have been Franklin, so the argument goes, who "encouraged," or even "persuaded," Paine to leave England, immediately recognizing him as a "kindred spirit" and as a secret weapon in the transatlantic war of words.[3] In fact, we do not know when and under what circumstances the two men first met and how well they came to know each other in London. Franklin's introduction was pointedly not based on personal acquaintance, but on the recommendation of an unnamed third party. Paine later identified that man as George Lewis Scott, a mathematician who was a member of the Royal Society, like Franklin, and served as a commissioner of the Board of Excise, where Paine had been employed.[4]

The extraordinary significance that some scholars have ascribed to Franklin's introduction of 1774 is at least in part a result of Paine repeatedly reminding Franklin of this letter and portraying himself as Franklin's protégé.[5] There is no doubt that Franklin's letter was extremely useful to Paine in starting a new life. Paine gratefully recounted to his patron how, after having "suffered dreadfully" from a "Putrid Fever" on the passage to America, the recommendation had secured him the special attention of a physician upon landing in Philadelphia. Moreover, Franklin's reference had gained Paine "many friends and much reputation."[6]

But precisely because Franklin's introductions were so useful, he was forced to write countless letters of this kind. In 1773–74, Franklin presented at least five other young, honest, and ingenious Englishmen to Richard Bache alone, in letters very similar to Paine's. Some of these young men became quite prominent in Philadelphia, like Robert Hare, the future speaker of the Pennsylvania State Assembly. Others failed in their endeavors, like the printer John Hewson, and still others remain obscure.[7] During his years in France, Franklin was asked to write introductions with such frequency, on behalf of people completely unknown to him, that he even composed a satire titled "Model of a Letter of Recommendation of a Person You Are Unacquainted with."[8] In 1783, Franklin apologized to Richard and Sarah Bache for having troubled them with such letters, emphasizing that "when I recommend a Person simply to your Civilities & Counsels, I mean no more than that you should give him a Dinner or two, & your best Advice if he asks it; but by no means that you should lend him Money: For many I believe go to America with very little; and with such Romantic Schemes and Expectations as must end in Disappointment and Poverty."[9]

Still, based on their assumptions about an immediate, special bond between Franklin and Paine, it has appeared only logical to many biographers that Franklin would direct Paine to write *Common Sense,* and that he also must have had a hand in reviewing and editing the manuscript.[10] When *Common Sense* was first published, anonymously, in January 1776, Franklin was indeed high on the list of rumored authors.[11] Yet Paine's own account of the pamphlet's genesis does not credit Franklin with anything other than general encouragement. According to Paine, Franklin suggested in October 1775 that Paine write a "history of the present transactions," and Paine, who had already begun work on *Common Sense,* "got it ready for the press as fast as I conveniently could, and sent him the first pamphlet that was printed off." Franklin himself appeared uncertain of the identity of *Common Sense*'s author as late as mid-February 1776.[12]

All these myths surrounding Franklin and Paine focus on the very beginning of Paine's stay in America and on his best-known achievement, *Common Sense*.[13] What they have obscured is that Franklin exerted a much more readily apparent and significant influence on Paine's second political career, in France. One reason for this oversight might be a desire to disassociate Franklin from the more controversial parts of Paine's oeuvre. Such a desire would also help explain the persistence of the patently absurd claim that Franklin urged Paine to burn the manuscript of *The Age of Reason,* a work that Paine did not begin to write until three years after Franklin's death.[14] Or the neglect might simply reveal how much research remains to be done on Franklin's and Paine's lives in Paris and on the social and political network to which Franklin introduced Paine in 1787.

Paine visited France for the first time in the spring of 1781, when he accompanied congressional envoy John Laurens. During the two and a half months Paine spent at Passy, a village on the outskirts of Paris (today part of the 16th Arrondissement), he rarely ventured beyond Franklin's residence down the street.[15] The following year, Franklin distributed "into good Hands" copies of Paine's *Letter to the Abbé Raynal,* and in return sent Paine a copy of Hilliard d'Auberteuil's *Essais historiques et politiques sur les Anglo-Américains,* which Franklin deemed to require as much correction as Raynal's work.[16]

Paine's and Franklin's correspondence took on a much more personal tone after Franklin's return to Philadelphia in September 1785. In response to Paine welcoming home "my Patron and Introducer," Franklin avowed, "I value my self on the Share I had in procuring for [America] the Acquisition of so useful and valuable a Citizen."[17] In 1787, both men became founding members of the Society for Political Enquiries, which convened at Franklin's home.[18] Paine was spending most of his time seeking patrons for his iron bridge, until he decided in early 1787 to submit his design to the Académie Royale des Sciences in Paris and the Royal Society in London. Since Paine knew no one in Paris apart from Lafayette and Jefferson, he once again turned to Franklin for recommendations: "As I had the honor of your introduction to America it will add to my happiness to have the same friendship continued to me in the present occasion."[19]

In contrast to the single, formulaic letter of introduction in 1774, Franklin's four warm recommendations of Paine in 1787 as "one of our principal Writers at the Revolution" and "a Friend of mine" have been largely ignored. In addition, Paine carried eight other letters by Franklin to Paris, all addressed to Franklin's closest friends. The twelve letters, dated between April 15 and 22, were more than Franklin had written in any week since his return. Even the few biographies of Paine that do mention these French recommendations discuss them only in the context of Paine's iron bridge. The recommendations' immediate purpose, in which they succeeded, was to ensure a favorable response to Paine's bridge project. But their more important long-term effect was to introduce Paine to Franklin's French circle of scientists, royal administrators, and philosophes. This circle included the duc de La Rochefoucauld, who had collaborated with Franklin on a French edition of the thirteen state constitutions and other founding documents; the comte d'Estaing, the famed admiral, who had been Franklin's neighbor at Passy; Louis-Guillaume Le Veillard, another neighbor of Franklin's; the comtesse d'Houdetot; the marquis de Chastellux; Jean-Baptiste Le Roy, a well-connected scientist; the political economist André Morellet; the marquis de Condorcet, who became one of Paine's closest French collaborators; and Thomas Jefferson, whom Franklin asked to further "introduce [Paine] where it may be proper, and of Advantage to him."[20]

These letters carried particular weight because it was the first time Franklin had written to most of these friends since leaving France almost two years earlier. They were crammed with news about politics (noting, for example, the coincidence of the Constitutional Convention in Philadelphia and the Assembly of Notables in Paris), science (the latest transactions of the American Philosophical Society), and Franklin's family and health (his continued affliction with bladder stone and gout).

As a result of these letters, Paine's reception in Paris was "abundantly made cordial and friendly," as Paine reported to Franklin.[21] "I will do all in my power to be useful and agreeable to someone whom you love," responded Le Veillard, who was going to see Paine again the following day at a dinner hosted by Franklin's former landlord, Jacques-Donatien Le Ray de Chaumont.[22] Jean-Baptiste Le Roy was even more effusive: "I am truly obliged to you for having introduced him to me. His mind lives up exactly to his reputation, and he seems to have an excellent character, which makes him very enjoyable company. You know how your recommendations are valued, but meeting him is enough to be inclined to do him all the little services that an old Parisian like myself can do for a foreigner." The day before, Le Roy had taken Paine to dine with Chretien-Guillaume de Malesherbes, one of the highest-ranking officers in the French state. Le Roy also introduced Paine to Jean-Rodolphe Perronet, the architect and engineer famous for his stone-arch bridges, whom Franklin had erroneously thought to be dead.[23] Morellet helped Paine to retrieve the model of his iron bridge, which had been confiscated by French custom officials, who, as Morellet quipped, "had not foreseen that one day a bridge would be built in Philadelphia or New York to be placed across the Seine in Paris."[24] In the preface to the first part of *Rights of Man,* Paine described his conversations with the Anglophile Morellet about their common desire for improved Anglo-French relations. Paine recounted conveying a letter from Morellet to Edmund Burke in the hope of combating old anti-French prejudices in England, only to find that Burke instead chose to create new ones in his *Reflections.*[25] As Paine summed up his reception in Paris in the last extant letter he ever wrote to Franklin: "It must have been a very strong attachment to America that drew you from this Country for your friends are very numerous and very affectionate."[26]

Franklin played a key role in facilitating Paine's entry into French reform circles. But what influence, if any, did these circles have on Paine's work? The surprisingly few scholars who have addressed this question generally agree that the early French Revolution had a radicalizing effect on Paine's ideology. Gary Kates and Richard Whatmore portray Paine as essentially copying the ideas of French friends like Nicholas de Bonneville and Condorcet, and as translating "for a British audience certain French writers' ideas about the nature of modern republicanism." Under the sway of French authors, Whatmore argues, Paine came to believe that Britain's mixed monarchy was not only a tyranny but also a much weaker and more unstable state than a new kind of republic based on commerce, equality of ranks, and popular sovereignty. By contrast, other British radicals adhered to the conventional wisdom that republicanism was viable only in small states, and they welcomed the French Revolution for making France more like Britain.[27]

Others have been more skeptical about the extent to which French revolutionaries shaped Paine's thought. Mark Philp suggested that Paine's French experience primarily confirmed for him the significance of the American model of reform, and that *Rights of Man* was aimed at a British audience, not a French or American one.[28] It is clear that for years after he began living in Paris, Paine's French was rudimentary at best. He wrote most of both parts of *Rights of Man* in England, and both works are predominantly concerned with British politics. They also reiterate some attacks on mixed government that Paine had first made in *Common Sense* and the *Crisis* series. Even Richard Whatmore remained rather vague about Paine's French sources, citing Diderot's call for the abolition of ranks, Raynal's writings on North American manners, attacks on the French nobility by the comte de Mirabeau and Nicolas Chamfort, and Paine's well-known ties to Condorcet, Jacques-Pierre Brissot, and Etienne Clavière.[29]

In trying to understand how moving in Franklin's French circle affected Paine, it is useful to consider how Franklin himself operated in it. Living among reform-minded French nobles directed both Franklin's and Paine's attention to a central issue of the age, the problem of aristocracy. The two Americans addressed this issue in remarkably similar terms, and there is even the possibility that Paine was emulating Franklin in his arguments. But where Franklin was circumspect and well versed in French court politics, Paine was confrontational and incapable of keeping up with the radical political changes in France. In the end, Franklin's introduction to France proved a mixed blessing for Paine: it provided Paine with a launch pad for a second political career, even more brilliant than the first; but by amplifying Franklin's critique of aristocracy in a Revolutionary context, Paine managed to render suspect not only the noble members of Franklin's circle but, through his association with them, also himself.

Franklin made his most comprehensive statement on aristocracy in 1784, in a satirical essay on hereditary privilege, ostensibly targeting the Society of the Cincinnati. Significantly, its composition and distribution involved some of his French associates, especially André Morellet, who would three years later befriend Paine.

In December 1783 news arrived in Paris of a recently founded American veterans organization called the Society of the Cincinnati. The society's charter provided for hereditary membership, passed on to the eldest son, and a decorative medal featuring a bald eagle. These distinctions created much controversy in America after a pamphlet by South Carolina Judge Aedanus Burke (no relation of Edmund) accused the Cincinnati of setting itself up as a hereditary aristocracy. The Cincinnati extended an invitation for membership to French generals and colonels, who proved eager to join, and the organization even won the endorsement of Louis XVI.[30]

On January 26, 1784, Franklin received copies of the society's charter and

Burke's pamphlet from John Paul Jones and, on the same day, began drafting a letter expressing his longtime beliefs about the absurdity of primogeniture and hereditary nobility.[31] The letter is best known today for Franklin's objections against the bald eagle as the emblem of America, the eagle being "a Bird of bad moral Character" and "a rank Coward," and his preference for the turkey, "a true original Native of America" and "tho' a little vain & silly, a Bird of Courage." Although it is commonly described as a letter to Sarah Bache, the discrepancy between Franklin's musings on the Cincinnati and other correspondence between him and his daughter, which tended to revolve around family matters, suggests that he composed the document with a wider audience in mind.

In March 1784, Franklin collaborated on a translation of the essay with Morellet, who advised Franklin to modify the text to avoid offending French readers. "Moreover," Morellet wrote, "if you permit me to say so, this paper, which is excellent in itself, might upset certain people whom you do not want to offend and for this reason it must not be given, unless you deem otherwise, to anyone but those who have enough philosophy to know and feel the entire absurdity and ridiculousness of the deadly prejudice that you are fighting so well." Franklin assured Morellet that the essay had "never been communicated to any one but yourself, and will probably not appear till after my Decease, if it does then."[32] Nevertheless, Franklin's close attention to the faithfulness of the translation clearly demonstrates that he intended it to be read by others in his French circle. Among this group were the comte de Mirabeau and Nicolas Chamfort, who incorporated parts of the essay in their *Considerations sur l'Ordre de Cincinnatus*, an expanded and annotated translation of Burke's pamphlet—however, at Franklin's behest, without attribution. Franklin enlisted Richard Price and Benjamin Vaughan to help Mirabeau find a publisher in London, where the book first appeared in December 1784.[33]

In July 1790, only a month after the news of Franklin's death had reached Paris, the author Philippe-Antoine Grouvelle, a member of Franklin's Masonic lodge (the Neuf Sœurs) and Chamfort's former secretary, contributed Morellet's translation of Franklin's letter to the *Journal de la Société de 1789*. The society was a political club of moderate supporters of the constitutional monarchy and counted many of Franklin's friends among its members, including Mirabeau, Lafayette, Condorcet, Du Pont de Nemours, and La Rochefoucauld. In his preface, Grouvelle suggested that the letter was already familiar to a number of the *Journal*'s readers but that current events had given it new relevance, "even for those who have read it in its day." Grouvelle evoked "Franklin's shadow" to bestow legitimacy on the new Revolutionary order, in particular on the recent and extremely controversial abolition of noble privileges. Franklin's reasons for attacking the cult of nobility at its inception in America, Grouvelle argued, were the same that led the French revolutionaries to fight it in its decline.[34]

At the moment when Franklin's Cincinnati letter was finally published in France, his "adopted political son" Paine was in the midst of writing the first part of *Rights of Man*. One of the pamphlet's most notorious passages, depicting English peers as an idle, parasitic elite, radically changed the terms of debate about privilege and social class in England.[35] Paine's scathing criticism of aristocracy was in many ways reminiscent of Franklin's satire. Among Paine's particular targets was primogeniture, a practice "against every law of nature" and "family justice" which led to corruption and waste of public resources.[36] In his Cincinnati letter, Franklin similarly denounced primogeniture as a "pest to Industry and Improvement of the Country" which bred an "odious Mixture of Pride & Beggary, & Idleness . . . , occasioning continual Extinction of Families by the Discouragement of Marriage and improvement of Estates."[37]

Paine ridiculed historical justifications of aristocratic privilege, claiming that even Edmund Burke "had not boldness enough to bring up William of Normandy and say, there is the head of the list, there is the fountain of honor, the son of a prostitute, and the plunderer of the English nation."[38] Much of Franklin's Cincinnati letter was devoted to a "mathematical Demonstration" that in only nine generations a future knight of the Cincinnati would be merely a 512th part of the current titleholder, whose full honor he inherited. Within those nine generations, 1,022 men and women would have been involved in the production of this one future knight, which caused Franklin to question whether, "after a reasonable Estimation of the Number of Rogues and Fools, & Royalists & Scoundrels & Prostitutes" among those ancestors, "Posterity will have much reason to boast of the noble Blood of the then existing Set of Chevaliers de Cincinnatus."[39]

Both texts were entirely devoid of the deference common among political writers of the time, which is why Morellet was so nervous about Franklin circulating his letter. Franklin speculated that the American veterans who founded the Cincinnati must have been "too much struck with the Ribbands & Crosses they have seen among them, hanging to the Button-holes of Foreign Officers." In itself, without the pretension to pass on their distinctions to posterity, this would have been merely silly: "if People can be pleased with small Matters, it is a pity but they should have them."[40] Paine wrote that titles were but nicknames, harmless in themselves, but degrading to the character of a man who "talks about [his] fine riband like a girl, and shows [his] garter like a child."[41]

We have no evidence that Paine ever saw Franklin's Cincinnati letter. Given Paine's penchant for dropping Franklin's name in his works, it seems probable that he would not have passed up this opportunity in *Rights of Man,* which already included effusive praise of Franklin.[42] Still, Paine's friendship with Morellet and acquaintance with many members of the Société de 1789 make it quite possible that he did know the letter. It is notable that Paine had little to say about the evils of hereditary aristocracy before *Rights of Man.* Nearly all his attacks on the hereditary principle in *Common Sense* were directed against the monarchical system in general and George III in particular. During the 1783–84 controversy in America about the Society of the Cincinnati, Paine's sole extant contribution was a letter to George Washington, bemoaning that the organization's noble intentions, namely, "the example of the late Army retiring to private Life," had been misunderstood. Even Paine admitted, however, that whether "every part of the institution is perfectly consistent with a republic, is another question." He also presented Washington with a song that he had composed in honor of the Cincinnati.[43]

One reason for Paine's focus on kingship might have been the absence of a titled aristocracy in America.[44] Yet, for Franklin, the true culprit behind the metropolitan policies against the colonies had always been Parliament, and in particular the House of Lords. In 1775, Franklin wrote that he considered an institution of hereditary legislators to be no less absurd than "(as in some University of Germany) Hereditary Professors of Mathematicks."[45] Paine used exactly the same analogy in *Rights of Man,* adding "hereditary judges" and a "hereditary poet-laureate" for good measure, although, again, there is no evidence that he borrowed it directly from Franklin.[46]

It was only in France that Paine, consciously or unconsciously, began to follow in Franklin's footsteps in criticizing hereditary privilege. Only in *Rights of Man* did Paine hold the aristocracies of England and other European nations responsible for the decline of their states, and only there did he define equality of ranks as essential to republican liberty. It was such "leveling doctrines" that shocked and inspired Paine's contemporaries in Britain and throughout Europe. Paine broke new ground by condemning the English aristocracy in terms previously reserved for its French counterpart and by holding up France as a model to England. In France, Paine pointed out, enlightened nobles had recognized the superiority of merit over birth and "brought their titles to the altar, and made of them a burnt-offering to Reason."[47] Of course, Paine's acquaintance with these "patriots of France" had been made possible by Franklin's introductions.

According to the common images of Franklin and Paine, the former was a moderate, accommodating pragmatist, and the latter a radical, utopian fanatic.[48] This contrast is implicit in the oft-repeated anecdote according to which Franklin once remarked, "Where liberty is, there is my country," whereupon Paine retorted, "Where liberty is not, there is my country."[49] However, the differences between Franklin and Paine had little to do with ideology, but, instead, with the two Americans' political acumen and with the historical moment in which their works appeared.

When Paine wrote *Rights of Man,* France had already set an example of the complete abolition of noble privilege. At the time Franklin wrote his letter on the Cincinnati, even he would have regarded such abolition as utopian. For Franklin, the Cincinnati's awkward attempts to transplant the trappings of European nobility to an American setting exposed the fundamental absurdity of all such distinctions and practices. But, characteristically, Franklin was careful and strategic in disseminating his views on such a sensitive issue, especially since it also involved Franco-American relations. He did not share his letter on the Cincinnati with other Americans in Paris, like John Adams and John Jay, who were openly critical of the organization.[50] Instead, he distributed it discreetly among hand-picked members of the French first and second estates. Franklin saw the creation of the Cincinnati less as a threat to the American republic than as an opportunity to question with reason and wit a cornerstone of the ancien régime.

Mirabeau and Chamfort's *Considerations sur l'Ordre de Cincinnatus* was largely ignored when it first appeared in France in 1785. Ironically, one review singled out Franklin's "mathematical Demonstration" as "one of the most original ideas of M. de Mirabeau's work."[51] But, according to William Doyle, the pamphlet was nonetheless a milestone, as it represented "the first overt and direct attack on the principle of nobility in Europe."[52] Moreover, the resurfacing of Franklin's letter in 1790 suggests that it made a lasting impression on its select readership.

If Franklin was ahead of his time, Paine had fallen behind the times when a French translation of the second part of *Rights of Man* appeared in April 1792. The translator, François Lanthenas, removed Paine's dedication of the second part to Lafayette, now shunned by most Revolutionary factions as a reactionary, and noted disapprovingly: "Paine, that uncorrupted friend of freedom, believed too in the sincerity of Lafayette. . . . Bred at a distance from courts, the austere American does not seem any more on his guard against the artful ways and speech of courtiers than some Frenchmen who resemble him."[53]

The ominous reference to deceitful courtiers and the emphasis on Paine's foreignness reflected an element of French political rhetoric that Paine himself had helped to popularize. Writing for a British mass audience, Paine adopted in *Rights of Man* the current French definition of aristocracy, as he explained to Edmund Burke: "The Term Aristocrat is used here, similar to the word Tory in America;—It in general means an Enemy to the Revolution, and is used without that particular meaning formerly fixed to Aristocracy."[54] This expanded definition had the advantage of uniting French, British, and American reformers in a universal struggle against inequality. The enemy was no longer just the French estates or the English House of Lords or American Tories, but nobility (or "no-ability," as Pained liked to pun) everywhere.

While appearing to deny the significance of the place and rank of one's birth, this definition of aristocracy in fact turned the accidents of birth into irredeemable stigmas.[55] If all enemies of the Revolution were aristocrats, then all aristocrats were potential enemies of the Revolution. Even the most progressive nobles, like Franklin's friends La Rochefoucauld, d'Estaing, and Condorcet, could not escape from the shadow of suspicion cast by their origins, and by 1794 they had all become victims of the Revolution. By that time, Paine himself had been imprisoned, and only by sheer luck did he escape the guillotine. His principal crimes were being born an Englishman and his inability to navigate the rapidly changing political landscape of France.

The end of Paine's political career in France, in the bowels of the Luxembourg prison, could not be in starker contrast to Franklin's departure from France as one of the most celebrated and beloved figures of the age. How could their persuasions have been so similar and yet their fates in France so different? Both the content and the distribution of Franklin's Cincinnati letter demonstrate that he was no less of a radical cosmopolitan than Paine. Conversely, despite his reputation in Britain and America, Paine actually occupied a moderate position within the spectrum of French Revolutionary politics. At a time when the French nobility seemed deeply entrenched, Franklin challenged the very foundations of hereditary privilege. After distinctions of birth had been officially abolished, Paine inadvertently helped to reify them as markers of political loyalty.

What made all the difference in the end was that Franklin was a much more skillful politician, ever careful in choosing his audience and in covering his tracks. Franklin spent his years in France making powerful friends. His intimacy with the French nobility aroused suspicions among his fellow Americans in Paris and in Congress but proved essential to securing and maintaining French support for the cause of American independence. Franklin passed on his French circle to Paine, and, for better or worse, without Franklin's introductions, Paine would never have become as deeply involved in French politics as he did. As a deputy in the highly polarized National Convention at a moment when France was engulfed in civil and foreign conflict, Paine was much more vulnerable than Franklin had ever been. Paine's limited French, his irredeemable foreignness, and the dizzying speed of Revolutionary politics prevented him from building alliances of his own that could have protected him once most of the French reformers he had met through Franklin were dead.

NOTES

1. The quote comes from the entry of 20 April 1787 in the journal of the artisan John Hall, describing a conversation with Paine. Hall emigrated from England to Philadelphia in 1785 and assisted Paine on the model of his iron bridge (see Moncure D. Conway, *The Life of Thomas Paine,* 2 vols. [New York: G. P. Putnam's Sons, 1892], 2:468).

2. Benjamin Franklin to Richard Bache, 30 September 1774, in *The Papers of Benjamin Franklin,* ed. Leonard W. Labaree et al., 40 vols. to date (New Haven, Conn.: Yale University Press, 1959–), 21:325–26.

3. Gregory Claeys, *Thomas Paine: Social and Political Thought* (Boston: Unwin Hyman, 1989), 22; Harvey J. Kaye, *Thomas Paine and the Promise of America* (New York: Hill and Wang, 2005), 28; Vikki J. Vickers, *"My Pen and Soul Have Ever Gone Together": Thomas Paine and the American Revolution* (New York: Routledge, 2006), 73; Joyce E. Chaplin, *The First Scientific American: Benjamin Franklin and the Pursuit of Genius* (New York: Basic Books, 2006), 245.

4. Paine to Henry Laurens, 14 January 1779, in *The Complete Writings of Thomas Paine,* ed. Philip S. Foner, 2 vols. (New York: Citadel Press, 1945) [hereafter cited as *Complete Writings*], 2:1162.

5. Paine, *The American Crisis III,* in *Complete Writings,* 1:88; Paine to Franklin, 16 May 1778, in *Papers of Benjamin Franklin,* 26:487; Paine to Franklin, 23 September 1785, in *Complete Writings,* 2:1251.

6. Paine to Franklin, 4 March 1775, in *Papers of Benjamin Franklin,* 21:515–17.

7. Franklin to Richard Bache, 6 April 1773, 25 July 1773, 17 February 1774, and 10 September 1774, ibid., 20:141, 320–21, 21:102, 302.

8. "Model of a Letter of Recommendation of a Person You Are Unacquainted with," 2 April 1777, in *Papers of Benjamin Franklin,* 23:549–50.

9. Franklin to Richard and Sarah Bache, 27 July 1783, in *Papers of Benjamin Franklin*, 40:392.

10. This claim was first made by Benjamin Rush, who also took credit for the title *Common Sense* (see *The Autobiography of Benjamin Rush*, ed. George W. Corner [Princeton, N.J.: Princeton University Press, 1948], 114; and *Letters of Benjamin Rush*, ed. L. H. Butterfield, 2 vols. [Princeton, N.J.: Princeton University Press, 1951], 2:1008).

11. Joseph Hewes to Samuel Johnson, 13 February 1776, in Paul H. Smith et al., eds., *Letters of Delegates to the Congress, 1774–1789*, 26 vols. (Washington, D.C.: Library of Congress, 1976–2000), 3:247. See also Thomas Jefferson [TJ] to Francis Eppes, 19 January 1821, in *The Writings of Thomas Jefferson*, ed. Andrew A. Lipscomb and Albert Ellery Bergh, 20 vols. (Washington, D.C.: Thomas Jefferson Memorial Association, 1904–5), 15:305.

12. Paine, *The American Crisis III*, in *Complete Writings*, 1:88–89; Franklin to Charles Lee, 19 February 1776, in *Papers of Benjamin Franklin*, 22:357.

13. For a dissection of the myths about the circulation and impact of *Common Sense*, see Trish Loughran, *The Republic in Print: Print Culture in the Age of U.S. Nation Building, 1770–1870* (New York: Columbia University Press, 2007), 33–103.

14. This tale has been repeated most recently in Ralph Frasca, *Benjamin Franklin's Printing Network: Disseminating Virtue in Early America* (Columbia: University of Missouri Press, 2006), 207. For a discussion of the Franklin letter in question, see *Papers of Benjamin Franklin*, 7:293–95.

15. Paine to Franklin, 31 March 1787, Benjamin Franklin Papers, American Philosophical Society, Philadelphia, Pa. [hereafter cited as APS]. Paine later claimed that he had intended to remain in Europe and never to return to America, despite the entreaties of Laurens, Franklin, and Jonathan Williams Jr. (see Paine to [Robert R. Livingston?], 19 May 1783, in Thomas Paine, *A Collection of Unknown Writings*, ed. Hazel Burgess [Houndmills, Basingstoke, Hampshire (England): Palgrave Macmillan, 2010], 39–40).

16. Robert R. Livingston to Franklin, 13[–14] September 1782, in *Papers of Benjamin Franklin*, 38:102; Franklin to Livingston, 5[–14] December 1782, ibid., 38:415–16.

17. Paine to Franklin, 23 September 1785, Benjamin Franklin Papers, APS; Franklin to Paine, 27 September 1785, Benjamin Franklin Papers, Library of Congress, Washington, D.C..

18. David Freeman Hawke, *Paine* (New York: Harper and Row, 1974), 169.

19. Paine to Franklin, 31 March 1787, Benjamin Franklin Papers, APS.

20. Explicit recommendations of Paine are included in Franklin to the duc de La Rochefoucauld, 15 April 1787, in *Memoirs of the Life and Writings of Benjamin Franklin . . .*, ed. W. T. Franklin, 3 vols. (London: Henry Colburn, 1818) [hereafter cited as *Benjamin Franklin Memoirs*], 2:97–99; Franklin to the comte d'Estaing, 15 April 1787, Benjamin Franklin Papers, Library of Congress; Franklin to Le Veillard, 15 April 1787, Pierpont Morgan Library, New York; Franklin to the Marquis de Chastellux, 17 April 1787, in *Ben-*

jamin Franklin Memoirs, 2:99–100; Franklin to TJ, 19 April 1787, in *The Papers of Thomas Jefferson,* ed. Julian P. Boyd et al., 39 vols. to date (Princeton, N.J.: Princeton University Press, 1950–) [hereafter cited as *Jefferson Papers*], 11:301–2. Paine undoubtedly delivered: see Franklin to the Abbés de Chalut and Arnoux, 17 April 1787, in *Benjamin Franklin Memoirs,* 2:100; Franklin to the Marquis de Lafayette, 17 April 1787, ibid., 2:100–102; Franklin to Michel-Guillaume St. John de Crèvecoeur, 17 April 1787, Benjamin Franklin Papers, Library of Congress; Franklin to the comtesse d'Houdetot, 17 April 1787, ibid.; Franklin to Jean-Baptiste Le Roy, 18 April 1787, in *Benjamin Franklin Memoirs,* 3:555; Franklin to the Abbé Martin Lefebvre de La Roche, 22 April 1787, Harkness Collection, New York Public Library; Franklin to Rodolphe-Ferdinand Grand, 22 April 1787, Benjamin Franklin Papers, Library of Congress; and Franklin to André Morellet, 22 April 1787, ibid.

21. Paine to Franklin, 22 June 1787, Benjamin Franklin Papers, APS.

22. Le Veillard to Franklin, 13 June 1787, ibid.

23. Le Roy to Franklin, 21 June 1787, ibid.

24. Morellet to Franklin, 31 July 1787, in *Lettres d'André Morellet,* ed. Dorothy Medlin, Jean-Claude David, and Paul LeClerc, 3 vols. (Oxford: Voltaire Foundation, 1991–96), 2:74.

25. Paine, *Rights of Man, Part the First,* in *Complete Writings,* 1:245–46. Morellet was only identified as the secretary of the archbishop of Toulouse, the French finance minister Loménie de Brienne. In September 1787, Paine also passed on greetings to the Earl of Shelburne from Morellet, "your Lordship's very good friend and mine" (Paine to the Right Honorable the Marquis of Lansdowne, 21 September 1787, ibid., 2:1265).

26. Paine to Franklin, 22 June 1787, Benjamin Franklin Papers, APS.

27. Gary Kates, "From Liberalism to Radicalism: Tom Paine's *Rights of Man*," *Journal of the History of Ideas* 50 (October–December 1989): 569–87; Richard Whatmore, "'A gigantic manliness': Paine's Republicanism in the 1790s," in *Economy, Polity, and Society,* ed. Stefan Collini et al. (New York: Cambridge University Press, 2000), 135–57 (quotation, 136).

28. Mark Philp, "Revolutionaries in Paris: Paine, Jefferson and Democracy," in this volume.

29. Whatmore, "'A gigantic manliness,'" 152–53, 154–55.

30. Cassius [Aedanus Burke], *Considerations on the Society or Order of Cincinnati* (Charleston, S.C.: A. Timothy, 1783); Minor Myers Jr., *Liberty without Anarchy: A History of the Society of the Cincinnati* (Charlottesville: University Press of Virginia, 1983), 24–44, 49–51, 145–48, 258–65; Markus Hünemörder, *The Society of the Cincinnati: Conspiracy and Distrust in Early America* (New York: Berghahn Books, 2006), 15–21, 26–28, 35–37.

31. John Paul Jones to Franklin, 26 January 1784, Benjamin Franklin Papers, APS; Franklin to Sarah Bache, 26 January 1784, Benjamin Franklin Papers, Library of Congress. Franklin, who in his *Autobiography* identified himself as "the youngest Son of the youngest Son for 5 Generations back," had published his first satire on titles of honor at the age of sixteen, in the second issue of the *New-England Courant* printed under his name (see *The*

Autobiography of Benjamin Franklin, ed. Leonard W. Labaree [New Haven, Conn.: Yale University Press, 1964], 46; and "On Titles of Honor," *New-England Courant,* 18 February 1723, in *Papers of Benjamin Franklin,* 1:51–52).

32. Morellet to Franklin, 16 March 1784, and Franklin to Morellet, 16 March 1784, both Benjamin Franklin Papers, APS.

33. Franklin journal entry, 13 July 1784, Benjamin Franklin Papers, Library of Congress; Franklin to Richard Price, 7 September 1784, Benjamin Franklin Papers, APS; Franklin to Benjamin Vaughan, 7 September 1784, Benjamin Franklin Papers, Library of Congress; W. R. Fryer, "Mirabeau in England, 1784–85," *Renaissance and Modern Studies* 10, no. 1 (1966): 43, 48–50.

34. *Journal de la Société de 1789,* 24 July 1790, 1–16; Mark Olsen, "A Failure of Enlightened Politics in the French Revolution: The Société de 1789," *French History* 6, no. 3 (1992): 303–34; Durand Echeverria, "Franklin's Lost Letter on the Cincinnati," *Bulletin de l'Institut Français de Washington,* n.s., 3 (1953): 119–22.

35. Amanda Goodrich, *Debating England's Aristocracy in the 1790s: Pamphlets, Polemic, and Political Ideas* (Woodbridge, U.K.: Boydell Press, 2005), 57–62.

36. Paine, *Rights of Man, Part the First,* in *Complete Writings,* 1:288.

37. Franklin to Sarah Bache, 26 January 1784, Benjamin Franklin Papers, Library of Congress.

38. Paine, *Rights of Man, Part the First,* in *Complete Writings,* 1:320.

39. Franklin to Sarah Bache, 26 January 1784, Benjamin Papers, Library of Congress.

40. Ibid.

41. Paine, *Rights of Man, Part the First,* in *Complete Writings,* 1:286.

42. Ibid., 1:300.

43. Paine to George Washington, 28 April 1784, in *The Papers of George Washington: Confederation Series,* ed. W. W. Abbot et al., 6 vols. (Charlottesville: University Press of Virginia, 1992–97), 1:319–20.

44. See Alfred Owen Aldridge, *Thomas Paine's American Ideology* (Newark: University of Delaware Press; London: Associated University Presses, 1984), 58–59.

45. Franklin to William Franklin, Journal of Negotiations in London, 22 March 1775, in *Papers of Benjamin Franklin,* 21:583. Franklin used the same analogy in a letter written in early 1784, sarcastically suggesting that Britain should make all of its "great offices of State hereditary" since evidently one could not "trust to nature for the chance of requisite talent" (Franklin to David Hartley, 7 January 1784, David Hartley Papers, William L. Clements Library, Ann Arbor, Mich.).

46. Paine, *Rights of Man, Part the First,* in *Complete Writings,* 1:289.

47. Ibid., 1:287.

48. Or, as Craig Nelson put it, Thomas Paine was "Benjamin Franklin unleashed" (see Nelson, *Thomas Paine: Enlightenment, Revolution, and the Birth of Modern Nations* [New York: Viking, 2006], 50).

49. The earliest appearance of this anecdote seems to be in Thomas Clio Rickman, *The Life of Thomas Paine* (London: T. C. Rickman, 1819), 179.

50. Lafayette to George Washington, 9 March 1784, in *Papers of George Washington: Confederation Series,* 1:190.

51. *Correspondence littéraire, philosophique et critique par Grimm, Diderot, Raynal, Meister, etc.,* . . . , notices, notes, general table by Maurice Tourneux, 16 vols. (Paris: Garnier Frères, 1877–82), 14:145–46.

52. William Doyle, *Aristocracy and Its Enemies in the Age of Revolution* (Oxford: Oxford University Press, 2009), 137.

53. "French Translator's Preface" in Paine, *Rights of Man, Part Second,* in *Complete Writings,* 1:347. For the French reception of *Rights of Man,* see Alfred Owen Aldridge, "*The Rights of Man* de Thomas Paine: Symbole du siècle des Lumières et leur influence en France," in *Utopie et institutions au XVIIIe siècle: Le Pragmatisme des Lumières,* ed. Pierre Francastel (Paris: Mouton, 1963), 285–87.

54. Paine to Edmund Burke, 17 January 1790, in J. T. Boulton, "An Unpublished Letter from Paine to Burke," *Durham University Journal* 43 (December 1950): 51.

55. Doyle, *Aristocracy and Its Enemies,* 284–93.

Revolutionaries in Paris
Paine, Jefferson, and Democracy

MARK PHILP

In "Discourse on the Love of Our Country," Richard Price wrote: "Be encouraged all ye friends of freedom and writers in its defence.... Behold the light you have struck out, after setting America free, reflected to France and there kindled into a blaze that lays despotism in ashes and warms and illuminates Europe."[1] Price's stirring celebration of the cause of liberty seems to endorse a view that became widely held between 1789 and 1792, namely, that the principles of the American Revolution had laid the foundation for a similar revolution in France that might also extend to Britain. Modern commentators have almost entirely resisted this view: some have treated the French Revolution as a modern, socially transformative, and progressive revolution (rather than as a classical revolution, involving the returning of political society to its original principles); others have seen America's as a limited, political revolution, in sharp contrast to the French, in which social issues derailed political reforms to produce a depth of political intrusion into the private world that opened the road to totalitarianism. But these contrasting perspectives have developed with the benefit (and the blinkers) of hindsight, and few who responded positively to the opening events of the French Revolution grasped that this might be a radically different set of events than those of America in 1776. Hence, in part, people's confusion over Burke's reaction.

This sense of America's contribution to France's revolution was important for both Thomas Paine and his friend Thomas Jefferson. Nevertheless, while the American experience exercised a powerful influence on Paine, I will argue that his experiences in Paris (in Jefferson's circles) and in London in the late 1780s and early 1790s had an independent impact, both on his understanding of America and its revolution and on his expectations for France and Britain. I focus here on the changes in Paine's position in the opening years of the French Revolution, the implications that this has for his understanding of the nature of democracy, and his subsequent reevaluation of America's implications for Europe in 1791–92. The main focus of the essay is on Paine rather than Jefferson, who left France in the autumn of 1789, but their intellectual kinship in the two years they overlapped in Europe helps us to understand why Paine's thinking took the direction it did in the aftermath of Jefferson's departure. Linking the interpretation of the writings of the two men in this period allows a clearer appreciation of the ways in which their affinities derived in large part from their interpretation—and reinterpretation—of America.

The argument of this essay touches on broader issues concerning political ideas in the American and French Revolutions at the end of the eighteenth century. On the one hand, it gives grounds for resisting the rather teleological account that drives a certain amount of American historiography—in which the movement for independence and the institutions of representative democracy are seen as the natural and inevitable outcome of the self-determination of the American people. For a number of writers on France, the French Revolution demonstrates a similar conceptual determinism, in which the events of 1792–94 are the unfolding of the logic inherent in claims by the National Assembly to embody the general will. However, where the American tendency is to see the institutions of democracy and representative government as the necessary consequence of commitments to rights and popular sovereignty, in the French case, the language of the people, the nation, and the nation's sovereignty opens the conceptual space for the emergence of the Terror.[2]

In contrast to such perspectives, this essay emphasizes the contingent development of ideas and the under-determination of events by language and theory. Both French and American historiography have emphasized the power of political language and discourse, but they have not, in my view, sufficiently acknowledged that, in this period at least (1776–1830), the Atlantic World undergoes massive political and social upheaval in which political discourses are dramatically transformed and reemerge in often unpredictable and contradictory ways that are not, for the most part, driven by any internal conceptual necessity or logic. The analysis undertaken here of Paine's developing position argues that his understanding of his world changes but that there is nothing predetermined about the process or the direction of these changes. It suggests that historians need to recognize that historical actors change their minds for reasons that are not always apparent to them, and that we should not assume that what seems an obvious entailment to us would also have been evident to them. Between 1787 and 1792, Paine's political vision broadens dramatically to encompass the possibility of a political transformation for Europe on the American model. In that process, however, his French and British experience leads him dramatically to revise his understanding of America's past and of its relationship to the future, and that, in turn, subsequently transforms his expectations of Europe's future.[3]

In 1774, after a history of successive failures in Britain, Paine secured letters of introduction from Benjamin Franklin, whom he had met in London, and using the money he had received under the Articles of Separation from his wife, he bought himself a passage to the United States.[4] In America he blossomed, becoming one of the most influential pamphleteers of the American Revolution and playing a part in both federal and Pennsylvania politics. He accompanied John Laurens on a short visit to France in 1781, but seems to have had few contacts among the French, associating chiefly with Laurens and Franklin and returning to America with Laurens several weeks later. In the aftermath of the American Revolution, and with the financial security to pursue his scientific interests, Paine developed a design for a single-span bridge made of iron, and finding it difficult to attract sponsors in America, he determined to take his model to Paris.

Paine arrived back in Paris in May 1787. He was quickly in touch with Jefferson.[5] While the full extent of his day-to-day contact with Jefferson is not wholly clear, we do know that he associated with Lafayette and others of Jefferson's circle.[6] Indeed, between 1787 and 1789, various discussions and exchanges took place involving Jefferson, Paine, Lafayette, and others, which covered a number of major political issues: they examined and responded to the proposals of the Federal Convention of 1787; they deliberated over the basic principles underlying the institutions and practices of popular government; they engaged in a pragmatic discussion of the constitution of France and how it might navigate through the difficulties that increasingly beset it from 1787; and they analyzed the relative merits and disadvantages of the British constitution as a potential model for France and America.[7] For example, on February 4, 1788, Lafayette reported that "Mr Jefferson, Common Sense and myself are debating (the proposed constitution) in a convention of our own as earnestly as if we were to decide upon it."[8] Through these discussions, both Paine and Jefferson began to rework and rethink their principles in ways that produced major developments in their positions and, in Paine's case, had a powerful subsequent effect on the development of his views between 1789 and 1792.

Paine's biographers have tended to see him, at this point, as obsessed by concerns relating to his bridge, but his correspondence demonstrates his involvement in a number of other domains. In the absence of an American minister in London, he affected to play the role, and sought out for discussion a number of leading Whigs, including Sir George Staunton, Stanhope, Fox, Burke, Portland, and Landsdowne.[9] His correspondence shows that his attention was engaged by events in Britain, France, and elsewhere. Indeed, his concern over the possible war over the Dutch Revolt led him to write *Prospects on the Rubicon* in August 1787.[10]

That Paine was engaged in thinking and deliberating about politics and its principles is also clear from the fact that at least three major themes, which are central to the first part of his *Rights of Man* (1791) but largely absent from his earlier writing, emerged for him in discussions in France in the late 1780s. The first concerns the language of rights.

No fully worked out account of natural rights by Paine was published until the first part of *Rights of Man* in 1791.[11] However, a draft of his distinction between types of rights appeared in a letter to Jefferson written in 1788/89, well before Burke's *Reflections*.[12] In that letter (referring to a discussion the previous evening at Jefferson's), as in *Rights of Man,* natural rights are distinguished into those where we have the power to execute them (as in the right to think for ourselves) and those that we need a civil power to support (as in the right to property). Although the discussion is fuller in *Rights of Man,* this earlier letter shows that, rather than responding to Burke's attack on "natural rights" by developing a new set of distinctions, Paine had already largely worked these out. Moreover, the impetus for doing so was a discussion of a pamphlet by James Wilson defending the federal constitution, in which Wilson saw individual natural rights in terms of the right to "act as his pleasure or his interest may prevail," which renders the state of nature "insupportable," requiring us to give up these rights to preserve our liberty.[13] Paine accused Wilson of muddling liberty and security, and the position he advanced was one in which natural rights are entrusted, the better to be exercised, rather than given up or alienated. It is this that disposes Paine to the idea of an enumeration of rights: in his view, all civil rights have at their basis a natural right that they seek more effectively to secure. This position was one shared by Jefferson and Condorcet. All three men regretted the omission of such a statement in the American case and argued for its inclusion, doing so in circles which subsequently influenced debates in France in the Estates General and National Assembly prior to August 1789, and it is clear that we should treat Paine's discussion in his letter as part of wider deliberations on America's Constitution.[14]

The second issue concerns the nature of constitutions and their relationship to government. The discussions of constitutional matters in relation to America, Britain, and France became increasingly linked in Paine's circles in Paris. There was a growing polarization between Anglophiles, who hoped that the failure to resolve the French state's financial problems would produce a political reform that would move the French constitution closer to that of the English, and those who despaired of any constitution that retained the independent power of the nobility in a system of checks and balances. The American case became central to one influential group of French thinkers, deriving originally from Turgot but subsequently associated with Condorcet, Mirabeau, Lafayette, La Rochefoucauld, Sieyès, Roederer, and Talleyrand.[15] Curiosity about America had been fueled by French involvement in the American Revolution, and in 1783, during Franklin's period as special minister to France, he persuaded Vergennes to allow him to translate and publish in France a complete set of constitutions from the American states that had sparked further interest. What united those in the Anglophobe group was a resistance to the idea of distinct orders within the state. They embraced the principle of the sovereignty of the people, without intermediary orders of political privilege, and they depicted America as a perfect example of a sovereign legislature and as a dramatic departure from the aristocratic order of England. One striking example of this commitment was their translation and extensive annotation of John Stevens's account of America, *Observations on Government, Including Some Animadversions on Mr. Adams's Defence of the Constitutions of Government of the United States of America: and on Mr. De Lolme's Constitution of England* (1787), which attacked Jean Louis DeLolme's and John Adams's laudatory accounts of English government and the principle of mixed government.[16] James Madison sent the pamphlet to Philip Mazzei, a close associate of Jefferson's, who worked with Du Pont, Condorcet, Jean Antoine Gallois and the Abbé Piattoli to turn it into a weapon for the Anglophobe view.[17] Jefferson does not mention the pamphlet, but he owned an annotated copy, and Appleby suggests that he played a part in diverting the printer employed to work on a French edition of John Adams's *Defence of the Constitutions of the Governments of the United States* (1786) to the task of publishing a translation of Stevens with an additional two hundred pages of closely argued notes.[18] We do not know if Paine read it—we do not know what Paine read!—but it seems very likely that he did so. Indeed, it seems likely that the evening Jefferson, Paine, and possibly others, spent in Paris in

1788 discussing James Wilson's pamphlet on America's federal constitution informed the notes of the highly annotated edition of Stevens's *Examen*.[19]

Although Stevens ended his pamphlet by broadly endorsing the two-chamber system of government, he expressly rejected the idea that bicameralism was rooted in or reflected some fundamental distinction between orders within society.[20] He attacked, that is, the idea of mixed government as a balance of different social orders in the states (which he associated with the English model), but he was open to the possibility of a bicameral legislature (a topic on which Paine usually argued for unicameralism, but often with the added idea of splitting the legislature in two, so that one part should debate and the other decide).[21] This distinction tended to be overlooked by those in France who were concerned to reject mixed government and to advocate a unitary assembly in the subsequent debates on the formation of the Estates General. As a result, Stevens's discussion of bicameralism is wholly ignored in the additional notes to the French edition.

Stevens also seems to have engaged the imagination of the French reformers on the principles underlying the construction of the state, with his distinction between the people, the constitution, and the government subsequently making an appearance in the first part of Paine's *Rights of Man*:

> The constitution of the state . . . is that original compact entered into by every individual of a society, whereby a certain form of government is chalked out and established unalterably, except by the people themselves: thus by a constitution then, when applied to civil society, we do not mean government itself, but the manner of its formation and existence. . . .
>
> The governments in these states are in fact nothing more than social compacts entered into for the mutual advantage of the individuals of whom the society is composed.[22]

This distinction between the constitution as an act of the people, and the government as "the creature of a constitution," is a central part of Paine's position in the first part of *Rights of Man*: "A constitution is a thing *antecedent* to government, and a government is only the creature of a constitution. The constitution of a country is not the act of its government, but of the people constituting a government."[23] But this is a new development for Paine. In his *Dissertations on Government; the Affairs of the Bank; and Paper Money* (1786), in which he gives one of his fuller discussions of political principles, the people are conceived of as the sovereign power, but their sovereignty is exercised in "electing and deputing a certain number of persons to represent and act for the whole."[24] That is, it is expressed in their electoral, rather than their constitutive or legislative capacity. Also, in his discussion of the character of the social compact, there is no discussion of constitutions. What is missing from the earlier position, which is present in 1791, is the view that the people's sovereignty is expressed in the creation of the constitution, rather than either directly in legislation, or by proxy through their representatives. Nonetheless, we can see Paine grappling with the idea in his insistence in *Dissertations* that "the sovereignty in a republic is exercised to keep right and wrong in their proper and distinct places. . . . A republic, properly understood, is a sovereignty of justice, in contradistinction to a sovereignty of will."[25]

What Paine does not have in 1786 is the distinction between a constituent power and the constituted power of government. Although the distinction is widely attributed to Sieyès, it figured substantially earlier in the debates on the formation of the state constitutions of America after 1776, with "the phrase and the thing" first emerging in the struggles to establish statehood for Vermont.[26] Although there are suggestive comments in *Common Sense* that imply something like the distinction, this is not something that Paine had worked out. But it is a principle and a distinction that he had firm control of by the end of February 1789, when he argued that Pitt ought to have held a national convention over the king's illness, "for if government be permitted to alter itself, or any of the parts permitted to alter the other there is no fixed Constitution in the country."[27] This suggests that it is the example of the creation of the federal convention itself, with, possibly, the theoretical defense of the distinction in Stevens, which convinces Paine of the point and gives him the terminology to articulate it. It also suggests that Stevens, the federal constitution, and Paine's Paris circles may subsequently have had an impact on French views as to the proper relationship between the people, the constitution, and the government, furnishing Sieyès with the distinction with which he is so often associated. Certainly, the group with whom Jefferson was most closely associated combined resistance to giving independent weight to any social order within the constitution with the view that the constitution should be understood as the expression of an original compact that established a form of government that could be changed only collectively by reference back to the people. Moreover, those views were central to some of the debates about unifying the three estates into a single National Assembly and arguing for a founding act of constitutional design for France.

The impact of the "American" argument is hard to tell—but it was certainly feared by many in the Estates General, for whom the English model seemed self-evidently appropriate. Norman Hampson quotes Clermont-Tonnerre, elected president of the assembly in mid-August 1789, on the threat to the English model: "One cannot pretend to do better than that nation (Britain). Not long ago, on the credit of several writers, people professed the most exaggerated admiration for the British constitution. Today they affect to despise it, following the opinion of an American writer who is full of contradictions." Hampson suggests the "American writer" is Paine, but there is greater probability that it is Stevens (although the uncertainty between the two is itself revealing).[28]

The issue of rights and the nature of constitutions were two central elements to Paine's attack on Burke, on which Paine's views develop in this crucial period between 1787 and 1789. The third was the issue of the sovereignty of each generation, which Paine later deployed to undermine Burke's claim that the British people unconditionally and in perpetuity willed their subjection to William of Orange and his successors. This claim can be linked to principles of natural right, but a link is not a deduction: natural rights theorists over the previous two centuries had failed to draw the implications that Paine and Jefferson did. Moreover, it seems clear that both men developed an interest in the issue and developed the principle around the same time. In Jefferson's case, he developed a set of arguments about the sovereignty of each generation in his correspondence with Madison in September 1789, with no evidence of such a commitment earlier in his writing. Paine gives the argument considerable prominence only eighteen months later in the first part of *Rights of Man*. Moreover, rather than thinking that the principle somehow originates without prompting in Jefferson, it is much more plausible to think that Jefferson was drawing on discussions he had had with others, that Paine was cognizant of those discussions, and that he was probably a participant in some of them between 1787 and 1789. Certainly, it is too much of a coincidence to think that Paine hammered out the principle wholly independently in responding to Burke's *Reflections,* while Jefferson (if one follows the editors of the *Jefferson Papers*) picked it up from his doctor, Richard Gem, and then restricted its discussion to his correspondence with Madison.[29] Moreover, McLean's claim that the principle is in fact derived from Condorcet's work, simply adds to the sense that this is an idea that is being generated in discussions that centrally involve the Parisian group that Paine and Jefferson were closest to. Indeed, it seems highly likely that such discussions were in turn drawing on Adam Smith's discussion in *Wealth of Nations*.[30]

Those troubled by the suggestion that Paine used Jefferson's and others' ideas without attribution should recognize that Paine adopted whatever ideas he found useful in the causes he promoted and was not at all troubled by taking them from others without attribution. The first part of *Rights of Man* (1791) includes Jefferson's description of Marshal de Broglio (i.e., the duc de Broglie) as a "high-flying aristocrat, cool, capable of every mischief"; and there is a letter from Paine to Jefferson describing a method for measuring the amount of wood in a tree that appears to have borrowed from Leonardo da Vinci![31] Similarly, Jefferson does not attribute the thought of generational sovereignty to Dr. Gem or Condorcet or Smith in his letter to Madison; his concern is with the idea, its validity, and its ramifications, not with who might claim to own it. For both, ideas were no man's property, and these ideas were very much in circulation, with each writer developing them in distinctive ways, having drawn from the common stock.

Paine and Jefferson shared the experience of the American Revolution and they shared a number of points of doctrine about the nature of political systems, among them the ultimate sovereignty of the people and the importance of a bulwark of rights by which to protect the people from those who governed them. They shared, I believe, two further positions, at least until Jefferson returned to America at the end of 1789. The first was a sense of American exceptionalism; and the second was a hesitation over how to describe the kind of order they hoped for in France. The exceptionalism is clear: before 1789, neither Paine nor Jefferson saw events in France as heading for an American system of government. Their response to the events of 1789 was to see them as a limitation of arbitrary power within a constitutional and representative system headed by a monarch. It is difficult to be wholly sure what Paine envisaged—partly because we do not have much evidence, other than letters prior to 1791, and partly because we cannot be sure how far the first part of *Rights of Man* (1791) fully expressed his beliefs about French developments, as against emphasizing the positive dimensions of those events as a rhetorical contrast to the picture he draws of the British constitution. Certainly, what he said about changes in Britain was largely compatible with a constitutional monarchy with a reformed House of Commons, and what he said about France was not hugely different.[32]

Jefferson was similarly limited in his expectations of the revolution in France. What united them was the view, which Paine captures in *Common Sense*, that America was exceptional and that the popular institutions that marked the American case were inappropriate for the substantial, luxurious, and corrupt commercial states of Old World Europe. In this respect, it is striking how reticent Paine was in his comments on monarchy until the very end of *Rights of Man* (1791), and it is important not to underestimate how his position on Europe is transformed after the late spring of 1791, and especially after the flight to Varennes. (Even in his letter of June 1791, he argues that "monarchy signifies in its primary meaning, *the despotic rule of one individual*. . . . In this relation France is not a monarchy."[33])

In January 1789 it is clear that he still thought that America was dramatically different from Europe:

> A thousand years hence . . . , perhaps in less, America may be what England is now! The innocence of her character that won the heart of all nations in her favour may sound like a romance, and her inimitable virtue as if it had never been. The ruins of liberty that thousands bled for, or suffered to obtain, may furnish materials for a village tale or extort a sigh from rustic sensibility, while the fashionable of that day, enveloped in dissipation, shall deride the principle and deny the fact. (And when it does fall it shall be said . . .) here, ah painful thought! The noblest work of human wisdom, the grandest scene of human glory, the fair cause of freedom rose and fell![34]

Paine did occasionally refer to the American example as having an impact on Europe, as when he sent the key to the Bastille to Washington as "one of the first ripe fruits of American principles transplanted to Europe," but this does not mean that he holds the view that American principles can be systematically applied elsewhere. That suggestion does not appear until the second part of *Rights of Man,* and Paine was clear that this work was a departure from the first part.[35] Jefferson's position was hardly different: he was attracted to France, but it bore no comparison to America; he compared an American education with a European one, with the latter corrupting the former's love of equality;[36] and, in a letter to George Wythe, he predicted that "if all the sovereigns of Europe were to set themselves to work to emancipate the minds of their subjects from the present ignorance and prejudices, & that as zealously as they now endeavour the contrary, a thousand years would not place them on that high ground on which our common people are now setting out." Like Paine and others, Jefferson thought that the American Revolution had "awakened the French nation"—or at least the thinking part of the nation—"from the sleep of despotism in which they were sunk." But, again, this did not mean they should or could imitate America. The end was a liberal constitutional monarchy, an end to arbitrary power, and a place for nobility of talents rather than birth.[37]

Paine and Jefferson also shared the language they used to describe the systems of government that they advocated. In his *Condition of the Working Class in England,* Frederick Engels referred to Paine as "the famous democrat," and that is a description that few today would hesitate to apply. But it was not a term Paine used. Indeed, there was no European use of the term prior to 1790 (and its use in America was rare and complex, being used by some interchangeably with "republican"—and, in the hands of most, signifying support for the popular self-government of small states, which tied in with a classical set of ambitions for a virtuous people).[38] When it was used in Europe, it was initially used pejoratively. People in eighteenth-century Europe saw democracy as referring to small city-states governed by the people, with a tendency to instability and succumbing to the control of demagogues; or (with Adam Smith) they used the term as a description for primitive forms of government for undeveloped societies; or, finally, and most commonly among reformers, they saw it as one component of government arranged in a balance between monarchy and aristocracy. In the first two cases, it was seen as wholly inapplicable to modern commercial societies of any size; in the latter case, it was an element of popular representation within a balanced constitution, but it was not one that necessarily demanded universal suffrage, secret ballots, or frequent elections. Later, in 1816, Jefferson insisted that "a democracy is the only pure republic, but impracticable beyond the limits of a town." At the same time, he acknowledged that "the full experiment of a government democratical, but representative, was and is still reserved for us . . . the introduction of this new principle of representative democracy has rendered useless almost everything written before on the structure of government."[39]

But that clarity was not present in the late 1780s while he was in France, and Paine was no clearer. Paine was an outspoken critic of mixed government in *Common Sense,* referring to the king as the remains of monarchical tyranny, and the House of Lords as the remains of "aristocratical" tyranny. But he made no positive case for democracy there. Much like the *Federalist Papers,* he preferred the language of "republic" to that of democracy. In 1786, he wrote:

> In republics . . . the sovereign power, or the power over which there is no control, and which controls all others, remains where nature placed it—in the people; for the people in America are the fountain of power. . . . This sovereignty is exercised in electing and deputing a certain number of persons to represent and act for the whole, and who, if they do not act right, may be displaced by the same power that placed them there, and others elected or deputed in their stead.[40]

Prior to the discussion in the second part of *Rights of Man* (1792), there is no explicit reference to democracy as the appropriate political form. Moreover, if we ask who puts "democracy" on the map of debates in the early 1790s, the answer is Burke, for whom the term formed a central plank of his attack on France, even though he attacks them for something they only later embraced. Neither Paine nor Jefferson advocated "democracy" for Europe or America in the late 1780s, and only later (in 1791–92) did Paine argue that representation had enabled a new democratic form to be applied in countries of any extent.[41] At the end of the 1780s that thought was still being worked out. And while Stevens did argue that the American states were "approaching nearer to perfect democracies than any we have accounts of," and denied that such governments would inevitably collapse, what drove his position was the view "THAT MAN IS ACTUALLY CAPABLE OF GOVERNING HIMSELF."[42] That is, what they agreed on in the 1780s was something like a principle of popular sovereignty, not as something to be exercised continuously through a general will, but as a basic principle underlying the formation of constitutions and thus, indirectly, of governments. Both insist, borrowing the phrase from Lafayette, that "for a nation . . . to be free it is sufficient that she wills it."[43] In 1792, Jefferson explained "the catholic principle of republicanism" as, "to wit, that every people may establish What form of government they please and change it as they please; the will of the nation being the only thing essential."[44] Sieyès would have wholly agreed, but that demonstrates that it was possible to secure unanimity on *this* fundamental principle when thinking about the people of America, France, and Britain, without anything necessarily following in terms of government forms, including the presence or absence of monarchy or the extent of popular participation in government. My sense is that this captures precisely the positions of both Paine and Jefferson in the late 1780s—they took from the American Revolution a principle of popular sovereignty, but they did not apply it identically in Europe and America, and in Europe they did not see it as opposed to the institution of monarchy. What did stick in their craws was aristocracy and arbitrary power.

Jefferson returned to America in the fall of 1789, but Paine's thinking developed further in significant ways, most notably in the second part of *Rights of Man,* in his *Letter Addressed to the Addressers* (1792), and in his *Dissertation on First Principles of Government* (1795).

The second part of *Rights of Man* is not a reply to Burke. It is a freestanding account of the nature and principles of government. It starts with the example of America, as the only place where the reform of government and man could begin, and as having introduced a revolution in the principles and practices of government. In 1791, he had defended the French reforms that produced a moderate constitutional monarchy; in 1792, he conceded that this was no longer relevant. Instead, the American Revolution became the fulcrum on which the political world could be made to turn, eradicating not simply the order of the nobility, but the very principles of monarchical and hereditary government, and replacing them with representative democracies. "Government founded on a *moral theory, on a system of universal peace, on the indefeasible hereditary Rights of Man,* is now revolving from west to east. . . . It interests not particular individuals, but nations, in its progress, and promises a new æra to the human race."[45] The contrast Paine drew in *Common Sense*—with liberty fleeing from east to west, and with the principles of the New World being of little relevance to the corrupt orders of the Old—was transformed by coming to see the American example as the instigator of a revolutionary change to wholly representative government throughout the Old World. The evidence strongly suggests that he did not hold this view before the spring of 1791 (shortly after July 14, 1789, he is predicting the whole thing will be settled), but it is absolutely clear that he did thereafter.[46] Accordingly, he developed a much more thorough account of representative government than had appeared earlier in his work.[47]

In doing so, he returned to the contrast between governments founded on reason and those founded on ignorance drawn in the "Conclusion" to part one, arguing that all hereditary government is in its nature tyranny and that it treats a people as hereditary property, as if they were flocks or herds.[48] In contrast, representative government is a new departure, one that is not to be equated with democratic government, which he takes to be direct popular government appropriate only to the small city-states found in the ancient world.[49] The principle of representation was unknown in ancient democracies, with the result that as those states grew, they collapsed into tyranny. In contrast, modern states engraft representation onto democracy, ensuring its suitability for any state, as America demonstrates.[50] In the *Federalist Papers*, Madison referred to states with representative government as "republics." That is a position close to Paine's own in his *Dissertations on Government* (1786) through to (and including) his "Letter to the Abbé Sieyès" in July 1791; but in the second part of *Rights of Man* Paine denies that republics are a type of *government*. Indeed, "what is called a *republic* is not any *particular form* of government. It is wholly characteristical of the purport, matter, or object for which the government ought to be instituted," and government that does not make this the end of its activity is neither republican nor good. Many governments claim the title, but "the government of America, which is wholly on the system of representation, is the only real republic ... that now exists. Its government has no other object than the public business of the nation, and therefore it is properly a republic." It is naturally opposed to the word *monarchy,* which essentially signifies "arbitrary power in an individual person; in the exercise of which *himself,* and not the *res-publica,* is the object."[51] Only representative democracy, then, can claim legitimacy. Hence the introduction of a sustained critique of monarchy at the end of chapter 3 of the second part.

Gary Kates sees Paine as having been influenced by those in France who were more radical than he was, and believes that Paine's definition of "republic"—as "wholly characteristical of the purport, matter, or object for which government ought to be instituted ... RES-PUBLICA, the public affairs, or the public good; or, literally translated, the *public thing*"—was "lifted practically verbatim from his friend Bonneville's daily newspaper, *Bouche de fer,*" in July 1791.[52] In fact, Paine used this phraseology in his "To the Authors of 'Le Républicain,'" written in June 1791 to Condorcet and others planning to establish a republican paper, and in doing so he was effectively reworking commitments from his *Dissertations on Government* of 1786, nearly two years before his major stay in France.[53] Kates is right that we should pay attention to Paine's involvement with reform circles in France, and is absolutely justified in thinking that the vast majority of Paine scholarship, with the notable exception of Aldridge, is almost entirely innocent of any such attention.[54] But the evidence for seeing Paine as simply absorbing the intellectual innovations of his French friends does not seem strong, especially given the way Paine's thinking was evolving. Moreover, we also need to consider Paine's value for his French friends: they were attracted in large part to his American experience and, in their turn, they reinforced in him a sense of the importance of that experience and its significance as a basis for reform in Europe—something that is evident even in the first part of *Rights of Man.*[55] Kates emphasizes the place of Sieyès in the second part of Paine's *Rights of Man,* but it is crucial to recognize that in 1791 and 1792 Paine was writing for a British audience, rather than a French or American one, and much as he was prepared to debate with Sieyès, he recognized that a British audience would have little interest in the detail of their disagreements and that he should focus directly on the principle of monarchy rather than giving Sieyès the detailed rebuttal that Burke had earned in 1791. Kates also points out that Paine parts company with Lafayette (as does Condorcet, in July 1791), but in Paine's case, he seems to have seen this as largely a matter of the pace rather than destination of reform (he was probably aware of Lafayette's letter to Washington, written in January 1790, that talks of preparing the nation for a convention in ten years or so to remedy the remaining defects of the Constitution), and there is evidence much earlier in his correspondence that he sees a divergence in judgment between himself and Lafayette.[56]

These various signs require careful, contextual reading. Paine's increasing confidence in the potential for change in Europe was partly a function of his reading of French events, in which his newer French friends were playing a significant part, but it was also probably influenced by his contacts in England, where the reform movement was spreading.[57] Moreover, the evidence suggests that it dates from the early months of 1791, when he was in England writing the conclusion to the first part of *Rights of Man*, where he settled on the contrast between government by reason, election, and representation, and that by ignorance and hereditary succession, with America epitomizing the former. Difficult as it is to establish influence, it is important to recognize that Paine's attitude to Britain (and France) changed dramatically in this period, and that the factors that might have influenced him, such as the rise of an extra-parliamentary radical movement, were ones in which he also played a significant role. In this sense, his own success may have proved deeply persuasive!

Even if we doubt that Britain is the source of his anti-monarchism—in the sense that it was Britain that persuaded him that a fuller move to a republican (American) model was possible in the spring and early summer of 1791—it does seem undeniable that it is the British context that encourages him to make the move from natural rights and popular sovereignty, which are present in the first part of *Rights of Man*, and from the advocacy of the representative system and American conventionism in the second part, to the demand for universal manhood suffrage that he makes in his *Letter addressed to the Addressers*, written in the summer of 1792: "As every man in the nation of the age of twenty-one years pays taxes ... out of the product of his labour ... so has every one the same equal right to vote, and no one part of a nation, nor any individual, has a right to dispute the right of another."[58] That move really does seem to derive not from France, which he had not visited for a year, but from his involvement with the Society for Constitutional Information and the London Corresponding Society, associated with and buttressed by his new sense that a fully representative form of government was possible for the ancien régime states of Europe.

My central contention is that Paine's intellectual position is a changing one and that we should understand these changes in part in relation to his experiences in Paris with Jefferson and his circles, where he is involved in debates in which the American experience became gradually universalized. In the process, it also became reinterpreted and reinflected with meanings that would not have been obvious to or recognized by these men a few years earlier. Paine's and Jefferson's European experiences reshaped their understanding of the American Revolution and of its fundamental principles: encouraging the elaboration of a theory of government based on the sovereignty of the people; distinguishing between that will and the constitutions and governments through which it was expressed; validating a set of natural rights claims to set limits to government action and increasingly coming to see these as demanding generational sovereignty and (eventually) universal manhood suffrage; and, finally, coming to espouse the language of representative democracy that over the next twenty or thirty years began to take root in America and in Britain.

One piece of evidence that underlines the danger of reading the radicalism of 1791 and 1792 back into earlier understandings and claims is Price's "effusion of zeal in the cause of human liberty and virtue," with which I opened this essay—the light struck out in America reflected to Europe.[59] What is rarely noticed is that Price himself insisted that it was not a clarion call for republicanism or democracy—and, in that sense, it was not an understanding of the achievement of America—that called for the kind of transformation of government that Paine came to see as essential by the spring of 1791:

> I cannot help taking this opportunity to remove a very groundless suspicion with respect to my self, by adding that so far am I from preferring a government purely republican, that I look upon our own constitution of government as better adapted than any other to this country, and in Theory excellent, etc. . . . I know not one individual among them (Protestant Dissenters) who would not tremble at the thought of changing into a Democracy our mixed form of government, or who has any other wish with respect to it than to restore it to purity and vigour by removing the defects in our representation, and establishing that independence of the three states on one another in which its essence consists.[60]

The account that I have given that sees an inching forward on the part of Paine and Jefferson, which is something they shared with their French friends into 1790 and 1791, is intended in part as a caution against seeing such changes as inevitable. The language of politics changed dramatically in France during the

Revolution, but rather than seeing this as in some way conceptually driven, it seems to me to make more sense to see it as a chaotic and complex process in which language was as much at the mercy of change as driving it. One example is the use of "democracy": secondary literature does not hesitate to use the term, but it was not widely used, and when it *was* used, either positively or negatively, it was almost entirely rhetorical and contentless. Moreover, insofar as it *was* used, it was because it was a negative term that became revalorized by being turned against the emergent enemy, the aristocrat (albeit that too was a relatively late manufacture—in the summer of 1789 and after).[61] This is clearly no more than a gesture, but there is a school of thinking on the Revolution that elevates its events into a battle of ideas and language, and in my view underplays the extent to which they were as much victims of a progressive collapse of order as they were its drivers.

A second issue concerns America. I have offered an account of American assumptions, about their gradual Europeanization. If we follow the story through to 1793–96, we can see that events in France, paradoxically, eventually began to reconfirm for Paine and Jefferson a sense of America's difference. But this is not a stable conception of America at work. The existing literature fails adequately to recognize the way in which positions that sound the same in 1785 as in 1805, have come to be attended by a host of new assumptions and implications; that in often very different ways the French Revolution made Americans in Europe (and many at home) think differently about their own Revolution, so that the future that they drew from it in the early nineteenth century was not one immanent to it, but rather involved considerable retrospective reinterpretation—much as, I have suggested, Paine's and Jefferson's senses of America are changed by their experience of France.

In the account I have given, Paine clearly changes his position—but not just as rhetorical sallies against opponents in pamphlet debates. The reading of *Rights of Man* that I have offered sees his position changing prior to Burke's *Reflections*—as arising from discussions of America influenced by developments in France and, later, in the light of his acquaintance with the English reform movement. In these developments, we have a process that includes experiences, intellectual exchanges, conceptual reworking, reactions to others, the reading and re-reading of events, and so on. In that process, it seems to me, we see people's thinking change and their intellectual commitments and positions take on new significance for them, and they draw conclusions which they did not see as there to be drawn earlier. And I emphasize this because I think that, while it is possible to read Paine wholly as a powerful rhetorician and pamphleteer, responding to circumstance and using whatever arguments he thinks will work with his audience, I hope to have established that a great deal more is in play in his work.

NOTES

My thanks are owed to the editors and to audiences in London and Warwick for their comments, and to Jonathan Clark for his careful reading of the piece, which corrected a number of errors.

1. Richard Price, "Discourse on the Love of Our Country," in *Richard Price: Political Writings*, ed. D. O. Thomas (Cambridge: Cambridge University Press, 1991), 196.

2. On the American front, see, for example, Edmund S. Morgan, *Inventing the People: The Rise of Popular Sovereignty in England and America* (New York: Norton, 1988). On France, this line has been developed and pursued by a number of interpretations, including the later work of François Furet. But see the closing remarks to what is one of the most important works on the discourses of political theory in the French Revolution: "To the extent that their acceptance of the suspensive veto implied a repudiation of Sieyès's arguments for a theory of representation based on the division of labour, the assembly was setting aside a discourse of the social, grounded on the notion of the differential distribution of reason, functions and interests in modern civil society, in favour of a discourse of the political, grounded on the theory of a unitary general will. In the most general terms, it was opting for the language of political will, rather that that of social reason; of unity, rather than of difference; of civic virtue, rather than of commerce; of absolute sovereignty, rather than of government limited by the rights of man—which is to say that, in the long run, it was opting for the Terror" (Keith Michael Baker, *Inventing the French Revolution* [Cambridge: Cambridge University Press, 1990], 305). See also Kenneth Margerison, *Pamphlets and Public Opinion: The Campaign for Union of Orders in the Early French Revolution* (West Lafayette, Ind.: Purdue University Press, 1998), 77–82, for comments on the similar positions of Furet and Halévi. Some of these ideas link to Hannah Arendt's reading of the two revolutions in *On Revolution* (London: Faber and Faber, 1964), and the themes are also picked up in Antonio Negri's *Insurgencies: Constituent Power and the Modern State* (Minneapolis: University of Minnesota Press, 1992).

3. In these notes, I suggest that a similar case can be made for Jefferson, although I lack the space to do so fully.

4. For the Articles of Separation, see the document acquired by the East Sussex Records Office in November 2009.

5. Paine was resident in Paris principally in the spring and summer of 1787; between December 1787 and February 1788; in the spring of 1788; in the winter of 1789–90; from April to July 1791; and from August 1792. He also corresponded with Jefferson and Lafayette (not always directly) when in England. It is also important to recognize the sig-

nificance of Paine's earlier trip and of the letters of introduction he secured from Franklin (with whom Paine seems to have become intimate only on that visit), which brought him into a range of circles he would have otherwise found difficult to reach. This issue is poorly discussed in most secondary sources, but see Philipp Ziesche's essay "Thomas Paine and Benjamin Franklin's French Circle" in this volume.

6. There is a question of when Paine met Condorcet. Paine's correspondence mentions a number of major figures, including the duc de Rochefoucauld, General Chastellux, Malesherbes, Le Roy, Buffon, Abbé Morley, M. Terenet, and others—but not Condorcet (see *The Life and Major Writings of Thomas Paine*, ed. Phillip S. Foner, 2 vols. [Secaucus, N.J.: Citadel Press, 1945], 2:1262–63). Does this mean they did not meet until 1789 or 1790? It should be noted that those listed appear in a letter to Franklin in which Paine is noting particular friends of Franklin. There is no firm evidence of contact with Condorcet, although he would have been aware of Paine's bridge project and he was closely associated with Jefferson, which makes some contact likely. See Jean-Paul Lagrave, "Thomas Paine et les Condorcet," in *Thomas Paine, ou, La République sans frontières*, ed. Bernard Vincent (Nancy: Presses Universitaires de Nancy; Paris: Ligue des Droits de l'Homme, 1993), 57–65, which suggests they were acquainted from 1787: "Paine et les Condorcet s'étaient connus dès 1787 et avaient pu s'apprécier. Mais ce n'est réellement qu'à partir de 1791 que l'action allait les souder de façon indéfectible" (57); see also Elisabeth Badinter and Robert Badinter, *Condorcet, 1743–1794: Un intellectuel en politique* (Paris: Fayard, 1988), 227–28. Certainly by 1789–91, Paine and Condorcet were close (see Alfred Owen Aldridge, *Man of Reason: The Life of Thomas Paine* [London: Cresset Press, 1960, ©1959], 145), but it is difficult to identify the starting point of their relationship (Paine first mentions Condorcet in a surviving letter of 16 April 1790). Phillip Foner attributes Paine's writing of *Prospects on the Rubicon* (1787) to the influence of Lafayette, Condorcet, and de Brienne (see *Life and Major Writings of Thomas Paine*, 2:620). Paine's contact with Lafayette is much clearer: he knew him from America and gravitated to him partly because of his fluency in English. One reason that Paine and Condorcet may have been less close in the initial stage of the Revolution was that Condorcet was a supporter of Brienne's reforms and did not see the need for calling the Estates General (see Keith Michael Baker, "Condorcet," in *A Critical Dictionary of the French Revolution*, ed. François Furet and Mona Ozouf [Cambridge, Mass.: Belknap Press of Harvard University Press, 1989]).

7. The evidence, discussed below, relies on various letters and texts—including the French edition of John Stevens's *Observations on Government, Including Some Animadversions on Mr. Adams's Defence of the Constitutions of Government of the United States of America: and on Mr. De Lolme's Constitution of England* (New York, 1787), published in France in 1789 under the title *Examen du gouvernement, comparé aux constitutions des États-Unis*; the two parts of Paine's *Rights of Man*; and a number of letters written by Jefferson, Lafayette, and Paine. John Stevens's *Observations on Government* was published in America under a pseudonym, "By a Farmer, of New Jersey," and was often attributed to

William Livingston; indeed, the French version of this work lists Livingston as the author. However, the Library of Congress copy bears a manuscript note in the hand of Thomas Jefferson attributing the work to "John Stevens of N. Jersey." In this essay, the French version of Stevens's work will be cited under his own name, rather than "Livingston."

8. Louis Gottschalk, *Between the American and French Revolution, 1783–1789* (Chicago: University of Chicago Press, 1950), 374.

9. See, for example, *Life and Major Writings of Thomas Paine,* 2:1265, 1270–71, 1283, 1300–1301.

10. On Russia, see ibid., 2:1271; on the Austrian Netherlands, ibid., 2:1288; and on the Turks, ibid., 2:1301.

11. It may seem surprising that there is no discussion of rights earlier in Paine, given that we associate the practice of drawing up a bill of rights with America. But, in fact, the language of rights had a rather uncertain place within American debates (enabling a generation of scholars to dismiss Locke's influence), until it was crystallized in the debates on the Bill of Rights in relation to the federal constitution in 1787 and 1788. Clearly, in one sense, an awareness of rights claims was a powerful current in American thought, but in the process of bringing them to the fore and grounding a wider political argument on them, those earlier commitments became reworked and reinterpreted—not least because they had traditionally been thought of as rights against a potentially tyrannical political power and there was widespread uncertainty as to whether such rights were required by, or legitimate in, a political order deriving from the sovereignty of the people. See, for example, Hamilton's resistance to a bill of rights in Federalist No. 84 (in *Federalist Papers,* Gideon Edition [Indianapolis, Ind.: Liberty Press, 2001], 445). There was a widespread sense that such a Bill would have a different function—one that "delimited certain areas of individual behavior over which the sovereign majority relinquished control" (see Willi Paul Adams, *The First American Constitutions: Republican Ideology and the Making of the State Constitutions in the Revolutionary Period,* 2nd ed. [New York: Rowan and Littlefield, 2001], 143). As late as the 1780s, only half of the American states had a bill of rights, and they were not used as the basis for judicial decisions. It seems plausible to claim that, while a sense of rights against an oppressive colonial power were clear, the place and meanings of rights within a republican polity were slow to emerge—as indeed, the discussion on the Bill of Rights in 1787–88 demonstrates. See also Keith Michael Baker, "The Idea of a Declaration of Rights," in *The French Idea of Freedom: Origins of the Declaration of the Rights of Man and of the Citizen,* ed. Dale Van Kley (Stanford, Calif.: Stanford University Press, 1994), 154–96.

12. Reprinted in *Life and Major Writings of Thomas Paine,* 2:1298–99. The letter refers to a meeting at Jefferson's house in Paris, which he left to return to America in October 1789.

13. *The Substance of a Speech Delivered by James Wilson, Esq.: Explanatory of the General Principles of the Proposed Faederal Constitution* . . . (Philadelphia, 1787), 7. See also note 18 below.

14. See Thomas Jefferson [TJ] to James Madison, 15 March 1789, in *Thomas Jefferson, Writings,* ed. Merrill D. Peterson (New York: Library of America, 1984) [hereafter cited as *Jefferson Writings*], 942–46; and Condorcet, *Letters from a Freeman of Newhaven to a Citizen of Virginia,* in *The Political Theory of Condorcet II,* trans. Fiona Sommerlad and Iain McLean, Social Studies Faculty Working Paper, 1/1991 (Oxford: University of Oxford, 1991), 26–73.

15. Joyce Appleby, "America as a Model for the Radical French Reformers of 1789," *William and Mary Quarterly,* 3rd ser., 28 (April 1971): 267–86, esp. 274. Paine sends his regards to Mazzei via Jefferson on 16 December 1788 (see *Life and Major Writings of Thomas Paine,* 2:1273).

16. See Appleby "America as a Model"; Jean Louis de Lolme, *The Constitution of England, or, An account of the English Government; in which it is compared with the Republican Form of Government and occasionally with the Other Monarchies of Europe* (London, 1775); and John Adams, *A Defence of the Constitutions of Government of the United States of America* (Philadelphia, 1787). See also Keith Michael Baker's discussion of Stevens's pamphlet in the French context, in "The Idea of a Declaration of Rights."

17. Filippo Mazzei, *Memoirs of the Life and Peregrinations of the Florentine, Philip Mazzei, 1730–1816,* trans. Howard Rosario Marraro (New York: Columbia University Press, 1942), 278.

18. Joyce Appleby, "The Jefferson-Adams Rupture and the First French Translation of John Adams' *Defence,*" *American Historical Review* 73 (April 1968): 1084–91.

19. See *Life and Major Writings of Thomas Paine,* 2:1298–99. Stevens's work concerns itself with Wilson's argument that a declaration of rights is superfluous (see *Examen du gouvernement,* 231n28). That argument is not in fact made in *The Substance of a Speech Delivered by James Wilson, Esq.,* but it does appear in Wilson's *Substance of an Address to a Meeting of the Citizens of Philadelphia, Delivered, October 6, 1787* (1888). It is possible that Paine's "Letter to Jefferson" (see *Life and Major Writings of Thomas Paine,* 2:1298–99) refers to this earlier pamphlet, but the phrasing does not quite fit. However, the editors of Stevens do seem to have been drawing on the (earlier) October speech. But the focus on Wilson does seem likely to have been something mediated through Jefferson and Paine's circle.

20. See Stevens, *Examen du gouvernement,* 51.

21. *Life and Major Writings of Thomas Paine,* 2:525–28.

22. Stevens, *Observations on Government,* 44, 50. Stevens addresses the issue of democracy and stability on pp. 50–53.

23. *Life and Major Writings of Thomas Paine,* 1:278.

24. Ibid., 2:369.

25. Ibid., 2:375.

26. On the attribution of the distinction to Sieyès, see Arendt, *On Revolution,* 162–63; on the Vermont distinction, see Willi Paul Adams, *First American Constitutions,* 63. Ad-

ams attributes to John Adams and Paine attempts to formulate the principle, in Paine's case referring to the discussion in *Common Sense* in which Paine suggests the formation of a continental conference to frame a Continental Charter (see Arendt, *On Revolution,* 28–29).

27. *Life and Major Writings of Thomas Paine,* 2:1280.

28. Norman Hampson, *Prelude to Terror* (Oxford: Basil Blackwell, 1988), 73.

29. See *The Papers of Thomas Jefferson,* ed. Julian P. Boyd et al., 39 vols. to date (Princeton, N.J.: Princeton University Press, 1950–) [hereafter cited as *Jefferson Papers*], 15:384–99.

30. Iain McLean, "Thomas Jefferson, John Adams, and the Déclaration des Droits de l'Homme et du Citoyen" (unpublished manuscript in author's possession). On Smith, see Adam Smith, *An Inquiry into the Nature and Causes of the Wealth of Nations,* ed. R. H. Campbell and A. S. Skinner (Indianapolis, Ind.: Liberty Fund, 1976), bk. III, chap. ii, sec. 6, 384–85.

31. See *Life and Major Writings of Thomas Paine,* 1:261; on Da Vinci, see Martin Kemp, *Leonardo* (Oxford: Oxford University Press, 2004), 138–41; and Paine to TJ [May? 1788], *Jefferson Papers:* 13:225–26.

32. Paine's letter to Thomas Walker, in February 1798, talks of the majesty of the nation being "collected to a centre and residing in the Person exercising the Regal Power," which follows a similar French view that the king is the representative of the nation as a whole (*Life and Major Writings of Thomas Paine,* 2:1279). Nonetheless, the suggestion that Paine is a monarchist, wildly inconsistent, or an opportunist, made by Hazel Burgess, the editor of *A Collection of Unknown Writings by Thomas Paine* (Basingstoke [England]: Palgrave, Macmillan, 2009), with respect to an attributed pamphlet of 1791, misses the extent to which, until then, Paine had had rather different assumptions about America than about Britain. Burgess bases the attribution of the pamphlet (addressed to the king) on the fact that it is signed "Common Sense," "the name no other would dare assume" (149), and on the grounds of phraseology and wording. Although there is no space here for a detailed refutation, neither claim really stands scrutiny—it is doubtful that Debrett would have published a pamphlet by Paine, and the use of "Common Sense" throughout the pamphlet is not a mark of Paine's British writings. On the other hand, we know that James Perry used that signature (see Perry's *Oxford Dictionary of National Biography* entry); the defense of mixed government goes against Paine's remarks in his letter to Walker; and the direct address to the king is not Paine's practice. Moreover, the database *Making of the Modern World* contains seven pamphlets published under the "Common Sense" signature between 1780 and 1830, only one of which Burgess attributes to Paine (and that, in my view, wrongly).

33. *Life and Major Writings of Thomas Paine,* 2:1316.

34. Ibid., 2:1276.

35. Ibid., 2:1303, 1321.

36. See TJ to James Monroe, 17 June 1785; *Jefferson Papers,* 8:227–35; TJ to John Ban-

ister Jr., 15 October 1785, ibid., 8:635–38; and TJ to George Wythe, 13 August 1786, ibid., 10:243–45.

37. TJ to George Washington, 4 December 1788, ibid., 14:328–32; TJ to Richard Price, 8 January 1789, ibid., 14:420–24.

38. For example, Patrick Henry described himself as "a Democrat on the plan of our admired friend J. Adams" (see Adams, *First American Constitutions*, 103).

39. TJ to Isaac H. Tiffany, 26 August 1816, in *The Writings of Thomas Jefferson*, ed. Andrew A. Lipscomb and Albert Ellery Bergh, 20 vols. (Washington, D.C.: Thomas Jefferson Memorial Association, 1903–4), 15:65–66.

40. Paine, *Dissertations on Government; the Affairs of the Bank; and Paper Money*, in *Life and Major Writings of Thomas Paine*, 2:369.

41. Ibid., 1:368–75.

42. Stevens, *Observations on Government*, 53. See also *The Substance of a Speech Delivered by James Wilson, Esq.*, 10, where Wilson essentially backs away from subscribing to the view that the Convention is recommending a democratic system, ending by an appeal to it being a form of government founded on and by the PEOPLE.

43. *Life and Major Writings of Thomas Paine*, 1:255, 322.

44. Jefferson, *The Anas*, http://www.history1700s.com/etext/html/texts/jefferson/jeff1a.txt.

45. *Life and Major Writings of Thomas Paine*, 1:356.

46. See Paine to Thomas Walker, 26 February 1789, ibid., 2:1278–81; Paine to Anonymous, 16 March 1789, ibid. 2:1285–86; and Paine to George Washington, 31 May 1790 ("complete and triumphant"), ibid., 2:1304.

47. Jefferson's views on French affairs are discussed by Conor Cruise O'Brien in *The Long Affair: Thomas Jefferson and the French Revolution* (London: Sinclair Stevenson, 1996), esp. chap. 2. O'Brien misses the point that Jefferson had dramatically different expectations of Europe than America, and so interprets the letters very unsympathetically. But there seems little doubt that Jefferson, like Paine, started with limited expectations; that he thought the French king a good man (see TJ to Edward Carrington, 16 January 1787, *Jefferson Papers*, 11:48–50); that he saw the existing regime as constructed on a despotic model (TJ to James Madison, 30 January 1787, ibid., 11:92–97); that he believed Brienne could "give the people as much liberty as they are capable of managing" (TJ to John Adams, 13 November 1787, ibid., 12:349–51); that he had doubts as to whether they would get a better constitution than the English (TJ to Richard Price, 8 January 1789, ibid., 14:420–24); that he anticipated that reform would leave the king "possessed completely of the Executive powers" (TJ to Diodati, 3 August 1789, ibid., 15:325–27); and that it is only after his return to America that he believed that the new regime would be a fundamental change that would affect the whole of Europe (TJ to George Mason, 4 February 1791, ibid., 19:241–43). Essentially, Jefferson's train of thinking ran remarkably parallel to Paine's.

48. *Life and Major Writings of Thomas Paine*, 1:364.

49. Ibid., 1:369.

50. Ibid., 1:371.

51. Ibid., 1:370, 369.

52. Paine's definition is in ibid., 1:369–70. See also Gary Kates, "From Liberalism to Radicalism: Tom Paine's *Rights of Man*," *Journal of the History of Ideas* 50 (October–December 1989): 581.

53. "To the Authors of 'Le Républicain'" (June 1791), in *Life and Major Writings of Thomas Paine*, 2:1315–18. I have rehearsed some of these points in my essay "Political Theory and History," in *Political Theory: Methods and Approaches*, ed. David Leopold and Marc Stears, (Oxford: Oxford University Press, 2008), 143. Kates also sees Sieyès as the real foil for Paine in the second part of *Rights of Man*, although it is striking that he makes only a brief appearance (being mentioned three or four times in a matter of a few pages, in the third chapter, in relation to the dispute over monarchy), and his appearance is briefer than that of Burke (in Part Two and, indeed, even in this chapter).

54. See Aldridge, *Man of Reason*, esp. chaps. 7–15. See also Aldridge's "Condorcet et Paine," *Revue de littérature compare*, no. 32 (1958): 47–65. Subsequently to Kates, see Richard Whatmore's Kates-influenced account in "A Gigantic Manliness: Paine's Republicanism in the 1790s," in *Economy, Polity, and Society: British Intellectual History, 1750–1950*, ed. Stefan Collini, Richard Whatmore, and B. W. Young (Cambridge: Cambridge University Press, 2000), 135–57.

55. "The American Constitutions were to liberty, what a grammar is to language: they define its parts of speech, and practically construct them into a syntax" (*Life and Major Writings of Thomas Paine*, 1:300).

56. Lafayette to Washington, 12 January 1790, *The Letters of Lafayette to Washington, 1777–1799* (Philadelphia: American Philosophical Society, 1976), 346; Lafayette to Washington, 23 August 1790, ibid., 349. On Lafayette's response to the federal constitution—for example, his comments on the need for a bill of rights—see Lafayette to Washington, 1 January 1788, ibid., 334. On Lafayette, see Paine's comments in his letters to William Short, 1 and 22 June 1790, in *Life and Major Writings of Thomas Paine*, 2:1306, 1309.

57. This, after having been initially dismissive of the political possibilities of the British people when he returned to Europe.

58. Thomas Paine, *"Rights of Man," "Common Sense," and Other Political Writings*, ed. Mark Philp (Oxford: Oxford University Press, 1995), 377.

59. This is Price's own description, in a letter to John Adams dated 1 February 1790 (in *The Correspondence of Richard Price*, ed. Bernard Peach and David Oswald Thomas, 3 vols. [Durham, N.C.: Duke University Press; Cardiff: University of Wales Press, 1994], 3:271).

60. Price to William Smith, 1 March 1790, ibid., 3:273 (Price is quoting from his treatise, *The Evidence for a future period of improvement in the state of mankind, with the means and duty of promoting it* [London, 1787], 30).

61. See William Doyle, *Aristocracy and Its Enemies in the Age of Revolution* (Oxford: Oxford University Press, 2009).

The Troubled Reception of Thomas Paine in France, Germany, the Netherlands, and Scandinavia

THOMAS MUNCK

Historians of ideas, and historians of the Enlightenment, have long since recognized the initial impact of Thomas Paine in France, pointing to his multiple election as deputy to the Convention parliament in 1792 as evidence of the extent to which his name and reputation had become well established in France. But we have not had such full accounts of his political role from the perspective of his fellow participants in the new French Republic, nor explanations of why his influence waned so rapidly in 1793. Equally, we lack understanding of why he had little impact in the German-speaking world, and virtually no impact at all elsewhere in continental Europe. The failure of his *Rights of Man,* in this respect, is particularly surprising, given that much of what he says might seem relevant to political life and social reform in the monarchies of continental Europe. While publication of his *The Age of Reason* may help to account for the reaction against Paine, especially in the Anglophone world, in the mid–1790s it cannot explain his earlier dwindling influence in France itself, nor the failure of his broader republican arguments to become integrated into the radical political traditions of other parts of Europe.

In seeking a fuller explanation of his uneven reception, we need to keep several obvious but fundamental points in mind. First, we should bear in mind that the deceptively expansive Anglophone book market, first defined by the London–Dublin–Edinburgh triangle, and then extended across the Atlantic, was not particularly well connected to continental Europe until relatively late in the eighteenth century. Since English was not the preferred language of international communication, English texts tended to reach a French audience quite quickly, by means of translation or adaptation, but often remained inaccessible in other language communities for much longer. Before the mid-eighteenth century, translation into German sometimes happened in the first instance via French (as the obvious international language of Enlightenment Europe), and translation into other European languages was often equally circuitous. Although knowledge of English in central Europe improved substantially after mid-century, and the Germans in particular became interested in the work of the Scottish writers, they were more conservative than the French in their choice of reading. This is not the place to discuss eighteenth-century theories and overall patterns of translation, nor to attempt to map in detail precisely how the Enlightenment became accessible to those broader layers of readers who did not have ready access to French or German, let alone to English.[1] It is worth noting that despite such language barriers, Enlightenment thinking traveled quite well, and a growing number of readers across at least northwestern and northern Europe gained access to a widening range of ideas from outside their own language community.[2] At the same time, we need to keep in mind that the impact of a particular text depended on a great variety of external factors, and that outside its own language area a text could be severely handicapped, either by inadequate or delayed translation, or by insufficient cultural contextualization. So even though events in America were well covered in the newspapers and periodicals of the late Enlightenment, we should not assume that the key texts and detailed commentaries relevant to an appreciation of such key figures as Thomas Paine or Thomas Jefferson were readily accessible to readers who lacked fluency in English.

The more explicit factor of censorship is generally better understood, in part because the elaborate and bureaucratic system of controls that were maintained in France until 1788 is well documented. However, it is again worth pointing out that France is not particularly typical of continental practices. In the Netherlands, censorship had mostly become unenforceable at the "national" level, even though religious controls (in particular) still operated sporadically at the local level. Sweden, on the other hand, formally abolished nearly all censorship in 1766, Denmark in 1770. And although neither monarchy maintained consistent support for freedom of the press over the following decades, both acquired a lively and far-ranging, if intermittent, public debate relating to a broad range of topics, including politics and religion. In the German-speaking lands, regulatory practices were much more diverse, but there is no doubt that both writers and translators were able to exploit advantageously the devolution of power within the Holy Roman Empire, either by publishing in those states where there were no substantial restraints, or (as happened in the Netherlands) exploiting local power networks to ensure that formal restrictions were evaded. Legal niceties, and the unpredictability of power networks, may have made publication of some controversial texts a matter of calculated risk (as was increasingly the case even in Prussia after 1786), but publishers did not lack experience, nor were they likely to miss good business opportunities. In the process, they may at times have exercised nearly as much self-imposed censorship as Le Breton notoriously did for the last ten volumes of Diderot's *Encyclopédie,* but they would also have recognized the potential for profit from topical best-sellers.[3] In any case, censorship or self-censorship primarily affected the discussion of domestic rather than foreign issues: the reporting and discussion of developments in America, for example, do not appear to have been particularly controversial.

On that basis, we might have expected the work of both Paine and Jefferson, in their different ways, to have gained recognition across continental Europe, but the evidence we have suggests a more limited and very uneven reception of their printed work. Admittedly, documenting the detailed business strategies of publishers is of course rarely possible, nor do we have the evidence to get a clear profile of actual readers. Some impression of patterns of reception, however, can be gained from a great variety of sources, and historians have paid considerable attention in recent years to formats and paper quality (indicative of the intended market), the rate of reprinting (it was uneconomical to store a large number of copies in anticipation of longer-term sale), citations in sales catalogues and advertisements, listings in libraries, and other indirect indicators of market diffusion. Surprisingly, historians of print culture have so far tended to overlook one major source of evidence regarding the reception of new work in print—namely, the summaries and discussions of books and pamphlets provided in the periodical press, and especially in the general literary reviews which were proliferating in later eighteenth-century Europe. The explicit raison d'être of the reviews was to acquaint readers with new trends in the intellectual and literary centers across Europe and to highlight the significance of particular work in a broader context, but the reviews' relative lack of originality may help explain why historical research has so far made little systematic use of this material for comparative purposes.[4] The literary review journals of eighteenth-century Europe constitute extremely voluminous, if largely descriptive, bodies of material suitable for both quantitative and qualitative analysis. If deployed systematically, this material can be used to supplement the more established methodologies of book history, as well as the range of ancillary evidence now available regarding commercial libraries and other market mechanisms. Equally, these journals can provide a broader reflection of the diffusion of ideas, extending well beyond the more content-focused analysis used by historians of ideas. Some of the journals, such as the *Allgemeine deutsche Bibliothek* (1765–1806), or the *Kiöbenhavnske Lærde Efterretninger* (1720–1810), even provide explicit information on conflicting translation practices, and will eventually allow continuous mapping of the changing cultural parameters of their own language community, reflecting not only what the editors assumed general readers might want to know about, but often self-consciously aiming to provide a remarkably diverse and sophisticated forum for the discussion of topics related to, but going far beyond, what the books that were being reviewed actually said.[5]

Since neither Jefferson nor Paine was widely read in Europe before 1790, this essay will undertake no reassessment of transatlantic communication in the previous decades (nor will I go over well-known debates relating to the broader representation of the American Revolution itself in Europe). Surprisingly, even in the wide-ranging debates of the 1790s, Jefferson continued to remain marginal and largely unnoticed in Europe: a few of his works were reprinted in English, in Paris and elsewhere, but nothing substantial appeared in translation, probably because his writings from this period were mostly very context-specific and not particularly relevant to European readers.[6] As we shall see in the case of Paine, a new and topical publication often generated interest in earlier writings by the same author, but in the case of Jefferson, his work from before 1789 was not revived in this way in Europe in the 1790s. By contrast, Paine had much more to say to European general readers, so it is his use of print, and his communicative strategies, that will be the main focus. This essay will first give an overview of Paine's role in France, based both on the traditional historiography and on a closer reading of the Revolutionary context there. I will then seek a clearer understanding of Paine's reception in continental Europe, not merely by applying the standard range of techniques used by historians of print culture, but also by initiating a systematic use of literary reviews and other evidence. This combination of approaches, it is argued, may help us understand the public perceptions of writers and activists such as Paine, and may be of particular use in deciphering the ambivalent and often changeable reception that Paine had in Europe in his own lifetime.

Unlike his slightly older contemporary and erstwhile friend, Edmund Burke, Paine took the trouble of observing events in Revolutionary France at first hand. He was there before the outbreak of the Revolution, and was back during the winter of 1789–90. When he returned once more in early 1791, he engaged directly with the Revolution: for example, he helped Brissot and Condorcet to form the Republican Society (July 1791) and took up the challenge to engage with Sieyès in a public debate concerning the merits of representative republican government as an alternative to monarchy.[7] In 1792, the charges and prosecution brought against Paine in Britain, concerning the second part of his *Rights of Man,* were noted in France and other parts of Europe, and no doubt helped consolidate his reputation in France.[8] His celebrity is clear from the fact that he was formally elected by several constituencies in the new French Convention, eventually choosing the seat for Calais. He spoke on the Convention's first full day of debate (September 21, 1792), and joined its Constitutional Committee on October 10.[9] He also wrote a letter on behalf of his constituency to congratulate the Convention on its decision to abolish the monarchy.[10] But it is worth noting something that seemed to remain a pattern throughout his French political career—namely, that this letter was read out to the Convention on his behalf (not by Paine himself, though he was present). Presumably, Paine lacked the ability to project his French text sufficiently clearly or fluently, at least in the face of the challenging acoustics of the Convention chamber.

The narrative outline of his problematic role in the trial of Louis XVI is well known. His substantive speeches regarding the trial (November 21, 1792, and again on January 14, 16, and 19, 1793, at the time of the votes on the king's fate) were reported in full, but they did not show much sensitivity to the political context. The last of these speeches also confirmed the problems faced by Paine because of his lack of fluency in French: having explained this handicap to the assembly, Paine stood on the tribune while Bancal (as secretary of the Convention) read out the French version of his speech. In it, Paine explained why he was calling for a reprieve (deferment of the death penalty) for the king. This reading was interrupted twice by none other than Marat. On the first occasion, Marat argued that as a Quaker opposed in principle to the death penalty, Paine should not speak on this matter; the second time, even more ominously, he denounced the speech as a deliberately deceptive translation distorting what Paine really meant. After some disruption, the secretary confirmed that he had the English original to hand, and that the rendition was in fact accurate. It seems that Paine himself did not fully grasp what was going on, and although we should refrain from exaggerating the real power of Marat at this point (he was widely loathed even by his fellow Jacobins), there is no denying the wider impact that such a confrontation, over such a sensitive issue, could have on popular opinion in Paris.[11]

Paine appears to have continued participating in the Convention in various ways (for example, helping to draft a formal letter to the British government, on February 1, 1793).[12] But as the Convention became increasingly torn by Girondin allegations against the Paris Commune and its extremist leadership, Paine became inadvertently embroiled. He had to appear at the Revolutionary Tribunal on April 24 as a witness in connection with the trial of Marat—a trial which was of course tactically very badly handled by the Brissotins, and where Paine himself was put on the defensive when publicly accused by Marat of association with the Brissotins.[13] Before jumping to any conclusions, however, we should remind ourselves, first, that Marat used accusations of this kind ad nauseam as a rhetorical device to further his own populist reputation; and second, that the putative distinction between Brissotins and Jacobins, more entrenched in the autumn of 1793, was at this stage neither clear-cut nor generally accepted by the majority of Convention deputies. In other words, it would be highly misleading to suggest that Paine had already become irretrievably linked to a "losing side" in the increasingly bitter struggle for control that beset the Convention during the summer of 1793. In fact, apart from these specific incidents, Paine became less active on the floor of the Convention, and seemingly not very influential in committee either. Like some of the other older deputies (Paine was fifty-five at the time of his election as deputy, well above the average in the Convention), he kept a low profile—increasingly stymied, no doubt, by his lack of fluency in French and his consequently limited ability to access the detailed information required for an effective understanding of the major political issues and the true scale of responsibilities weighing on the deputies.[14]

During its first year of operation, the Convention, taking everything into account, functioned much better as a parliament than historians have often allowed. Detailed scrutiny of the daily debates suggests there were a large number of deputies who spoke frequently, some of them to considerable effect. During the period from September 1792 to June 1793, some forty deputies spoke substantively on twenty or more occasions, and Cambon, making altogether eighty-seven significant speeches covering a wide range of topics, held the record. The debates on the floor of the Convention were lively and outspoken, often dominated by deputies who were not openly taking sides in the emerging split between the extremist Montagnard deputies (such as Marat, Saint-Just, and Robespierre) and their opponents. There is no obvious reason why Paine could not have taken a more prominent role in this while retaining both significant independence and even some authority. But the records suggest that he spoke only six times during this nine-month period, and only once on a topic other than the trial of the former king. We can only assume that he was out of his depth in the complex republican politics that must otherwise have seemed so important to him.[15]

Even after the purge of the Convention by the Paris Commune (May 31–June 2), Paine does not appear to have been at any particular risk. The existing accounts suggest that he was still regarded by some deputies across the political spectrum as a useful asset in the quest for closer links with the new American republic—and, politically, as an eccentric rather than a threat. The federalist revolts during the summer significantly changed the nature of the factional rivalries in the Convention, but Paine's idealistic belief in constitutional government may well have made it difficult for him to commit strongly to the rebel Girondin cause. Equally, he was unable to engage in the complex political bargaining that led to shifts of balance in the newly reconstituted Committee of Public Safety of July 1793 and in the other increasingly powerful organs of government. As a foreigner, he would always have been vulnerable to accusations of either ambivalence or misunderstanding, and to navigate these treacherous waters would undoubtedly have required much greater political skills than he seemingly possessed—not least since Revolutionary politics, built on Rousseauist assumptions that factionalism was a form of corruption, increasingly turned to denunciation as a key tool in politics.

The first formal denunciation of Paine came on June 18, by a deputation from Arras.[16] While it is difficult to unravel such incidents, not least because they were relatively commonplace, this particular denunciation was not followed up either by the Convention or (it seems) by any of the key committees. As before, any possible involvement of either Marat or Robespierre is difficult to document; equally, further discussion of the role of Gouverneur Morris is unhelpful, since he seems to have had little traceable influence on French parliamentary politics. We can be fairly certain, however, that the war itself was bound to make Paine's British origins an issue that could increasingly easily be exploited by his critics. He was again formally denounced (in absentia) before the Convention in October, and when Bourdon returned to the attack in the Convention on December 27, 1793, he publicly noted that Paine had consistently absented himself from the assembly since the time of arrest of the core Brissotins in October.[17] Even so, the formal confirmation of his arrest, announced in the Convention on January 2, 1794, points more toward the growing paranoia of the Convention, coupled with misunderstandings and political misjudgment on the part of Paine himself, than to any strong conviction among his fellow deputies that he represented any real threat to the current French regime. An American delegation appealed to the

Convention on January 27, 1794, but the case was simply referred to the Committee of Public Safety, and then ignored.

It is worth reminding ourselves that it was at precisely this time that Paine was rewriting *The Age of Reason,* a short version of which had appeared in French earlier in 1793, but which he now extended, ostensibly in part to influence the then current French debate over de-Christianization. If it had been pitched at the right level, and if Paine had established stronger points of contact in real politics, such a book could have had a significant impact on what was a crucial balancing act in French politics at this moment, between on the one hand the increasingly vociferous and populist de-Christianizers outside the Convention, and on the other, those supporting the policy of compromise which both Robespierre and Danton saw as essential. In the event, Paine's work seems to have had little traceable impact on its intended French readers—no doubt either because he had not made the necessary political connections, or because the whole issue of de-Christianization rapidly became snarled up in the personal denunciations and purges of February and March 1794. Instead of its intended impact, the book caused well-known substantial collateral damage among Anglophone readers on both sides of the Atlantic. So, in effect, Paine had doubly miscalculated: he had failed to judge political realities in France in such a way as might have allowed him to play a significant role in forging a much-needed middle road for the embattled Convention leaders; and he had made himself deeply suspect to many observers outside France, who would now assume that Paine had become a convinced exponent of the iconoclasm of revolution.

Paine's continued imprisonment in Paris until November 5, 1794—that is, long after Thermidor—is not inconsistent with the fate of other deputies who had stepped out of line with the volatile opinions of the time: in context, this detention provides no reliable indication of his perceived influence or reputation. Most of the seventy deputies who were arrested during the Terror but survived, took a remarkably long time to secure liberation, and (as with the forty or so who were arraigned or denounced but evaded actual arrest) waited longer still before they were able to return to their seats in the Convention. Paine's illness may have explained part of his long absence, but when he did return to the Convention, in July 1795, he seemed to have lost none of his appetite for political idealism: his speech criticizing the current conservative revisions to the draft constitution was once more read out on his behalf by one of the secretaries, but proposals to have it printed were squashed by objections from the floor.[18] Paine then largely disappeared from the official records and newspapers of the Revolution, and naturally lost his formal status as deputy once the Convention came to an end a few months later. Although he remained in France through the subsequent reactionary phases, and continued to write intermittently, he was rarely noted in the press—his political idealism and radical republicanism were no longer relevant in the fast-moving Revolutionary politics.

A conventional political account, such as the one outlined above, can take us only part of the way. Even the extant political narratives of the Convention itself—formally outlined in minutes, in the daily reports of the *Moniteur*, in the summary accounts of other newspapers, and in printed material of various kinds (including individual speeches), not to mention in letters and personal accounts which give a much stronger flavor of personal allegiances and strains—tend to become too fragmentary during Year II to allow detailed analysis of particular political plans or personal alliances. Fear of being compromised or denounced, and the paranoia of conspiracy, made it essential for everyone who was politically active to cover their tracks as much as possible. Paine was in any case always liable to be on his own, and far more so when he emerged from prison late in 1794. By then, even the newspapers—whose freedom had already been curtailed in March 1793, and whose careful wordings, a few brave exceptions aside, offer little usable insight into the most radical phase of the Revolution—had difficulty gauging political developments within France, let alone sustaining substantive debate. Any critical review of Paine's published work (or that of any of his contemporaries) was, of course, out of the question during Year II, and authors were naturally hesitant to relaunch political debate after Thermidor. The anarchic post-Thermidor period, with its "White Terror," offered new kinds of opportunities for some categories of writers (Paine himself did attempt to join in), but continuing uncertainty ensured that imprints, title page information, and authorship indications were as misleading as they had been during the ancien régime. This, combined with uneven library holdings, makes it very difficult to track the actual profile of any one particular publication in France.

A wider comparative context, drawing on those parts of continental Europe with extensive print industries and somewhat less political disruption, may provide a more reliable indication of changing demand for books. Paine's impact across several language communities is of enormous interest, not just from his own perspective, but also in terms of mapping political shifts in Europe in reaction to events in France. Paine himself had relatively little direct input into this process of diffusion: he never went back to Britain and, until his return to America, never traveled outside northern France. It therefore seems appropriate to shift our main focus of analysis away from the writer and toward his individual texts and his likely readers across some of the other language communities in Europe. Such an approach also allows the application of the more diverse set of tools developed in recent work on early modern print culture. Although Robert Darnton's methodology (not least because of his reliance on books alone, without newspapers or periodicals, and his rather loosely elastic chronological framework) cannot be made to work satisfactorily for the period after 1789, and is only partly adaptable to the rest of continental Europe, the debate his work has engendered has nevertheless created a much keener awareness of how much care we need to take over the publication history and reception of any particular work (whether "canonic" in status, or not).[19] It soon becomes clear (as measured by the standards of more-recent research in print history) that Paine's political influence, and his ability to communicate effectively with his readers, is not as straightforward anywhere in Europe as one might have expected.

This is apparent even from within the British print market itself. William St. Clair, in his thorough and methodologically very significant study of *The Reading Nation in the Romantic Period* (2004), questioned the enormous circulation figures claimed by some of Paine's supporters regarding the *Rights of Man* in the English original. The actual evidence is sparse, and even establishing the precise number of distinct editions is problematic; nevertheless, the case for several hundred thousand copies is no longer sustainable.[20] The first edition of both the first and second parts sold at 3s. 6d. unbound, in a format to match Burke's *Reflections* exactly (so they could be bound together): such relatively upmarket presentation was clearly not intended for mass circulation. The cheap reprints (at 6d. or less) which were distributed soon after, some of them on Paine's own initiative, were designed to meet requests from various towns, resulting in documented print-runs of at least 20,000 copies (not including American reprints).[21] Such a conservative figure may well underestimate actual circulation, but would still bring Paine roughly level with the figures claimed for Burke's *Reflections;* and given the much lower price (within access of manual laborers), coupled with a likely multiple readership, would be enough to explain British government panic. Fear of his impact on wider opinion in Britain is even more clearly underscored by the government's ill-disguised attempt to buy the copyright of the second part for 1,000 guineas, in order to stop further publication. St. Clair himself acknowledges that the documented print-run totals in Britain represent a very considerable success, and that sales would undoubtedly have been much higher had the government not imposed severe penalties from May 1792 onward. No less significantly, *Rights of Man* directly or indirectly inspired an impressive array of responses, rebuttals, and commentaries, keeping Paine's core arguments alive (even when explicit mention of the work had become an offence liable to prosecution). Significantly, this process lasted for several years, even after his trial and his involvement in the republican revolution in France had ceased to be newsworthy.

Equally, we might note local evidence of unusually active debate across Britain: for example, there is ample evidence in the newspapers serving Glasgow and its hinterland that during the autumn of 1792 and spring of 1793 a number of informal groups and societies sprang up dedicated to electoral reform, some of them devoting entire evening meetings to the explicit study of Paine's work.[22] The loyalist fear of these events is entertainingly illustrated in the *Glasgow Advertiser* in January 1793, when the report of the resolutions drafted by a select committee of two societies of the Friends of the People in Kilbarchan, compiled on January 14, 1793, and calling for Painite constitutional reform, led to a response, a few issues later, by a "Select Committee from the two Societies of the Foes of the People of Barkingkill," signed by "Roberspier, President, and Marrat, Secretary."[23] Yet the prosecution of Paine and his supporters, and the heavy-handed clampdown on other radical activity in Britain from the spring of 1793 onwards, seem to have been essentially successful: the *Rights of Man* became more difficult to obtain, and was apparently removed from commercial libraries and other collections where it might trigger penalties. In this light, the demand for English-language copies of *The Age of Reason* is more impressive than we might have expected: it ran to at least a couple of reprints in England, probably totaling between two and three thousand copies, somewhat more in Philadelphia, and it, too, triggered a vigorous range of responses among contemporary writers on both sides of the Atlantic. By comparison, the English versions of Paine's *Decline and Fall of the English System of Finance*, of 1796, and *Agrarian Justice*, of 1797, seem to have made much less impact among contemporary readers.[24]

At the moment, the compilation of bibliographical data comparable to that available for the English-speaking world before 1800 (via the English Short Title Catalogue) has not been completed for most of continental Europe, so direct comparison of publication records across these different markets must be treated with caution. In the case of France itself, the complexity of the ancien régime book trade so clearly delineated by Darnton and others, combined with the very uneven state of printers' records from the Revolutionary period, suggest that it will take some time before we have available tools equivalent to the English Short Title Catalogue. Fictitious or missing imprints, the absence of date of publication, and other obstacles make the precise enumeration and dating of separate editions exceptionally problematic. What is clear is that both parts of *Rights of Man* were rendered into French with the customary speed of translators there, appearing very soon after the English original (alongside new translations of *Common Sense* and other writings). A trawl of the holdings of the Bibliothèque Nationale and other libraries indicates several translations/reprints of this text, probably issued in 1793, and no doubt aided by Paine's initially high profile in the Convention. His outspoken criticisms of British corruption (in the second part) ensured that both parts would have been appreciated in France, and newspaper advertisements confirm that impression. As noted earlier, however, the upheavals of the Terror left little room for the luxury of reviews, so the critical reception in France is not readily documented. The fate of like-minded friends of Paine, such as the philosophe Condorcet (who was arrested and died early in 1794), confirms what we already know from the Revolutionary press: namely that by Year II there was little or no scope for any kind of serious discussion of even relatively non-sensitive matters. Even if Paine's alleged links to the Brissotin faction were neither clear-cut nor politically decisive, assumptions to that effect would have added to perceptions of irrelevance that soon made his publications all but disappear from sight in French debate. This may have been the outcome even for *Rights of Man*—though until we have detailed comparisons of all available versions, we cannot be sure. In such a context, it is easier to understand why his *The Age of Reason,* although revised in direct response to the de-Christianization campaign in France in the autumn of 1793, did not even seem to generate the publicity of rebuttal and rejection that it had in the English-speaking world.

In the rest of continental Europe, the printing trade suffered less direct disruption, but certainly did not escape harassment from government. Three sample areas will serve as indicators of the print history of Paine's major work: first, the Netherlands, which continued to act as a little-regulated haven both for French authors and publishers, and for the European book trade more widely; second, northern (Protestant) Germany, where political disunity and a keen interest in print had allowed the development of the best newspaper and periodical coverage available anywhere in the world; and third, the two Scandinavian states, both of which were monarchies where parts of Paine's message might have been relevant but where liberal censorship policies came increasingly under siege as reactions to events in France became more pronounced. All of these areas had high levels of literacy across a wide cross-section of the population, and all had (at various times) benefited from lively internal political and social debate and enthusiasm for moderate reform, so would appear good testing grounds for the wider diffusion of Paine's ideas.

The summary data (see table 1) creates no particular surprises. *Common Sense* was widely translated in the early 1790s, no doubt because of its renewed relevance at the start of the French Revolution, or perhaps because it could sell alongside *Rights of Man* (the first part of which served as a response to demands for histories and explanations of the early French Revolution). Both parts of Paine's *Rights of Man* seem at first to have met a positive reception: they appeared in Dutch in 1791 and 1793, respectively; in German in 1792–93; and the first part appeared in Swedish in 1792. Interestingly, the Danes had to make do with a German version of *Rights of Man* (published in Copenhagen in 1793), but they may also have used a French version published in Hamburg. Not surprisingly, *The Age of Reason* had less success. Apart from the French translation already noted, a German version was completed by 1796; but the Dutch had to wait until 1798, and there is no trace of either a Danish or a Swedish translation. Some of Paine's other late work failed to reach very far, but it is interesting that the proceedings of his in-absentia English trial for *Rights of Man* (late in 1792) were themselves translated into French and German. We can observe that French and German interest in Paine's work is sustained into the later 1790s, including his work on English public finance, but that Scandinavian readers did not seem to sustain enough demand to make translations viable.

In recent years, historians have become more aware of the need to expand book history to include other forms of printed material. We now have some very important studies of major informative newspapers (such as the *Gazette de Leyde,* the *Gazette d'Amsterdam,* and *Der Hamburgische Correspondent*[25]), and research has also been done on Spectator-type journals, advertisers, and other printed ephemera. As noted above, however, historians of the Enlightenment have made less-effective use of the literary reviews, often regarding them as material suitable primarily for literary studies rather than for social history or the history of the public sphere/opinion. Although attempts have been made to cherry-pick choice morsels from the more famous reviews, often to sustain arguments regarding the reception of a particular work that has since acquired canonic status, genuinely systematic analysis of the major reviews remains underdeveloped. Even for the English-speaking world, the reception of Paine has been analyzed mostly by means of other books and pamphlets written in response to his works.

Focusing our attention on the literary reviews may make our analysis more dependent on the idiosyncrasies of critics and the accidents of journal pub-

TABLE 1
European diffusion of foreign-language translations of select writings of Thomas Paine

Title of work (publication date)	Year translation became available in:				
	French	German	Dutch	Danish	Swedish
Common Sense (1776)	1776 1791 1793	1794	1794	—	—
Letter to the Abbé Raynal (1782)	1783	—	—	—	—
Rights of Man I (1791)	1791 1792 1793	1791 1792 1793	1791	—	1792
Rights of Man II (1792)	1792 1793	1793	1793	—	not known
The Age of Reason I/II (1794-96)	1793-95	1794-96	1798	—	—
The Decline and Fall of the English System of Finance (1796)	not known	1796	1796	—	1797
Agrarian Justice (1797)	1797	—	—	—	—

lication. As already noted, these journals are often descriptive rather than analytical, even resorting to extensive quoting from the books under review, perhaps in order to avoid alienating readers (or government authorities) by taking a more explicit approach. Nonetheless, using these journals places us in a better position to compare the reception of a range of works in any one language, and to compare the reception of translations of the same text into several different languages. Those literary reviews that ran for considerable periods of time also allow us to map more clearly changes in supposed reader interests over time, and (especially for the smaller language communities) actual linguistic developments to suit growing public debate and evolving political cultures. No less importantly, literary reviews can give a more convincing impression of the expectations sustained by a socially more diverse readership who might not themselves feel qualified to enter actively into formal discussion in print. Although the review journals developed from a genre specifically intended for the traditional Republic of Letters of the later seventeenth century, some of them became more inclusive in approach as the market expanded rapidly after 1763, beginning to reflect the interests of a wider readership who may have wanted to know about a book before taking the trouble of obtaining a copy, or who may simply have wanted a general impression without going to the trouble of reading widely and intensively for themselves.

As we would expect, the reception of Paine reflected in these journals varied greatly across the Dutch, German, and Scandinavian reading population. The Dutch and Danish review journals generally took particular trouble over the kinds of books that had direct practical and social relevance, and this emphasis may have reflected what the readers found most interesting (or at least what the editor thought they would). The best-known German periodicals had a wider reader community, which may have allowed them to focus on more demanding and abstract intellectual interests in areas where scholarly innovation was a priority and where the interests of readers might be more specialized. Compared with relatively "safe," or mainstream, authors such as Montesquieu, Adam Ferguson, Adam Smith, Voltaire—or for that matter, Benjamin Franklin—radical campaigners such as Paine were in any case bound to be read in part for the emotional rhetoric and communicative powers, for relevance in terms of key contemporary issues, and perhaps even for breaking out of established styles of writing. The reception of particular texts is therefore likely to tell us as much about the host community as about the original work and/or its translation.

Not surprisingly, the high-profile public debate between Paine and Sieyès regarding the relative merits of monarchical and republican forms of government (which, as we observed earlier, was announced and published in the French press in July 1791) was widely reviewed across Europe. The *Deutsches Magazin* immediately published a long article in 1791 that translated the French press releases by both Sieyès and Paine, but that also gave Sieyès a clear advantage, in that it printed his lengthy critique of Paine and thus gave Sieyès the last word without balancing it with Paine's.[26] Other journals joined in: early in 1792 the Göttingen *Historisches Magazin* published a very similar version of Sieyès's review of Paine's ideas on monarchical and republican government, openly recognizing Paine as a distinguished contributor to both the American and now the French Revolutions, but without citing him in detail. At this stage, as the journal made clear through the voice of Sieyès, the fundamental problems of monarchy and the French constitution could still be discussed as a question of intellectual and political principle, alongside questions of representation, electoral franchise restrictions, and fundamental rights in both revolutions.[27] Naturally, the Danish press also covered the Sieyès-Paine debate (albeit in much less detail) as part of their reporting of the early stages of the Revolution.

As regards the individual works of Paine, the initial reception in the Netherlands was bound to be particularly positive, not least because of influences from France. With a major Huguenot émigré community there, many of whom remained active French speakers, and a print industry that continued to supply large sections of the French market, the Dutch would have had fairly ready access to French material even without any translations. But they also did translate a substantial proportion of French work, just as they demonstrated a consistent interest in translation from English during the later years of the Enlightenment. Most of Paine's works thus became available, and some of them were reviewed in detail in the main Dutch review journal, the *Vaderlandsche Letter-Oefeningen*.[28] *Common Sense* appeared only belatedly, in 1794 (on the back of publicity surrounding his European role), and was not reviewed until 1796, when *VLO* noted Paine's fiery language and commended the text as a worthy supplement to his major works. For the Dutch, the most important text, naturally, was *Rights of Man,* both parts of which had been translated quickly into Dutch and published in Amsterdam/Rotterdam. Already in 1791 the *VLO* had devoted four pages to a review of the first part, siding wholly with Paine against what they saw as Burke's total misrepresentation of the early Revolution: noting Paine's convincing explanation of the legitimacy of fundamental rights, the reviewer praised the actions of the French National Assembly "against the low reproaches and libelous accusations" made by Burke. The review then focused on the remarks Paine had made on the role of the aristocracy in France, quoting extensively from the translation itself, without further comment. The second part was given a fuller treatment in 1793. The review noted the radical tone of Paine's critique, characterizing the work's discursive organization as "full of witty and sharp insights," and emphasizing key points by once more simply quoting substantial sections of text. The *VLO* noted the fundamental nature of Paine's criticisms of the English system of government and constitution, the corrupting dependence on patronage, and the disproportionate costs of the monarchy as an institution. This, it observed, would explain not only why Paine was prosecuted in England, but also why the book itself was "hated, cursed and damned," and reputedly burned by loyalists there (December 1792).[29]

Because of its Mennonite orientation, and the natural Dutch avoidance as far as possible of religious sensitivities and divisions, the reaction of the *VLO* to *The Age of Reason* was profoundly different. This work was reviewed in 1798, and from the outset the tone was clear: the reviewer greeted "with disgust and indignation . . . this despicable creation of the sumptuous and outrageously misapplied ingenuity of a writer, [in] overthrowing the Christian doctrine, which has brought comfort to thousands of people for centuries." Paine was castigated for his total lack of understanding in this area and his lack of knowledge of the old biblical languages, ensuring that he totally misinterpreted the issues he had tackled, and even misquoting the Bible itself. His poor education and the subversive influence of the Quakers were deemed partly to blame, but Paine was particularly denounced for mocking those who held traditional beliefs. He had made "a statement of things which he does not believe in, and of the reasons he does not believe them," and had denounced Revelation as possibly true, but only to those "to whom it occurs," as if there was "truly no considerable difference between mere fictitious stories and clear facts." For good measure, the translator was blamed for adding notes to the text "which do him as little credit as the foul venture of bringing a work like this into being."[30] Of course we are not surprised to see the *VLO* reacting against this text; but the sheer violence of that reaction, from a journal that normally used much more mundane language, and which had been so positive toward the *Rights of Man*, certainly confirms that it was *The Age of Reason* that really undermined the influence and reputation that Paine had enjoyed until then in one of the most liberal societies in Europe.

The German journals were never as positive toward Paine, even in respect of his earlier works. Although the *Minerva* had carried Paine's engraved portrait as a frontispiece in 1793, referring to him (in an article later in that year) as "the famous author of Rights of Man," the reception of *Rights of Man* was decidedly mixed with regard to the first German translation of first part in 1791, the second translation the following year, and the translation of second part, which followed in 1793. Readers of the *Allgemeine deutsche Bibliothek* were left in little doubt that even the first part was unbalanced, and the translator was berated for not having included sections of Burke to act as an antidote to the interesting but misguided view of the Revolution perpetrated by Paine. In the eyes of the reviewer, the tone of the second part indicated that Paine had seriously misread the political instincts and public consensus prevailing in Britain: rather than trigger a response there equivalent to the effect *Common Sense* had had in the colonies, the second part (in the eyes of the reviewer) was likely to have the opposite effect, and might even devalue what worthwhile points might be contained within the basic argument. Paine's book was meant for readers of the lower sorts, and parts of it would be of no interest to German readers. Although no detailed analysis of the content was provided, the reviewer suggested that the book was so dangerous and socially irresponsible that the British government had been entirely justified (if perhaps not altogether wise) in trying to ban it and prosecute the author.[31]

Even allowing for the possible political considerations in northern Germany of not wanting to cause offense to the British monarchy, these hostile reactions to *Rights of Man* seem to reflect a revulsion closely resembling that of the political classes in much of Europe against the radical turn taken by the Revolution from 1792 onward. The translation of any highly topical work will always, by its very nature, be a hostage to fortune because it will appear some time after the original—and by 1793 both the British suppression of radicalism and the widespread violence in France were clear to everyone across Europe. Other journals, for example the *Historische-politische Magazin* in 1794, followed this cue. Significantly, the responses to a translation of *The Age of Reason* (published in Lübeck in 1796) were not couched in enough detail even to acquaint the reader with the core arguments of the text itself. Instead, this and other major journals preferred to concentrate on those authors (Lord Erskine, Seiler, and others) who produced substantive rebuttals of *The Age of Reason* in order to shore up the established churches against the threats of Deism.[32]

The Swedes published a translation of at least the first part of *Rights of Man,* and they had also in 1797 tackled *The Decline and Fall of the English System of Finance*. Reviews and discussion of these works have not yet been located, but it is likely that both of these works were deemed relevant in the context of the highly unstable political situation in Sweden in the 1790s and the reversal of some reform policies. However, further south, in Denmark, the *Rights of Man* was in effect hushed up altogether. No Danish translation ever appeared of this or any other of Paine's major works, and although some readers would have been able to access the German version of *Rights of Man* in 1793, they were also treated to an instant rebuttal by a member of the Danish-Norwegian landowning elite, Caspar Wilhelm von Munthe af Morgenstierne, which for good measure was published both in German and in French, but not in Danish.[33] Once again, this reaction seems to be soured by knowledge of actual events in France by this time: after all, the Danish monarchy had initiated an impressive range of reforms of its own, since 1785, and had maintained a wide degree of freedom of the press even when many other governments had begun to panic after 1792. Events in France were still being reported in some depth in the Danish press, and a number of other politically innovative texts were published (at some risk) in Copenhagen right up to 1795. The fact that the Danish intellectual scene was more readily influenced by German intellectual currents, rather than by French or even English-language ones, may help to explain the extent to which Paine was simply ignored. *The Age of Reason* was neither translated nor reviewed in Denmark, and Paine never became (indeed, never has become) a household name there.

This essay has revisited some of the long-standing assumptions concerning the reputation and reception of Paine's work outside the Anglophone world. His contribution to the French Revolution takes on a somewhat different complexion if seen firmly in the context of the politics of the first year of the Convention parliament. His lack of fluency in French was of course a fundamental problem, and may at least in part explain the succession of misjudgments he made as a deputy in the Convention. But I have also argued that his supposed association with the Girondins is not quite what it seemed, and was certainly not in itself sufficient to explain why he was so rapidly sidelined from the spring of 1793 onward. We need perhaps to retain a clear distinction (as arguably we need to do also in the case of independent thinkers such as Condorcet) between, on the one hand, those who have the kind of rational and analytical mind to comment on politics and the theory of government, and on the other, those who have the ability to engage in practical politics with sufficient sense of timing, and sufficient political instinct, to be able to make themselves heard. Paine, like Condorcet, clearly belonged in the former category, and had no talent for the latter. He was clearly better on paper than he was in the debating chamber; and while the role of international revolutionary was not an easy one to bring off, he clearly did not make the most of the opportunities available to him. In any case, such contrasting careers as those of Sieyès and Marat remind us that those with a flare for pamphleteering and journalism were not necessarily the most effective politicians.

The reception of Paine's major works in the rest of Europe highlights some further general points. Most obviously, it reminds us yet again of what scholarship in the last few years has already established: that the process of enlightening in many parts of Europe did not imply abandonment of religious belief, though for many it modified the way such beliefs were voiced and interpreted. The well-established assumption among historians that it was, above all, *The Age or Reason* that ruined Paine's reputation in the Anglophone world, seems to be corroborated when we look at his reception in the Netherlands and the German lands. The double failure of the book, both in terms of its purpose at a critical juncture in French politics, and in terms of its rejection even by liberal opinion elsewhere, underlines the surprisingly stark inability of Paine to understand the public opinion that he had previously been so skilled at exploiting.

That said, Paine clearly did attract significant attention, both for his *Rights of Man* and as a foreigner contributing directly to a crucial stage in the French Revolution. Comparison with Jefferson is instructive: unlike Paine, Jefferson had little to say to Europeans in the 1790s, either in the form of relevant ideas for reform or as a practical politician. Paine tried both, and although success eluded him in the rapidly shifting politics of the French Revolution, his contemporaries both in France and the Netherlands at first greeted his ideas with some enthusiasm, German readers more cautiously. It is possible that similarly ambivalent reactions surround those few translations of Paine into other languages (for example, Italian) that can be found in the 1790s; but without comparably robust journals and relative freedom of discussion, the conclusions we can draw for southern Europe will be more tentative. What the present study has demonstrated is that, in those societies where print culture gained real momentum in the late eighteenth century, it is worth exploiting a full range of source material appropriate for each particular language-community and likely readership. As the difficulties experienced by Paine clearly demonstrate, translation itself was not as straightforward as it might appear. In addition, the fundamental political vocabulary, and the relative levels of freedom of expression and debate, varied so much across Europe in the 1790s that ideas and practical reform proposals by no means always crossed cultural borders unscathed.

NOTES

1. There is a growing literature on the history of language in early modern Europe, but see, notably, Fania Oz-Salzberger, *Translating the Enlightenment: Scottish Civic Discourse in Eighteenth-Century Germany* (Oxford: Oxford University Press, 1995); Fania Oz-Salzberger, "The Enlightenment in Translation: Regional and European Aspects," *European Review of History* 13, no. 3 (2006): 385–409; and Peter Burke, *Languages and Communities in Early Modern Europe* (Cambridge: Cambridge University Press, 2004).

2. On, for example, the Netherlands as a focal point for exchange (both in newspapers and in the book trade), see Margaret C. Jacob and Wijnand W. Mijnhardt, *The Dutch Republic in the Eighteenth Century: Decline, Enlightenment, and Revolution* (Ithaca, N.Y.: Cornell University Press, 1992); Jeremy D. Popkin, *News and Politics in the Age of Revolution: Jean Luzac's "Gazette de Leyde"* (Ithaca, N.Y.: Cornell University Press, 1989); and G. C. Gibbs, "The Role of the Dutch Republic as the Intellectual Entrepôt of Europe in the Seventeenth and Eighteenth Centuries," *Bijdragen en Mededelingen betreffende de Geschiedenis der Nederlanden,* no. 86 (1971): 323–49. Scandinavia will be discussed more fully below.

3. For a survey of censorship and self-censorship practices, see Thomas Munck, *The Enlightenment: A Comparative Social History, 1721–1794* (London: Arnold, 2000), 76–105.

4. See Norman S. Fiering, "The Transatlantic Republic of Letters: A Note on the Circulation of Learned Periodicals to Early Eighteenth-Century America," *William and Mary*

Quarterly, 3rd ser., 33 (October 1976): 642–60; Frank Donoghue, "Colonizing Readers: Review Criticism and the Formation of a Reading Public," in *The Consumption of Culture, 1600–1800: Image, Object, Text*, ed. Ann Bermingham and John Brewer (London: Routledge, 1995), 54–74; Geraldine Sheridan, "Irish Literary Review Magazines and Enlightenment France, 1730–1790," in *Ireland and the French Enlightenment, 1700–1800*, ed. Graham Gargett and Geraldine Sheridan (Basingstoke, Hampshire, U.K.: Palgrave Macmillan, 1999), 21–46; and Antonia Forster, "Review Journals and the Reading Public," in *Books and Their Readers in Eighteenth-Century England: New Essays*, ed. Isabel Rivers (Leicester: Leicester University Press, 2001), 171–90.

5. For further discussion, see my article on "Eighteenth-Century Review Journals and the Internationalization of the European Book Market," *International History Review* 32, no. 3 (2010): 415–35.

6. Morellet had issued Jefferson's *Observations sur la Virginie* in 1786, but apart from a few minor papers and addresses, non-English speakers would have had no access to his writings (see Durand Echeverria and Everett C. Wilkie, *The French Image of America: A Chronological and Subject Bibliography of French Books Printed before 1816 Relating to the British North American Colonies and the United States* (Metuchen, N.J.: Scarecrow Press, 1994).

7. Their respective points of view were reported in some of the papers, such as the *Gazette Nationale, ou, Le Moniteur Universel*. Throughout this essay, references are to the reprinted version of this newspaper (see *Réimpression de l'Ancien Moniteur* [Paris: Henri Plon, 1858–70] [hereafter cited as *AM*], in this case, vol. 9, pp. 137–39. Paine defines "monarchy" as any government that is hierarchical and unaccountable, in contrast to representative systems.

8. The *Moniteur* noted the publication of reports of his trial in absentia (*AM*, 14:470), and elsewhere in Europe (as we shall see below), the trial also attracted attention.

9. *AM*, 14:182.

10. *AM*, 14:310–11.

11. *AM*, 14:535, 15:156, 200, 248.

12. *AM*, 15:338.

13. *AM*, 16:275–80.

14. The pattern of activity for all the deputies in the Convention, as reported in the *Moniteur* and in the formal minutes, is highly revealing of the political profile of the assembly during the first year of the Republic. A few of Paine's exact contemporaries (Ruhl, Sillery, Guyton-Morveau) spoke much more frequently than he did; equally, until May, the Brissotins (Girondins) were far from reduced to silence.

15. These and the following specific observations are based on my prosopographical study of the Convention during its first year of operation. Its parameters are described more fully in Evan Mawdsley and Thomas Munck, *Computing for Historians* (Manchester, U.K.: Manchester University Press, 1993), 101–13.

16. *AM*, 16:683. The Arras group also denounced three other deputies.

17. *AM*, 19:54.

18. *AM*, 25:171.

19. A good overview can be found in Haydn Trevor Mason, *The Darnton Debate: Books and Revolution in the Eighteenth Century* (Oxford: Voltaire Foundation, 1998).

20. The claims are summarized in Gregory Claeys, *Thomas Paine: Social and Political Thought* (Boston: Unwin Hyman, 1989), 111–12.

21. William St. Clair, *The Reading Nation in the Romantic Period* (Cambridge: Cambridge University Press, 2004), 623–24.

22. Carolyn Albert, "The Impact of the French Revolution on Local Activity in West Central Scotland in 1792 and 1793" (M.Phil. thesis, University of Glasgow, 1998).

23. *Glasgow Advertiser*, 18–21 January 1793 and 28 January–1 February 1793, cited in Albert, "Impact of the French Revolution," 101–2.

24. St. Clair, *Reading Nation*, 624–25.

25. Popkin, *News and Politics in the Age of Revolution*; Pierre Rétat, *La Gazette d'Amsterdam: Miroir de l'Europe au XVIIIe Siècle* (Oxford: Voltaire Foundation, 2001); Brigitte Tolkemitt, *Der Hamburgische Correspondent: Zur öffentlichen Verbreitung der Aufklärung in Deutschland* (Tübingen: Niemeyer, 1995).

26. *Deutsches Magazin*, 2 (1791): 193–216.

27. *Neues Göttingisches Historisches Magazin* (1792): 341–49 (pt. 1).

28. This journal, founded in 1761 by a Mennonite preacher, survived into the nineteenth century as the most important journal of its kind for the Dutch-language community.

29. *Vaderlandsche Letter-Oefeningen* (1791): 572–75, (1793): 32–38.

30. Ibid., (1798): 430–35. For a full discussion of the Dutch debate, including in other journals, see P. van Gestel, "Dutch Reactions to Thomas Paine's *Age of Reason*," *Studies on Voltaire and the Eighteenth Century*, no. 378 (1999): 271–301.

31. *Allgemeine deutsche Bibliothek*, 117 (1794): 469–73; *Neue Allgemeine deutsche Bibliothek*, 8 (1794): 119–23 (pt. 1), 15 (1795): 77–81 (pt. 2).

32. *Deutsches Magazin*, 15 (1798): 180–87; *Neue Allgemeine deutsche Bibliothek*, 84 (1803): 283–88.

33. *Kiöbenhavnske Lærde Efterretninger* (1794): 23–24, 43–44, 145–53.

COMMONALITIES AND DIFFERENCES
*Paine and Jefferson,
Paine versus Jefferson*

Empire without Colonies
Paine, Jefferson, and the Nootka Crisis

EDWARD G. GRAY

It is hard to imagine a more apposite opening paragraph than that which graces Harold Adams Innis's monumental *The Fur Trade in Canada:* "The history of Canada has been profoundly influenced by the habits of an animal which very fittingly occupies a prominent place on her coat of arms. The beaver (*Castor Canadensis*) was of dominant importance in the beginnings of the Canadian fur trade. It is impossible to understand the characteristic developments of the trade or of Canadian history without some knowledge of its life and habits."[1] So it is, with the lowly beaver, that the nation of Canada rises from the beaten plains and icy fjords of far-north America. At first glance, Innis's logic—that a single animal can be given so pivotal a role in a modern nation's past—seems strikingly quaint. Can it really be said that any animal—let alone the waddling beaver—can be so central to a nation's history?

While there may be some exaggeration in Innis's particular characterization, it turns out that, in fact, the modern world has been to a very large extent shaped by the habits and characteristics of mammals. In addition to the beaver, we might add the horse, the pig, and the dog to the list of historically important mammals. And if we move into the nineteenth century we find at least one upon which an entire, integrated industrial economy was built: that is of course the whale.[2]

It may seem perverse to begin an essay about Thomas Paine and Thomas Jefferson with a disquisition on the historical impact of mammals, but in fact, the particular episode I wish to describe centers on fur-bearing mammals.

Those mammals—or really, one particular mammal, the Sea Otter (*Enhydra lutris*)—accounts for the first serious diplomatic crisis faced by the young United States. That crisis—familiarly known as the Nootka Sound Crisis—involved a standoff between Spain and Britain over a tiny, incredibly remote fur-trading factory on the Pacific coast of Vancouver Island. Had it not been for other concurrent events that distracted Spain's principal Bourbon ally—the convening of the Estates General, the declaration of independence of the *Assemblée Nationale,* the storming of the Bastille, and the effective imprisonment of the French monarch—the flap over Nootka could well have sparked the eighteenth-century's third world war.

To anybody concerned with the prospects of the new American republic, the whole affair was enormously unsettling. For Jefferson, the dangers were fairly obvious. There was, on the one hand, the ever-present fear of foreign entanglement. Should Britain declare war on Spain, was neutrality at all a realistic option for the United States? The dilemma was particularly acute in light of the continued presence of British troops in the west and the likelihood that those troops would seek passage through American-claimed territory. But perhaps of equal concern was the possibility that whatever lay between North America's Pacific Coast and the Mississippi River, if not the Appalachian spine, was becoming an arena for European colonial conquest. Would the new nation survive the colonization of its vast western flank? The question lingered for Jefferson like a bad cold. For Paine, the issues were quite different. He cared little or not all about the affairs of a distant colonial periphery—or its fur-bearing treasures. Nor was he particularly fearful for the fate of the new United States in a world at war. Republicanism, he presumed, had already survived such trials in America and would likely do so again. What concerned Paine, rather, was the possibility that the Pitt government would exploit the conflict to crush reform at home.[3]

Nothing about any of this is particularly surprising. Paine, the transatlantic radical, was pleased with events in France, but by 1790 the prime target of his radical ambition was increasingly Britain. And insofar as war against Spain, and possibly its Bourbon "friend" France (whom the Pitt administration was feverishly and covertly trying to draw to its side by claiming, among other things, that Spain was much more dangerous to the cause of republicanism than the constitutional monarchy across the English Channel) could strengthen reactionary forces in Britain, the prospect of such a war deeply troubled him. Similarly, Jefferson, while he had much invested in the course of events in France and Britain, had much more invested in the American hinterland. The dangers of instability and imperial annexation in the American West had been a preoccupation for him at least since the end of the Revolutionary War. Staring out across the hills of central Virginia into those contested lands that had already drawn his generation of Virginians into one—and arguably two—devastating imperial wars, he could not help but be unsettled by events surrounding the Nootka Crisis.

All of this is to suggest that in their responses to the Nootka affair, Jefferson and Paine betray expected differences. Jefferson, the Virginian, statesman, and politician, is concerned above all with national security. Paine, the radical and the dissenter, is concerned with the progress of his constitutional ideals. But of course Paine and Jefferson are often understood to be fellow travelers when it comes to the ideology of eighteenth-century reform. They both despised monarchy; they both argued fervently for government by law; they both regarded institutionalized religion with a deeply jaundiced and skeptical eye; they both had a profoundly optimistic understanding of human nature; they both embraced rationalism as the only valid path to truth. One could go on. What is perhaps less often recognized is that beyond these familiar commonalities lay additional and generally overlooked points of convergence, points that emerged with particular power in 1790. Despite their varying concerns with respect to the Nootka Crisis, Paine and Jefferson articulated a very similar kind of statecraft. The comparison suggests much less about Jefferson than it does about Paine, a figure rarely thought of as exhibiting anything so coherent with respect to the organization and distribution of international power as "statecraft."[4] But what I would like to claim in what follows is that, in fact, Paine was very much concerned with the central subjects of early modern statecraft: taxation, trade, and defense. And Paine's discussion of these matters suggests a vision very similar to that articulated by Jefferson. Given Paine's urban, artisanal associations, it may seem strange to associate him with the agrarian, utopian Jefferson. But one of the things this analysis suggests is that the common binary, distinguishing trade from manufactures, or agriculture from manufactures, does not really hold for Paine, and may be less important for Jefferson than many scholars have suggested.[5] With regard to political economy, Paine regarded himself as, above all, a friend of commerce. His perspective on both manufactures and agriculture was shaped by a faith in the civilizing power of what Adam Smith famously called the human "propensity to truck, barter, and exchange one thing for another."[6] Insofar as manufactures could facilitate trade—by creating infrastructure on which to move goods and by building navies with which to defend that infrastructure—Paine can be properly identified as a promoter of manufactures. But there is little in Paine's writings to suggest any interest in a Federalist-style export economy dependent on large-scale production of consumer goods and the coercive maintenance of markets at home and abroad. Rather, for him, manufactures were constructive insofar as they served commerce, but they could not be ends in and of themselves. And commerce, according to most of Paine's writings, primarily entailed the export of natural produce—naval stores, minerals, and agricultural products—rather than manufactured goods.

This perspective is consistent with an important aspect of Jeffersonian political economy, namely that whatever the new nation's economy looked like, it would be sustained by the vast American hinterland. Space, as so many historians have observed, would prevail over time as the crucial ingredient in Jeffersonian economic development. This was as true for Paine as it was for Jefferson. For an earlier generation of scholars, this expansive political economy was primarily a function of Jefferson's brand of republicanism. By curtailing manufactures and attendant urban growth, it fostered natural virtue, which, in turn, made the agrarian republic possible. In recent years, Peter Onuf and others have begun to explore an alternative basis for this Jeffersonian vision. As indebted as it was to republicanism (or the latter's liberal contortions, *pace* Joyce Appleby), this work has suggested, it was equally if not more indebted to an alternative model of empire that arose out of the eighteenth-century critique of the British Empire. That model depended, above all, on the abolition of the subordinate-colony/mother-country relationship. In its place would be an entity whose evolution was organic and whose parts were bound by commerce. In place of plantations or colonies, its constituent parts would be individuals encouraged by the fraternal legal and institutional affiliations of the state to expand the geographic scope of that state.[7]

While this imperial ideal may have emerged out of a general Anglo-American critique of the British Empire, it contained within it elements that in the British context were merely utopian but in the American context were quite real. As we all know, Jefferson's vision would never have been realized (the degree to which it actually was realized is obviously a contentious question) were it not for one crucial fact: America was a continent, with abundant, cheap land. And according to the Jeffersonian ideal, it was land that would allow ordinary people to be part of commercial society, and it was land that would ultimately secure the gains of commerce by facilitating independence from corrupting domestic and international politics. This famous agrarian ideal was obviously impossible for an island nation with limited landed resources, and insofar as Jefferson's ideal was the result of circumstances—as opposed to the ideals inherited from the broader pre-Revolutionary debate over empire—the geographical circumstances of the United States cannot be ignored.

PAINE, JEFFERSON, AND THE NOOTKA CRISIS

There is no doubt that Paine's imperial vision was also shaped by the specific geographic context of American empire.[8] At the end of the day, the fact that America was a continent and not an island was exactly what would allow it to achieve its imperial destiny. But Paine saw barriers to that destiny with which Jefferson never much concerned himself. Paine's efforts to address those barriers—as much as any single argument advanced in his writings—betray his fundamental faith in the kind of continental empire Jefferson envisioned.

Nootka Sound opens onto the Pacific Ocean roughly halfway up the coast of Vancouver Island. Just beyond the inlet, on the Sound's northern bank, lies a modest cove, named by Captain James Cook "Friendly Harbor." For Cook, the name was emblematic of the generous reception accorded him and his men by the local Mowachaht peoples (whom Cook called the "Nootka," after what he believed to be the Native name for the sound into which his ships sailed). After a month's time at Nootka in the early spring of 1778, Cook's two ships, *Resolution* and *Discovery,* sailed out into the Pacific and turned northward to continue their futile quest for the Northwest Passage—the principal object of this (Cook's third) Pacific voyage. But their month at Nootka Sound would prove to be among the most momentous of the expedition's more than fifty months. Although the voyagers would discover the Hawaiian Islands (named by Cook the Sandwich Islands, after Lord Sandwich, First Lord of the Admiralty), and Cook would meet his end on those same islands in the winter of 1779, the discoveries at Nootka would prove much more immediately significant.[9]

Upon the expedition's return to England in the fall of 1780, its esteemed commander's body parts having been buried at sea off the island of Hawaii, news quickly spread that Cook and his men may have stumbled upon the mother-lode of early modern empire: a foolproof path to the markets of China. As a byproduct of the usual haggling for food, tools, labor, and sex, Cook's crew had accumulated some 1,500 sea otter pelts during their stay at Nootka. While the crew were well aware that furs could fetch fair sums in Europe and Asia, they had no idea just how prized the supple sea otter pelts would be in the markets of Canton. Spanish merchants had introduced the pelts to China—from Baja California via Manila—in the first half of the eighteenth century. But supplies dwindled as Native hunters abandoned the trade. Russian traders continued the trade, but they were only able to supply a fraction of what the Chinese market demanded.[10] It was thus with enormous good fortune that Cook's crews disembarked with their pelts. What they discovered was the possibility of immense profits, as much as thirty guineas per pelt. As Second Lieutenant James King recalled, "The rage with which our seamen were possessed to return [to Nootka] and buy another cargo of skins to make their fortunes at one time, was not far short of mutiny."[11]

By 1787, no less then seven British-flagged ships had come to Nootka Sound to trade for otter pelts. At the same time, both Britain's oldest and newest imperial rivals—France and the United States—were preparing Northwest Coast expeditions of their own.[12] All of this was happening despite longstanding Spanish claims to North America's Pacific coast, and by the 1780s the stampede for sea otter—now consisting of British, French, American, and Russian traders—was clearly threatening Spanish hegemony, such as it was, over most of the American Pacific rim. Though it had spent the previous two hundred years trying, Britain had yet to establish any kind of lasting presence from which to encroach on Spain's Pacific activities, particularly the Manila Galleon trade. But in Nootka it appeared to have found the place for just such a presence. The Sound provided an enclosed deep-water harbor; vital naval stores, including fresh water and timber; valuable furs; and, perhaps most important, a Native population willing to trade. Indeed, the Mowachaht, in addition to being skilled fishermen and hunters, were people of the potlatch, which gave them a seemingly limitless outlet for European trade goods.[13]

Still, even if Britain were able to establish some sort of outpost at Nootka, it would likely be primarily commercial rather than military. And Spain had little interest in the Northwest Coast fur trade. To Spanish officials, a much more immediate problem presented itself in the guise of the new United States.[14] Aside from the obvious dangers of American republicanism, especially as Spain's Bourbon relation faced a republican surge of its own, the Spanish Crown—which was struggling to secure the sweeping Bourbon imperial reforms—feared the fiscal impact of expanding American empire. The contraband trade had already cost the Spanish Empire dearly (primarily in the form of Spanish reales winding up in the coffers of America and Britain) and was among the principal reasons for the Bourbon Reforms. But an American Empire, vastly enriched by the China trade, would almost certainly—and perhaps fatally—expand the contraband problem. As one Spanish official wrote:

> We should not be surprised if the English colonies of America, republican and independent, put into practice the design of discovering a safe port on the South Sea, and try to sustain it by crossing the immense land of this continent above our possessions of Texas, New Mexico, and the Californias.... In truth, it would obtain the richest

trade of Great China and India if it were to succeed in establishing a colony on the west coasts of America.[15]

The idea that Americans might build a Western empire on the back of the North Pacific fur trade raised the specter of a complete collapse of the Spanish imperial system in North America, and perhaps even the rest of the Americas. The problem was less the potential Anglo-American annexation of Spanish claims in North America than the rapid expansion of the contraband trade between an imperial United States and Spain's New World possessions. For Spain, the specter of a new American Pacific empire raised the horrifying prospect—surely as horrifying to Spain as the potential loss of its West Indies possessions was to Britain earlier in the century—of losing vital silver and colonial tax revenues. As part of a broader program to secure empire from within and protect it from without, Spain thus undertook to reassert sovereignty on North America's Northwest Coast.

To this end, on February 17, 1789, two ships carrying 28 soldiers, 4 Franciscan priests, and 163 other men sailed from the port at San Blas, Mexico, for Nootka Sound. Fearful that too bold a gesture might offend local natives, Spanish officials instructed the voyagers to build some kind of fort but to occupy it only during the day. Presumably, the structure would stand as sufficient indication of Spanish intentions even once the expedition returned to San Blas. Unfortunately, traffic to Nootka had increased such that when the Spanish ships finally reached the Sound, there were already two American ships in the region. And over the course of the next few months, a parade of vessels sailed into the area, including four owned by the recently founded British firm, the King George's Sound Company.[16] Thus, rather than spending their time establishing some kind of permanence on New Spain's far northern frontier, the Spaniards found themselves struggling to address these intrusions into what was putatively Spanish territory. The culmination of the whole business—disastrous for Spain—was the capture of two British ships and one American. The latter ship was soon released at San Blas, but the other two remained in Spanish hands until July 1790.

It is interesting to note that these British ships, which had sailed from Macao some months earlier, carried provisions and laborers to build a permanent settlement at Nootka. These included Chinese carpenters, bricklayers, blacksmiths, shoemakers, tailors, and a cook—twenty-nine artisans in total. The King George's Sound Company, under the direction of a former naval lieutenant and merchant seaman, John Meares, had every intention of laying permanent British claim to the Northwest Coast sea otter trade. Indeed,

Meares would later claim that this venture was simply meant to provision a fur-trade factory he had already established several years earlier. Meanwhile, in London, one of the company's founders was exploring ways to extend to Nootka the penal colonization already begun at New South Wales. Jefferson's fears that Britain intended to recolonize North America from west to east were not, it turns out, so far-fetched.[17]

For the Pitt administration, reaction to the Spanish capture of two of His Majesty's ships and their crews was dictated largely by two circumstances. The first was the ever-pressing quest to maintain British naval hegemony in the face of a continued Bourbon threat. And the second was the fact that events in France, while alarming, had not yet induced the full-scale reorientation of domestic and foreign policy that would begin after the appearance of Burke's *Reflections on the Revolution in France* (1790).[18] Pitt's administration thus regarded Spanish actions less as a threat to specific British interests than as a possible threat to Britain's capacity for naval deterrence. Though a military response would be costly, the costs of inaction could thus be greater, insofar as inaction risked strengthening those factions in France and Spain inclined to challenge Britain's naval dominance. None of this is to suggest that there were not true strategic interests at play. Since the end of the American war, if not before, the government had been working to extend the British presence in the Americas. The latter quest fueled a host of initiatives, including talk of allying with Latin American independence fighters under the leadership of the Venezuelan radical Francisco de Miranda. To this end, the administration suggested that Britain could do for Latin America what France had done for the United States. And through this kind of revolutionary alliance, it could recover a semblance of its former influence in America, dispose of another of its imperial rivals there, and establish a new and much less politically fraught American market for its manufactures.[19] By the end of the following year, such an alliance would be impossible. Nonetheless, in the relative quiet of the spring of 1790, all of these factors fed the British government's incredible truculence. Encouraged by East India trading interests, particularly John Meares himself, the administration began preparing for war almost as soon as news of the Nootka seizure reached London.[20] Gouverneur Morris, the unofficial American special envoy in England, wrote in early May of 1790 that "two ships of the line are put in commission a hot press is carrying and the two Houses of Parliament are at this instant debating upon a message from his Majesty which speaks of the Dignity and Honor of his Crown. The Rights of the Nation & c."[21]

PAINE, JEFFERSON, AND THE NOOTKA CRISIS

As Britain prepared for war, Paine was traveling back and forth between London and Paris, attempting to monitor events in the latter while seeing to the construction of an iron-bridge prototype in the former. Paine had been working on the iron bridge at least since 1785, and after abandoning hopes for American financing, he traveled to France and then England in 1787. After meeting Edmund Burke, an early supporter of the bridge project, Paine formed a partnership with the Walker Brothers, proprietors of one of Britain's largest iron works, and by early 1790, the Walkers had cast components for Paine's largest prototype to date. During the summer of 1790, as the Nootka affair reached its crescendo, Paine found himself overseeing a small work crew as they assembled a 110-foot iron bridge on a bowling green near the intersection of Edgware Road and the new Marylebone Road on London's far-northern fringe.

While the bridge was Paine's principal occupation, he was still as consumed with the march to war as any politically aware Londoner at the time. And virtually all of his correspondence from 1790 contains references to the looming crisis. But with two correspondents in particular, he seems to have given the matter much greater attention. The first of these was his friend Edmund Burke. Paine's rupture with Burke after the November publication of Burke's *Reflections* is familiar enough. But prior to this, the two maintained a cordial friendship. While they disagreed about whether the French Revolution was merely a movement of constitutional reform or a step down the road to anarchy, they agreed that iron bridges offered a promising solution to one of the era's central technological problems. They also appear to have more or less concurred on the behavior of the Pitt administration with respect to Nootka. Of course the Whig Burke was no friend of the administration, as his struggle to impeach Warren Hastings made all too plain, but given the direction his friendship with Paine would soon take, it is difficult to imagine the two would have found common ground on the Nootka affair. But, in fact, that appears to have been the case. In early May 1790, Paine met with Burke to discuss the matter and to urge the great orator to—as he had done so many times before—awaken his somnambulant fellow MPs before a corrupt administration and an ineffectual sovereign led the nation to war. Far from dismissing Paine, Burke simply suggested that Paine take his plan elsewhere, not because it was worthless, but because Burke had expended too much political capital cutting a deal with the administration to allow the continuation of the Hastings trial.[22]

While Paine's correspondence with Burke was very limited, he left a much more substantial correspondence with Jefferson's former secretary and the current chargé d'affairs in Paris, William Short. Whether at Short's urging or simply on Paine's own initiative is unclear, but Paine clearly functioned as an unofficial intelligence gatherer and American agent in London. Much of what he learned of the Nootka affair found its way into his letters to Short, and it was from Short that Jefferson learned many details of the crisis. What is clear from this correspondence is that Paine's primary fear was Great Britain. Should the last bastion of "courtly and . . . aristocratical hatred against the principles of the French Revolution" defeat Spain and its allies, the European economy would collapse. And with that collapse, resulting partly from the absorption of Spanish silver by Great Britain, the French Revolution (which at that point remained largely a revolution in constitutional principles as far as Paine was concerned) would surely collapse as well. And with the fall of that domino would go the forces for reform within Britain. Given such risks, Paine was even prepared to sacrifice the growth of republicanism in the Americas. "Such a transfer of property and Dominion" as would follow British victory— even British victory with the aid of Latin American republicans—would simply prolong "the bondage" of those Latin American countries, and "it is better for themselves and the World, that they remain as they are," bound by the yoke of monarchical empire.[23]

At the same time, the possibility that revolution in France could be stalled by foreign war was almost as troubling. It was a difficult problem for Paine. The failure of revolution in France or the successful assertion of British power in Europe and America would have the same ultimate effect. They would strengthen the counter-revolutionary Pitt government at the expense of a beleaguered Whig opposition. In the end, it seems, Paine concluded that the only way to stop the administration was French war against Britain, or at least the threat of such a war. Perhaps he was encouraged in this view by the popular sentiment, communicated to him by Short, that revolution is akin "to those disorders of the human body after which purgation is indispensable." For the body politic, "war either civil or foreign is the only [purgation] that will suffice, & the latter is to be preferred to the former."[24] In late June, Paine thus sent—via Short—a paper to the Marquis de Lafayette, which he urged the latter to translate and see into print. The transaction was all very secretive, and Paine was clearly terrified by the possibility that what he had written, and the identity of its author, would find its way back across the English Channel. Judging from a remark by Gouverneur Morris some months later, Paine had every reason to be fearful. Rather than simply follow Spain in a defense of its imperial holdings, Paine was urging the French to take a very different tack and do what their Spanish allies had tried to compel them to do during the American War for Independence: namely, to lead the combined Franco-Spanish fleet in an attack on England's Channel defenses.[25]

Paine's intent is fairly clear. At the very least, his pamphlet would raise for the English the danger of naval action in the Channel, something he was convinced they were totally unprepared for. The English are, he wrote Short, "unaccustomed to wars at home or on their own coast," and as a consequence, "they have no idea of a war but at a distance, and that they are only to read the accounts of it in the news-paper. Of this sort of war they make a mere trade and ever will." Having conveniently forgotten the Jacobite rising of 1745, not to mention a variety of other recent domestic rebellions, Paine concluded that the terror of facing an assault on her home shores would put an end to Britain's march to war. Describing his paper, which he had enclosed in one of his letters to Short, he noted—precisely as Spain had hoped when it pushed for the same action during the American War—that "the contents . . . will operate to detain their fleets at home, for such will be the fears and clamours of the John Bulls that the coast must be guarded at the risk of all other enterprises, and whether their views are to the Baltic, the West Indies, or else where the same event will follow, that is the fleet must be kept at home."[26]

Paine continued to call for the threat of attack from the French through the spring and summer of 1790, citing among other things the common belief that the Royal Navy was grossly undermanned and that the sailors it did have—forced into service by the hopelessly corrupt press gangs—were unskilled landsmen. He further claimed that British tactics favored war in distant parts where small enemy detachments could be confronted and overwhelmed. If faced with the full Spanish and French fleets, he was certain, Britain would retreat. "There is no instance I believe to be found in which the English fully risk an action at Sea but when they have the superiority of ships. In every case of inferiority or equality they either avoid an action or fight shy."[27] At first glance, it is hard to imagine that even Paine thought his anonymous pamphlet would have the desired effect. But Paine did wield the sword of persuasion—the quill pen—as well as virtually anyone of his age, even Burke, whose distinction at this time remained largely oratorical. And it is possible—since the full contents of the essay have been lost, we cannot know for certain—that Paine thought this pamphlet would do for Revolutionary France what the *Crisis* essays had done for war-torn America: namely, mobilize a hesitant populace for war. If this was in fact Paine's thinking, it was astonishingly naive and in some sense ill considered. A British enemy seeking to reclaim far-distant colonies was one thing; but a Britain defending her homeland altogether another. Indeed, the latter might have had precisely the consequence—through French defeat—Paine was trying to avoid in the first place. But the very fact that Paine was prepared to propose such a war, and to do so in such a way as to implicate both the Marquis de Lafayette and Short, is indicative of just how high the stakes in the Nootka Crisis had become for him.

By late summer, as the great powers appeared paralyzed with indecision and the danger of war dimmed, Paine turned more of his attention to the building of his bridge, and this would remain his principal undertaking until the appearance of Burke's *Reflections* in the fall. But Paine's effort to influence international politics, brief though it was, offers some important insight into his larger imperial vision. Consider his suggestion that the Franco-Spanish assault be a naval assault. Here, the most fervent republican radical of his age is proposing not just war, but war using that most vital pillar of old-fashioned empire: naval power. Like most Anglo-American political thinkers, Paine was no friend of standing armies. But navies were a different matter. Power deployed for national defense—as opposed to domestic coercion—was necessarily naval power. And, for Paine, navies were not only essential ingredients in the familiar matrix of trade and security, they were also a vital outlet for domestic commerce and manufactures. It was precisely this fact, in his view, that explained the fundamental limitations of British power and the astounding promise of American power.

He first developed the point in his most familiar political statement, *Common Sense,* particularly the pamphlet's second half, which concerns not so much the failures of the British Crown or the collapse of the relationship between the mother country and her colonies, but rather the distinct qualities that made an independent American nation both possible and necessary. Paine was making an argument to people well-versed in the structural defense of empire, and it is to that defense that he turned when trying to convince his countrymen that, far from staring into a post-monarchical abyss, they were looking toward a new and prosperous world order. Regarding the possible loss of Britain's blue-water protections, for instance: "No country on the globe is so happily situated, so internally capable of raising a fleet as America," for "tar, timber, iron, and cordage are her natural produce. We need go abroad for nothing." Who needs the British Navy when everything needed to make a navy—and indeed the very same commodities on which British sea power had begun to rely—represented an independent America's imperial bounty?[28]

And it was not just in defense that these goods could benefit a newly independent America. It was also in the realm of commerce and manufactures. Shipbuilding, especially in an environment rich in naval stores, could give

America the commercial advantages formerly enjoyed by only the great trading powers of Europe. Indeed, it could do this to a degree unknown even to those European powers: "The Dutch, who make large profits by hiring out their ships of war to the Spaniards and Portuguese, are obliged to import most of the [ship-building] materials they use." America would have no such obligation. Hence, in building a navy, it could defend and enrich itself in a way that the empires of the Old World could only dream of. For it was precisely "the natural manufactory of this country [America]" which, at immense cost, gave the British Empire power to protect its colonial possessions. It was as if America could be no other than a great empire. It would need no hazardous and unpredictable Baltic or colonial trade for masts or cordage or tar. All of this could be supplied domestically, an advantage enjoyed by no European state (with the partial exception of Russia).[29]

This talk of ships and navies hardly sounds like the stuff of Painian statecraft, whatever form that might have taken. But in fact it was integral to Paine's understanding of the new order, particularly in the United States. Paine's point—aside from persuading skeptics that America would be safe after leaving the British Empire—was to establish the advantageous interconnectedness of trade, manufactures, and security. Like all Atlantic nations, America would have to build a navy. But unlike existing powers, it would be able to do so through free domestic commerce and manufactures. This is what we might call the perfect circle of Painian political economy. As Paine put it in *Common Sense,* in an America with abundant landed resources, "commerce and protection are united." Nothing could contrast more sharply with the political economy of the British Empire, where commerce and manufactures were entirely a function of protection. With no Royal Navy, there would be no safe Atlantic sea-lanes, and without safe sea-lanes, the cost of imports would rise, manufacturing would suffer, the populace would fall to idleness, and the government would be left to expend its limited resources on protecting itself from enemies within. To put the equation a little differently, it is clear that whatever form Paine's American Empire would take, it would rest on the capacity of Americans to extract commodities from the American hinterland. Doing so would facilitate national security, but also, crucially, commerce.

And of course Paine shared the liberal notion that trade was a fundamentally pacifying force. This kind of market sentimentalism is especially pronounced in *Common Sense,* where Paine struggles to counter two seemingly intertwined dangers of independence: that it could yield chaos and civil war, and that it could leave America vulnerable to imperializing European powers. The problem was that an armed populace wracked by the divisive imperial crisis would likely come to blows, but an unarmed populace would be vulnerable to foreign invasion. To address this conundrum, Paine orchestrated an exceptional pas de deux. On the one hand, America need not fear civil war as long as it had commerce, for "the more a country is peopled, the smaller their armies are." The reason is that trade is a "consequence of population," and the more people engage in trade, the more they "become too much absorbed in trade to attend to any thing else. Commerce diminishes the spirit, both of patriotism [a term analogous for Paine to 'tribalism'] and military defense."[30] Free countries have commensurately small armies because their populations are too distracted with the demands of trade to threaten the standing order. Commerce, in other words, may be fed by the material requirements of hard power, but ultimately it diminishes the need for hard power. This sort of "creative destruction"—liberalized commerce leading to the demise of the coercive instruments of old empire—remained integral to Paine's thinking and casts his call for war in a somewhat more reasonable light. Much as Spanish diplomats had tried to persuade their French counterparts eleven years earlier, he assumed that the interconnectedness of trade and security meant that the mere threat of Franco-Spanish attack would play devastatingly on British vulnerabilities. As long as the Royal Navy was detained defending its home shores, it was not protecting the very trade channels from which it drew material sustenance. And without that free movement of goods, the dominoes of Painian political economy fall: manufactures decline; populations become underemployed and restless; governments expend increasingly scarce resources maintaining order at home; and the security sustaining overseas trade collapses. The larger point here is that, much like that of Smith, Jefferson, and other exponents of sentimentalizing trade, Paine's statecraft presumed the interdependence of commerce and security.

For Jefferson, the Nootka Crisis was really the first serious international incident of his term as secretary of state. After returning to the United States in the fall of 1789 and traveling to New York to assume his secretaryship in March of 1790, he was initially consumed with the familiar problems of British posts in the Old Northwest, control of the Mississippi River, and the British trade monopoly. But not long into his term, he began to receive reports that the Pitt administration was preparing for war. Among the first such reports was that of John Rutledge, who sat in the House gallery as Pitt delivered the king's address to the Commons. The speech put forth the claims against Spain and called for immediate mobilization for war. Rutledge reported to Jefferson that he had dined with a group of British gentlemen after the speech and, not surprisingly, was mortified by their sympathy, not to say blind enthusiasm, for the Crown's position:

> In my life I do not remember to have been amongst such insolent bullies. They were all for war, talked much of *Old England* and the *British Lion,* laughed at the Idea of drubbing the Dons, began to calculate the millions of dollars they would be obliged to pay for having insulted *the first power on Earth,* and seemed uneasy lest the Spaniards should be alarmed at the British strength, ask pardon for what they have done and come immediately to terms.[31]

Jefferson likely received this letter and additional updates from Gouverneur Morris by early June, and within a month he was advising the president on how best to proceed.

Amid the usual political intrigue of the Washington cabinet—Hamilton, it seems, was colluding with a British agent to steer American policy toward Britain[32]—Jefferson formulated the administration's position on the impending war. Officially, it would be one of neutrality. But unofficially, it would favor Spain. The opportunity to leverage some kind of covert alliance in exchange for free use of the Mississippi was something Jefferson and Washington simply could not refuse.[33] Similarly, the possibility that Spain would make additional concessions, such as the granting of independence to Florida or Louisiana, also appealed to the administration. Continued British recalcitrance on Atlantic trade only heightened the importance of a freer, more independent American periphery. Of course, the real engine of policy was not the promise of victory's spoils but the fear of British empire. Should Britain prevail and displace Spain from North America, it would control the Floridas, the entire Mississippi basin, and the port of New Orleans. For Jefferson, the perils were obvious. Britain would then

> take from the remaining part of our States the markets they now have for their produce by furnishing those markets cheaper with the same articles. Tobacco, rice, indigo, bread, lumber, naval stores, furs.
> She will have then possessions double the size of ours, as good in soil and climate.
> She will encircle us completely, by these possessions on our landboard, and her fleets on our sea-board.[34]

In terms of unofficial policy, then, neither Jefferson nor Washington was particularly interested in the far Northwest and its sea otters. The threat of war was fundamentally a threat to inland American commerce and, in turn, a threat to continued American independence. This was not, as we have seen, some sort of irrational Jeffersonian paranoia. The Americans appear not to have known about the advances of the King George's Sound Company, but they well knew about Cook's voyages and subsequent British efforts to fill the commercial and geopolitical vacuum that was the North Pacific. They also well knew that British success could have staggering implications for the global power balance. As Edmund Burke remarked in May of 1790:

> I do indeed apprehend, that if [Spain] thought we had formed a Systematick Scheme of a connected chain of establishments, beginning at [Tierra del Fuego], and ending at Nootka Sound, and by a port in the Sandwich Islands commencing a regular establishment in the South Sea, that Court [of Spain] would rather put every thing to hazard, than suffer such a line of circumvallation to be drawn about their colonies, which must put them to an expence above their powers, to prevent smuggling in time of peace, and to provide for their security in time of War. On the South Sea side, they are beyond imagination weak; and our vast Strength in the East Indies adds to their comparative debility.[35]

The prospect that the Pacific would displace the Atlantic as the chief locus of British empire building, in other words, was entirely plausible. If we step back from the hothouse of wartime policy making and look at Jefferson's broader perspective on the West, it is thus difficult not to conclude that he was deeply troubled by the prospect of any sort of British colonization in North America—whether in Florida or at Nootka Sound. As early as 1783 he had questioned the widely broadcast scientific character of British exploration in the Pacific. The British "pretend it is only to promote knowledge," he wrote to George Rogers Clark, but "I am afraid they have thoughts of colonizing into that quarter."[36] Aside from the possibility that such ventures would lead to permanent settlements, there was the added fear that they would uncover the long-sought strategic river passage linking the Mississippi to the Pacific. This, in turn, could afford Britain the very same kinds of colonizing possibilities the Ohio River had afforded the United States. Except that with Pacific access such colonies would be able to dispose of their produce in the enormous and lucrative markets of China. The possibility of such a water route west—disproved only after the Lewis and Clark expedition—even further heightened the dangers of British control of the Mississippi. Not only would it mean sharply limited outlets for American farmers in the Old Northwest, it would also mean the prospect of enormous enrichment of the British Empire. To be able to freely move goods from the American hinterland to Asia was precisely the prospect that made Nootka Sound and the Northwest Coast trade of such vital strategic potential.

Jefferson's policy, intended as it was to avoid open war while allowing continued American expansion westward, was fundamentally an effort to forestall these dangerous eventualities. Of course, as Hamilton never tired of observing, it was all very utopian—the idea that simple trade and the organic, self-generated expansion of settlements would produce the effects that colonies had achieved for other empires. But, if nothing else, Jefferson's imperial vision—as Peter Onuf and others have observed—was fundamentally anti-British. In other words, Jefferson's "Empire for Liberty" was not simply an artifact of political expediency or an ex post facto rationale for an expansionist political economy. Nor did it represent the kind of anticolonial posture scholars have begun identifying in Enlightenment-era figures such as Kant, Diderot, Rousseau, and Hume. This critique rests on its own alternate imperial vision.[37] That vision is imperial without being coercive, commercial without being mercantile, and expansive without being colonial. That is, in place of formally established colonies, it rested on an organic process of settlement and assimilation. That process was to be facilitated by commerce. Through trade, inconvenient ethnic or cultural conflicts (such as that between Native peoples and European settlers) would be overcome; sociability would be rewarded; and diverse communities unified under a halo of shared commercial interests would forge just, stable, and noncoercive institutions of government.

Thus, the familiar British imperial order is set on its head: governments do not precede trade, they are its byproduct. And for this reason, such governments—as conceived by sentimental liberals of the Jeffersonian and (as is being suggested in this essay) the Painian stripe—rest on the natural, sociable inclinations of commercial people rather than the coercive mechanisms of imperial states. Fundamental to this imperial vision was free commerce—which is, of course, very different from free markets. And free commerce required those arteries of circulation, rational intercourse, or whatever other bodily metaphor we might employ to signify the gentle, civilizing effects of human truck and barter. One need not probe too deeply into the eighteenth-century inclination to understand political economy in terms comparable to those that appeared to drive the biological universe to see that Jefferson's imperial vision was one dependent on natural circulation. Hence his position with respect to the Mississippi: it was not only that farmers inhabiting the American hinterland would have an outlet for their produce, it was also the logic and symmetry of it all: goods moving down the Ohio to the Mississippi and then to markets in New Orleans and the West Indies would flow much like fluids in the body. And that flow—rather like water on a plant—was precisely what allowed the slow, organic, and peaceful expansion of Jeffersonian empire.

As should now be fairly clear, Paine's concerns with respect to the Nootka Crisis did not in any obvious way cross the Atlantic. To be sure, he feared the reassertion of British empire, but he never much struggled with the precise implications of this for the United States. This should not lead us to conclude that Paine had simply left the New World. His principal preoccupation during the months of the Nootka Crisis—the iron bridge he was building—is indicative of his own sense of just how a large-scale commercial empire would come to be. Much like Jefferson and Washington, Paine saw the new republican imperial process as a function of infrastructure—the mechanisms by which producers would move goods to consumers. But unlike Jefferson and Washington, he understood those mechanisms to be unnatural. That is to say, the corresponding expansion of American settlement and commerce would occur not *because* of the continent's grand river routes, but in spite of those routes. For Paine, rivers were as much inhibitors of commerce as they were its facilitators, and only when farmers, miners, artisans, and other producers could safely and freely cross them—without fear of extortionist ferrymen or deadly spring floods and winter ice floes—would commerce move freely across the American continent. If Jefferson's notion of continental empire was in part a function of his experience as a Virginian, so Paine's appears to have been partly a reflection of his time in Philadelphia. For at some level, the prospects of Pennsylvania and its capital city would rise and fall with the riverine barriers its citizens daily confronted.

The problem was made acutely clear to Paine as he contemplated the party divisions that seemed to paralyze the Pennsylvania legislature in the years after the War for Independence. As he put it in a letter to his political ally Daniel Clymer of Berks County, "It was my intention at the conclusion of the war to have laid down the pen, and satisfied myself with silently beholding the prosperity of the country, in whose difficulties I had borne my share, and in the raising of which to an independent Empire, I had added my mite." But wishes only seldom come true. Paine now confronted no independent empire, but a factionalized and economically stagnant collection of commercial and political islands. One of the problems was that familiar inhibitor of rational circulation and fruitful commerce, the Susquehanna River.

For this natural obstruction meant that those backcountry residents of Pennsylvania who by all natural inclination ought to be invested in the commercial life of the provincial capital at Philadelphia, instead took their business to Baltimore. They are simply "beyond the reach and circle of that commercial intercourse which takes place between all the counties on [the east] side [of] the Susquehanna," Paine wrote. Their representatives thus come to Philadelphia with no particular interest in the commercial welfare of the state as a whole. So vested are their voters' interests in Baltimore's markets that they "may probably think it would be no disadvantage to their situation if the Delaware, through which all the produce of the Counties east of the Susquehanna were exported, were shut up."[38]

A more vivid illustration of the Achilles heel of continental empire can hardly be imagined. Unable to do business in the capital of their province, these Pennsylvania farmers grow politically alienated. In place of citizens with vested interests in their political communities, they become a faction whose allegiance will only be secured through politics and force. The pacifying, civilizing effects of commerce are lost. And all because western Pennsylvanians are unable to cross a river. Paine's iron bridge, originally intended for the Schuylkill, would solve such problems. It would transform an inland archipelago into the kind of integrated continental empire he and Jefferson assumed would be the foundation of American nationhood.[39]

Among the most lasting assessments of Tom Paine was John Adams's view that the corset maker turned pamphleteer appeared to have had "a better Hand at pulling down than building." The perspective persisted for at least two centuries. As Bernard Bailyn wrote of *Common Sense* thirty years ago, the pamphlet's aim was not to "probe difficult, urgent, and controversial questions and make appropriate recommendations," but to "tear the world apart—the world as it was known and as it was constituted."[40] Another perspective, more common among Paine's many biographers and modern admirers, is that Paine somehow transcended his age, that his ideas were so trenchant, so modern, so powerfully formulated that they tell us as much about who *we* are as they do about Paine. In this vein, Paine's most recent biographer has written, "It could be said that the most significant reason to read the works of Thomas Paine today is as an act of fealty, for anyone living in a modern nation will already know by heart every one of his ideas and innovations, as they have been so completely adopted by modern government and society as to seem as though never needing invention, as sui generis as Newton's gravity or Priestley's Oxygen."[41]

The purpose of this essay has not been to disprove either of these interpretations. Paine certainly loathed the old order and perhaps more than any of his contemporaries was prepared to advance its destruction; similarly, none of us with an interest in Paine can help but be moved by the incredible modern resonance of much that he wrote. Nonetheless, there is value in detaching Paine from some of the clichés that have so shaped contemporary interpretations of his particular radicalism. In aligning him with Jefferson, I am not suggesting that he was a Jeffersonian in any strict sense of the term; nor am I suggesting that Jefferson the planter and slaveholder was a Painite. Rather, I am suggesting that, much like Jefferson, Paine practiced a distinctly eighteenth-century brand of statecraft, inflected on the one hand by the kinds of utopian notions about commerce, markets, and governments so familiar among the so-called "system-builders" of the age. And on the other, that statecraft betrayed a genuine concern with the realities of power and its disposition. Armaments, naval stores, iron bridges, taxation, the global jockeying for power, and the recognition that America's principal asset was not technology, not liquid capital, not underemployed masses, but its hinterland, was as central to Paine's vision of American development as it was to Jefferson's. In this sense, Paine was more Jeffersonian than we have recognized. But perhaps more importantly, Jefferson was more of a Painite than we conventionally assume. As Gordon Wood has observed, "If Jefferson had ever written out in any systematic way what he believed about politics, it would have resembled much of [Paine's] *Rights of Man*."[42] At the end of the day, even the most radical of revolutionaries must find the way to institutional stability and longevity. They must, in other words, become builders—builders of governments and builders of the infrastructure that make governments sustainable.

NOTES

For his careful reading of this paper and for saving me from several interpretive and factual errors, I am deeply indebted to Professor P. J. Marshall. I am also grateful to Professor H. T. Dickinson for his immensely helpful suggestions about the British side of the Nootka Controversy. I, of course, am alone responsible for any remaining errors.

1. Harold Adams Innis, *The Fur Trade in Canada: An Introduction to Canadian Economic History* (1930; repr., Toronto: University of Toronto Press, 1999), 3.

2. See, for example, Virginia DeJohn Anderson, *Creatures of Empire: How Domestic Animals Transformed Early America* (New York: Oxford University Press, 2004); Andrew C. Isenberg, *The Destruction of the Bison: An Environmental History, 1750–1920* (New York: Cambridge University Press, 2000); and Eric Jay Dolan, *Leviathan: A History of Whaling in America* (New York: W. W. Norton, 2007).

3. It should be acknowledged that Paine also feared that the British mobilization for war would delay his efforts to build an iron-arched bridge across the Thames (see Paine to Washington, 31 May 1790, in *The Complete Writings of Thomas Paine,* ed. Philip S. Foner, 2 vols. [New York: Citadel Press, 1945] [hereafter cited as *Complete Writings*], 2:1305).

4. For a rare exception to this tendency, see David M. Fitzsimons, "Tom Paine's New World Order: Idealistic Internationalism in the Ideology of Early American Foreign Relations," *Diplomatic History* 19, no. 4 (1995): 569–82.

5. The classic and still influential account is Drew R. McCoy, *The Elusive Republic: Political Economy in Jeffersonian America* (Chapel Hill: University of North Carolina Press, 1980).

6. Adam Smith, *An Inquiry into the Nature and Causes of the Wealth of Nations: A Selected Edition* (Oxford: Oxford University Press, 1993), 21.

7. Peter Onuf, *Jefferson's Empire: The Language of American Nationhood* (Charlottesville: University Press of Virginia, 2000), esp. chap. 2; Onuf, "'Empire for Liberty': Center and Peripheries in Postcolonial America," in *Negotiated Empires: Centers and Peripheries in the Americas, 1500–1820,* ed. Christine Daniels and Michael V. Kennedy (New York: Routledge, 2002), 301–17; Robert W. Tucker and David C. Hendrickson, *Empire of Liberty: The Statecraft of Thomas Jefferson* (New York: Oxford University Press, 1990). Also, J. G. A. Pocock, "States, Republics, and Empires: The American Founding in Early Modern Perspective," in *Conceptual Change and the Constitution,* ed. Terence Ball and J. G. A. Pocock (Lawrence: University Press of Kansas, 1988), esp. 66–73. For the colonial antecedents of these debates, see Jack P. Greene, *Peripheries and Center: Constitutional Development in the Extended Polities of the British Empire and the United States, 1607–1788* (Athens: University of Georgia Press, 1986), esp. chap. 6; J. G. A. Pocock, "Political Thought in the English-speaking Atlantic, 1760–1790, Part 1: The Imperial Crisis," in *The Varieties of British Political Thought, 1500–1800,* ed. J. G. A. Pocock (Cambridge: Cambridge University Press, 1993), 246–82; David Armitage, *The Ideological Origins of the British Empire* (Cambridge: Cambridge University Press, 2000), chap. 7; Craig Yirush, *Settlers, Liberty, and Empire: The Roots of Early American Political Theory, 1675–1775* (New York: Cambridge University Press, 2011); and Joyce Appleby, *Capitalism and a New Social Order: The Republican Vision of the 1790s* (New York: New York University Press, 1984).

8. Although it should be noted that Paine's *Agrarian Justice* (1797) is no defense of European continental cultivation, but an argument for natural equality, drawn from natural jurisprudence and a liberal commercial ideal (see Gregory Claeys, *Thomas Paine: Social and Political Thought* [Boston: Unwin, Hyman, 1989]).

9. On Cook at Nootka, see Robin Fisher, "Cook and the Nootka," in *Captain James Cook and his Times,* ed. Robin Fischer and Hugh Johnson (Vancouver: Douglas and McIntyre, 1979), 81–98.

10. Warren L. Cook, *Flood Tide of Empire: Spain and the Pacific Northwest, 1543–1819* (New Haven, Conn.: Yale University Press, 1973), 43–44.

11. James King, *Captain Cook's Third and Last Voyage to the Pacific Ocean* (Philadelphia, 1793), 248.

12. Cook, *Flood Tide of Empire*, 100–107; Edward G. Gray, *The Making of John Ledyard: Empire and Ambition in the Life of an Early American Traveler* (New Haven, Conn.: Yale University Press, 2007), chap. 6.

13. See Tom McFeat, comp., *Indians of the North Pacific Coast* (1967; Seattle: University of Washington Press, 1971), esp. 72–80; and Leland Donald, *Aboriginal Slavery on the Northwest Coast of North America* (Berkeley: University of California Press, 1997).

14. This is not to say that Spain had no reason to fear British aggression in far-distant lands of no obvious strategic value. Indeed, the Nootka Crisis bore a striking resemblance to a similar struggle over what Samuel Johnson called "a few spots of earth, which in the deserts of the ocean had almost escaped human notice." Twenty years earlier, Britain threatened war against France and Spain after the governor of Buenos Aires ordered Spanish troops to evict a British garrison from the island of West Falkland. I am indebted to Professor Gabriel Paquette of the Johns Hopkins University History Department for pointing this out to me. Johnson is quoted in Nicholas Tracy, "The Falkland Islands Crisis of 1770; Use of Naval Force," *The English Historical Review* 90 (January 1975): 40. For a useful interpretation of the eighteenth-century Anglo-Spanish rivalry, see Alan Frost, "The Spanish Yoke: British Schemes to Revolutionise Spanish America, 1739–1807," in *Pacific Empires: Essays in Honour of Glyndwr Williams,* ed. Alan Frost and Jane Samson (Vancouver: UBC Press, 1999), 33–52.

15. Quoted in Cook, *Flood Tide of Empire,* 130. On Spanish economic concerns, see ibid., 88–89; and J. H. Elliott, *Empires of the Atlantic World: Britain and Spain in America, 1492–1830* (New Haven, Conn.: Yale University Press, 2006), 353–68.

16. The firm's name, the King George's Sound Company (also known as the London Company), was based on Cook's initial name for what soon thereafter came to be called Nootka Sound.

17. On Meares's colonizing scheme, see Barry M. Gough, *The Northwest Coast: British Navigation, Trade, and Discoveries to 1812* (Vancouver: UBC Press, 1992), chap. 6; and on the proposal to found penal colonies on the Northwest Coast, see Pat Wilson and Richard H. Dillon, "Documents: A Plan for Convict Colonies in Canada," *The Americas* 13 (October 1956): 187–98. Alan Frost sees Britain's plans for colonial advance on the Northwest Coast as part of a larger, more concerted, and more entrenched plan to capture Spanish American markets for British manufactured goods (see, for example, Alan Frost, *The Global Reach of Empire: Britain's Maritime Expansion in the Indian and Pacific Oceans, 1764–1815* [Melbourne: Miegunyah Press, 2003], 217–29).

18. Boyd Hilton, *A Mad, Bad, and Dangerous People? England, 1783–1846* (Oxford: Oxford University Press, 2006), 58–59.

19. Samuel Flagg Bemis, *The Jay Treaty: A Study in Commerce and Diplomacy,* rev. ed. (New Haven, Conn.: Yale University Press, 1962), 71, 70–85. More generally on Britain and the Nootka Affair, see William Ray Manning, "The Nootka Sound Controversy," *Annual Report of the American Historical Association for the Year 1904* (Washington, D.C.:

Government Printing Office, 1905), 279–478; Vincent Todd Harlow, *The Founding of the Second British Empire, 1763–1793* (London: Longmans, Green, 1952), vol. 2, chap. 7; Jeremy Black, *British Foreign Policy in an Age of Revolution, 1783–1793* (Cambridge: Cambridge University Press, 1994), chap. 5; Frost, *The Global Reach of Empire,* chap. 9; and Stanley Elkins and Eric McKitrick, *The Age Federalism: The Early American Republic, 1788–1800* (New York: Oxford University Press, 1993), 212–23. More generally on the role of British naval deterrence, see Paul Kennedy, *The Rise and Fall of British Naval Mastery* (London: Allen Lane, 1976), esp. 121–22. Though not dealing with the Nootka Crisis specifically, two additional essays have shaped my interpretation of the government's response: P. J. Marshall, "Britain's American Problem: The International Perspective," and Paul W. Mapp, "The Revolutionary War and Europe's Great Powers," both in the *Oxford Handbook of the American Revolution,* ed. Edward G. Gray and Jane Kamensky (New York: Oxford University Press, 2013).

20. On Meares's skillful exploitation of the government's political vulnerabilities to his own advantage, see John M. Norris, "The Policy of the British Cabinet in the Nootka Crisis," *English Historical Review* 70 (October 1955): 562–80.

21. *A Diary of the French Revolution by Gouverneur Morris, 1752–1816,* ed. Beatrix Cary Davenport, 2 vols. (Boston: Houghton Mifflin, 1939), 1:510.

22. *Address to the Addressers,* in *Complete Writings,* 2:497–98.

23. Paine to Short, 1 June 1790, ibid., 2:1306–7; also see Harold W. Landin, "Some Letters of Thomas Paine and William Short on the Nootka Sound Crisis," *Journal of Modern History* 13 (September 1941): 357–74.

24. Short to Paine, 8 June 1790, in Landin, "Some Letters of Thomas Paine," 368.

25. In Morris's diary entry for 15 August 1790 he writes that "Paine, who was with me [at a meeting with the French agent in London], had shown a paper which he had written, and which Lafayette had caused to be translated and published, recommending an attack in the Channel by the combined fleets." Morris may have been mistaken—perhaps misled by Paine—since no evidence of any such translation exists (see *The Diary and Letters of Gouverneur Morris,* ed. Anne Cary Morris, 2 vols. [New York: C. Scribner's Sons, 1888], 1:340–41; see also Howard V. Evans, "The Nootka Sound Controversy in Anglo-French Diplomacy—1790," *Journal of Modern History* 46 [December 1974]: 609–40). On earlier Franco-Spanish plans to attack England, see Jonathan R. Dull, *A Diplomatic History of the American Revolution* (New Haven, Conn.: Yale University Press, 1985), 108–9; and Margaret Cotter Morison, "The Duc de Choiseul and the Invasion of England, 1768–1770," *Transactions of the Royal Historical Society,* 3rd ser., 4 (1910): 83–115.

26. Paine to Short, 22 June 1790, in *Complete Writings,* 2:1309–10.

27. Paine to Short, 24 and 25 June 1790, ibid., 2:1312.

28. *Common Sense,* in *Thomas Paine: Collected Writings,* ed. Eric Foner (New York: Library of America, 1995) [hereafter cited as *Collected Writings*], 38.

29. Ibid., 38–39. Also, on Paine's political economy, see Donald Winch, *Riches and*

Poverty: An Intellectual History of Political Economy in Britain, 1750–1834 (Cambridge: Cambridge University Press, 1996), esp. 127–56.

30. Paine, *Common Sense,* in *Collected Writings,* 42.

31. Rutledge to Thomas Jefferson [TJ], 6 May 1790, *The Papers of Thomas Jefferson,* ed. Julian P. Boyd et al., 39 vols. to date (Princeton, N.J.: Princeton University Press, 1950–) [hereafter cited as *Jefferson Papers*], 16:414.

32. See the "Editorial Note," ibid., 17:35–108. On Hamilton's role in the crisis, also see John Lamberton Harper, *American Machiavelli: Alexander Hamilton and the Origins of U.S. Foreign Policy* (Cambridge: Cambridge University Press, 2004), chaps. 5–6.

33. For a superb synopsis of Jefferson's concerns about navigation in the Mississippi, see Jenry Morsman, "Securing America: Jefferson's Fluid Plans for the Western Perimeter," in *Across the Continent: Jefferson, Lewis and Clark, and the Making of America,* ed. Douglas Seefeldt et al. (Charlottesville: University of Virginia Press, 2005), 45–83.

34. Secretary of State [TJ] to the President, enclosing Opinion, 12 July 1790, *Jefferson Papers,* 17:109.

35. Paine to the Earl of Charlemont, 25 May 1790, in *The Correspondence of Edmund Burke,* ed. Thomas W. Copeland et al., 10 vols. (Cambridge: Cambridge University Press; Chicago: University of Chicago Press, 1958–78), 6:118.

36. TJ to Clark, 4 December 1783, *Jefferson Papers,* 6:371. On Jefferson's fears about British activity in the Pacific, see Alan Taylor, "Jefferson's Pacific: The Science of Distant Empire, 1768–1811," in *Across the Continent,* ed. Douglas Seefeldt et al., 16–44.

37. On Enlightenment anti-imperialism, see Sankar Muthu, *Enlightenment against Empire* (Princeton, N.J.: Princeton University Press, 2003); and Emma Rothschild, "David Hume and the Seagods of the Atlantic," in *The Atlantic Enlightenment,* ed. Susan Manning and Francis D. Cogliano (Aldershot, U.K.: Ashgate, 2008), 81–96.

38. Paine to Daniel Clymer, [September?] 1786, *Complete Writings,* 2:1256.

39. On Paine's iron bridge, see Edward Gray, *Thomas Paine's Iron Bridge: A Story of Architecture, Politics, and the Invention of a Revolutionary New Society* (New York: W. W. Norton, forthcoming).

40. *Adams Family Correspondence,* ed. L. H. Butterfield, Marc Friedlaender, and Richard Alan Ryerson, 10 vols. (Cambridge, Mass.: Harvard University Press, 1963–2011), 1:363; Bernard Bailyn, "*Common Sense,*" in *Fundamental Testaments of the American Revolution* (Washington, D.C.: Library of Congress, 1973), 20.

41. Craig Nelson, *Thomas Paine: Enlightenment, Revolution, and the Birth of Modern Nations* (New York: Viking, 2006), 338.

42. Gordon Wood, *Revolutionary Characters: What Made the Founders Different* (New York: Penguin Press, 2006), 213.

Thomas Paine and Jeffersonian America

EMMA MACLEOD

> The independence of America, considered merely as a separation from England, would have been a matter but of little importance, had it not been accompanied by a revolution in the principles and practice of governments. . . . Government founded on a *moral theory, on a system of universal peace, on the indefeasible hereditary Rights of Man*, is now revolving from west to east, by a stronger impulse than the government of the sword revolved from east to west.
>
> —Thomas Paine, *Rights of Man, Part Second*

THUS THOMAS PAINE opened the second part of his best-selling work, *Rights of Man*, which was published in February 1792 and which is often characterized as a key text in the British debate on the revolution in France, but in which Paine was in fact much more concerned to present America as a model republican government than to defend Revolutionary France.[1] To Paine, America was a glorious demonstration of republican principles successfully at work, a practical example for other states to imitate. His aspirations for the new republic were expressed in a prolific stream of journalism and personal correspondence from the time he arrived in America in 1774 until the end of his life. However, he had left the United States in 1787 and did not return until 1802, having spent most of the intervening period in France. During that time, the new American Constitution had been ratified and the administrations of George Washington and John Adams had governed America. Paine was highly critical of both administrations in certain respects, and he feared that the American republic was drifting from his view of its founding principles. In March 1801, however, Paine's friend, Thomas Jefferson, was sworn in as the third American president. Paine hoped that under him the United States would return to his understanding of its original vision. This essay is an attempt to explore how far Jeffersonian America matched up to Paine's hopes for the republic.

Paine's personal history and experience of America naturally colored his views substantially. On the one hand, as an enormously influential propagandist during the American Revolution, he took great pride in the new republic, and he was convinced that the United States had an extremely important role to play in the world. He had also known, corresponded with, and admired Jefferson, the American minister in Paris, at least since Paine had arrived in that city in 1787.[2] In turn, Jefferson had invited Paine to return to America in 1801 in the face of powerful detractors, and had treated him with respect and sympathy. However, Paine was bitter about his treatment by many other Americans, including the Washington administration, which had allowed him to languish in the Luxembourg prison in Paris, in fear for his life, at the height of the French Revolutionary Terror, not pressing the case that Paine was an American citizen, rather than British, and ought to be released. Paine was also unhappy with Congress in general for failing to honor him properly, either verbally or materially, for his services during the American Revolution. His unhappiness was further extended to the various individuals who had crossed him throughout his American career. He therefore balanced great enthusiasm for his adopted country and its government under Jefferson with a sense of resentment and disillusionment. "America is not the same agreeable Country as when I left it," he wrote in October 1803.[3]

Paine's experience of Revolutionary Europe between 1787 and 1802 is also relevant to his opinions on the United States. How his experience of Revolutionary America was brought to bear on his thinking on the political situations in France and Britain in the 1790s is relatively familiar—for example, his attack on monarchy and hereditary government, his argument that no generation can dictate to its successors, and his demand for popular sovereignty and representative government. He himself emphasized the importance of America to his political thought thereafter.[4] Less often considered, perhaps, is how Revolutionary Europe affected his attitudes toward the new American republic.[5] Gary Kates and Mark Philp, on the other hand, have argued that Paine's thinking was at least crystallized, and perhaps even made more radical, by his experience of the French Revolution, which raises the question of to what extent he applied these ideas in turn to republican America.[6] Paine expressed the hope, in the first part of *Rights of Man* (1791), of "seeing the New World regenerate the Old."[7] Did his reflections on the Old World of the 1790s help to "regenerate" his ideas about the New?

The wider group of British and Irish radicals who emigrated to America to escape the political turbulence of Britain in the 1790s, whose stories Michael Durey has so helpfully uncovered, were sometimes disappointed with the reality of the new American state. It is difficult to study the careers of many of these men and their families without realizing that the America they experienced was often rather different from the republican utopia they had so eagerly anticipated. Ironically, this was perhaps partly because of the very optimistic analysis of the American government presented in Paine's *Rights of Man*.[8] While there are certainly prominent examples of British and Irish radical immigrants who flourished in their adopted country, such as the lawyers Thomas Addis Emmet and William Sampson and the physician William James MacNeven, "a wider focus . . . strongly suggests that failure was as common as triumph among the exiles." The radicals had escaped to America just as the French Revolution was inspiring fear of radicalism and repression there, as well as in Britain.[9] Was Paine, who had regarded himself as an American citizen since 1776, able to draw on greater reserves of optimism than some of the other British exiles as he viewed his adopted country in the Jeffersonian era?[10]

This essay will therefore begin by surveying Paine's aspirations for the American republic. It moves on to examine his criticisms of American government in the 1790s, before studying his analysis of the state of the union in the first decade of the nineteenth century, concluding that, on balance, Paine's personal investment in America, together with his disappointment in France and his general satisfaction with the work of the Jefferson administration, allowed him to find a greater measure of contentment concerning American politics by that time.

Paine's ambitions for the American republic naturally developed and expanded over the years, partly as a result of his experience of Revolutionary Europe between 1787 and 1802. Self-government was, of course, his original aim for America, as he argued in *Common Sense* (1776); but already in *Common Sense*, and then in successive publications, as the need to demand self-government became redundant, he moved on to discuss the nature of the American constitution.[11] Paine urged the need for a formal constitution, agreed upon by representatives of all the states acting in concert. "The American constitutions [state and federal]," he famously wrote in *Rights of Man*, "were to liberty, what a grammar is to language."[12] He insisted that the form of this autonomous American government must be representative and rest entirely on popular sovereignty, rather than contain any hint of hereditary rule. "When we are planning for posterity," he warned the Revolutionary generation, "we ought to remember that virtue is not hereditary," and therefore safeguards needed to be raised against power being abused by any element of the government.[13] Popular sovereignty was both designed by nature and established by right after the Revolution, and it was the best method of ensuring good and just government. "It is always the interest of a far greater number of people in a nation to have things right," Paine wrote in 1792, "than to let them remain wrong."[14] Representative government, in turn, was the best means of guaranteeing popular sovereignty in a nation too large to accommodate the simple democracy of the ancient city republics—so that, as he wrote, "What Athens was in miniature, America will be in magnitude."[15]

Paine's experience of the revolution in France, however, seems to have persuaded him that government should be based not just on a large and equal representation, but upon universal manhood suffrage. He had not specified the desirability of a vote for every man in *Common Sense* or his other political writings of the 1770s and 1780s: it might not always happen, he had pointed out in *Common Sense,* that the multitude should be "a body of reasonable men." Moreover, although he argued in "A Serious Address to the People of Pennsylvania" (1778) that all independent men (whom he defined as those not in service with a family or in public office), even those who were poor, should be qualified to vote, he was heard to express doubts as late as 1790 about the wisdom of allowing the majority to rule.[16] The events of the French Revolution, however, propelled him to the view that a universal male franchise was necessary in order to protect the people from arbitrary government and to ensure the protection of the interests of all, and not just of those qualified to vote. Kates shows that after Louis XVI's flight to Varennes in October 1791, Paine became convinced of the need for a fully democratic republican system of government.[17] By the time he wrote his *Dissertation on First Principles of Government* (1795), he was even more explicit:

> The true and only true basis of representative government is equality of rights. Every man has a right to one vote, and no more in the choice of representatives. . . . It is dangerous and impolitic, sometimes ridiculous, and always unjust to make property the criterion of the right of voting. . . . The right of voting is the primary right by which other rights are protected. To take away this right is to reduce a man to slavery.[18]

In the second part of *Rights of Man,* Paine confidently asserted that "it is on this system that the American government is founded. It is a representation ingrafted upon democracy." When he came to write the much more detailed and precise defense of universal suffrage in the *Dissertation on First Principles of Government,* however, he made no such direct comparison with or claim for the American republic. Nonetheless, he later declared that he had been anxious and "watchful" while he wrote these works, lest the American republic diverge from its libertarian beginnings.[19]

Paine also argued persistently that religious toleration should be enshrined in the new American constitutions. He insisted that the "free exercise of religion, according to the dictates of conscience" was to be secured to all men, "above all things."[20] Americans had observed the disadvantages of uniting church and state in England, and had separated the two in their new republic.[21] Paine also wanted freedom of the press, the rights to security of the individual and of his property, the rule of law, and low taxation.

Evidence that "the individual" in this case should include black men as well as white is not substantial, despite Paine's reputation for supporting the abolition of slavery, though he clearly opposed slavery in his private writings. He briefly attended meetings of the antislavery society in Philadelphia in 1787, and he expressed careful sympathy with the slave rebellion on Santo Domingo in 1791. Presumably, he approved of the French abolition of slavery there in 1794, although he does not seem to have discussed either this or Napoleon's reintroduction of slavery there in 1802. James V. Lynch has cast serious doubt on Paine's reputation as an abolitionist based on his assumed authorship of two essays published in 1775 and of the preamble to the Pennsylvania Emancipation Act of 1780.[22] Even had he written all three, however, the evidence for Paine's abolitionism is relatively slight.

Next, Paine wanted to see America sustained by expansion across the rest of the North American continent, and by flourishing commercial relationships with other nations, rather than by any involvement in European military or political alliances. "Besides, what have we to do with setting the world at defiance?" he asked in *Common Sense*. "Our plan is commerce, and that, well attended to, will secure us the peace and friendship of all Europe."[23] In 1792, nearly a decade after American independence, and before the outbreak of war between Britain and Revolutionary France seemed likely, he suggested a naval alliance between Britain, France, America and, possibly, Holland, which would, he thought, in effect impose peace on the rest of the world and promote unprecedented commercial growth everywhere.[24]

More important than its more temporal international relations, however, Paine became convinced that America had a profoundly significant purpose to fulfill in the world. This was the dual role of providing an asylum for political and religious refugees fleeing persecution elsewhere, and of modeling a pattern of republican government for peoples elsewhere to learn from and emulate. In 1776, Paine had reminded his readers that since their earliest days, the American colonies had offered asylum to "the persecuted lovers of civil and religious liberty," and he urged the new republic to continue in this vocation.[25] However, at this stage, as Philp has pointed out, Paine believed the governments of Europe were too corrupted to be reformed, and he saw America as atypical in its youth and purity.[26] As he watched the trajectory of the French Revolution, however, he came to see America as a political exemplar to the world. America had "made a stand, not for herself only, but for the world, and looked beyond the advantages herself could receive." America's was a revolution of international proportions and implications that had shaken up the science of government for the first time in many generations.[27] By 1791, the American Revolution had inspired another dramatic political transformation, in France, and Paine hoped that both would inspire the institution of representative government throughout Europe. "Never did so great an opportunity offer itself to England, and to all Europe, as is produced by the two revolutions of America and France."[28] Later, when the French political upheaval became a difficult model to defend, he emphasized the credibility and stability of the American pattern.

"I am not an ambitious man," Paine told James Monroe in 1794, "but perhaps I have been an ambitious American. I have wished to see America the *Mother Church* of government, and I have done my utmost to exalt her character and her condition."[29] He watched his adopted country intently and anxiously during the 1790s and beyond for evidence that it was living up to his hopes for its safeguarding of political and civil liberties, and for its place in the world.

Paine's main criticisms of the American republic were directed at the domestic and foreign policies of the Washington and Adams administrations during the 1790s. This was for perhaps three reasons. One was his personal bitterness toward America during these years; another was the urgency with which he needed America to stick to what he saw as its founding principles, once the French Revolution had been sucked into the vortex of terror and violence; and the third was his genuine disagreement with the constitutional and foreign policy inclinations of the Washington and Adams administrations.

In fact, Paine sympathized with the Federalists' support for strong central government over the power of individual states, as did Jefferson. Eric Foner goes so far as to say that "Paine, like Jefferson, was a Federalist in 1787," and Paine himself argued that he would have voted for the new constitution had he been in America in 1790.[30] Moreover, although his direct comments specifically upon the American Bill of Rights are surprisingly few, it is difficult to imagine that the document did not please him.[31] Indeed, he had dedicated the first part of *Rights of Man* to Washington with a glowing endorsement. None of this, however, was enough to soften his criticism of the Washington and Adams governments. "There was a time," he wrote in 1796, "when the fame of America, moral and political, stood fair and high in the world. . . . The politics of Washington had not then appeared."[32] He went on to foresee the eventual decline and fall of America—admittedly, perhaps a thousand years on—but it is difficult to imagine a more complete contrast to the view of America he had put forward in the second part of *Rights of Man* just four years earlier.

In what ways, then, did Paine think that Washington and the Federalists who came after him had become, as he said in 1803, "apostates from the principles of the Revolution?"[33] First, although he agreed that Congress should have authority over state legislatures, he was highly critical of any attempt to strengthen the presidency. He thought that both Washington and Adams became fond of presidential power and tried to enhance its status, suggesting that Adams and Alexander Hamilton had wanted to make Washington president for life.[34] Paine was also generally critical of a bicameral legislature, thinking it likely to strengthen any elitist elements in government, and he censured Hamilton for suggesting that senators should hold office for life during good behavior.[35] Moreover, he accused the Federalist administrations of contemplating government "as a profitable monopoly, and the people as hereditary property," of planning "to overthrow the liberties of the New World, and place government on the corrupt system of the Old." Thus, they had increased taxation, instituted a standing army, and persuaded the people that these were necessary by spreading rumors of a French invasion, the likelihood of which Paine ridiculed.[36]

Second, Paine condemned persecution on religious grounds, giving much of his time after his return to the United States in 1802 to supporting the growing Deist movement in America.[37] Moreover, he attacked the Federalist administrations for their suspicion and harassment of political radicals, both Americans and those who were political refugees from Britain in these years. Federalists were increasingly wary of the French Revolution and its sympathizers by 1793, especially after the execution of Louis XVI, and they were apprehensive of political unrest breaking out in America in fraternity with France, and of French atheism crossing the Atlantic. By 1798, public opinion was in sufficient agreement with this analysis to allow the passing of the Alien and Sedition Acts against domestic opposition. All forms of oppression, in Paine's view, were directly contrary to the Revolutionary genesis of the United

States and to its original character as a provider of asylum to those persecuted elsewhere. He later claimed that a "Reign of Terror" had "raged in America during the latter end of the Washington Administration, and the whole of that of Adams," dubbing them "Terrorists of the New World."[38]

Moreover, the negative attitude to political radicals from Britain and Ireland was directly related to the Federalists' foreign policy. Paine's detestation of the British government was renewed by that government's violent hostility to Revolutionary France, and he argued that America should shun any dealings with Britain, and that, if anything, it should pursue alliance with France, which had supported America's struggle to throw off British sovereignty. He was, therefore, dismayed to find the Washington administration negotiating with Britain and signing the Jay Treaty in 1794, which offered Britain considerably more favorable commercial terms than the country was prepared to offer France. In Paine's view, the British "monopoly" over American ships damaged American trade badly and it disrupted American relations with France.[39] The leaders of the Federalists, Paine said, were "an English faction," which followed, "like a satellite, the variations of their principal."[40] As a result of the disadvantages he believed America suffered because of the Jay Treaty, in 1800 Paine formulated a plan for a maritime compact to protect the trade of neutral nations, which he had presented to the ministers of various of these nations then in Paris, and which he said was only foiled by the untimely death of the Russian emperor Paul.[41]

Paine had hoped not to see the development of party politics in America,[42] and he criticized the emergence of party politicking and corruption, blaming, of course, the Federalist supporters of Washington and Adams for this innovation.[43] Nevertheless, his own intransigent hostility to the Federalist Party was plain. This was informed by his bitterness about his neglect in Paris by the Washington administration, his personal resentment of American foreign policy, and his outrage about his persecution in America because of his Deism and his sympathy for the French Revolution. His open letter to George Washington (1796) was a blistering personal assault on the man for whom he had once worked closely, but his hostility to John Adams was also scathingly expressed ("John was not born for immortality," he observed in 1802; later, he called him "a counter revolutionist").[44] Paine was, as Dr. Johnson once said approvingly of his friend Richard Bathurst, "a very good HATER."[45]

Mark Philp, summarizing all of this neatly, has suggested that "the idea of America, interpreted to serve radical ends by Paine in Europe in 1791–2, comes back to America, with the émigrés, and eventually with Paine himself, to articulate a critique of the corruptions of the Adams era and the dangers of Hamilton's ambitions and the Federalists' factionalism."[46] The question remains, however, whether Paine thought that Jeffersonian America was returning to his vision of the American republican founding principles—or whether he believed that in some respects it had moved beyond the point of complete return to these? He had, after all, in *Common Sense,* pointed out to the Americans at the start of the Revolutionary struggle that "youth is the seed time of good habits, as well in nations as in individuals."[47] Had America missed its opportunity to fulfill its promise? Indeed, did Paine by 1801 hold the United States of America to a more radical understanding of its founding principles, in some respects, than he had held himself when he had left it in 1787?

John Keane has suggested that as late as 1805, Paine was disillusioned with the state of the union and pessimistic about America's loyalty to what he understood to be its founding principles.[48] Certainly, Paine had been dismayed to find that vicious personal criticism of him continued after his return to America, mainly for his Deistic best-seller, *The Age of Reason* (1795), as well as (among Federalists) for *Rights of Man* and his "Letter to George Washington."[49] Moreover, Paine was deeply hurt to be denied a vote in 1806 in an election at New Rochelle, where he had a house and a small estate that had been gifted to him by the State of New York in 1784 in recognition of his service to the United States. He was ruled not to be an American citizen, on the grounds that he had not been considered to be an American citizen when he was imprisoned in Paris in 1794, and had therefore been judged ineligible for American help.[50]

Paine published his own most prolonged public attack on the Federalist Party in a series of eight *Letters to the Citizens of the United States,* most of which were written shortly after he arrived back in America.[51] In them, he explained—injecting his post–French Revolution, cosmopolitan view of the American Revolution—that even the independence of America was not as important as the American attack on political corruption throughout the world, and that this was why he was opposed to the Federalists, who were, in his view, unprincipled and corrupt.[52] Peter Onuf and Leonard Sadosky have recently argued that the Jeffersonian Republicans claimed, and perhaps even believed, that they were the true representatives of the American people rather than a mere political party offering an alternative to the Federalist Party. The Federalists, by this token, were a small faction, and enemies of the people: the "vicious few" in opposition to the interests of the "virtuous many."[53] It is difficult, from Paine's writings, to discern how large he believed the force he was struggling against to be. "They have never declared what their principles are, or for what purpose they are federalized," he complained in 1806. "Their language is abuse instead of argument; and as far as their conduct discovers their motives, their leaders are an English faction disaffected to the peace of the United States."[54]

More constructively, Paine acknowledged that the American constitutions, national and federal, were not finished articles, but required ongoing attention. He commented in the press on the debate in Connecticut in 1803–4 over the Republican attempt to overturn the old royal charter of that state, granted by Charles II, which had not yet been replaced with a constitution. Paine advised the Republicans to stop trying to reform the legislature before creating a constitution. "This round-about way," he told them, adhering to the principles of popular sovereignty, "besides the tediousness and uncertainty of it, was fundamentally wrong; because as a Constitution is a law to the legislature, and defines and limits its powers, it cannot, from the Nature of the Case, be *the act* of the legislature; it must be the act of the people *creating a legislature*."[55] Furthermore, his last political pamphlet was addressed to the citizens of Pennsylvania as a contribution to the debate in that state over a potential reform of its constitution. In it Paine displayed his European-born commitment to universal suffrage, arguing that the 1790 Pennsylvania constitution was less democratic than that of 1776,

> for it makes artificial distinctions among men in the right of suffrage, which the principles of equity know nothing of; neither is it sound policy. We every day see the rich becoming poor, and those who were poor before, becoming rich. Riches, therefore, having no stability, cannot and ought not to be made a criterion of right. Man is man in every condition of life, and the varieties of fortune and misfortune are open to all.[56]

Moreover, he wrote, a unicameral legislature (with appropriate safeguards) was preferable to two chambers, the governor had a dangerously strong executive power, and civil disputes should be solved by arbitration rather than by court action. However, both the Pennsylvania and Connecticut situations demonstrated the benefits of the principle of not being bound by the pronouncements of previous governments, and Paine emphasized the sound American republican sense in pursuing reform peacefully rather than, as happened elsewhere, by bloodshed.[57] A. Owen Aldridge has argued that Paine was not entirely wedded to the unicameral system, citing, for instance, his advice to the Marquis of Condorcet on the French Constitution in 1791–92, in which he advocated a single legislature divided into two equal sections. Aldridge's view is that Paine had been disillusioned by the Pennsylvania experiment with unicameralism. This does not seem to be borne out by his advice to the Pennsylvanians in 1805, and it may be that he never quite abandoned his long preference for simpler forms of government over more complex forms involving bicameralism and the separation of powers.[58] In acknowledging the need in practice to exercise patience and to accept incremental progress toward his ideals, however, Paine demonstrated a pragmatism and forbearance with which he is not usually credited.

Clearly, Paine was more comfortable with Jeffersonian America than he had been with Federalist America. At the end of his caustic eighth *Letter to the Citizens of the United States*, in 1805, he wrote "The country at this time, compared with what it was two or three years ago, is in a state of tranquility," ending on a note of hopefulness for American politics under Jefferson. No doubt his essential contentment was reinforced by his deep disappointment in the outcome of the revolution in France, which led him to endorse the fundamental political health of the United States. "Republic! Do you call this a republic?" he asked Henry Redhead Yorke, of France, in 1802. "I know of no republic in the world except America. . . . I have done with Europe and its slavish politics."[59] Even in the midst of his press battles with the Federalists, he was not always dominated by moods of rage or black pessimism, but was sometimes able to write with humor and wit, as, for instance, in his piece for the *Philadelphia Aurora* of August 23, 1804, "Nonsense from New York," in which he satirized an item in a July edition of the *New York Gazette* and pulled the Federalists' legs as well as hounding them mercilessly.[60]

Paine retained a continuing sense of his own purpose in America throughout these last years of his life, writing pamphlets and newspaper articles until late in 1807, when his health began to fail in earnest, corresponding with Jefferson, offering to serve as American envoy to France in January 1806, and regularly presenting Jefferson with advice on the aspects of policy which interested him most. For instance, Paine had suggested the purchase of Louisiana from the French, knowing that Napoleon required the money he would receive in return, but not realizing that Jefferson already had a similar, if less far-reaching, plan in train. In the end, it was Paine's proposal, to buy the entire territory of Louisiana and not just the land around New Orleans, which was pursued.[61] Paine continued to send advice on what he considered to be the best ways to incorporate Louisiana as an American state and to establish representative government and acceptable religious practices there.[62]

Jefferson had not wanted to endorse Paine's proposed maritime compact of 1800, although he agreed with its principles, because he was unwilling to commit America to obligations in Europe.[63] As the Napoleonic Wars progressed, however, and the British expanded their policy of stopping and searching American ships and impressing seamen suspected to be deserting British sailors, Paine urged Jefferson to put his foot down, asserting that America was the only neutral nation with the power to resist the so-called British right of search.[64]

Paine has tended to receive significant credit from historians for maintaining an abolitionist position on slavery, perhaps partly because the radical exiles in general did not have a consistent record on the matter, much less the young republic itself. Possibly, many British radical writers on America were too preoccupied with securing political rights for Britons and praising those of their white counterparts in the United States, to engage with the awkward fact of black slavery—or, as Colin Bonwick suggests, to prioritize socioeconomic issues over political representation.[65] Or perhaps, as Anthony Page has suggested with respect to Richard Price, British radicals did not wish to offend their American friends who were slaveholders.[66] Even Paine, although he sustained his opposition to slavery, did not write about it at any great length or appear to spend much time campaigning against it. In his case, this may have been because he identified too strongly with the liberals in Congress who, although they were in many cases opposed to slavery themselves, recognized that if they forced the case for abolition, it was likely to split the new and fragile union of the thirteen states, and therefore put the issue aside.[67] Paine was as anxious as any congressman to preserve the union, and he does not seem to have complained that the federal constitution did not deal with slavery. James Lynch convincingly suggests that he may not even have had any more advanced views on racial equality than other liberals of his day. He did attempt to convince Congress to abolish slavery in Louisiana after the territory had been purchased from France in 1803, and he may also have tried to persuade Jefferson to allow slaves escaping from Santo Domingo to find refuge in America.[68]

Although he was not an official adviser to Jefferson and not all his schemes were adopted by the president, Paine was a staunch supporter, both of Jefferson personally and of the Republican Party generally. This is interesting, in view of the attitudes to the Jefferson presidency of other British and Irish radicals who had settled in America. Joseph Priestley expressed great satisfaction with the administration before he died in 1804; and others were content, under Jefferson, to take more moderate political positions and accept his policy of political conciliation. Some, however, were less easily satisfied, including two newspaper editors with whom Paine often worked, William Duane (of the *Philadelphia Aurora*) and James Cheetham (of the *New York American Citizen*). These more militant democrats refused to participate in Jefferson's reconciliation agenda and often thought that Jefferson's policies in office did not go far enough.[69] It is true that, as an inveterate grumbler, Paine himself had private complaints to make about Jefferson's treatment of him. Moreover, he continued to ask for financial compensation for his previous service, either because he needed the money or because he needed to feel that his contribution was still acknowledged.[70] Moreover, as Foner suggests, Paine's thinking in the 1800s was overshadowed by the events of the previous decade in Europe and America, leaving him out of step with Jefferson's efforts to promote political unity, which caused the president to withdraw from Paine.[71] Jefferson had other reasons for being guarded in his relationship with Paine, such as the damage that Paine's outspoken religious views did to his reputation, but even under these circumstances, it is striking how often the president indulged Paine with meetings and correspondence.[72] Paine remained deeply grateful to Jefferson for having written, just two weeks after he had become president, to invite him to return to America from France,[73] and his pen was ever ready to produce newspaper articles to back Jefferson publicly against Federalist press attacks: "I have now gone, calmly and deliberately through all the charges and calumnies raised against Mr Jefferson; but I have not done it for the purpose of defending him. I have done it to expose the baseness of the federal faction, and to hold it up to public detestation. Mr Jefferson's conduct needs no defense."[74] Paine also seems to have kept out of the struggles among the Jeffersonian Republicans, except where he had personal quarrels with individuals.

Paine had been accused by Federalists of trying to import French Revolutionary principles into the young American republic. His European experiences had certainly confirmed him in his enthusiasm for republican America, and perhaps this allegation was less slanderous than his supporters claimed.[75] He now favored universal manhood suffrage more than most Americans did, and he now saw a radical cosmopolitan, universalist role for America in the world. His European sojourn had reinforced his belief in the process of ongoing constitutional reform and his approval of the American republican mechanism for such continued reform, and indeed his conviction that universal manhood suffrage was necessary. It had also persuaded him that America, of all places in the world, was fitted to provide a model to the world of representative government. These conclusions gave him cause for fundamental optimism in the final years of his life.

And in general it can be argued that Paine continued to take great pride in the American republic—"the country of my heart"—and in America's place in the world.[76] "The experiment has now been made," he pronounced in an 1804 pamphlet, *To the People of England on the Invasion of England*. "The practise of almost thirty years, the last twenty of which have been of peace, notwithstanding the wrong-headed tumultuous administration of John Adams, has proved the excellence of the representative system, and the NEW WORLD is now the preceptor of the OLD. The children are become the fathers of their progenitors."[77] Writing to Jefferson early in 1805, Paine repeated his claim that the United States was now "the Parent of the Western world," and that it was more able to mediate in European disputes with peoples throughout the Americas than was any country in Europe.[78] A few weeks later, he told him: "As everything of public affairs is now on a good ground I shall do as I did after the War, remain a quiet spectator, and attend now to my own affairs."[79] Jefferson cannot have believed that Paine would keep this resolution—only the final descent into crippling ill health in 1807 prevented Paine from continuing to comment on public affairs. He had been forced by the emergence of the Federalist Party and its inveterate opposition to him personally, as well as to Jefferson, to engage in party politics, and he was clearly disturbed by their presence in American political life.

Nevertheless, far from being monochromatically pessimistic and disillusioned with America under its third president, Paine ended his life in his adopted country, certainly with black episodes of self-pity and rage brought on by a combination of his temperament, illness, and other personal circumstances, but against a brighter backdrop of greater contentment regarding the political state of America. His long individual investment in America, together with his positive comparison of American politics with those of Revolutionary France, and his general satisfaction with the Jefferson administration, gave him reason to hope that his vision of the American republic was being materially fulfilled.

Paine's years in Europe between 1787 and 1802 had made his aspirations for the American republic more radical and more earnest. If Paine believed that America was exceptional, he did not think it was unique in being able to create and sustain republican government: he acknowledged that it was atypical—in its youth, its geographical extent, and in its remoteness from Europe—but he continued to hope that it could be a model for the rest of the world rather than an anomaly. The cosmopolitanism and universalism of the French Revolution were honored in Paine's view of America, while the darker side of French events also contributed to his desire to see the United

States lead the nations of the world into the light of political and social liberty. Paine's reflections on the revolution in France intensified and broadened his thinking about the new republic in America. Rather than regenerating his views on the New World, it seems that Paine's reflections on the Old World of the 1790s led him to hope still more profoundly to see "the New World regenerate the Old."[80]

NOTES

1. See Mark Philp, "The Role of America in the 'Debate on France' 1791–5: Thomas Paine's Insertion," *Utilitas* 5 (November 1993): 221–37.

2. Alfred Jules Ayer says Paine went to Paris in December 1787 to "cement" his friendship with Jefferson (see *Thomas Paine* [London: Secker and Warburg, 1988], 52). It seems possible that the two men had been acquainted with each other since at least the Congress of 1776, at which Paine had lobbied delegates to vote in favor of Independence (see John Keane, *Tom Paine: A Political Life* [London: Bloomsbury, 1995], 135–37).

3. Paine to Elisha Babcock, 10 October 1803, in Richard Gimbel, "New Political Writings by Thomas Paine," *Yale University Library Gazette* 30 (January 1956): 97.

4. See Paine, "To the Citizens of the United States" (Letter I), 15 November 1802, in *The Complete Writings of Thomas Paine*, ed. Philip S. Foner, 2 vols. (New York: Citadel Press, 1945) [hereafter cited as *Complete Writings*], 2:910; A. Owen Aldridge, *Thomas Paine's American Ideology* (Newark: University of Delaware Press, 1984); and David A. Wilson, *Paine and Cobbett: The Transatlantic Connection* (Kingston: McGill-Queen's University Press, 1988), 18–19, 67–76, 184, 186.

5. Although see Eric Foner, Introduction to Thomas Paine, *Rights of Man* (Penguin: Harmondsworth, U.K., 1984), 17, 20.

6. See Gary Kates, "From Liberalism to Radicalism: Tom Paine's *Rights of Man*," *Journal of the History of Ideas* 50 (October–December 1989): 569–87; Mark Philp, Introduction to Thomas Paine, *"Rights of Man," "Common Sense," and Other Political Writings* (Oxford: Oxford University Press, 1995), xxvi; and Mark Philp, *Paine* (Oxford: Oxford University Press, 1989), 72.

7. Paine, *Rights of Man, Part the First*, in *Complete Writings*, 1:244.

8. Michael Durey, *Transatlantic Radicals and the Early American Republic* (Lawrence: University Press of Kansas, 1997), 165.

9. Ibid., 205–6, 211, 221, 292. Of the hundred and six exiles examined by Durey, thirty returned to the British Isles.

10. See Jack Fruchtman Jr., *Thomas Paine: Apostle of Freedom* (New York: Four Walls Eight Windows, 1994), 439–40.

11. Ayer, *Thomas Paine*, 42.

12. Paine, *Rights of Man, Part the First*, in *Complete Writings*, 1:300. For similar lan-

guage, see also Paine, *Common Sense,* ibid., 1:28–29, 36–36; and Paine, *Rights of Man, Part Second,* ibid., 1:390.

13. Paine, *Common Sense,* ibid., 1:38.

14. Paine, *Dissertations on Government; the Affairs of the Bank; and Paper Money,* ibid, 2:369. See also Paine, *Rights of Man, Part Second,* ibid., 1:381.

15. Paine, *Rights of Man, Part Second,* ibid., 1:369–72 (quotation, 371–72).

16. Paine, *Common Sense,* ibid., 1:45; "A Serious Address to the People of Pennsylvania," *Pennsylvania Packet* (Philadelphia), 1 December 1778, ibid., 2:285–87. See also Aldridge, *Thomas Paine's American Ideology,* 132–33; Philp, *Paine,* 34; and Keane, *Tom Paine,* 302.

17. Kates, "From Liberalism to Radicalism."

18. Paine, *Dissertation on the First Principles of Government,* in *Complete Writings,* 2:577–78, 579.

19. Paine, *Rights of Man, Part Second,* ibid., 1:371; Paine, "Letter to George Washington," 30 July 1796, ibid., 2:694.

20. Paine, *Common Sense,* ibid., 1:29, 37.

21. Paine, *Rights of Man, Part the First,* ibid., 1:293.

22. James V. Lynch, "The Limits of Revolutionary Radicalism: Tom Paine and Slavery," *Pennsylvania Magazine of History and Biography* 123 (July 1999): 180–93; Paine to William Short, 2 November 1791, in *Complete Writings,* 2:1321.

23. Paine, *Common Sense,* in *Complete Writings,* 1:20. On expansionism, see Wilson, *Paine and Cobbett,* 62–63.

24. Paine, *Rights of Man, Part Second,* in *Complete Writings,* 1:447–49; Paine, "To Mr. Secretary Dundas," 6 June 1792, ibid., 2:452.

25. Paine, *Common Sense,* ibid., 1:19, 21, 30–31; Paine, *Rights of Man, Part the First,* ibid., 293–94n.

26. Philp, Introduction to Paine, *"Common Sense," "Rights of Man," and Other Political Writings,* xxvi.

27. Paine, *Rights of Man, Part the First,* in *Complete Writings,* 1:244; *Rights of Man, Part Second,* ibid., 1:354, 360; *Dissertation on First Principles of Government,* ibid., 2:571.

28. Paine, *Rights of Man, Part the First,* ibid., 1:299–300; Paine, *Rights of Man, Part Second,* ibid., 449.

29. Paine to James Monroe, 10 September 1794 (from the Luxembourg Prison), ibid., 2:1350. On America and France, see Paine, *Rights of Man, Part the First,* ibid., 1:156–62.

30. Eric Foner, *Tom Paine and Revolutionary America* (New York: Oxford University Press, 1976), 205; Paine, "Letter to George Washington," 30 July 1796, in *Complete Writings,* 2:691–93.

31. Or perhaps, by 1791–92, he was simply preoccupied with the upheaval in France, escape from Britain and publishing *Rights of Man,* and his bridge-building project. On strong central government over the power of individual states, see Paine to TJ, February

1788 [misdated 1789], in *Complete Writings*, 2:1299; it is David Wilson (in *Paine and Cobbett*, 70) who gives the February 1788 date (citing *The Papers of Thomas Jefferson*, ed. Julian P. Boyd et al., 39 vols. to date [Princeton, N.J.: Princeton University Press, 1950–], 13:4–5).

32. Paine, "Letter to George Washington," 30 July 1796, in *Complete Writings*, 2:691; see also ibid., 2:694, 707, 715.

33. Paine, "To the Citizens of the United States" (Letter VI), 14 May 1803, ibid., 2:935.

34. Paine, "To the Citizens of the United States" (Letter II), 22 November 1802, ibid., 2:916; Paine, "To the Citizens of the United States" (Letter VIII), 7 June 1805, ibid., 2:955–56; Paine, "Remarks on Gouverneur Morris's Funeral Oration on General Hamilton," 7 August 1804, ibid., 2:960; Paine to TJ, 1 April 1797, ibid., 2:1390–91.

35. Paine, "To the Citizens of the United States" (Letter III), 29 November 1802, ibid., 2:918. On Paine's thinking in terms of "people" versus "aristocracy" rather than in class terms, see Wilson, *Paine and Cobbett*, 186–87.

36. Paine, "To the Citizens of the United States" (Letter I), 15 November 1802, in *Complete Writings*, 2:910; Paine, "To the Citizens of the United States" (Letter II), 22 November 1802, ibid., 2:917; Paine, "To the Citizens of the United States" (Letter III), 29 November 1802, ibid., 2:919; Paine, "To the Citizens of the United States" (Letter IV), 6 December 1802, ibid., 2:925; Paine, "To the Citizens of the United States" (Letter VI), 12 March 1803, ibid., 2:949–50; Paine, "To the Citizens of the United States" (Letter VIII), 7 June 1805, ibid., 2:951–53. See also Paine, "A Challenge to the Federalists to Declare their Principles," 17 October 1806, ibid., 2:1007–1010; and Paine, "Of the Comparative Powers and Expense of Ships of War, Gun-Boats, and Fortifications," 21 November 1807, ibid., 2:1075.

37. He wrote seventeen essays for *The Prospect*, edited by Elihu Palmer (see Foner, *Tom Paine and Revolutionary America*, 259).

38. "To the Citizens of the United States" (Letter III), 29 November 1802, in *Complete Writings*, 2:918, 920; "To the Citizens of the United States" (Letter VI), 12 March 1803, ibid., 2:936.

39. Paine, "Letter to George Washington," 30 July 1796, ibid., 2:691–723; Paine, "Observations on Jay's Treaty," 2 July 1795, ibid., 2:568–70; Paine, "The Recall of Monroe," [addressed to the editors of the *Bien-informe*], 27 September 1797, ibid., 2:613–15. On Federalist funding by Anglo-American commerce, which explains the Jay Treaty from the American perspective, see Wilson, *Paine and Cobbett*, 117–18.

40. [Paine], "A Challenge to the Federalists," 17 October 1806, in *Complete Writings*, 2:1009.

41. Paine, "To the Citizens of the United States" (Letter VII), 21 April 1803, ibid., 2:939–48.

42. Ayer says that Paine had not foreseen them (see Ayer's *Thomas Paine*, 96), but Paine, in his *Dissertations on Government; the Affairs of the Bank; and Paper-Money*, gave the impression rather that he did not wish to see them, and certainly did not wish to be

attached to one (see *Complete Writings,* 2:368, 390, 409; see also Paine to General Lewis Morris, 16 February 1784, ibid., 2:1247; Paine to Daniel Clymer, September 1786, ibid., 2:1255; and Foner, *Tom Paine and Revolutionary America,* 201–21).

43. Paine, "To the Citizens of the United States" (Letter VII), 21 April 1803, in *Complete Writings,* 2:948.

44. Paine, "To the Citizens of the United States" (Letter II), 22 November 1802, ibid., 2:913; Paine, "To the Citizens of the United States" (Letter VIII), 7 June 1805, ibid., 2:955.

45. Cited in Hester Lynch Piozzi, *Anecdotes of the Late Samuel Johnson during the Last Twenty Years of His Life* (London, 1786), 83.

46. Philp, "The Role of America," 236.

47. Paine, *Common Sense,* in *Complete Writings,* 1:36.

48. Keane, *Tom Paine,* 510.

49. Gregory Claeys, *Thomas Paine: Social and Political Thought* (Boston: Unwin, Hyman, 1989), 35, 111–12, 184–93, 209. On reaction to his religious views, see also Keane, *Tom Paine,* 475–79.

50. On the New Rochelle election incident, see Bernard Vincent, *The Transatlantic Republican: Thomas Paine and the Age of Revolutions* (Amsterdam: Rodopi, 2005), 112–14.

51. The letters were written between 15 November 1802 and 21 April 1803 (see "To the Citizens of the United States" (Letters I through VIII), in *Complete Writings,* 2:908–57.

52. Paine, "To the Citizens of the United States" (Letter VIII), 7 June 1805, ibid., 2:956. Cf. the opening quotation to this chapter (from *Rights of Man, Part Second,* 1:364, 356).

53. Peter S. Onuf and Leonard J. Sadosky, *Jeffersonian America* (Malden, Mass.: Blackwell, 2001), chap. 1.

54. Paine, "The Emissary Cullen, Otherwise Carpenter," 28 October 1806, reprinted in A. Owen Aldridge, "Thomas Paine and the New York *Public Advertiser,*" *New-York Historical Society Quarterly* 37 (October 1953): 368–69.

55. Paine to Elisha Babcock, 27 August 1804, in Gimbel, "New Political Writings by Thomas Paine," 99. See also [Paine], "To the People of Connecticut, on the Subject of a Constitution," 2 August 1804, ibid., 100–102; and Fruchtman, *Thomas Paine,* 406, 414.

56. Paine, "To the Citizens of Pennsylvania on the Proposal for Calling a Convention," August 1805, in *Complete Writings,* 2:1001.

57. Ibid., 2:992–1007.

58. Aldridge, *Thomas Paine's American Ideology,* 234; *Thomas Paine's Answer to Four Questions on the Legislative and Executive Powers,* in *Complete Writings,* 2:526.

59. Henry Redhead Yorke, *Letters from France in 1803,* 2 vols. (London, 1804), 2:342, quoted in Claeys, *Thomas Paine,* 34.

60. [Paine], "Nonsense from New York," 23 August 1804, in Gimbel, "New Political Writings by Thomas Paine," 102–5.

61. Paine to TJ, 25 December 1802, in *Complete Writings,* 2:1431; Keane, *Tom Paine,* 473–74.

62. Paine to TJ, 2 August 1803, in *Complete Writings,* 2:1441; Paine to John C. Breckenridge, 2 August 1803, ibid., 2:1443–46; Paine to TJ, 23 September 1803, ibid., 2:1447–48; Paine to TJ, 25 January 1805, ibid., 2:1456–64; Paine, "To the French Inhabitants of Louisiana," 22 September 1804, ibid., 2:963–68. See also Keane, *Tom Paine,* 482, 487–89, 490.

63. TJ to Paine, 18 March 1801, quoted in Paine, "To the Citizens of the United States" (Letter VII), 21 April 1803, ibid., 2:946–47.

64. Paine, "On the Question, Will There Be War?," 14 August 1807, in *Complete Writings,* 2:1012–17.

65. Colin Bonwick, *English Radicals and the American Revolution* (Chapel Hill: University of North Carolina Press, 1977), 217–18. Cf. Christopher Leslie Brown, *Moral Capital: Foundations of British Abolitionism* (Chapel Hill: University of North Carolina Press, 2006), 126–34, on the British debate about slavery at the start of the American War of Independence.

66. Anthony Page, "'A Species of Slavery': Richard Price's Rational Dissent and Antislavery," *Slavery and Abolition: A Journal of Slave and Post-Slave Studies* 32, no. 1 (2011): 53–73.

67. See Joseph J. Ellis, *Founding Brothers: The Revolutionary Generation* (London: Faber, 2002), chap. 3.

68. Lynch, "The Limits of Revolutionary Radicalism," 193–96. On Louisiana, see Paine, "To the French Inhabitants of Louisiana," *Complete Writings,* 2:968; cf. Paine to TJ, 25 January 1805, ibid., 2:1456–64. On Santo Domingo, see Claeys, *Thomas Paine,* 35. Paine's standing as an abolitionist has also been claimed on the basis of two black men traveling to attend his otherwise small funeral (see Claeys, *Thomas Paine,* 36).

69. Durey, *Transatlantic Radicals,* 260–61, 274.

70. Keane, *Tom Paine,* 513–14, 529–30; Ayer, *Thomas Paine,* 178. And see, for example, Paine to TJ, 12 January 1803, in *Complete Writings,* 2:1439; and Paine to TJ, 20 April 1805, ibid., 2:1465–66.

71. Foner, *Tom Paine and Revolutionary America,* 258.

72. Claeys, *Thomas Paine,* 35; Keane, *Tom Paine,* 469–73. Note also Jefferson's continued respect for the radical editor William Duane despite Duane's militancy during Jefferson's presidency (see Durey, *Transatlantic Radicals,* 275).

73. Paine, "To the Citizens of the United States" (Letter III), 29 November 1802, in *Complete Writings,* 2:922. Jefferson's letter was published by Paine in "To the Citizens of the United States" (Letter VII), 21 April 1803, ibid., 2:946–47.

74. Paine, "Another Callender—Thomas Turner of Virginia," 23 and 24 July 1805, ibid., 2:989. See also Paine, "To Mr. Hulbert, of Sheffield," 12 March 1805, ibid., 2:975–80; and Paine, "A Challenge to the Federalists," 12 March 1805, ibid., 2:1007–10.

75. Vincent, *The Transatlantic Republican,* 26.

76. Paine, "To the Citizens of the United States" (Letter IV), 6 December 1802, in *Complete Writings,* 2:926.

77. Paine, *To the People of England on the Invasion of England,* 6 [May] 1804, ibid., 2:683.

78. Paine to TJ, 1 January 1805, ibid., 2:1454.

79. Paine to TJ, 25 January 1805, ibid., 2:1459.

80. Kates, "From Liberalism to Radicalism"; Philp, Introduction to Thomas Paine, *"Rights of Man," "Common Sense," and Other Political Writings,* xxvi; Philp, *Paine,* 72; Paine, *Rights of Man, Part the First,* in *Complete Writings,* 1:244 (quotation).

Thomas Jefferson's Portrait of Thomas Paine

GAYE WILSON

A PORTRAIT OF THOMAS PAINE was among the artwork from Thomas Jefferson's personal collection sent to the Boston Athenaeum for exhibition and sale in 1828. The small painting had been a gift from the artist John Trumbull to Jefferson in late 1788 and had remained a part of Jefferson's collection until after his death and the dispersal of his estate. It was not listed as one of the pieces sold at the Athenaeum, yet its whereabouts following the sale were unknown until it was identified in 1955. The only bit of its intervening history on record was the portrait's purchase at an auction in Concord, Massachusetts, in 1912. The purchase was made quite by accident, as it was among several items sold as a lot and only discovered later, upside down, in the bottom of a "button" box. When the painting was found, the pupils of the eyes had been gouged out and the figure, painted on a wood panel, had been pierced three times in the chest. Dr. Theodore Sizer, curator from the Yale University Art Gallery and an expert on the artist, John Trumbull, had identified the portrait. He very tactfully suggested that the vandalism was probably the work of a child, and certainly it may have been.[1] Still, this small painting with its curious history is intriguing as an icon of Paine's vacillating public image and his relationship with Thomas Jefferson.

Jefferson commissioned a portrait of Thomas Paine after the two men met in Paris in 1787. How well Jefferson knew Paine before then is not certain, although Jefferson was well aware of Paine the pamphleteer and readily acknowledged his contributions during the American Revolution "and the effect his writings produced in uniting us in independance." While still in

John Trumbull. *Thomas Paine* (before restoration), 1788. Oil on wood. (Thomas Jefferson Foundation at Monticello, photograph by Edwin S. Roseberry)

Philadelphia preparing for his assignment to France, Jefferson had proposed to James Madison that the Virginia Commonwealth should consider a stipend to Paine, "the author of Common sense," for "the grateful impressions which his services have made on our minds." He repeated the proposal from Paris: "I still hope something will be done for Paine. He richly deserves it."[2] Along with his advocacy for a state stipend, Jefferson's desire to obtain a portrait of Paine indicated that he believed him of substantial merit and repute and wanted to include Paine's image in his own growing portrait collection, which he referred to as his "principal American characters," and on another occasion, "my pictures of American Worthies."[3] This decision did not rest necessarily on the friendship that had developed while both were in Paris, but rather upon considerations of Paine's contribution as a thinker and a writer. It was genius and merit, not personal affability, that secured a place in a pantheon of worthies.

Jefferson was following a centuries-old tradition in building a collection of likenesses of celebrated men. A portrait, whether sculpted or painted, had served since the preeminence of Greece and Rome as a means of memorializing and demonstrating honor. Such collections had been scarce in the American colonies, but with the success of the Revolution there was an impulse to celebrate and preserve history through the images of patriots. A "Worthy" in eighteenth-century public portraiture was someone who had displayed a "genius" that served mankind, one who represented honor and good character, and, perhaps most importantly, one who inspired "virtue" in contemporaries.[4] Ironically, British collections served as primary examples, and American collectors such as Jefferson would have been aware of the discourse that had persisted throughout the century regarding the public function of art and its contribution to civic virtue. In his library, Jefferson had the works of the English artist and writer Jonathan Richardson, one of the earliest British authors to publish his thoughts on the goal of painting and portraiture, in his *Essay on the Theory of Painting*. Richardson concluded that in addition to preserving the faces of great men, a portrait should also exhibit the subject's character, so that, therefore, "a picture, besides its being a pleasant ornament, is useful to instruct and improve our minds, and to excite proper sentiments and reflections." He continued this thought, writing, "I know not what influence this has, or may have, but methinks 'tis rational to believe that Pictures of this kind are subservient to Virtue: that Men are excited to imitate Good Actions, and persuaded to shun the Vices of those whose Examples are thus set before them."[5] But was Thomas Paine a worthy example to set before the public? Some would not be as convinced as Jefferson appeared to be in that summer of 1787.

Paine responded promptly to Jefferson's request for a portrait, saying he would be honored.[6] When calling upon Jefferson at his Paris residence, the Hôtel de Langeac, Paine had the opportunity to view the beginnings of Jefferson's collection of painted and sculpted images of men notable to the American Revolution and the founding of the republic. Most notable were two portraits of George Washington—a three-quarter-length portrait by the American painter Joseph Wright, and a full-length one by Charles Willson Peale. There was also a bust portrait of John Paul Jones by the renowned French sculptor Jean-Antoine Houdon, and a copy of the famous Duplessis portrait of Franklin, among other paintings and prints. The significance of Jefferson's intent for this collection would not have been lost on Paine. To have his portrait join those of other outstanding Revolutionary heroes would serve to validate his own contribution to the American cause.

Paine felt he had earned his place in the republic of letters with *Common Sense* and his "Crisis" series, which had fueled and then bolstered the revolution in America, and he welcomed that recognition. With the end of the Revolution, however, his provocative style was no longer needed, as most Americans welcomed a return to normality after the uncertainties of war. This led Paine to a new project: designing a bridge. His *Common Sense* had united Americans in revolutionary ideas, and now Paine turned to uniting the new nation geographically with a design for a single-arched iron bridge that could span a river with no supports.

Upon his arrival in Paris in 1787, Paine presented himself more as a man of science than as a revolutionary writer. He had left Philadelphia for Europe with the hope of generating interest either in Paris or London that could assist him in realizing a prototype of his bridge model. Even though his initial nomination to the American Philosophical Society, in 1781, had been blocked, his admission in 1785 legitimized his position as a man of science.[7] Topics in the Jefferson–Paine correspondence at this time focused as much on science as politics, yet in Jefferson's mind, Paine's identity remained unchanged. When he placed the commission for a portrait, he identified the sitter as "Mr. Paine, author of common sense." This was the achievement that interested Jefferson, and that made Paine eligible to be figuratively placed alongside Washington.

Occupied with plans for his bridge, Paine left Paris for London in the fall of 1787 before Jefferson acted on the portrait commission. It may have been Jefferson's intent all along to employ an artist in London, as he had done in spring 1786 when he visited that city and had his own portrait taken by the American-born artist Mather Brown and commissioned a portrait of John Adams by Brown. These portraits had not been delivered, and apparently his idea was to place a third commission with Brown.[8] This put him in the awkward situation of relying on an acquaintance in London, John Trumbull, who was also an artist, to act as go-between. Jefferson seemed aware that this could be uncomfortable for Trumbull, and wanted to make sure there was no "gaucherie" in his request. He admired Trumbull's work, but bypassed him in favor of Brown. When Brown was falling far behind in executing the commissions, Trumbull was suggested as a possible artist for the Adams portrait. But Jefferson was not in agreement, and replied, "With respect to Mr. Adams's picture, I must again press it to be done by Brown, because Trumbul does not paint of the size of life, and could not be asked to hazard himself on it."[9] Apparently, the only portraits Jefferson had seen from Trumbull to that point were small studies created to support the artist's ideas for large history paintings based upon scenes from the American Revolution. Jefferson fully supported this intent to illustrate scenes from American history, especially Trumbull's plan for a large work recording the moment of the presentation of the Declaration of Independence to the Continental Congress, which placed Jefferson as the central figure. But what he wanted was a life-sized portrait of Paine, and he questioned Trumbull's ability to work in that scale. Trumbull dutifully placed the commission, reporting back that Brown had agreed to take Paine's portrait.[10]

After frustrating delays, Jefferson finally received John Adams's portrait from Brown, along with his own, in September 1788, more than two years after the original commission. He was relieved to be able to add the *Adams* to his collection, and possibly displayed this portrait at the Hôtel de Langeac, but he still had no image of Thomas Paine. There was no explanation as to why Brown had not yet executed the commission for Paine's portrait. Perhaps there had been little time for a sitting—Jefferson knew that Paine was spending time in Yorkshire attempting to have a prototype made of his iron bridge. Then, without further prompting, he received the portrait of Paine, but from Trumbull rather than Brown, and not in life size, but in a small, 3½ inch by 4 inch format.

Jefferson's commission for Paine's portrait had been very explicit as to size: "I would wish it of the size of the one he [Brown] drew of myself." Mather Brown's portrait of Jefferson measured 28 inches by 36 inches, the size known in England as a "kit-kat."[11] This was slightly larger than a bust portrait, which showed head only, and so allowed for a hand, and therefore a gesture, and, in the case of Brown's *Jefferson* and his *Adams,* props as well.[12] Nevertheless, when Jefferson received Trumbull's gift of the small painting of Paine, he responded promptly ("I am to thank you a thousand times for the portrait of Mr. Paine") and added that it was a perfect likeness. He made no comment about the size.[13]

The portrait of Paine did not arrive alone. Trumbull's preceding letter alerted Jefferson to expect a little case containing two pictures, one for him and another a gift for his eldest daughter, Martha.[14] Joining the portrait of Paine was a portrait of Jefferson identical in size, and both painted in oil on wood panels. Although Trumbull did not elaborate upon the portraits, he apparently resorted to the small sketch of Jefferson he had made on a previous trip to Paris as a part of his study for the *Declaration of Independence.* It is probable that Trumbull took Paine's image from life, as it does not closely resemble portraits of Paine known to have been available in London at the time and so is not likely to be a copy.[15] This could account for the features appearing somewhat more modeled and finished, as opposed to the sketchy quality of the *Jefferson,* with a hasty shadow defining the nose.[16] Trumbull hinted that these may have been intended as studies until he could complete more-finished portraits, commenting that "it is all I can do untill I have the happiness to see you again."[17]

Jefferson's response that Trumbull had achieved a "perfect likeness" was

John Trumbull. *Thomas Paine*, 1788. Oil on wood.
(Thomas Jefferson Foundation at Monticello)

not disingenuous, as the portrait compares well to other extant works of Paine. The figure is conservatively dressed in a dark, blue-grey frock coat with simple buttons and a fashionably high collar. This is worn over a pale buff, single-breasted waistcoat. At first glance, the hair might appear loose, thus confirming Paine's unkempt image. Actually, it is a result of Trumbull adding a final wash of gray over the background but leaving the umber underpainting around the head. The hair disappears into this uneven shadow, and what might at first appear unkempt is in fact a conservatively dressed hair or wig with the standard queue, side-curls, and moderate dusting of hair powder. The dominance of gray tones gives a quietness and solidity to the small portrait. The head is in three-quarter profile, with the expression calm, the mouth relaxed, but the gaze direct. The figure who stares back at the viewer could have been any comfortably established British or American gentleman.

The portrait as it appears today is the result of careful restoration. The gouged eyes are repainted and the piercings in the chest covered, yet there is no doubt that Paine's eyes always looked straight at the viewer. Contemporaries of Paine remarked upon his eyes. Following their first meeting in 1776, General Charles Lee pronounced, "He has genius in his eyes." One who met him in France years later remarked that "his eyes are full of fire," and another that "his dark eye still retained its sparkling vigour."[18] Was Trumbull taken

THOMAS JEFFERSON'S PORTRAIT OF THOMAS PAINE

John Trumbull. *Thomas Jefferson*, 1788. Oil on wood.
(Thomas Jefferson Foundation at Monticello)

with the "vigor" of Paine's glance, or was it instinctive for Paine to turn face-on regardless of the circumstances? No matter how the pose was decided, Paine looks back at the viewer with a level and unwavering glance.

The portrait of Jefferson does not engage the viewer as directly: his eyes are turned away to an undetermined point. The expression is thoughtful, while more enigmatic than Paine's open gaze. This mood is offset, however, with a livelier color palette than the dominant grays used for Paine, with the dark green of Jefferson's frock coat complementing the gold of his waistcoat and the warm tones of his hair and skin. Jefferson's hair is far more casual than Paine's, with the absence of powder and the sides left loose rather than dressed with curls. This reflects closely the image Trumbull took for his study for the *Declaration of Independence* and gives Jefferson an even more distinctly "American" look than the artist's gentlemanly interpretation of Paine. Trumbull's familiarity with Jefferson's features allowed him to work quickly and produce a painting that appears very spontaneous. This would support his hint that the small paintings were intended as studies, with more-formal portraits to follow. The small portrait of Jefferson would undoubtedly remain with Martha Jefferson as a personal memento. If this had been the plan, it was never implemented: the lives of all involved took very different directions.

When the portraits of Jefferson and Paine are placed side by side, the initial impression is of two well-dressed Anglo-American gentlemen of the late eighteenth-century. On closer examination, the variation in each pose and the interaction—or lack of interaction—with the viewer implies character differences that might seem prophetic and insightful but that were expected of a good portrait artist. Trumbull's *Jefferson* appears thoughtful, cautious, and reserved. His *Paine* is far more direct and immediate. Whether by intent or by serendipity, Trumbull suggested character traits in the portraits of each man that would play out in their lives and public careers.

Trumbull's portrait of Paine admitted him to the class of gentleman, and at that particular time, he could claim such a position. His correspondence with Jefferson during this period reveals that things were going well for Paine. The prototype for his bridge was moving forward and he felt positive about the progress. "I am in some intimacy with Mr. [Edmund] Burke," he reported, noting that Burke had promised to introduce him to the new ministers of the British government. Paine had already made the acquaintance of the likely future head of the Treasury, the Duke of Portland, "at whose seat in the Country I was a few days last summer." The following month, Paine could report more interest in his model and another new acquaintance, Lord Fitzwilliam, heir to the Marquis of Rockingham, who invited him to his home of Wentworth. Paine frequently mentioned corresponding with Sir Joseph Banks of the Royal Society, and he appeared to be enjoying the attention given him and his bridge design.[19]

Jefferson was not the first to include an image of Thomas Paine in a collection of "American Worthies." The artist and patriot Charles Willson Peale began one of the earliest American collections of outstanding men of the Revolution, painting them himself and displaying the portraits in his Philadelphia studio (later the Peale Museum). Peale's rationale embraced the eighteenth-century expectations of such collections, as he explained that he was "ever fond of perpetuating the Remembrance of the Worthies of my time, as I conceive it will be a means of exciting an Emulation in our Posterity." He foresaw these images as integral to the telling of the history of the American Revolution, "the Likeness being added to the Historic page giving it more force and the Reader more pleasure."[20] Both Peale and Jefferson were guided by a tradition in Western art that sought to preserve history by preserving images of its illustrious men, and both considered Thomas Paine within this tradition.[21]

Existing evidence suggests that Peale painted two portraits of Paine, though both are unlocated today. The original was commissioned by Henry

Laurens, and then Peale made a copy for his own collection from the Laurens original. It was documented in a gallery list of 1784, and then again in 1795 in "An Historical Catalogue of Peales' Collection of Paintings," which included a brief biography of Paine.[22] The final listing was in the sale catalog of 1854 that marked the dispersal of the Peale Museum collection, where it sold for $6.50.[23] The 1854 sale catalog evidences that Paine remained a member of Peale's "Worthies" despite the fluctuations of public opinion.

The original portrait made for Henry Laurens had a more interesting history, traveling to London with Laurens. Prints subsequently made there from this painting provide the only evidence of Peale's work. Laurens left for Europe in the autumn of 1780 with a commission from the Continental Congress to negotiate a loan and commercial treaties with Holland. Not surprisingly, he acquired a full-length portrait of Washington as he prepared for this assignment, just as Jefferson would bring a *Washington* with him to Europe four years later. George Washington was the undisputed icon who would keep American artists busy for many years to come. In wartime Philadelphia Charles Willson Peale wrote that "my last large Canvas is now before me with outlines of Gen Washington traced on it," gratefully accepting Laurens's offer to send much-needed art supplies from Europe.[24]

The *Paine* as a second portrait for Laurens's mission is more surprising. By 1780, some Americans were beginning to find Paine bothersome, even if they did respect his writing. But Laurens demonstrated his continuing support for Paine by choosing the author of *Common Sense* and the *American Crisis* as a partner for the *Washington*.[25] However, Laurens's mission was cut short when he was captured at sea and then imprisoned in the Tower of London. The *Washington* portrait was confiscated, but the *Paine* apparently followed Laurens to London, where prints made from the original preserved some idea of Peale's work. The most widely circulated print, by the noted London engraver James Watson, shows Paine holding a book or tablet inscribed, "In the Cause of / LIBERTY / AND / MY COUNTRY / The Crisis / Common Sense." Peale thus identified his subject, picturing him as an author and a scholar. Paine's elbow rests on a table with quill and paper, and he holds his chin in his hand with a finger pointing to the cranium, the source of thought.[26] Though seated in the traditional three-quarter profile, the head is turned directly to the viewer and the face displays a relaxed expression and slight smile. The outstretched arm holding the tablet, and the thumb pointing to the title, guide the eye to the inscription, and so establish the importance of the figure gazing from the portrait.

The setting is not typical. The figure sits in a landscape with a tree and

James Watson after Charles Willson Peale. *Thomas Paine,* 1783. Mezzotint on paper.
(National Portrait Gallery, Smithsonian Institution)

foliage replacing the usual drapery; the tabletop is plain, and there is no ornate chair-back to suggest opulence. Peale did use nature as a backdrop in some of his full-length standing portraits, and, as could be expected, he placed Washington on a battlefield. It was not as common in the early 1780s, however, to see a figure seated at a desk placed outdoors under a tree rather than on a portico or simply with nature visible through an open window. It is impossible to know whether Watson's print accurately replicates the original portrait. If it is indeed Peale's work, perhaps he found the very essence of Paine's personality and thinking more in keeping with the freshness and honesty of nature than a traditional setting with heavy drapery and fine upholstered chairs. Certainly, eighteenth-century portraiture used every element of the painting to reveal the subject's character and status.

Peale's inclusion of *Common Sense* and *The Crisis* helped identify the subject, as the engraver, James Watson, made a major mistake in titling the print as "Edward Payne, Esq." The explanation under the title, that it is "From an Original Portrait in the Possession of Henry Laurens, Esq.," and the name of "C.W. Pele Pinx. Philadelphia," ties the print to the original portrait, but suggests that Paine's name was not as universally known as he might have hoped. Nevertheless, Watson's work connected Paine with the peace negotiations taking place in Paris that would end the War for Independence. The publication of the print was dated January 1, 1783, and so preceded the preliminary signing of a treaty on January 18. The final negotiations were not concluded until the following September; nevertheless, the release of the new print was timed to take advantage of Paine's participation in American independence.[27]

A second print that claimed to be from the original portrait of Paine was advertised for sale in a London newspaper in July 1791. Even though Laurens had returned to the United States by this date, the original Peale could be the source, since Laurens left the portrait in London with a Paine admirer, Thomas Brand Hollis.[28] The engraving advertised in the *Gazetteer* by Thomas Bassett rode on the notoriety of Paine's recently published work, *The Rights of Man*, and there was no mistake made in the name this time. The advertisement promised "A highly finished portrait of Thomas Paine, Esq."[29]

Some in America may have questioned the "Esq." attached to Paine's name. Before leaving Philadelphia for Paris in 1787, Paine had made enemies, and his name was appearing already in newspapers in its shortened, deliberately ungentlemanly form of "Tom" Paine. His notoriety began shortly after his anonymous publication of *Common Sense,* which was followed by a vitriolic dispute with his first publisher. The controversy publicized Paine's authorship of the popular pamphlet, but some observers found his behavior reprehensible even though they embraced his sentiments.[30] A member of Congress concluded that "Poor Payne" was "not the most prudent man in the world."[31]

Paine's self-assessment did not agree with the negative views held by others. In 1782, he stressed his republican virtue in placing public need before his own: "If there is any one circumstance in my character which distinguishes itself from the rest, it is personal disinterestedness, and an anxiety to serve a public cause in preference to myself."[32] These were traits expected in a gentleman, but to trumpet them publicly was to negate them. True disinterestedness must be practiced but not touted. Paine could be hard to take, as Sarah Franklin Bache made clear in a letter to her father, Benjamin Franklin: "There was never a man less beloved in a place than Paine is in this, having at different times disputed with everybody. The most rational thing he could have done would have been to have died the instant he had finished his *Common Sense,* for he never again will have it in his power to leave the world with so much credit."[33]

To some, Paine was repugnant; to others, he was an interesting, noteworthy figure. While visiting Philadelphia, the marquis de Chastellux made a point of calling upon Paine, and added his own pen-portrait to his *Travels in North-America.* He identified Paine as "that author so celebrated in America, and throughout Europe, by his excellent work, entitled, *Common Sense,* and several other political pamphlets." Chastellux was joined by the Marquis de Lafayette when they visited Paine at his apartment and found him in "a room pretty much in disorder, dusty furniture, and a large table covered with books lying open, and manuscripts begun." Chastellux described Paine's appearance as being as disheveled as his room: "His person was in a correspondent dress, nor did his physiognomy belie the spirit that reigns throughout his works." But he could accept Paine's appearance, the dust, and the disarray as "attributes of a man of letters." Another talent he admired in Paine was his "agreeable and animated" conversation.[34]

It took another revolution for Paine to once again hit the stride he had experienced with *Common Sense.* When he encountered Jefferson in Paris, Paine was amusing himself as a man of science and designer of bridges. But, as he recognized early on, "I know but one kind of life I am fit for, and that is a thinking one, and, of course, a writing one."[35] The French Revolution provided the cause that inspired his next important work, *The Rights of Man.*

The interest surrounding the publication of the two-part *Rights of Man* in 1791–92 in London generated a market for new images of Thomas Paine. As previously noted, a second print was taken from the Charles Willson Peale portrait made for Henry Laurens and advertised for sale in July 1791, but this portrait looked back to the Paine of *Common Sense* and the *Crisis.* A new image by the London portrait artist George Romney captured the Paine of *The Rights of Man* and was then made more widely available through publication of a fine engraving by William Sharp in April 1793.

The original painting by Romney is unlocated, but Sharp's engraving is extremely well modeled and detailed. It was credited as a good likeness by a British traveler who had sought out the infamous Thomas Paine in 1802, shortly before he left Paris for the United States. He pronounced: "The portrait of him engraved by Sharp from Romney's picture of him is a good likeness" (even though he found Paine's general appearance "mean and poverty-stricken").[36]

Romney placed Paine in three-quarter profile in front of a table covered with objects appropriate to a thinker and writer: quill pens, inkwell, and sheets of paper. The words "Common Sense" are visible on the sheet of paper lying on the desk. Standing over this, propped against the inkwell and thus making it even easier to read, is a second sheet, with the words "Rights of Man." The placement of the papers does not imply that *Rights of Man* had superseded *Common Sense,* suggesting instead that the earlier work serves as

William Sharp after George Romney. *Thomas Paine,* 1793. Engraving on paper.
(National Portrait Gallery, Smithsonian Institution)

the foundation of its recently published successor. Romney used the same convention as Peale to identify his subject and justify his celebration in a formal portrait.

As in the previous works by Peale and Trumbull, Paine's eyes meet the viewer. He is similarly seated, but strikes a more expansive pose than in the earlier portraits. This is achieved through the openness of the coat as it curves toward the back, perhaps held back by a hand, out of view, resting on the hip. With this gesture, more of the chest is exposed, giving a greater sense of breadth to the figure. Without the original painting, it is impossible to know the color palette, but Sharp has skillfully captured the lustrous surface of the double-breasted waistcoat. The fringe that outlines the lapels and front opening contributes a visual interest and adds to the richness suggested by the sheen of the fabric. The deep "V" of white created by the shirt and the cravat connect the fine waistcoat to the face. Sharp indicates a very simple ruffle without lace attached to the shirt front. Paine's hair is more loosely dressed than in the Peale or Trumbull, but it is in keeping with the trend toward less powder and less formality.

The simplified hair dressing, sometimes accompanied by more radical changes in clothing, was worrisome to some. Sir Nathaniel William Wraxall, a writer and member of the British House of Commons, connected clothing and appearance to his apprehensions attached to the Age of Revolution, and wrote in his memoirs that "the sinister events of the American war had already begun to shed a degree of political gloom over the capital and the kingdom; but this cloud, dark as it was, bore no comparison with the terror and alarm that pervaded the firmest minds in 1792 and 1793, after the first explosion of the French Revolution." He obviously did not share Paine's enthusiasm for revolution, and blamed political events for the leveling trends that resulted in more casual styles in hair and clothing. He wrote: "Dress never totally fell till the era of Jacobinism and of equality in 1793 and 1794. It was then that pantaloons, cropped hair, and shoe-strings, as well as the total abolition of buckles and ruffles, together with the disuse of hair-powder, characterized the men."[37]

Romney's original painting of Paine was taken on the cusp of the changes outlined by Wraxall. Certainly, Paine claimed a leadership position in the leveling process, and the Romney/Sharp portrait shows him adopting a less formal style of dressing the hair as well. It is difficult to say whether his hair is cropped or still pulled into a queue, but he had eliminated the side curls of his earlier portraits, along with the hair powder. Sharp's print definitely indicates a natural hairline and not a wig.

As the Romney/Sharp is a half-length portrait, it is impossible to say if Paine had taken up the more radical styles in clothing by exchanging his knee breeches for pantaloons, or shoes that laced rather than buckled. What is visible to the viewer is a very fine frock coat and waistcoat that ensure the same attributes of a gentleman displayed in the earlier Peale and Trumbull. The subtle difference in the Romney/Sharp portrait comes from the confident air of his pose. This confidence could stem from the "rightness" of the ideas put forward, first in *Common Sense,* and more fully elaborated in *The Rights of Man.*

The publication of the first part of *The Rights of Man* in 1791 in Philadelphia brought the name of Thomas Paine back into the American political scene, and linked his name with that of Thomas Jefferson. This was not intentional on Jefferson's part, resulting instead from a miscalculation. Jefferson did not intend the note he included when returning a borrowed copy of the London publication of *Rights of Man* to the Philadelphia printer to become a preface of the new American edition. His remarks—"that something is at length to be publicly said against the political heresies which have sprung up among us," and "I have no doubt our citizens will rally a second time round the standard of Common Sense"—generated a polemical firestorm. Jefferson explained to family members that he was not prepared for the "dust Paine's pamphlet has kicked up here." As he told James Monroe, he agreed with Paine's principles, but "never meant to have entered as a volunteer into the cause."[38]

Jefferson's reaction to the *Rights of Man* controversy reflected the demeanor captured by John Trumbull's small portrait of a few years earlier. Jefferson—thoughtful, contemplative, gazing into an undisclosed distance—was now publicly linked with the Paine who faced his audience with a direct and unblinking gaze (see figs. 2 and 3). Jefferson could not retreat to the more comfortable position of working quietly behind the scenes to promote his political agenda. The impetuous James Monroe saw some benefit in Jefferson's mistake: "Your sentiments indeed, if they had been previously question'd, are made known as well by the short note prefix to Paines pamphlet, as a volume could do it."[39] Jefferson's opinions were now public, and his connection with Paine was publicized vigorously by the Federalist press. While rebutting *The Rights of Man*, a writer in Boston's *Columbian Centinel* linked the "parent of this production" and "the gentleman who has stood its sponsor in this country."[40]

A visual link between Jefferson and Paine was established through Jefferson's portrait collection, which had moved with him to his Philadelphia residence. Paine's portrait was noticed by the British consul, Edward Thornton, who remarked in a 1792 letter to a correspondent in England that, "I do not know whether I ever mentioned that a miniature of Payne has a place in Mr. Jefferson's collection." To Thornton, the supposed dignity that this should afford did not match his view of Paine's character. For him, Paine was "a picture already tolerably deformed, of ingratitude, of imprudence and vulgarity," and he accused Paine further of "affected nicety and real meanness." According to Thornton: "He was accustomed to drink with the lowest blackguard in any dirty public house; of course was generally in distress for money and sometimes for necessaries. He yet affected such a delicacy, that his friends were afraid of alarming his feelings by any direct offer of assistance, but were under the necessity of putting the continental money into his breeches pockets at night, which he however had prudence enough to use the next day without hesitation or inquiry."[41] These habits observed by Thornton questioned any pretence of gentlemanly status as suggested by Jefferson's small portrait and its placement in a collection of Worthies.

Thornton's comments substantiate that Jefferson continued to display Paine's portrait and that it was the same small portrait from John Trumbull. Obviously, he had never obtained a portrait of life size. If this had remained a real interest, he could have commissioned a copy from Charles Willson Peale of the Paine portrait that hung in the Peale gallery. As Jefferson never made further reference to a second portrait of Paine, it is impossible to say if the lack of motivation stemmed from Paine's rising notoriety or simply that Jefferson was not as avid a collector once he returned from Europe. He continued to add occasional pieces to his collection, but not with the interest he had displayed while still in Paris.

It is doubtful whether Trumbull, who broke with Jefferson over many of the same issues that propelled Paine, would have been willing to paint Paine again in the wake of the deep partisan divisions of the 1790s. In his *Autobiography*, Trumbull wrote that the atrocities of the French Revolution—unlike the "calm splendor of our own Revolution"—repelled him, "while he [Jefferson] approved or apologized for all. He opposed Washington—I revered him—and a coldness gradually succeeded." The final break came at a dinner party in 1793 when Trumbull felt he had been offended by a dinner guest from Virginia and Jefferson as host did not attempt to stop the "attack" but only smiled and nodded. The debate had been over religion, with Trumbull defending Christianity. "From this time my acquaintance with Mr. Jefferson became cold and distant."[42] Trumbull's disgust with the French Revolution, his fealty to Washington, and defense of Christianity would make any relationship with Thomas Paine even more distasteful.

Since Trumbull's painting of the small portrait for Jefferson in late 1788, Paine's life had changed dramatically. Charged with sedition for his *Rights of Man,* he had been forced to leave London. During his retreat to France, he experienced first the exhilaration of the Revolution's early days, but was then caught up in the vortex of ever-shifting power struggles and thrown in prison. He left prison ill, weak, and extremely angry, blaming Washington for a lack of American support and lashing out in an open letter that condemned the president personally and politically. During this same period, he produced a new work, *The Age of Reason,* in which he attacked organized religion and questioned the divinity of Jesus and the authority of the Bible. No doubt John Trumbull would have been among the many Americans who rejected Paine's continued defense of the French Revolution, as well as among the even greater number of Americans outraged at Paine's public attacks on Washington and Christianity.

Despite the growing public resentment against Paine, as president, Jefferson supported Paine in his request to return to America in 1802. Jefferson had to realize that public knowledge of his offer to allow Paine passage on a United States frigate would be controversial, but he must have felt confident enough that his popularity would minimize the political risk. Once more, Jefferson's name was linked with that of Paine, now a reviled "infidel," and no longer known as the great champion of American independence. His reputation was even more in question than Jefferson's accidental public endorsement of *The Rights of Man*.

American newspapers quickly announced Paine's arrival in Baltimore Harbor on October 30, 1802: "Tom Paine, the infidel; the vile condemner and most bitter enemy, of the Christian religion, the libeler of WASHINGTON, and the particular friend and correspondent of Mr. Jefferson, patron of all that is base, has at length arrived in the United States." Some predicted grim consequences from Paine's influence and placed the blame directly on Jefferson: "It is inconceiveable what motives could have prompted Mr. Jefferson to an act which will plunge his country into disgrace . . . which will pollute the minds of the rising generation, and give a scope to vice and unlimited licentiousness."[43]

The Thomas Paine who returned to America in 1802 with Jefferson's encouragement hardly resembled the gentleman of Trumbull's small portrait. Still, the physical descriptions by Jefferson's opponents were as outlandish as their newspaper references to "the infidel" Paine. Eli Whitney encountered Paine in a Washington boardinghouse in 1802 and left a most detailed and repulsive description of rotting teeth, discolored skin, and a nose covered with carbuncles. He reported Paine as meanly dressed and "his whole appearance rather slovenly," and seemed satisfied that Paine had met his expectation as "the same filthy old sot that he has ever been represented."[44] From the other camp, a staunch Jeffersonian-Republican, Dr. Samuel Mitchill, met Paine at a dinner party in Washington given by Secretary of the Treasury Albert Gallatin and left a more generous word portrait. He saw "a red and rugged face," which, to Paine's credit, "looks as if it had been much hackneyed in the service of the world." But despite the worn look, Mitchill added, "his eyes are bright and lively." Obviously, the "vigour" that once described Paine's eyes had not been lost. Mitchill also noted that his aquiline nose "corresponded in colour with the firey appearance of his cheeks."[45] The redness of Paine's nose, and the amount of brandy he consumed, were noted by many. A member of the British legation in Washington observed that "he had but a bad character for sobriety," and a couplet from the publication *Salmagundi* ran: "Tom Paine is come from far, from far; His nose is like a blazing star!"[46]

Paine's visits to the presidential mansion did not go unnoticed. New Hampshire Senator William Plumer was outraged when he called upon Jefferson and "Thomas Paine entered, seated himself by the side of the President, and conversed and behaved towards him with the familiarity of an intimate and an equal."[47] His actions would suggest that in Paine's mind he and Jefferson were equal—just as when Trumbull had pictured them both as gentlemen in his dual portraits. To Senator Plumer, and much of the rest of the world, Paine had fallen far below the status of gentleman. The political opposition suggested that their president could be tainted by the presence of Paine. An editorial in the November 15, 1802, issue of the *Gazette of the United States* asked its readers to consider the morality of their president in light of his association with "Tom Paine."[48]

Jefferson may have been able to disregard the warnings that he was compromising his moral standing, but he was certainly aware that Paine's presence was politically dangerous. Jefferson's discomfort may have been perceived by Paine, who accused the president of "a sort of shyness, as if you stood in fear of federal observation." Jefferson denied Paine's accusation and blamed an extremely pressing work schedule. This may have mollified Paine. Even though he left Washington the following month never to return, he continued a cordial correspondence with Jefferson. Paine traveled north, eventually arriving in New York City, where his last portrait was taken.

In New York, Paine met an artist who matched him in eccentricity: John Wesley Jarvis. The artist and writer William Dunlap knew Jarvis and commented upon his friendship with Paine in his *History of the Rise and Progress of the Arts of Design in the United States*. According to Dunlap, Jarvis and Paine were house-mates and became close friends. Dunlap's reference to Paine is not flattering, as he identifies him as "Thomas Paine, who wrote 'Common Sense,' and played the fool." He made the interesting observation that Jarvis could not help admire Paine's genius, suggesting, however, that "few things are more dangerous than admiration of a misled man of uncommon talents." Notwithstanding Dunlap's misgivings, Jarvis left a fine portrait of an older Thomas Paine with a kindly expression. The bust-sized portrait shows only head and shoulders, and so concentrates upon Paine's unassuming face. His hair is now thin, lank, and beyond any concern for the latest style. Paine wears a greatcoat with double cape collar, and Jarvis has painted him with a very white cravat and a ruffled front to his shirt. Given Paine's economic condition at the time, it is possible that the greatcoat belonged to Jarvis, and the white linen may have been added by the artist as well. Paine's eyes are the most arresting feature—still dark, intense and gazing straight at the viewer. Apparently, Paine's directness never changed, even when he was failing in health and destitute.

Long after Paine's death in 1809, Jefferson continued to hold the man and his work in high regard. Jefferson told his grandson Francis Eppes that Paine was an honest man and a great advocate for human rights, and that no one had ever exceeded him in ease of style or simple and unassuming language.

John Wesley Jarvis. *Thomas Paine,* ca. 1806/7. Oil on canvas.
(Courtesy National Gallery of Art, Washington)

Paine's problem was that he had made "bitter enemies of the priests and Pharisees."[49]

Jefferson's feelings toward Paine were best expressed to Madame Bonneville, an old friend of Paine's who had cared for him in his final illness. Paine had left her his papers, and she hoped to publish the correspondence between Paine and Jefferson. But at seventy years of age, Jefferson did not want to risk stirring up old animosities. He asked that the letters not be published during his lifetime.[50]

Jefferson confessed to Bonneville that "while he [Paine] lived I thought it my duty, as well as a test of my own political principles to support him against the persecution of an unprincipled faction."[51] Paine was a "duty" and a "test" for Jefferson. His encounters with Paine often placed him in uncomfortable situations. Yet Paine was the man of *Common Sense,* and for Jefferson he remained an "American Worthy."

Jefferson never obtained a full-size portrait of Thomas Paine, yet he never gave up displaying his image among other eminent men and figures important to history. His "Catalog of Paintings &c. at Monticello," prepared between 1809 and 1815, lists only one artwork with Paine as its subject, the Trumbull portrait. The catalog indicates that the painting hung in the parlor in the lower tier. The works in Monticello's parlor were arranged in three tiers, with the most illustrious at the top. The fact that Paine's portrait rested on the lower tier probably had more to do with the size than negative notoriety, as he was flanked by small prints of the Polish hero, Thaddeus Kosciuszko, and the man of science, Count Rumford. Jefferson's catalog does list other miniature portraits in the public rooms of the house, but these hung in the tearoom, adjacent to the dining room. Jefferson chose to place the Paine portrait in the parlor, which made it available to a larger number of visitors.

Thomas Paine's image continued to be displayed at Monticello until Jefferson's death. The small oil sketch of Paine was not one chosen by Jefferson's family to keep and so was packed along with others for shipment to Boston, where the family had become convinced the artworks would be better received and bring a better price. It was listed in the Boston Athenaeum Sale Catalogue as "No. 316—Thomas Paine-an original on wood,—Trumbull," and then it disappeared until identified in 1955. Whether the vandalism it suffered in the interim was intentional, with symbolic blinding and piercing through the chest, or as Sizer has suggested, the prank of a child, may never be known. Still, it is ironic how the small portrait parallels the life of its subject, from a position in a pantheon of American Worthies, to being vilified, before finally being restored to its former position in the parlor of Monticello, where it hangs today.

NOTES

1. Jefferson's receipt of the Paine portrait was acknowledged in a letter, Thomas Jefferson [TJ] to John Trumbull, 12 January 1789, in *The Papers of Thomas Jefferson,* ed. Julian P. Boyd et al., 39 vols. to date (Princeton, N.J.: Princeton University Press, 1950–) [hereafter cited as *Jefferson Papers*], 14:440–41. The information on the damaged Paine portrait is from Theodore Sizer's report published in the *Yale University Library Gazette* (30 April 1956) and reprinted in Theodore Sizer, *Works of John Trumbull: Artist of the American Revolution* (New Haven, Conn.: Yale University Press, 1967), appendix A.

2. TJ to James Madison, 25 May 1784 and 8 December 1784, *Jefferson Papers,* 7:289, 558.

3. TJ to William Stephens Smith, 22 October 1786, ibid., 10:479; TJ to William Short, 6 April 1790, ibid., 16:318.

4. For the use of the term "worthy," see Brandon Brame Fortune, "Portraits of Virtue and Genius: Pantheons of Worthies and Public Portraiture in the Early American Republic, 1780–1820" (PhD diss., University of North Carolina, 1986). Fortune has published many outstanding works on early American art, and though her dissertation remains

unpublished, it is still one of the most complete studies on collections of worthies in the early American republic.

5. Jonathan Richardson, *An Essay on the Theory of Painting,* 2nd ed. (London, 1725), 14, quoted in Ellen G. Miles, "Portraits of the Heroes of Louisbourg, 1745–1751," *American Art Journal* 15 (Winter 1983): 64.

6. Thomas Paine to TJ, 18 August 1787, *Jefferson Papers,* 12:45. The letter from Jefferson to Paine requesting the portrait has not been located.

7. John Keane, *Tom Paine: A Political Life* (Boston: Little, Brown, 1995), 206.

8. For discussion of the Adams portrait commission, see TJ to William Stephens Smith, 31 December 1787, *Jefferson Papers,* 12:485; and William Stephens Smith to TJ, 16 January 1788, ibid., 12:517.

9. TJ to William Stephens Smith, 2 February 1788, ibid., 12:558.

10. John Trumbull to TJ, 30 October 1787, ibid., 12:297.

11. Susan Stein, *The Worlds of Thomas Jefferson at Monticello* (New York: Harry N. Abrams, 1993), 126.

12. TJ to John Trumbull, 4 October 1787, *Jefferson Papers,* 12:207. The "kit-kat" was originated by Sir Godfrey Kellner and named for the many portraits created in this size for members of London's famous Kit Kat Club. The information on the "Kit-Kat" portrait is from Carolyn Kinder Carr and Ellen G. Miles, *A Brush with History: Paintings from the National Portrait Gallery* (Washington, D.C.: Smithsonian Institution, 2001), 32; and Fortune, "Portraits of Virtue," 17.

13. TJ to John Trumbull, 12 January 1789, *Jefferson Papers,* 14:440.

14. John Trumbull to TJ, 19 December 1788, ibid., 14:364.

15. The print of Paine taken from C. W. Peale's portrait by John Watson in 1783 may have been familiar to Trumbull, but the appearance of the figure in Trumbull's work is decidedly different.

16. The discussion of these two portraits is based upon an on-site comparative study. They are currently displayed in Jefferson's Monticello and are owned and preserved by the Thomas Jefferson Foundation. There are excellent black-and-white reproductions and descriptions in Stein, *Worlds of Thomas Jefferson,* 124–25.

17. John Trumbull to TJ, 19 December 1788, *Jefferson Papers,* 14:365.

18. All references are from Keane, *Tom Paine,* 128, 371, and 608n160.

19. Paine to TJ, 15 January 1789 and 16 February 1789, *Jefferson Papers,* 14:454, 564. Paine's activities at this time are discussed in Keane, *Tom Paine,* 275–82.

20. Charles Willson Peale, as quoted in Charles Coleman Sellers, *Charles Willson Peale* (New York: Scribner, 1969), 183–84.

21. See Guilhem Scherf, "The History Portrait," in *Citizens and Kings: Portraits in the Age of Revolution, 1760–1830,* curated by Robert Rosenblum, English ed., redesigned with new material (London: Royal Academy of Arts, 2007), 112–13.

22. An electronic version of this catalogue is available through *Early American Imprints, Series I: Evans,* no. 29281.

23. Charles Coleman Sellers, *Portraits and Miniatures by Charles Willson Peale* (Philadelphia: American Philosophical Society, 1952), 156.

24. Charles Willson Peale to Henry Laurens, 6 March 1780, *The Papers of Henry Laurens,* ed. Philip M. Hamer et al., 16 vols. (Columbia: University of South Carolina Press, 1968–2003), 15:243–44.

25. Peale did not invoice Laurens for the portraits until 20 February 1787. He charged: "for a portrait of General Washington a whole length (a Coppy) thirty Guineas"; "To Portrait of Mr. Paine an original picture in 3/4 size Ten Guineas" (see *The Selected Papers of Charles Willson Peale and His Family,* ed. Lillian B. Miller, 5 vols. [New Haven, Conn.: Yale University Press, 1983–2000], 1:467).

26. For a discussion of traditional poses for scholars, see Brandon Brame Fortune with Deborah J. Warner, *Franklin and His Friends: Portraying the Man of Science in Eighteenth-Century America* (Washington, D.C.: Smithsonian Institution, National Portrait Gallery; Philadelphia: In association with the University of Pennsylvania Press, 1999), 26–29, 128–29.

27. For dates of the negotiations resulting in the Treaty of Paris, see Stacy Schiff, *A Great Improvisation: Franklin, France, and the Birth of America* (New York: Henry Holt, 2005), 325–26; 349–50; for the publication of the Paine print, refer to Sellers, *Portraits and Miniatures by Charles Willson Peale,* 156.

28. Sellers, *Portraits and Miniatures by Charles Willson Peale,* 156.

29. Advertisement for the print from the *Gazetteer,* 28 July 1791, reprinted in David Freeman Hawke, *Paine* (New York: Harper and Row, 1974), 231; and in Sellers, *Portraits and Miniatures by Charles Wilson Peale,* 156.

30. For Paine's feud with publisher Robert Bell, see Trish Loughran, *The Republic in Print: Print Culture in the Age of U.S. Nation Building, 1770–1870* (New York: Columbia University Press, 2007), 85–88.

31. Keane, *Tom Paine,* 170–76 ("Poor Payne" quotation, 182).

32. Hawke, *Paine,* 110.

33. Sarah Franklin Bache to Benjamin Franklin, 14 January 1781, Gimbel Collection, American Philosophical Society, Philadelphia, cited in Keane, *Tom Paine,* 206. See also the discussion of Paine's personal traits in Gordon Wood, "Thomas Paine, America's First Public Intellectual," in *Revolutionary Characters: What Made the Founders Different* (New York: Penguin Press, 2006).

34. Marquis de Chastellux, *Travels in North-America, in the Years 1780, 1781, and 1782 . . . Translated . . . by an English Gentleman . . .* (Dublin, 1787), 310.

35. Paine to Henry Laurens, 14 September 1779, *Papers of Henry Laurens,* 15:166.

36. M. T. S. Raimback, ed., *Memoirs and Recollections of Abraham Raimback* (London, 1843), 78–80, cited in Keane, *Tom Paine,* 608n160.

37. *The Historical and the Posthumous Memoirs of Sir Nathaniel William Wraxall, 1772–1784*, ed. Henry B. Wheatley, 5 vols. (London, 1884), 1:98–99.

38. TJ to Thomas Mann Randolph, 3 July 1791, *Jefferson Papers*, 20:295–96; TJ to James Monroe, 10 July 1791, ibid., 20:297.

39. James Monroe to TJ, 2 July 1791, ibid., 20:304.

40. "Publicola, No. 1," reprinted from *Columbian Centinel* (Boston) in *Journal & Patriotic Register* (New York), 6 July 1791.

41. Edward Thornton to James Bland Burges, 28 April 1792, as reprinted in S. W. Jackman, "A Young Englishman Reports on the New Nation: Edward Thornton to James Bland Burges, 1791–1793, *William and Mary Quarterly*, 3rd ser., 18 (January 1961), 107–8.

42. *Autobiography, Reminiscences, and Letters of John Trumbull, from 1756 to 1841* (New York, 1841), 168–72.

43. *United States Chronicle* (Providence, R.I.), 18 November 1802, from the *Virginia Gazette* and reprinted in *The Republican; or, Anti-Democrat* (Baltimore), 17 November 1802.

44. Reprinted in *Citizen Paine: Thomas Paine's Thoughts on Man, Government, Society, and Religion*, ed. John P. Kaminski (Lanham, Md.: Rowman and Littlefield, 2002), 29.

45. From "Dr. Mitchill's Letters from Washington" as quoted in Keane, *Tom Paine*, 470.

46. The reference to Paine's sobriety is from Augustus John Foster, *Jeffersonian America: Notes On the United States of America, Collected In the Years 1805–6–7 and 11–12*, ed. Richard Beale Davis (San Marino, Calif.: Huntington Library, 1954), 303; the couplet is from William Irving, James Kirke Paulding, and Washington Irving in the nineteenth-century periodical *Salmagundi* (24 January 1807).

47. William Plumer to Judge Smith, 9 December 1802, in *Life of William Plumer, by His Son, William Plumer Junior* (Boston, 1856), reprinted in Keane, *Tom Paine*, 470.

48. "Tom Pain and His Friend Thomas Jefferson," *Gazette of the United States*, reprinted in *Boston Commercial Gazette*, 15 November 1802.

49. TJ to Francis Eppes, 19 January 1821, in *The Family Letters of Thomas Jefferson*, ed. Edwin Morris Betts and James Adam Bear Jr. (Charlottesville: Published for the Thomas Jefferson Memorial Foundation by the University Press of Virginia, 1986), 437–38.

50. Margaret B. Bonneville, 13 March 1813, in *The Papers of Thomas Jefferson: Retirement Series*, ed. J. Jefferson Looney et al., 9 vols. to date (Princeton, N.J.: Princeton University Press, 2009–), 6:8.

51. TJ to Margaret B. Bonneville, 3 April 1813, ibid., 6:47.

Two Paths from Revolution
Jefferson, Paine, and the Radicalization of Enlightenment Thought

MICHAEL ZUCKERT

Thomas Jefferson and Thomas Paine shared an enthusiasm for the revolutions of the late eighteenth and early nineteenth centuries. Both, of course, were strong partisans of the American Revolution; both were among the strongest non-French supporters of the French Revolution. Both called for and welcomed future revolutions. No American citizens played a greater role in the French Revolution than Jefferson and Paine. The former was much involved in the early stages of the Revolution, consulting with the Lafayette circle and advising on the *Declaration of the Rights of Man and of the Citizen.* Paine was even more heavily engaged, serving in the French Convention, writing on behalf of the Revolution, and debating the most pressing questions, including the fate of Louis XVI. Moreover, Paine came within a hair of sharing the ultimate fate of a great number of the French revolutionaries—the guillotine.[1]

Both Jefferson and Paine had an effect on the French Revolution, but I wish to explore the possible effect of the French Revolution on them. A prima facie case can be made for such an effect, for we see in both of them a radicalization of their political thinking suggestively related to their engagements with the Revolution. Their political thinking moved in rather different directions, however. Jefferson's most striking shift occurred in his political thinking proper, with his development of a theory of ward republicanism and his strenuous call for a participatory republicanism far beyond anything he had earlier favored, and beyond what any others of that generation of Americans contemplated. Paine's shift came in the development of a new theory of economic rights, a theory that has often been called (plausibly) a precursor to the theory of the welfare state.[2] Paine's "welfarism" marked a distinct shift from his early, libertarian emphasis on the limited role of government and the dominance of negative rights. Although the two men moved in somewhat different directions, we can discern a common concern with the problem of consent in modern philosophy in the evolution in the thought of both of them.

THE EARLY PAINE

Paine began his career with a position very like that of a modern libertarian. He put natural rights at the forefront of his political thinking (see the title of his chief book), he understood rights to be negative rights, and he believed that the task of government was limited to protecting citizens from violations of their rights. Paine's early position was thus rather like that of John Locke, but Paine was more doctrinaire than Locke in limiting the legitimate scope of governmental action. Accordingly, his position was more full-bodied in developing a theory to account for the positive achievements of civilization independent of government. One must appreciate, Paine insisted, the difference between government and society. The former operates via coercion, the latter by voluntary action. As Paine so incisively put it: "Society is produced by our wants and government by our wickedness." Society and the voluntary actions (such as market exchanges) undertaken to meet our wants supply all the positive things that contribute to human happiness. Government contributes to happiness only in a negative way, by preventing or punishing the evil that men would do that interferes with happiness. Even more strongly than Jefferson, Paine pronounced government merely a "necessary evil." He would certainly have agreed with Thoreau's Jeffersonian dictum that "that government is best which governs least."[3]

Yet in his later works of the 1790s—roughly two decades after his early work—Paine laid out a program that sounds like that of a modern welfare state: progressive taxation, property redistribution for the sake of greater equality in society, old-age pensions, and other proposals, some of which we shall discuss in more detail below.[4] Perhaps most striking is his insistence that those provisions should not be seen as charity or prudent policy, but as a matter of right.[5] Recognizing Paine's affirmation of these welfare provisions as a matter of right helps set us on track to understand the political philosophic significance of his late doctrine. The arguments that emerged in the nineteenth century in favor of the welfare state were actually quite different from those Paine presented, as they depended on utilitarian or German idealist grounds. Paine, however, attempted to develop his case for welfare rights out of the womb of the kind of Lockean rights he deployed in his early libertarian days.[6] Paine is thus particularly interesting, for he implicitly claimed that the negative rights doctrine in and of itself generates welfare rights.[7] If true, Paine made an argument of first-rate importance, both philosophically and politically.

Paine burst on the world with *Common Sense,* his 1776 tract in favor of American independence. Like most of the American pamphlets and official documents in the period leading up to the Revolution, *Common Sense* begins with some brief reflections on political fundamentals. Most of the Americans expressed these fundamentals in Lockean terms—an original "state of nature," or state of equality, which, for various reasons, degenerates into a state of insecurity, requiring the establishment of government by means of a social contract to protect the rights endangered in the state of nature.

Paine sees things in much the same way.[8] He begins by positing human beings as living without government. He even thinks of them without society.[9] "In this state of natural liberty, society will be their first thought."[10] In what is probably his most characteristic idea, Paine firmly distinguishes between the making of society and the making of government. Society comes first; human wants are such that solitary men cannot satisfy them. Paine does not accept Rousseau's effort to show that human beings could have survived a very long time in a solitary state of nature. Human wants, according to Paine, move men into society: "necessity, like a gravitating power" leads them to seek "the reciprocal blessings of society." Human beings are driven into society not only by these sorts of external necessities, but also because the human "mind [is] so unfitted for perpetual solitude."[11]

Paine seems to affirm, then, that in a very deep sense human beings are social animals, for they need others, not only as means or instruments for the satisfaction of their individual wants, but as part of their nature as intellectual beings. Contrary to the views of thinkers like Aristotle, government is responsible for very little of the goods of civilization. "Society performs for itself almost everything which is ascribed to government."[12] Let us call this the descriptive, or sociological, presumption against government. More important is the moral presumption against government, for it is this that allows Paine to call most government an "imposition," a morally illegitimate intrusion. The source of the moral presumption is the doctrine of natural rights. To possess natural rights, Paine implies, is to possess, among other things, a presumptive immunity against the use of force and violence against oneself. With this presumption comes to light the true meaning of the state of nature in Paine (as well as in Locke and Jefferson): being born with or possessing inherent natural rights, men have an original and inherent immunity against the use of coercion; all coercive authority, all government, stands in need of moral justification in order to achieve legitimacy; and positing a state of nature as the beginning point is largely a way of expressing that demand.

Thus, it is not inconsistent in any way to affirm both natural sociability and a state of nature. Conceptually, if not chronologically, society precedes government. "Government, like dress, is the badge of lost innocence; the palaces of kings are built on the ruins of the bowers of paradise." At the beginning of society, human beings, conscious of their needs for each other and of the mutual benefits of their relations, will be just to each other. As long as they remain so, government, law, and coercion are not needed. However, this kind of spontaneous society is not self-sustaining. "As nothing but heaven is impregnable to vice, it will unavoidably happen, that in proportion as they surmount the first difficulties of emigration, which bound them together in a common cause, they will begin to relax in their duty and attachment to each other; and this remissness will point out the necessity of establishing some form of government to supply the defect of moral virtue." Social men are virtuous at first because the necessities that drive them into society are visible and fully felt by them.[13]

The tragedy of society, as Paine sketches it, follows from the paradox that the more successful society is in meeting needs, the more likely men are to forget the necessities prompting to society. They feel less dependent on each other and thus are more tempted to take advantage of others. Although human beings have a natural love for the society of others, nonetheless, the chief forces producing society are the self-interested drive of need of others. Under the conscious reign of necessity, men appreciate the connection between their own needs and the need to be just to others in order to procure their willing cooperation in the social division of labor. When the success of society dims their consciousness of the necessities underlying society, then government must be formed. Its purpose is to produce an artificial necessity of a second order to replace the lost first-order natural necessity that underwrote the original moral virtue. Government, law, coercion through imposition, or threat of punishment: these produce the new necessities that make men just.

Government is, then, a late arrival, and one with completely remedial functions, to make up for "the inability of moral virtue to govern the world." Its design and end are to provide nothing but "freedom and security."[14] Clearly, Paine had in mind a political system very like the "night-watchman state"—a government that protects individual liberty and free voluntary social action by maintaining basic rules of justice, thereby providing security. Paine affirms a state with limited tasks on both deontological and consequentialist grounds. Unlike many who write in the liberal tradition, Paine gave more of his space and explicit attention to the consequentialist argument—he took special pride in his discoveries of the government–society distinction and of the great independent role of society. But this is not to say that natural rights play little role in Paine's thinking—witness the title of his chief work, *Rights of Man*, which phrase, Paine is clear, means natural rights. The first part of that work contains what is probably Paine's most extensive discussion of natural rights, a discussion that probes the important questions of the origin or source of rights and the relation between natural rights—that is, claims human beings can raise in a state of nature—and civil rights—claims they can raise within society.[15] Paine supplemented that theoretical discussion in his text of 1797, *Agrarian Justice*, where he explained the right to property and attempted to demonstrate that the right to property implies the robust welfare rights that he described in his later works.

PAINE: FROM NIGHT WATCHMAN TO POSITIVE STATE

Before we attempt to probe Paine's rights theory, we require some notion of the rights claims and public duties beyond the night-watchman state that he identified in his later work. It is only in his writings of the French Revolutionary era—in the second part of *Rights of Man* and in his short but powerful essay *Agrarian Justice*—that these broader rights claims emerge.

The two works in which he laid out his notion of economic rights are quite different from each other in one crucial respect. The rights and policies laid out in the second part of *Rights of Man* are particularly tied to England. Both the policies proposed and the rationales put forward for them are tied specifically to English historical practices. Although Paine insisted that his proposals here are matters of right, not of charity, nonetheless, the rights involved are heavily affected by specifics that make them less than universally relevant.[16] Quite different is the case made in *Agrarian Justice*. In a prefatory inscription addressed to "the Legislature and the Executive Directory of the French Republic," Paine implicitly distinguished this work from his earlier treatment of economic rights: "The plan contained in this work is not adapted for any particular country alone; the principle on which it is based is general."[17]

Given its universality, *Agrarian Justice* will be of greater interest here, but the discussion in *Rights of Man* in some ways gives a firmer picture of the breadth of policy Paine was prepared to recommend: He would subsidize all poor families with a per-child allowance, which would also serve to subsidize education, for each of the poor children so supported would be required to attend school. He would give an old-age pension to all above age fifty, and a larger pension to all above age sixty. He would give a small maternity allowance to all mothers when they gave birth. He would subsidize the funerals of poor persons who died away from their local parish. He would set up homes for the urban homeless and subsidize work for the urban unemployed. He would establish a pension fund for demobilized soldiers and sailors, of which he thought there would be a great many once the revolutionary era of universal peace arrived. He would give tax relief to the middle class and would pay for his welfare plans by instituting a steep inheritance tax on landed wealth. The aim of the tax was not merely to raise revenue, but to break up the large estates of the aristocracy and thereby reduce or annul the outsized influence of the aristocrats. The rest would be paid for by increased savings and reduction of waste in government spending (*plus ça change, . . .*). The "waste" he would save on would include such things as the monarchy. That is to say, the economic welfare rights he would underwrite would require a thorough constitutional transformation of England.

The proposals vetted in *Agrarian Justice* are simpler. Each citizen is to receive, on coming of age, a fairly substantial payment (in Paine's proposal, 15 pounds), which could be a stake for all new citizens. At the other end of one's working life, Paine would have the state pay every person, on reaching age fifty, an old-age annuity (of 10 pounds per year in his proposal).

PAINE: NATURAL RIGHTS AND WELFARE RIGHTS

Although natural rights play a pivotal role in Paine's thinking, his discussions of them are few and somewhat disappointing. In line with the practical/polemical character of his calling, he paid far more attention to the question of the practical implications of human rights than to their nature, origin, and ground. This fact may derive from his (unacknowledged) connections to earlier rights thinkers like Locke, who, Paine might have thought, had laid out the philosophic dimension of rights, leaving the development of the full implications and implementation to others, like himself.

The polemical setting of his works supplied the context for his most extensive discussion of rights. Edmund Burke's attack on the French Revolution drove Paine to speak more theoretically of rights than he normally did. In his *Reflections on the Revolution in France*, Burke questioned the idea of natural rights as appealed to by the French and by the English admirers of the French. Burke challenged them by claiming that all English rights, and one supposes, by extension, all rights, simply had a historical source. "It has been the uniform policy of our constitution," said Burke, "to claim and assert our liberties, as an extended inheritance, delivered to us from our forefathers and transmitted to our posterity; as an estate specially belonging to the people of this kingdom, without any reference whatever to any other more general or prior right."[18]

Paine's hopes for his native land were quite the opposite of Burke's, for he wished to see the American and French Revolutions spread there and produce a genuine representative republic, without the king and nobles that Burke saw as the glories of the existing British constitution. The chief agenda of the first part of *Rights of Man,* therefore, was to reaffirm the naturalness and the universality of rights in the face of Burke's effort to historicize them.[19]

His efforts to refute Burke lead Paine to think through the nature and origin of rights in such a way that, as we shall see, it contributes importantly to his later formulation of welfare rights, and, perhaps serendipitously, brings him close to one of the main themes of the late Jefferson. Paine's first retort to Burke consists of an outright rejection of the idea that Parliament, or anybody else in 1688 or 1689, had the right to irrevocably commit the nation to the constitution adopted at that time, as though that generation had powers and rights later generations lacked, or as if it had the power to alienate the rights of later generations. As Paine put it: "There never did, there never will, and there never can exist a parliament, or any description of men, or any generation of men, in any country, possessed of the right or the power of binding and controlling posterity to the '*end of time,*' or of commanding for ever how the world shall be governed, or who shall govern it." The "rights of man," Paine concludes, were but imperfectly understood at the Glorious Revolution, for these rights disallow what the men of the seventeenth century attempted to do.[20]

In looking for a historical source of rights, Burke is assuming that some past generation had specially binding powers and thus was unequal in authority to other generations. But what could authorize one generation over another? How could we identify this privileged generation? In looking for a specially privileged generation, retorted Paine, we must go back to the very beginning: "We shall come then to the time when man came from the hand of his maker"; we come then "to the divine origin of the rights of man at the creation."[21] Paine may have had in mind a version of Locke's well-known workmanship argument: "Men being all the workmanship of one omnipotent and infinitely wise maker, all the servants of one sovereign master, sent into the world by his order and about his business, they are his property, whose workmanship they are, made to last during his, not another's pleasure."[22] "Man," Paine says, "has no property in man; neither has any generation a property in the generations which are to follow."[23] That claim is congruent with the implications of the divine ownership argument, and with another position Locke also affirms—that men are self-owners. As Paine says, "Personal rights . . . are a species of property of the most sacred kind." If so, nobody can dispose of the rights of others and no generation can govern another.[24]

Paine is particularly concerned to develop one of the implications of his thesis about ownership. The main point he seems to want to make by appealing to creation and the first man is that all men are equal, that there is a "unity in man." All men derive from the creator, and reason gives us no basis for distinguishing one from another in the crucial respect of deriving from the creator. Whatever authority one generation or individual has, all generations must have, for rights inhere in all men by virtue of what Paine refers to here as their relation to their source. The claims of natural rights are claims inhering in their humanity—that is, in whatever it is that makes them human—and therefore in these claims men must be equal. As Paine put it: "Every generation is equal in rights to the generations which preceded it, by the same rule that every individual is born equal in rights with his contemporary." Paine thus establishes that men are equal in their rights; he needs to specify more precisely what rights they have.[25]

Natural rights are to be distinguished from civil rights, which are different but "originate out of" natural rights. According to Paine's most comprehensive definition, "Natural rights are those which appertain to man in right of his existence," of which there are two kinds: "the intellectual rights, or rights of the mind," on the one hand, and "all those rights of acting as an individual for his own comfort and happiness, which are not injurious to the natural rights of others," on the other. Paine's list of rights readily follows from the idea of men as self-owners. They have the right to dispose of themselves, control themselves in thought and deed, so long as they do not infringe on the property, that is, the rights, of others.[26]

In his *Rights of Man,* Paine does not speak of property in the external world. He will turn to that task in *Agrarian Justice.* Paine's discussion of rights—that is, of what rights there are—can easily be compassed within Jefferson's list in the Declaration of Independence (life, liberty, and pursuit of happiness) if we add in Paine's notion of intellectual rights. The rights Paine identifies in *Rights* are intimately related to the individual—his mental and physical capabilities and actions. He sees the need to make a somewhat different case for the right to property. It is important to emphasize that Paine, despite his affirmation of welfare rights, does not deny a right to property, nor does he believe that equality of resources is the standard of justice in holdings. In the prefatory material to *Agrarian Justice* he identifies two kinds of property—natural, "that which comes to us from the Creator of the Universe—such as the earth, air, water," and "artificial or acquired property—the invention of men."[27] What Paine calls here "artificial property" cannot be equal in society, for it depends on the differential talents and efforts of men. What he calls natural property, however, is such that all do have a certain claim to equality or its equivalent.

Paine's doctrine of property is thus complex. It is also clearly meant as a variant on the Lockean theory.[28] He begins with a conception similar to Locke's affirmation that "God . . . hath given the world to men in common."[29] As Paine puts it, "The earth, in its natural uncultivated state, was and ever would have continued to be the COMMON PROPERTY OF THE HUMAN RACE." Locke, in his famous discussion of property, identified a two-stage process by which first the fruits of the earth and then the earth itself can become private property. Paine's view is similar to Locke's but differs in one very significant way: he refuses to go along with the idea that the earth itself can become fully private property. Like Locke, Paine put great weight on the role of labor in producing private property. The earth in its natural or uncultivated state is not very productive. It can support at best one-tenth of the population that the cultivated earth can support. The plenty that cultivation can produce requires the labor of individuals. This labor is an expenditure of what are men's own—their bodies, plans, inventions. They labor on what is not theirs (the earth) to produce more than otherwise would exist. The earth, however, is not theirs. "There could be no such thing as landed property originally. Man did not make the earth, and though he had a natural right to *occupy* it, he had no right to *locate as his [exclusive] property* in perpetuity any part of it: neither did the creator of the earth set up a land-office, from whence the first title-deeds should issue." When Paine affirms that men had a right to occupy the land, he means that men have a right to use it, to glean from it what it produces and what they require for their preservation. But when he denies a right to "locate as his property in perpetuity any part of it," he means that men have no kind of exclusive right over it, that is, to exclude others from it. Since property proper includes such a right of exclusion, they do not have property in it.[30]

At this point, Paine's account faces a conundrum of sorts. Despite what he claims, men have almost everywhere recognized exclusive rights of ownership to the earth itself. Given Paine's principles, it would seem to follow that he should denounce this development and call for the re-communization of the land, but he pointedly does not do this. He insists that it is not possible to return from the property arrangements characteristic of civilized society to the property arrangements characterizing the natural situation. The "carrying-capacity" of the uncultivated earth is much less than that of the cultivated earth, so social ownership of the means of production, while just in some sense, would be disastrous.

Instead, Paine tries to show how private ownership arose in a quasi-legitimate manner—legitimate enough, at least, so that it does not cry out to be overturned. When men began to cultivate and thus increase the produce of the earth, they required some bit of earth on which to work. "The idea of landed property" arose "from the impossibility of separating the improvement made by cultivation [to which they have a right] from the earth itself upon which the improvement was made." Since cultivation added much greater value than the earth held in an uncultivated state, the value of the latter was easily absorbed into the total value of the cultivated earth. "The common right of all [to the earth] became confounded in the cultivated right of the individual [to the product of his labor]." But that common right was not extinguished, even if it was forgotten. All those who do not have "rights" to the earth now have a right to compensation for the right that they no longer can exercise, although, in order to avoid "invidious distinctions," Paine would make indemnification payments to all.[31]

Paine opens his *Agrarian Justice* by calling attention to the great material disparities that exist in civilized nations between the rich and the poor. "The most affluent and the most miserable of the human race are to be found in the countries that are called civilized." The depth of poverty one finds in these nations is greater than anything one finds in "the natural and primitive state of man."[32] In other words, some day laborers are worse off than American Indian chiefs. The Lockean defense of property, and especially of the appropriation of the earth, depended on his claim that everyone (more or less) was indeed better off (materially) than they would be in a state without property. That material gain is the compensation the non-owners gain for their loss of access to the commons. Paine agrees that the aggregate of wealth is much greater, but the distribution of that wealth does not live up to Locke's view of the gains derived from property. Some men now in civilized society would have been better off if the original commons had remained common, even if many or most are better off.[33]

To understand the differences between Locke and Paine on the original commons, one must for a moment have recourse to a technical distinction pioneered by the political philosopher Samuel von Pufendorf. The earth may be thought to be "in common" in two different ways, Pufendorf pointed out: negatively and positively. To say that the earth is common in the positive way is to say that the earth is jointly owned by all mankind. To say that it is a negative commons is to say that it is unowned by any, but this in itself says nothing about whether it can somehow come to be privately owned by some individuals. Paine decrees the earth originally a positive commons. Every man in the natural state "would have been a *joint life-proprietor* with the rest in the property of the soil, and in all of its natural productions, vegetable and animal."[34] When some appropriate the land by improving it through their labor, they at the same time exclude the others from their share in the original joint property. For this, the expropriated deserve compensation.

Locke, on the other hand, sees the original commons to be a negative commons. It belongs to no one, but may be appropriated by individuals.[35] Since men are not joint owners originally, but only joint non-owners, no one is expropriated when land is appropriated by some. Thus, Locke does not think that non-owners are due compensation for land they had some prior ownership claim to. Moreover, if the original condition is one of positive commons, it is not clear that property could ever arise legitimately. As we have seen, every appropriation would be an expropriation. At the least, such an appropriation would require the agreement of the other co-owners. As Locke points out, "If such consent . . . was necessary, man had starved."[36] If there is to be property (even of the primitive sort) involved in eating the fruit and nuts we can gather in a state of nature, then it is not possible to conceive the original commons as a positive commons. But both Paine and Locke maintain that property is possible, and indeed is a right. So it is not open to either to posit a positive commons. Paine is thus guilty of a self-contradiction. To stick consistently to his notion of positive commons, he would have to conclude with Proudhon that all property is theft.

Paine has presented two different and conflicting grounds for inferring a right to indemnification. On the one hand, he has argued that the earth inherently cannot become owned (since it is not made by men) and what men are being compensated for in the payment they receive on coming of age is their loss of a right they possessed to hunt and gather on the commons, or even to cultivate it. Because they have lost this right, Paine concludes, some are worse off in the civilized condition than they would have been in a state of nature.[37] On the other hand, the argument from the positive commons affirms that the earth can be owned, but by all men jointly. In this case, they are being compensated for being dispossessed of their share of ownership.

The two arguments are inconsistent in evident ways, but there is a common concern underlying both, and that concern deserves separate consideration. As we have noticed in *The Rights of Man,* Paine is greatly concerned to affirm the equality of men across the generations, a concern he shares with Jefferson.[38] The latter moved toward his "earth belongs to the living" doctrine requiring a reconsideration of all laws in every generation so that the present generation is always able to give or withhold consent for the laws by which it is governed. Paine too accepted such a scheme, but he carried this idea of intergenerational equality into nearly every nook and cranny of his political thinking, including his adumbration of a theory of welfare rights.[39] It would even be fair to say that it was this point, more than any other, that accounted for his disagreement with Burke. In effect, the latter argued that decisions and actions taken by past generations had binding authority on the present, implying, Paine thought, an inequality among generations. Paine saw his age, the "age of revolution," differently: "We have it in our power to begin the world over again."[40] Paine's faith or hopes for a revolutionary new beginning and remaking of the world both derived from and required the complete equality of the generations, for only then would it be right that the inheritance of the past could so readily be cast aside.

Much of Paine's political theory is shaped by his efforts to think through and apply his doctrine of human equality in rights in the political sphere. Thus, his theories of republicanism, constitutionalism, and revolution can all be seen as inferences from the equality in rights of all individuals and generations.[41] The economic rights that Paine develops in the second part of *Rights of Man* and in *Agrarian Justice* are efforts to extend that idea to the sphere of property relations.

While there is land in common (negatively or positively understood), men have a right, according to Paine, to take from it what they need or want. It is part of their primary right of preservation. Where there is no longer a commons, men have lost that right, a loss that weighs much more heavily on some (the poor) than on others. According to Locke, this loss is made up by all sharing in the greater plenty made possible by the system of private ownership and commerce. In effect, Locke concedes that all do not share equally in the benefits of the new order, but that all share sufficiently so as to give an equivalent means to preservation and make up for the loss of the original right. In insisting that all do benefit, Locke is expressing the same concern as Paine did for the equality of rights and the need for some compensation for loss of rights affecting prospects for survival in the new circumstances of private ownership.

Paine has a reply to Locke: it is not a necessary, but a contingent, outcome that all are better off. Observation tells Paine that it is by no means certain that all are in fact better off in modern-day Europe. In response to the mere contingency of what Locke appears to have treated as a necessity, Paine posits the positive commons as a way of guaranteeing that all are indeed better off. The positive commons, which must be, in effect, purchased by society from its joint owners every generation, serves as an ongoing manifestation of the equal rights of every generation to its share in the rights of the commons: the right to use the external world in service of one's right of preservation. I suspect, in other words, that Paine knew quite well what he was doing in transforming Locke's negative commons into a positive commons, despite the several theoretical difficulties that transformation entails.

Despite the sophistication of Paine's position, I believe Locke still has the better of this argument. It is true that in the *Second Treatise* Locke makes some special assumptions about the operation of his propertied commercial society, most especially, that it is a full-employment economy with other conditions that allow markets to operate adequately. When he identifies as the chief task of statesmanship the wise management of the economy, Locke concedes that there are contingencies that may prevent the commercial society from achieving what it might for all.[42] His response to the problem of concern to Paine is more narrowly focused, however, and on the whole better tailored to the problem it is meant to solve. For Locke, the general solution to the loss of right to gather the fruits of the no longer existing commons is the right to share in the increased plenty produced by the commercial economy through the labor market. Nobody is completely without property: individuals have property in their body and its labor-power, which they are free to sell and, thereby, both to contribute to the production of plenty and to derive some share of it.[43] But Locke recognizes that some are disabled and thus unable to labor. He also recognizes the possibility of a less than full-employment economy in which laborers cannot find employment. There are also some—orphans are a good example—who cannot be taken care of by the market. In his essay on the poor law, Locke outlines a scheme of public welfare to remedy those cases where the labor market is not adequate to recompense those who have lost a right to the original commons. Public welfare in the form of targeted care for the infirm, the young, and the unemployed is Locke's version of what Paine is attempting to accomplish in his welfare scheme. Locke too recognizes the ongoing equal right of every generation and of all men, but does so in a way that responds specifically to those who specifically have a claim of right.

It is not difficult to speculate what led Paine in the direction he went. His own thinking, like the agenda of the American and then the French Revolutions, was at first essentially political. He gave little thought to economic rights until the drafting of the second part of *Rights of Man,* published in 1792. His more intensive thinking and his development of a more general theory, as expressed in *Agrarian Justice,* took place over the course of the years between 1792 and 1797. The subtitle of *Agrarian Justice,* "Opposed to Agrarian Law, and to Agrarian Monopoly, Being a Plan for Meliorating the Conditions of Man," gives a good indication of the germ out of which the text grew. One of the two opponents announced in the subtitle is "agrarian monopoly"— the situation he described in the text according to which some owned the land and all others were dispossessed without recompense. The other opponent was François-Noël Babeuf, the self-styled "Gracchus" after the Roman politician-brothers who proposed an agrarian law for redistribution of land in ancient Rome.[44] Babeuf had written in a widely circulated pamphlet: "Nature has given to every man the right to the enjoyment of an equal share in all property." Paine clearly disagrees with that assertion, for he unequivocally affirms the legitimacy of unequal property holdings.[45] *Agrarian Justice* must be seen as an attempt to lay out an alternative to Babeuf that at the same time pays attention to the issues of distributive justice that the latter raises.[46]

Although Paine targets Babeuf in *Agrarian Justice,* it is unlikely that his theory of property rights was developed directly in response to Babeuf. He claims in his "Preface" that the work was written in the "winter of 1795–1796" while he was convalescing at the home of James Monroe, the American minister to France, after his long spell in prison. Because of part two of *Rights of Man,* we can confidently say that his thoughts were moving in the direction of economic rights well before he knew of Babeuf. It is more likely that Paine and Babeuf were both responding to the same phenomenon—the irruption into the French Revolution during the 1790s of what Hannah Arendt called "the social question"—that is to say, the questions of poverty, the distribution of property, and the misery of the poor. Paine attempted to develop a response to this "social question" on the basis of the tools he had in hand—the basically Lockean liberal political theory with which he had been operating at least since *Common Sense.* The kind of Lockean response to the social question that he developed was greatly shaped, however, by the particular themes the debate with Burke brought to the fore—in particular, the theme of the equality of the generations. Later generations had a right to indemnification for their lost access to the original commons. Thus, Paine developed a theory of property rights that departed substantially from Locke's, and that, despite its great differences from the argument in *Rights of Man,* retained great similarity to the general character of the argument in that earlier book. In some ways, *Agrarian*

Justice was closer in character to part one of *Rights of Man* than it was to part two, despite the fact that the second part was the place where Paine made his first foray into a theory of welfare rights. The social question posed challenges to Lockean philosophy, for it is clear that the socioeconomic situation in France fell short of what Lockean theory promised. One response would have been to say "Apply the Lockean theory correctly and see what happens." Paine (and Babeuf) took different paths. Babeuf rejected the Lockean position altogether; Paine attempted to modify it substantially, a modification prompted by the impact on him of the Revolution.

JEFFERSON: THE DAWN OF SUNSET (LAWS)

Jefferson's early thought had many points of contact with the thought of Paine from the period of the Revolution. Like Paine, he understood the fundamentals in an essentially Lockean way—he accepted the basic story of pre-political human rights, of consent- or social contract–based government, of limited purposes to government grounded in the purported purposes for which the social contract was made—and he accepted the same idea of a right to revolution. He had a somewhat more conservative, we might say, theory of constitution than Paine at first. Where Paine in *Common Sense* emphasized the simplicity of constitutional theory and urged the adoption of simple models of government, Jefferson sided with those who favored relatively complex systems based on republicanism and separation of powers. Thus, he famously derided the legislative-supremacy-leaning constitutionalism of the Revolutionary period and favored a more sophisticated rather than a simple approach to constitutional design.[47] Like Paine, however, the experience of the French Revolution led to important shifts in his thinking.

There was conversation between the two men, and evidence of cross-fertilization of thought as well, for not only common themes, but common phrases and ideas, appear in their writings from this period. Thus, Paine, in his 1791 tirade against Burke, points out: "as government is for the living and not for the dead, it is the living only that has any right in it. . . . Man has no property in man; neither has any generation a property in the generations which are to follow. . . . [E]very generation is and must be competent to all the purposes which its occasions require. It is the living, and not the dead, that are to be accommodated."[48] In September 1789, Jefferson had written his famous letter to Madison in which Jefferson poses the question "whether one generation of men has a right to bind another." It was, he thought, a question never yet raised in either America or Europe.[49] That letter contained the famous phrase by which the letter is normally known: "the earth belongs in usufruct to the living." In almost the same language that Paine later used, Jefferson asserted that "the dead have no powers or rights over [the present]."[50]

In that letter, Jefferson develops his famous proposal for limiting the effective life of laws and public debts to nineteen years, the period at which, according to his actuarial tables, one generation replaces another. It is clear that the two have been exchanging ideas and have come to some common conclusions. Yet, this moment of convergence is a prelude to a later divergent development of thinking. Paine moved on to his theory of welfare rights and Jefferson to his theory of ward republicanism. The two Thomases take these divergent paths almost certainly in part because they have different fields of vision to contemplate in their later years. Paine remained in France until late 1801, well after *Agrarian Justice*. Jefferson, having left France in 1789, spent the rest of his days in America. The "social question" impinged on Jefferson to a much lesser degree. America was literally a place where the original commons still existed in part. Jefferson's purchase of the Louisiana Territory would greatly increase that commons. There was little urgency for Jefferson to think of ways to indemnify latecomers for loss of rights to the commons.

Yet Jefferson was not at all oblivious to the problem of property in France, and his reaction to it was different from Paine's from the outset, suggesting that the later differences in direction of their thinking had some basis other than the differing situations of America and Old Europe. In October 1785, Jefferson wrote to James Madison of "the wretchedness" he had seen among the poor in France. Why, he asked himself, were so many consigned to begging who were "willing to work, in a country where there is a very considerable proportion of uncultivated lands?"[51] The reason, Jefferson thought, lay in the tremendous inequality, or rather in the tremendous concentration of wealth: the owners had so much that they happily kept great amounts of land out of cultivation because they no longer had an incentive of making more profits from their lands. They valued wild land for hunting or for prestige reasons more than the extra income they might earn from farming more of their land. The result, however, was the "misery of the bulk of mankind" in France, who could not find work and whose surplus numbers drove down wages for those who did work.

Jefferson did not emphasize the loss of the original commons, as Paine did, but rather the distorted result of the particular distribution of land in France. His response was also much different from Paine's. Because the source of the problem was not private property per se, but excess concentration and inequality of holdings, the solution was "subdividing property" and progressive taxation. The former was to be done by expropriating the landowners by measures that "go hand in hand with the natural affections of the human mind." He had in mind the kind of reforms he had earlier proposed for Virginia: "the descent of property of every kind therefore to all the children, or to all the brothers and sisters, or their relatives in equal degree, is a politic measure and a practicable one." In his autobiography, Jefferson described these sorts of reforms as "the best of all Agrarian Laws" and as capable of being "effected without the violation of a single natural right of any one individual citizen."[52] Jefferson's solution to the problem of property was from the outset market oriented, in that he would remove the artificial legal impediments that prevented individuals from distributing their property as they would if they freely could. From the start, he resisted Babeuf's solution ("an equal division of property is impracticable"[53]) and he did not consider anything like Paine's proposal of a right to payment.

It was not merely the unequal and concentrated distribution of property that caught Jefferson's attention in 1789, but the larger question of the claims of vested rights altogether: may the nation change legally vested rights, and in particular, may current holders be divested? Thus, he asks "whether the nation may change the descent of lands holden in tail."[54] This question was already implicated in his efforts to abolish the law of entailment in Virginia as part of his "revisal" of the laws. But in 1789 he has in mind a much larger array of feudal inheritances: "Whether they may change the appropriation of lands given antiently to the church, to hospitals, colleges, order of clergy, and otherwise in perpetuity? Whether they may abolish the charges and privileges attached on lands, including the whole catalogue ecclesiastical and feudal? It goes to hereditary offices, authorities, and jurisdictions, to hereditary orders, distinctions and appellations; to perpetual monopolies in commerce, the arts or sciences; with a long train of et ceteras."[55]

Jefferson's questions and his answers can be read in two somewhat different ways. The great efforts at reform in France can be seen as attempts to free society and economy from the dead hand of the feudal past, to free society and economy to operate according to what Adam Smith called the principles of natural liberty. That is to say, the effort to free France from the legal straitjacket of the past can be seen, for example, as Marx saw it: as an effort to "modernize" France, to make it capable of being a market or capitalist society by freeing up resources to move freely in commerce. On the other hand, Jefferson's questions, and even more, his solution, can be seen more radically, as Richard Matthews did, as a proposal open to, if not quite embracing, socialism.[56] If the majority at any moment has the right to undo and reshuffle existing property rights, then it has the right to socialize and, in effect, to control entirely all the property and economic relations within society. Jefferson's argument is perhaps open to this latter interpretation, but it is doubtful that he had this radical a view in mind. Among other things, it would conflict with his frequent affirmation of a right to property, with his generally libertarian-leaning politics, and with his care that land redistribution be effected by laws that do not infringe on natural rights. He would free individuals to leave property where their own hearts dictated rather than having the laws prevent this free choice or expropriate those with much wealth.[57]

The most thorough and historically well-informed treatment of Jefferson's statement is Herbert Sloan's article and book on the topic.[58] Sloan emphasizes Jefferson's stress within the letter on the problem of debt, both personal and public. He traces this concern in part to Jefferson's own situation as a deeply indebted man, and also to his more public concern that long-term public debt is a temptation or a facilitator of substantial political evils, such as the temptation to wage "wars of choice." Sloan certainly has a point, for the discussion of debt does take up much of the space in Jefferson's letter. Indeed, he sees the imposition of strict limits on debt for the just-launched new government under the constitution to be the chief immediate practical application of his new principle. Yet I would suggest that we focus attention somewhat differently. Jefferson identifies the topic of his letter as "whether one generation of men has a right to bind another." This formulation includes the question of debt that Sloan foregrounds and the question of France's inherited encumbrances that receive so much attention in the letter, but it is broader than both. Indeed, the entire theme "the earth belongs to the living" is but a subcategory of this broader question.

The letter can readily be misread, or the proper emphasis missed, because Jefferson spends disproportionate space on the subheads of his larger question and less space on the most general conclusion at which he arrives. That conclusion comes about two-thirds through the letter and takes up only a brief paragraph: "On a similar ground it may be proved that no society can make a perpetual constitution or even a perpetual law."[59] Jefferson would set limits to the public debt and free society from feudal carryovers, but more than that, he would establish universal sunset laws. Every legal enactment would expire at the end of nineteen years and would go out of effect unless reenacted or refashioned. As Sloan perceptively notes, the idea of a new constitutional convention must have horrified Madison, who had just lived through and been impressed by the immense good fortune of having had one successful such convention.[60] Nonetheless, that was what Jefferson's proposal implied, for "every constitution, then, and every law, naturally expires at the end of 19 years. If it be enforced longer, it is an act of force and not of right."[61] To understand that conclusion, one must advert to the Lockean fundamentals of Jefferson's understanding of what makes for legitimate governance, as expressed, for instance, in the Declaration of Independence.

The beginning point in the Declaration, as well as in the 1789 letter, is natural rights: "The earth belongs always to the living generation. They may mange it then, and what proceeds from it, as they please, during their usufruct. They are masters too of their own persons, and consequently may govern them as they please."[62] The earth belongs to the present generation precisely because they have rights, including especially the right to life. Since the right to life can be satisfied only via appropriating external goods from the earth, the personal right to preservation is the ultimate source of the right to property. But it is only currently living individuals who possess the rights (and needs) of preservation, so it must follow that rights to property must inhere in the present generation. No previous generation can rightly encumber the earth in such a way that it can no longer serve the preservation needs of the present generation. At the same time, individuals are "masters of their own persons"—that is, they have the right to "govern" themselves as they please. They are self-owners (and therefore slavery is always contrary to natural right), and from this fact derives the right to liberty.

Despite the natural right to liberty—the right to do as they wish with themselves—government exists to regulate and control actions as well as property. What gives government the right to do this when it seems so contrary to basic natural rights? "The earth belongs to the living" letter only assumes the answer to that question, and thus fails to bring to explicitness what is actually the driving thought of Jefferson's entire theory. According to the Declaration of Independence, governments "derive their just powers from the consent of the governed." Over time, Jefferson interpreted that requirement of consent ever more strenuously. In the Declaration itself, it seems that consent applied to the establishment of government but was not an ongoing requirement. Thus, the Declaration affirms the right of a people to make government "in such form, as to them shall seem most likely to effect their safety and happiness." Monarchy is not ruled out, for the text emphasizes not the illegitimacy of monarchy per se but the misdeeds of "the present king of Great Britain." In this relative openness on legitimate forms of government, the Jefferson of 1776 differs from the Paine of 1776 in that the latter rejects monarchy as per se illegitimate, a conclusion Jefferson does not endorse in the Declaration.[63]

Over time, Jefferson came to see the unacceptability of this understanding of the place of consent. If the consent of the rights holders—that is, of all human beings—is required to constitute rightful political power, then it can never be the consent of a previous generation. As rights holders, the present generation, acting through the present majority, must in all cases endorse measures that are to have the force of law, and to rightfully limit and define the rights of individuals within civil society. Without such consent, "it is an act of force and not of right." The requirement of present consent is the central idea in Jefferson's new theory.

Although they use similar language, there is thus a significant, although nuanced, difference between Paine's affirmation of generational equality and Jefferson's insistence on the consent of the present generation. Paine's thinking is more limited than Jefferson's, for it is shaped largely by the polemical confrontation with Burke, whose doctrine in effect privileged the power of past generations to bind the present. Paine retorted with his insistence on the equality of generations. Jefferson, not bound by the Burkean context, went further and traced the requirements of legitimacy to the active consent of individuals.

JEFFERSON: THE FATE OF CONSENT

Madison sent Jefferson a tactful but firm critique of the idea that the "earth belongs to the living" as, for the most part, impracticable, socially disruptive, and suppressive of valuable individual initiative and action. But Jefferson never entirely gave up on it: he had hit on a theoretically important idea, despite the formidable practical difficulties Madison exposed. Still, it was not possible for him not to be unnerved by Madison's objections. How could his chief insight, that consent needed to be actualized, be reconciled with the impracticability of his original proposal? I would propose that the answer Jefferson arrived at finally was the pet scheme of his later years: the proposal for ward republics. The idea is sufficiently well known and discussed in the literature that it requires no exposition here.[64] I wish only to connect it up briefly with the concerns that animated Jefferson's thinking in 1789.

Jefferson's proposal for a "graduated system" where governing tasks and political power would remain at the lowest level compatible with the actual accomplishment of the tasks of governance, was based, in turn, on the very strenuous definition of the republican principle he promulgated in his later years. "Were I to assign to this term [republicanism] a precise and definite idea, I would say, purely and simply, it means a government by its citizens in mass, acting, directly and personally."[65] Rule by will of the people is the mature version of the concern with active "consent of the [currently] governed" that motivated the "earth belongs to the living" agenda: so far as governing could be devolved to the lower levels—the wards, the counties, the states, where the people could be more active, engaged, and knowledgeable—their will could be effective in governing. The ward republic idea is in one respect more sober than the universal sunset law requirement that Jefferson proposed in 1789. It did not require the extraordinarily disruptive expiration of every law and constitution nineteen years after its adoption, and it affirmed a clear principle of democratic rule while at the same time including compromises with that principle when these were needed for effective governance. Thus, Jefferson did not believe that the active will of the people could rule as effectively at so distant a level as the federal government, but he willingly assigned certain tasks, such as foreign affairs, to that government, for they could not be well done anywhere else.

In another respect, however, Jefferson's later republicanism is more radical than his proposal for a universal sunset requirement. His 1789 idea was inspired by theoretical need for "consent of the governed," that is, by the majority of those actually being governed. Consent is agreement to; it involves agency by the governed, but not to the degree that governing by the active will of the governed does. The 1789 proposal still implicitly conceptualized government on a model of a (somewhat) separate governing will—the government, proposing, and the people, more passive, consenting. The later idea breaks that model down and renders consent, more than agreement, to the will of others.

Despite, or perhaps because of, the radicalization of the consent idea in the idea of rule by the active will of the governed, or the affirmation of thorough self-government, we can still discern in Jefferson's ward republicanism the radicalizing impetus of the French Revolution. The French situation raised for him in a profound way the question of how one could get out from under the rule of the so-called dead hand of the past, of what made existing modes and orders legitimate and binding. The American experience had not raised the issue in the same way for the Americans—not even for Jefferson, who had the idea for a thorough "revisal" of the laws of Virginia. He had not felt there was as much to get out from under in America as the French and French sympathizers like Jefferson himself and Paine thought there was in France. But the train of thought triggered by the French situation led both Jefferson and Paine to ideas that were more universal, that were pertinent not only to France but to America as well. Paine's radicalized idea remained more pertinent to Europe, where there was no free land, and Jefferson's to America, where there was—and where there was, in addition, a set of well-developed republican institutions in place. By the mid-1790s, when Paine wrote *Agrarian Justice,* there were reasons to wonder whether France would ever succeed at establishing the republic it had been striving for in one constitutional attempt after another. It was natural, then, for Paine's ideas to move in the direction of welfare rights that would be good against any form of government, while Jefferson moved toward an ever more intense form of republicanism.

Each ended up considerably more radical in his thinking than the majority of his fellow Enlightenment thinkers; both remind one more than a little of positions that would emerge with force much later in political thought: Jefferson of the participatory democracy idea, and Paine of the welfare state. It would be too simple, we have now seen, to attribute the shift in thinking in either simply to the French Revolution, for in both cases the shift occurred over an arc of ideas already present in the thought of each well before 1789. However, it would be too simple to dismiss the impact of the Revolution, for the revolution in France forced to the front problems that remained much in the background in America, especially the problem of social justice and rights of property. In the two paths taken by them, we see prefigured the different paths later taken by the major democracies—Jefferson toward a state insisting on liberty and democratic control, and Paine toward the social welfare state. The radicalization of Lockean ideas we see in these two beyond what we see in other thinkers of the period, ironically, derived from the fact that the dead hand of the past weighed so heavily in France that they could not ignore it.

NOTES

Preparation of this paper was made possible by a Visiting Fellowship at the Social Philosophy and Policy Center, Bowling Green, Ohio. Thanks also to Mary Dilsaver and Kelli Brown for their expert typing, and to Peter Onuf for his incisive editorial work.

1. Paine, *Rights of Man, Part Two,* in *Thomas Paine: Collected Writings,* ed. Eric Foner (New York: Library of America, 1995) [hereafter cited as *Collected Writings*], 649, 652, 657.

2. Gareth Stedman Jones treats Paine in the context of radicalized Enlightenment policies aiming at the eradication of poverty (see his *An End to Poverty: A Historical Debate* [New York: Columbia University Press, 2005]). Paine's proposal has been revived in modern guise in Bruce Ackerman and Anne Alstott, *The Stakeholder Society* (New Haven, Conn.: Yale University Press, 1999). They would stake every young person coming of age

to a grant of $80,000 (in 1999 dollars), a proposal similar to what Paine put forward in *Agrarian Justice.*

3. Paine, *Common Sense,* in *Collected Writings,* 6.

4. Consider Jack Fruchtman Jr., *Thomas Paine: Apostle of Freedom* (New York: Four Walls Eight Windows, 1994), 228.

5. Paine, *Rights of Man, Part Two,* in *Collected Writings,* 628.

6. Fruchtman, *Thomas Paine,* 139.

7. But, consider Fruchtman's claim that Paine in the 1790s wrote under the spell of Rousseau, a forerunner of the German idealists. However, Rousseau does not spell out a welfare state doctrine (see Fruchtman, *Thomas Paine,* 251–52).

8. On Paine's Lockeanism, see ibid., 5–6, 225, 228. For a relatively late statement of this basic Lockean story, see Paine, *Dissertation on First Principles of Government,* in *The Writings of Thomas Paine,* ed. Moncure David Conway, 4 vols. (New York: G. P. Putnam's, 1894–96) 3:265–67.

9. Paine, *Agrarian Justice,* in *Collected Writings,* 401; Paine, *Rights of Man, Part Two,* ibid., 597.

10. Paine, *Common Sense,* in *Collected Writings,* 7; John Locke, *Second Treatise of Government,* ed. Peter Laslett (Cambridge: Cambridge University Press, 1960), par. 4.

11. Paine, *Common Sense,* in *Collected Writings,* 7.

12. Paine, *Rights of Man, Part Two,* ibid., 551; Paine, *Common Sense,* ibid., 7.

13. Paine, *Common Sense,* ibid., 7, 7–8.

14. Ibid., 8, 8–9.

15. Paine, *Rights of Man, Part Two,* ibid., 464, 461.

16. Ibid., 628.

17. Paine, "To the Legislature and the Executive Directory of the French Republic," in *Writings of Thomas Paine,* 3:324; John W. Seaman, "Thomas Paine: Ransom, Civil Peace, and the Natural Right to Welfare," *Political Theory* 16 (February 1988): 129.

18. Edmund Burke, *Reflections on the Revolution in France,* in *Select Works of Edmund Burke: A New Imprint of the Payne Edition,* foreword and biographical note by Francis Canavan, 3 vols. (Indianapolis: Liberty Fund, 1999), vol. 2, par. 203. Burke includes along with his theory of the origin and nature of rights some mockery of the French Declaration of the Rights of Man, a mockery that sets Paine off into a frenzy of denunciation (see Paine, *Rights of Man, Part Two,* in *Collected Writings,* 461).

19. Paine's agenda was thus similar to Leo Strauss's effort to reaffirm "natural right" in the face of historicist challenges (see Leo Strauss, *Natural Right and History* [Chicago: University of Chicago Press, 1953], 191–93).

20. Paine, *Rights of Man, Part One,* in *Collected Writings,* 438 (Paine's emphasis).

21. Ibid., 462.

22. Locke, *Second Treatise of Government,* par. 6.

23. Paine, *Rights of Man, Part One,* in *Collected Writings,* 438.

24. Paine, *Dissertation on the First Principles of Government*, in *Collected Writings*, 265.

25. Paine, *Rights of Man, Part One*, ibid., 463.

26. Ibid., 464.

27. The prefatory material for *Agrarian Justice* can be found in *Writings of Thomas Paine*, vol. 3.

28. Seaman, "Thomas Paine," 12, 22, 30. See also Mark Philp, *Thomas Paine* (Oxford: Oxford University Press, 2007), 60.

29. Locke, *Second Treatise of Government*, par. 26.

30. Paine, *Agrarian Justice*, in *Collected Writings*, 398, 399.

31. Ibid., 399, 401.

32. Ibid., 397.

33. Gregory Claeys, *Thomas Paine: Social and Political Thought* (Boston: Unwin Hyman, 1989), 198–99.

34. Paine, *Agrarian Justice*, in *Collected Writings*, 398; William Parsons, "Thomas Paine: Conscience of Liberalism" (PhD diss., University of Toronto, 2007), 75.

35. This is a contested claim in the Locke literature. See, for example, James Tully, *A Discourse of Property: John Locke and His Adversaries* (Cambridge: Cambridge University Press, 1980), 64–98; and Gopal Sreenivason, *The Limits of Lockean Rights in Property* (Oxford: Oxford University Press, 1995), 24–32. But see also Locke, *Second Treatise of Government*, par. 28, 30; and Parsons, "Thomas Paine," 74.

36. Locke, *Second Treatise of Government*, par. 28.

37. Paine, *Agrarian Justice*, in *Collected Writings*, 397.

38. Paine, "Dissertation on the First Principles of Government," in *Collected Writings*, 260–63.

39. Paine, *Rights of Man, Part One*, ibid., 438, 441.

40. Paine, *Common Sense*, ibid., 52.

41. See, esp., Paine, "Dissertation on the First Principles of Government," ibid., 263.

42. Locke, *Second Treatise of Government*, par. 42.

43. Ibid., par. 44.

44. Fruchtman, *Thomas Paine*, 355–56; Parsons, "Thomas Paine," 71.

45. Paine, "Dissertation on the First Principles of Government," in *Collected Writings*, 7–8.

46. See Paine, "To the Legislature and Executive Directory," in *Writings of Thomas Paine*, 3:324.

47. For one among many treatments of Jefferson's political thought at the time of the American Revolution, see Michael P. Zuckert, *The Natural Rights Republic: Studies in the Foundation of the American Political Tradition* (Notre Dame, Ind.: University of Notre Dame Press, 1996), 13–89, 202–43.

48. Paine, *Rights of Man, Part One*, in *Collected Writings*, 441, 438.

49. Thomas Jefferson [TJ] to James Madison, 6 September 1789, in Thomas Jefferson,

Writings, ed. Merrill D. Peterson (New York: Library of America, 1984) [hereafter cited as *Jefferson Writings*], 959.

50. Ibid.
51. TJ to Madison, 18 October 1785, ibid., 841.
52. *Autobiography,* ibid., 44–45.
53. TJ to Madison, 28 October 1785, ibid., 841.
54. Ibid., 963.
55. Ibid., 963–64.
56. Richard Matthews, *The Radical Politics of Thomas Jefferson* (Lawrence: University Press of Kansas, 1984).
57. Darren Staloff, *Hamilton, Adams, Jefferson: The Politics of Enlightenment and the American Founding* (New York: Hill and Wang, 2005), 304.
58. Herbert E. Sloan, *Principle and Interest: Thomas Jefferson and the Problem of Debt* (New York: Oxford University Press, 1995); Sloan, "The Earth Belongs to the Living," in *Jeffersonian Legacies,* ed. Peter S. Onuf (Charlottesville: University Press of Virginia, 1993), 281–315.
59. TJ to Madison, 6 September 1789, *Jefferson Writings,* 963.
60. Sloan, "Earth Belongs to the Living," 300.
61. TJ to Madison, 6 September 1789, *Jefferson Writings,* 963.
62. Ibid.
63. It must be noted, however, that Jefferson was speaking in the Declaration of the "American mind" and not his own views. The latter were closer to Paine's in their commitment to republicanism and hostility to monarchy.
64. For one among many accounts, see Zuckert, *Natural Rights Republic,* 227–39.
65. TJ to John Taylor, 28 May 1816, *Jefferson Writings,* 1392.

Conclusion
Thomas Paine in the Atlantic Historical Imagination

SETH COTLAR

Thomas Paine and Thomas Jefferson have long been associated with one another in the American historical imagination. Their many detractors have tended to regard them as unrepresentative radicals who were profoundly out of step with their fellow citizens, especially in regard to their religious beliefs. Their admirers, on the other hand, have lauded Paine and Jefferson as foundational articulators of what would become the egalitarian, democratic, and inclusionary commitments at the heart of the American political tradition. As the political winds have shifted over the past two centuries, so have Paine and Jefferson's reputations, sometimes in tandem, sometimes not. The essays in this collection offer numerous new interpretations of the historical relationship between these two revolutionaries. In doing so, they cast fresh light on both the age these men helped to shape and our contemporary investments in them. Indeed, understanding these two founders in particular enables us to think more clearly about what democracy has meant to Americans over the past two centuries, and what it means for us today.

This essay will focus primarily on Thomas Paine's place in the American historical imagination, and only obliquely on Jefferson, yet many of the observations offered here could apply to both men. Both Jefferson and Paine were socially embedded thinkers who were uniquely attuned to the new political cultures emerging around them in their Revolutionary age. Both were key articulators of a new, American nationalism, yet they were also cosmopolitan thinkers who drew political inspiration from the French Revolution. Finally, while both of them have served as inspirational figures (and, at times, objects of derision) for generations of politically minded Americans, their ideas do not map neatly onto our present-day ideological divides. The historical Paine and the historical Jefferson still repay our attention. They remain good to think with in our efforts to understand both the legacy of the Revolutionary Era and our contemporary moment.

Of all the founders, Thomas Paine must claim the most diverse fan club. A quick survey of the Internet uncovers a polyglot collection of Paine devotees—libertarians, socialists, pacifists, atheists, hyper-patriotic American conservatives, cosmopolitan progressives, multiculturalists, opponents of multiculturalism, rural survivalists, technophilic bloggers, and many more. The Paine impersonators who attended Tea Party rallies in 2009–10 draped themselves in "Don't Tread on Me" flags and called upon the American people to defend their exceptional system of small government and economic freedom from the misguided devotees of European-style socialism. Meanwhile, the Paine invoked by contemporary progressives is an urbane critic of narrow-minded Christian fundamentalism and an advocate of taxing the wealthy so the government can ensure economic opportunity for the poor and security for the elderly and infirm.[1] It is hardly surprising to see a figure from America's founding generation appropriated for political purposes, but Paine is unique in his ability to resonate with people across the political spectrum. What does it say about Paine's place in the Atlantic historical imagination that he can serve as an authentic personal hero for figures as diverse as Glenn Beck on the right, Tony Benn on the left, and Christopher Hitchens, the quintessential political iconoclast?[2]

Paine's contemporary allure derives in part from the fact that he seems like the founder with whom one would most like to drink a beer. His unimpeachable populism is evident in both the accessibility of his writings and the unpretentiousness of his personal life. Thomas Jefferson drank fine wine as he discussed philosophical treatises in the most exclusive of Parisian salons, while Thomas Paine downed cheap brandy in taverns frequented by workingmen who peppered their conversations with quotes from well-thumbed newspapers. John Adams's major political work was a three-volume tome aimed at other learned men; the stoic George Washington addressed his fellow citizens from an Olympian perch; James Madison was bookish, shy, and disinclined to play the role of the peoples' tribune; and Alexander Hamilton considered the bulk of his fellow citizens profoundly unqualified to discuss serious political matters. Thomas Paine, however, invited his readers to join as equal participants in a friendly and often jocular debate about the central issues of their day. He ridiculed those who thought they were better than others;

he grounded his arguments not on revered authorities but on the "common sense" of artisans and farmers; and the ultimate aim of his life's work was to dismantle the political and social arrangements that preserved the power of the elite few at the expense of the many. If, as Gordon Wood has argued, the founders were profoundly different from us, Paine is probably the founder who most defies that rule.³ In a political age when self-effacing populism is the unquestioned idiom of both the Left and the Right, it is no wonder that the political stock of Paine the plain-speaking ex-stay-maker has risen while that of Jefferson the plantation-owning philosophe has fallen.

But if Paine's populism explains the ease with which he is appropriated by people across the contemporary political spectrum, we are still left with the question of how his corpus of writings could be put to such contradictory purposes. How can Paine have been a patriotic believer in American exceptionalism, small government, and the beneficence of the free market *and* a tolerant cosmopolitan who advocated energetic government and economic regulation to serve the public interest? The simplest explanation is that Paine's progressive and conservative admirers tend to emphasize different parts of his career. Conservatives focus on Paine's early writings, such as *Common Sense* and the *Crisis* papers, with their damning indictment of governmental tyranny, strenuous defense of personal liberty, and inspirational paeans to American exceptionalism. Progressives, meanwhile, are drawn to what Eric Foner has called Paine's "social charter," a bundle of ideas he first articulated in chapter 5 of the second part of *Rights of Man* (1792) and then developed further in *Agrarian Justice* (1795).⁴ In these texts, Paine advocated policies such as old-age pensions, progressive taxation, and state subsidies to fund educational and economic opportunities for all citizens. Where the Paine of 1776 had described government as "a necessary evil," the Paine of the 1790s declared it the positive duty of the state to reduce poverty and create a more just society.

Before fully committing to the distinction between the early and the late Paine, however, it is important to note that neither he nor any of his contemporaries recognized a significant transformation in his thinking. John Adams disliked having Paine as a political ally in 1776, criticizing *Common Sense* as "so democratical, without any restraint," that it would inevitably "produce confusion and every evil work." Thirty years later, Adams had not changed his mind, lamenting to a friend that no "man in the World has had more influence on its inhabitants or affairs for the last thirty years than Tom Paine. There can be no severer Satyr on the Age. For such a mongrel between Pigg and Puppy, begotten by a wild Boar on a Bitch Wolf, never before in any Age of the World was suffered by the Poltroonery of mankind, to run through such a career of mischief."[5]

Just as Adams and other conservatives regarded Paine as a trouble-making demagogue for the entirety of his thirty-year career in the public eye, Paine, for his part, was proud of his consistency. One of his last significant contributions to public debate occurred in 1805 when he weighed in on the question of whether Pennsylvania should revise its state constitution. Paine peppered his argument with references to the principles of 1776, and his central contention was that the state constitution his close political compatriots had constructed in that year (and which had subsequently been scrapped) should be resurrected and ratified with only a few minor changes. Nothing over the previous three decades—years that had witnessed an Atlantic-wide revolution in which he had played a significant role—had made him rethink the fundamental political principles he had supported as a neophyte political pamphleteer thirty years earlier. In sum, if he were alive to speak for himself, he would concur with Simon Newman's assessment that "Paine changed very little between 1776 and 1809."[6]

Rather than offering another attempt to isolate Paine's "real" political principles, conservative or progressive, that should guide us in the present, this essay shifts the focus away from Paine the provider of clear and consistent answers to Paine the poser of foundational and enduring problems. Focusing on Paine's central questions enables us to assess the continuities in his life work as well as the important transformations in his thinking. Over the course of his thirty-year career of political writing, Paine explored the implications of concepts like equality, rights, and popular sovereignty, that were central to the Age of Revolution. We return to his writings, especially *Common Sense* and *Rights of Man*, because they articulated these foundational ideals with great clarity, simplicity, and conviction. In the years between the two revolutions that inspired these texts, as political and social conditions changed around him, Paine took those ideas in directions that neither he nor anyone else could have foreseen. We must resist the temptation to see "the real Paine" in *Common Sense* and then regard what followed as merely a French-influenced diversion. Likewise, we should also be careful not to see the later, more progressive Paine lurking in embryo beneath the surface of *Common Sense*. Paine's writings continue to be relevant and contested because they invited all of his fellow citizens to ponder some of the most important questions that we continue to debate today: What exactly do we mean when we say we believe in equality? What are the legitimate and most effective ways for a government of "the people" to exert its authority so as to further the common good? What do we consider a right, and how can governments best nurture and protect those rights? Whether we align ourselves alongside or against him, Paine continues to serve as a useful interlocutor as we work out our own answers to these open-ended and essentially unresolvable questions that lay at the heart of the political culture bequeathed to the Atlantic World by the eighteenth century's Age of Revolution.

For the past one hundred years, progressive historians have been drawn to Thomas Paine in large part because he was the founding generation's most forceful advocate of equality. Six months before Thomas Jefferson penned the famous phrase "All men are created equal," Paine opened *Common Sense*'s attack on hereditary monarchy with a similar claim: "*Mankind* being originally equals in the order of creation, the equality could only be destroyed by some subsequent circumstance." Whereas Jefferson the slaveholder's espousal of equality has struck many observers as suspect, Paine's seems more authentic. He had published an antislavery magazine article a few months before writing *Common Sense;* he had close ties to the politicized militia organized by Philadelphia's artisans (an organization some historians have compared to Cromwell's New Model Army); and he was an important figure in the city's robust community of radical intellectuals and professionals who sought to replace the state's traditional elite with leaders more attentive to the interests and aspirations of ordinary farmers and artisans.[7]

It was this coalition that produced the ultra-democratic Pennsylvania Constitution of 1776 that Paine spoke of so glowingly in 1805. Paine admired that constitution because it put political power firmly in the hands of "the people." He favored the 1776 constitution's unicameral legislature because he saw no need for a supposedly wiser upper house that was insulated from the populace through less-frequent elections. Instead of putting the power to check unwise legislation in the hands of a small elite (as was later done with the U.S. Senate, modeled after the British House of Lords), Paine preferred Pennsylvania's system, where every law had to be printed and publicly posted for citizens to consider before it could be approved by their representatives. Just as the legislative check was in the hands of the people, the tasks of constitutional revision and supervision also belonged to them, in the form of an elected and rotating Council of Censors. Where most of the other "founding fathers" worried that giving ordinary citizens so much sway over their government would lead to anarchy, Paine rejected their elitism and put great faith in his fellow citizens' reasonableness and intelligence.

Most historians regard Paine's commitment to equality in 1776 as a long-standing and fairly stable component of his political vision, something he brought with him across the Atlantic when he had emigrated two years earlier at the age of thirty-eight. Considering the radical company he chose to keep in his early days in Philadelphia, the clear espousal of fundamental human equality in *Common Sense,* and the direction his politics would eventually take, this would seem like a safe assumption. Nonetheless, due to the paucity of evidence regarding Paine's life before 1776, any account of the origins and nature of his egalitarianism will always require some degree of speculation. One of Paine's biographers, John Keane, dealt with this source problem by carefully reconstructing the broader social context in which Paine had been socialized. Keane's opening chapters paint a picture of the sort of violence and injustice Paine would have encountered in his early life—young men hanged for petty crimes, the ravages of rural and urban poverty, the narrow-minded pomposity of the English aristocracy, and other similar horrors so effectively satirized in William Hogarth's eighteenth-century caricatures. Like other biographers before him, Keane identified three influences that help explain why Paine developed a critical relationship to contemporary British society: his Quaker upbringing; his attendance at scientific lectures in London where urban artisans encountered Enlightenment ideas; and his participation in a debating society in Lewes, a town known for its legacy of political radicalism that stretched back to the English Civil War. Even though we have almost no direct evidence of Paine's early egalitarian radicalism, either in his own words or in his recollection, Keane and other biographers have made a strong circumstantial case that Paine sailed to America with a well-developed critique of Old World hierarchies and the ways they stifled the ambitions and killed the souls of the world's downtrodden masses.[8]

This argument offers a compelling explanation for why Paine was so open to the most egalitarian ideas of his age, yet it runs the risk of portraying Paine's political commitments as more deeply rooted, fully developed, and consistently radical than they may have actually been. Paine the lifelong crusader for equality, in other words, might be a back-formation, something we can see early in his life because we know the direction his thinking eventually took. This possibility is implied in Phillip Ziesche's essay in this volume, where he points out that Paine did not offer a critique of aristocracy as an illegitimate form of inequality until the late 1780s. Indeed, in 1784 he even composed a song in honor of the Society of the Cincinnati, an organization that many Americans derided as quasi-aristocratic. Compared to Benjamin Franklin, who was a scathing critic of the Cincinnati from the moment of its inception, Paine hardly looks like someone at the vanguard of egalitarian sentiment in the mid–1780s. Perhaps Paine had shed the deep-seated hatred of aristocracy that Keane attributes to him as a young man, or perhaps the early Paine's radicalism was confined largely to the realm of politics and had not yet been extended to a broader critique of social and economic inequality.[9]

A close reading of *Common Sense* bears out Ziesche's point about the partial nature of Paine's early egalitarianism. After stating his opening assumption of fundamental human equality, Paine took several steps backward in order to defuse the inevitable counterargument that he was an unrealistic leveler. "The distinctions of rich, and poor," he asserted, could "in a great measure be accounted for ... without having recourse to the harsh, ill-sounding names of oppression and avarice." Likewise, "Male and female are the distinctions of nature, [and] good and bad the distinctions of heaven." With qualifying statements like these, Paine reassured his readers that his espousal of equality would not lead to a melting down of all social distinctions. The wealthy need not be concerned about the security of their property, the poor should not look forward to some future redistribution, husbands need not worry about their future sway over their wives or daughters, and ministers should feel secure in their moral authority. *Common Sense* depicted only "the distinction of men into *kings* and *subjects*" as ludicrous and in need of reconsideration. Paine's use of the language of equality, therefore, was arguably as limited in intent as Jefferson's in the Declaration of Independence. While equality served as an important starting premise for both of these 1776 texts, hereditary monarchy was the only structure of power to which Paine directly applied it, just as the imperial relationship with Britain was the only structure of power Jefferson explicitly sought to dismantle. Using the language of equality as Paine and Jefferson did in 1776 was certainly provocative, and the future implications of this terminology were immense. We must distinguish, however, between unpredictable future implications on the one hand, and historically specific intentions on the other.[10]

The historian most responsible for developing and cementing the image of Paine the staunch egalitarian is E. P. Thompson. His 1963 classic, *The Making of the English Working Class,* has been required reading for all aspiring historians since its publication. Thompson saved Paine from the condescension of a historical profession that, with the notable exception of Philip Foner, had regarded him as an effective but derivative popularizer at best, a drunken, "filthy little atheist" who wrote simplistic propaganda at worst. Where most American historians had paid scant attention to Paine's later European career and saw him primarily as a tribune of American nationalism, Thompson offered a fresh interpretation of Paine's social and economic radicalism. Thompson's

Paine comes across as an organic intellectual, a man whose humble origins and populist instincts enabled him to speak the mind of an English working class angry about its historical exclusion from politics and anxious about the direction of economic change in their increasingly market-oriented society. In the context of the social movements of the 1960s, Paine's disregard for the social proprieties of his day and his affection for the neighborhood tavern no longer seemed like embarrassments to be delicately ignored, for they now appeared to be of a piece with his social radicalism.[11]

Paine and Jefferson's reputations fared quite differently in the new social history of the 1970s and 1980s that was inspired by Thompson's work. As the historical significance of slavery became increasingly apparent, Jefferson's espousal of equality in 1776 appeared ever more problematic and performative. Meanwhile, as scholars became more interested in the dynamics of radical social movements, Paine's egalitarianism looked more earnest and unimpeachable. Thanks to Thompson, Paine gained a new prominence as one of the key founding fathers of a modern social democratic tradition that shaped British and American dissenting politics from the late eighteenth century on. In this narrative about the latent possibilities of the Atlantic World's foundational principles, Paine plays a central role as the embodiment of his age's social and political conscience.[12]

Thompson's interpretation of Paine has not gone unchallenged, but it is still widely regarded as a canonical work. By viewing Paine from the perspective of his politicized working-class readers in the 1790s, Thompson brought to light facets of Paine's radicalism and its influence that had previously gone unnoticed.[13] That said, the shorthand version of Thompson that depicts Paine as a lifelong champion of the dispossessed, a depiction that is now arguably the dominant one in the American historical imagination, has hidden from us some of the complexities and uncertainties that marked Paine's evolution as a thinker. Indeed, if one did not have the image of Paine the working-class hero in mind, then Ziesche's account of him sending a fawning song about the Society of the Cincinnati to George Washington would not provoke such cognitive dissonance. Mark Philp's essay in this collection offers a similar reminder that Paine's political commitments were refined significantly in the late 1780s and 1790s. As late as 1791, it seems that Paine thought a reformed constitutional monarchy in both France and England was an admirable political goal—hardly the sentiments of an uncompromising radical who believed in fundamental human equality. Similarly, Armin Mattes's essay shows that Paine, a figure usually regarded as a key democratic thinker of the eighteenth century, rarely used the term himself until the early 1790s. These three authors offer important new insights on Paine because they looked for evidence of change, rather than taking his egalitarian and democratic bona fides as the starting point for their analyses.

The static image of Paine as a man of the people has also made many features of his personal life difficult to comprehend. In the 1770s and 1780s, Paine counted among his closest American friends and political patrons the wealthy financier Robert Morris as well as two members of South Carolina's largest slaveholding family, Henry and John Laurens. While the younger Laurens held relatively enlightened ideas about slavery and eventually convinced his father to manumit their slaves, the notoriously high-living Robert Morris arguably embodied the most antidemocratic, counter-revolutionary, and elitist impulses of his era.[14] Paine, the clear-eyed and unpretentious revolutionary represented in the portraits Gaye Wilson discusses in her essay, is hard to square with the world of Morris and his associates.[15] Yet when Paine's compatriots in the Philadelphia militia organized a violent protest in 1779 against the economic policies of the hated Robert Morris and his ally James Wilson, Paine sided with the state's financial elite, not the disgruntled citizenry. Likewise, when he returned to England in the late 1780s, Paine lived happily for several months at the estate of his friend Edmund Burke, the person who would become his age's most important critic of egalitarianism and defender of aristocracy and monarchy with the publication of his *Reflections on the Revolution in France* in 1790. Even after Paine rejected Burke and embarked upon his career as an advocate for revolution in 1790s London, Paine met and dined almost exclusively with the well-heeled and more moderate reformers of the Society for Constitutional Information rather than the artisans who comprised the London Corresponding Society. He did not shun his working-class compatriots, but neither did he make a point of joining their organization or regularly attending their meetings. In sum, even though Paine began his life in the working-class world of Georgian England and ended it being ostracized by "respectable" Americans and embraced by only a handful of plebeian radicals in New York City, during the intervening years Paine's social connections and aspirations were quite diverse.[16] Like Jefferson, he attended his share of exclusive Parisian salons and formal state dinners, yet he also spent weeks on end reading newspapers and composing political tracts in the workingmen's taverns of Philadelphia, London, and New York City.

To bring up Paine's links with the likes of Morris and Burke is not to establish his hypocrisy or guilt by association.[17] Rather, the point is to draw attention to how our contemporary investments in Paine and the broader Age of Revolution can sometimes overdetermine our interpretations of his life and writings. The power of these investments are well illustrated by the scholarly response to a 1999 article by James Lynch on the limits of Paine's political vision. Lynch did not deny the authenticity or significance of Paine's radicalism; he merely examined Paine's writings and actions in regard to slavery and concluded that his subsequent reputation as an abolitionist was not well deserved. Lynch raised doubts about the two unsigned antislavery pieces that had been attributed to Paine (and upon which his abolitionist reputation largely rests), and he clarified Paine's modest record of activity with the antislavery societies of his day. Lynch did not claim that Paine endorsed slavery or was a slaveholder himself, but simply that he resembled most of his white contemporaries in thinking slavery was wrong but doing little to bring about its end. He was an appropriately appalled observer, but that hardly merits his later promotion to the ranks of "abolitionist." Lynch's article was met largely with silence by other scholars. Some have engaged with the empirical question of whether Paine was actually the author of two anonymous antislavery pieces from 1775, but none have directly addressed Lynch's larger point about Paine's thin credentials as an abolitionist.[18]

Why do we so want Paine to have been an abolitionist? In 1874 James Parton famously noted that "if Jefferson is wrong, America is wrong," and a similar sentiment seems to prevail in regard to Paine. In this case, however, it is not the entirety of America that is at stake; it is the validity of the democratic, dissenting tradition that contemporary progressives trace back to Paine. For Paine to stand as a key founder of an American progressive tradition that runs from the Revolution through the civil rights era, it seems imperative that his credentials as an unqualified advocate of equality remain intact. What we risk losing when we jealously guard Paine's reputation as a consistent progressive (a task carried on in recent years by the Paine Anti-Defamation League[19]) is an understanding of him as a complex human whose political ideas evolved over time and in dialogue with circumstances and the various political communities of which he was a member. When we encounter Paine's complaints in *Common Sense* that the British had "stirred up the Indians and Negroes to destroy us," we need not feel disappointed or try to explain away such assertions as simply the conventional rhetoric of the day. Nor should we rush (as some readers might be doing at this moment) to come up with good reasons as to why Paine would befriend a figure like Robert Morris, at times support economic policies opposed by struggling farmers and artisans, or remain largely aloof from the abolitionist societies to which his friends in Philadelphia, London, and Paris devoted so much of their time. While the historical Thomas Paine resists Glenn Beck's efforts to turn him into an eighteenth-century version of a Reagan Republican, we should not shrink from admitting that the same historical Paine was not always the man of (all) the people that we might wish him to have been. To raise this point is not to say that Paine's egalitarianism was a sham, but that when investigated closely, it had limits, like every espousal of equality at the time or since. The historical Paine, the complex and contradictory human, can simply not bear the pressure that subsequent generations have put on him to embody their most cherished principles, whether those principles be conservative or progressive.

When we loosen our grip on Paine the symbol, it allows us to see him more sympathetically as a socially embedded thinker whose effectiveness derived not from the emblematic clarity and consistency of his thought, but from his ability to shift his ground as the world changed around him. Seeing Paine in this way is difficult, in part because it departs from the highly individualistic account he himself offered of his political theory. Paine famously (and probably spuriously) claimed not to have read much, and the private manuscripts he left behind offer little reflection about how his ideas germinated or evolved over time. Yet as the essays by Philp, Zuckert, Mattes, and Ziesche show, Paine was heavily influenced by his time in France and the company he kept there. His friends described him as a voracious newspaper reader and avid talker.[20] Though Paine himself gives us no indication of how his writing process worked, it appears as if his pamphlets were extended glosses or even rough transcriptions of real conversations he was having with his contemporaries. Thus, the voice we hear in *Common Sense* is not that of the abstracted "American people," as some commentators imply. Rather, as both Trish Loughran and Sophia Rosenfeld have recently argued, *Common Sense* speaks largely in the voice of the small but influential community of Philadelphia radicals in which Paine found himself in 1775–76.[21] In the late 1770s and 1780s, when an ambitious Paine's primary social world was comprised of a patriot elite more concerned with winning a war and maintaining order than remaking American society, his writings were more modest in scope, and have thus remained largely forgotten and unread ever since. In contrast, Paine's creative resurgence in the first half of the 1790s, when he produced *Rights of Man*, *Age of Reason*, and *Agrarian Justice*, can be attributed, in part, to his sustained engagement with an intellectual community in London and Paris comprised of the Atlantic World's leading visionaries and activists. Reading Paine's works as extended dialogues with specific communities solidifies his reputation as a writer with a unique ability to speak the minds of his contemporaries.

That said, two recent works on Paine have offered deeply contextualized readings of *Common Sense* that explore the limits of Paine's representativeness, exposing the partisan coercions and occlusions that the text's inspirational rhetoric masked. Rather than taking *Common Sense*'s iconic and representative status for granted, Trish Loughran and Sophia Rosenfeld have examined the process through which Paine's text was elevated and sought to elevate itself into a political symbol, a mystification that claimed to embody a moment of national unity and populist political awakening. Loughran's research into the history of *Common Sense*'s publication and dissemination revealed that the claims that the text instantly transformed British colonists into American patriots turned out to be wildly exaggerated, and rested almost entirely upon Paine's own boastful assertions. While acknowledging that it was a "novel publication" that sold better than any other political tract of its day, Loughran argues that the legendary story of "simultaneous and spontaneous dissemination" scholars attach to *Common Sense* has very little basis in reality. All but one of the editions of *Common Sense* were published north of Philadelphia, and the evidence regarding its circulation suggests that it was most popular in localities that were already radicalized and thus needed little convincing. Leading patriots shipped dozens of copies to their friends in distant places, but many of those shipments miscarried or were significantly delayed. It was January after all, and many rivers were frozen shut. Despite Paine's later claims that *Common Sense* sold hundreds of thousands of copies, Loughran points out that no colonial printer had the capacity to produce a print run larger than 3,000, thus making it nearly impossible that the twenty-five editions resulted in more than 75,000 physical copies being produced in 1776. Given that the white population was 2.4 million and that there is little evidence that the text made it much beyond the poorly maintained post roads that connected the colonies' largest settlements, the claim that Paine's text was one of the central forces pushing the entire nation toward independence merits rethinking.[22]

What *Common Sense* did well and continues to do well, Loughran argues, is project an alluring fantasy about national unity that beguiled some of his contemporary readers and has seduced a much larger number of his latter-day readers, especially those who are the subjects of the nation Paine projected. Seen from this perspective, Paine was not so much the mouthpiece for some preexisting political community of incipient Americans; rather, his text "naturalize[d] the not-yet realized nation" by turning readers' attentions away from the deep divisions that marked the would-be nation. Paine was well suited to this rhetorical task since he was an outsider with a limited understanding of the imagined nation on whose behalf he spoke. He was blissfully

CONCLUSION

ignorant of the intercolonial rivalries and local jealousies that shaped the dynamics of patriotism, loyalism, and neutrality within every community. And as a relative stranger to Philadelphia, he risked far less in publishing a pamphlet advocating independence than one of his more well-known and socially embedded radical compatriots. It was precisely Paine's status as an outsider, not the representative "man on the street," that made his text as successful as it was. Likewise, it may be *our* subsequent ignorance of the text's history as a produced and consumed object, as well as our nationalistic tendencies to overlook the divisions within the patriot movement, that leave us vulnerable to claims about its magical influence. Loughran's work suggests that our investments in a print-centered vision of American nationalism and the power of representative writers like Paine to speak the mind of "the people" have led otherwise careful scholars to fall prey to an oversimplified account of the cultural and political work Paine's text actually did.[23]

Where Loughran questioned the assumed connection between *Common Sense* and American nationalism, Sophia Rosenfeld has reexamined the place of *Common Sense* in the genealogy of democratic politics. Rosenfeld's transatlantic intellectual history of the phrase "common sense" unearthed meanings for the term that cut against the traditional reading of Paine's pamphlet. American historians have tended to trust Paine's claim that his pamphlet really did express the "common sense" of his day. The text's plain language seems to embody the world-changing historical moment when ordinary citizens finally found their voice and cut through the obfuscations that had long justified their exclusion from the political process. According to Rosenfeld, however, the eighteenth-century discourse of common sense usually had little to do with the expression of a preexisting popular consensus, but was most frequently a rhetorical device writers used to mask their deeply partisan intentions. Thus, a small community of radical Deists in 1760s Amsterdam described their scathing attacks on Christianity as a commonsensical critique of religious dogma. As Rosenfeld argues, however, their writings did not speak the minds of their overwhelmingly devout contemporaries, most of whom would have vehemently rejected the supposed "common sense" of enlightened Deism. Seen in this context, we must ask exactly *whose* common sense Paine was articulating in 1776. Was the language of common sense as bullying, haughty, and exclusionary in Revolutionary America as it was in eighteenth-century Amsterdam? If this was even partially the case, then it would seem imperative for us to reconsider the relationship between *Common Sense* and the American democratic tradition. Perhaps Paine was not giving voice to a previously suppressed longing for national self-determination and self-rule, but rather voicing a minority position and using the language of "common sense" to hide the deeply partisan nature of his argument.[24]

Approaching Paine in this way offers us a better vantage point from which to view his role as the tribune of American nationalism and democratic self-rule. In one of the most famous passages from *Common Sense,* Paine imagines people leaving the state of nature to gather under a tree that doubles as their statehouse. This is how governments are formed, Paine tells his readers. Independent, rights-bearing people come together en masse, agree upon the rules under which they will all live, and then disperse to enjoy freedom and tranquility. It is an inspirational and affirming story, a stark contrast with the violent history of conquest and exploitation that produced Europe's monarchies. It is, however, an utterly untrue, naive, and deceptive picture of how the American colonies mobilized for their war of independence. Paine's bucolic tree imagery suppresses the intellectual disagreements, unresolvable conflicts of interest, and physical violence that marked the movement toward independence. The beguiling image of self-governance as a social gathering under a tree—literally, a picnic—also implies that policy making is a simple matter that any citizen could do as well as any other. Rosenfeld sees the legacy of this Painite populism in the twentieth-century conservative movement that favors minimal government and disdains professional civil servants, intellectuals, and scientific experts. Paine's tree parable, written at precisely the moment when the explosion of commercial capitalism would introduce ever more complexity and diversity into the social and political world, encourages readers to repress those complications and flee into a world where a few honest citizens sitting around a tree can solve their problems in an afternoon. By pointing out the gulf between *Common Sense*'s lofty oversimplifications and the complex social and political world it sought to transform, Loughran and Rosenfeld, like James Lynch before them, have challenged the iconic vision of Paine in order to offer a more nuanced, critical account of his politics.

While Lougran and Rosenfeld emphasize the gap between rhetoric and reality exemplified in *Common Sense*'s tree parable, I would argue that we can read Paine's later writings as an extended, if unfinished, effort to fill in that gap by thinking through how modern societies could work toward realizing that parable's ideal of literal self-rule. In the second part of *Rights of Man* and *Agrarian Justice* in particular, Paine sought to identify and make manifest the background social conditions necessary to sustain the sort of radically egalitarian, inclusive, and participatory democracy implied in that primal scene of popular sovereignty under the metaphorical tree. It is in this sense that Paine's career can be read as an effort to work through a set of problems articulated in his earliest writings.

Michael Zuckert's essay in this collection effectively illustrates how this dynamic played out in Paine's later work. Both the Declaration of Independence and *Common Sense* revolved around the idea of consent, using Lockean ideas to justify the dissolution of British rule in America and the construction of new, legitimate political authority. During Paine's and Jefferson's respective stays in Revolutionary-era France more than a decade later, they returned to the idea of consent with a new set of questions and concerns. Consent was no longer simply a legitimating abstraction for them, but now posed important problems of institutional design. *Common Sense* had not paused to consider if every person actually had the ability to show up at that tree, nor did it seriously imagine what politics would look like under that tree in the months and years that followed. Paine's and Jefferson's writings from the late 1780s and early 1790s address precisely the questions of what sort of political and economic arrangements were necessary to make consent a truly robust, lived ideal. Jefferson addressed the political gap with his speculative writings about ward republicanism, a thickly institutionalized vision of politics where ordinary citizens exerted their literal consent on an ongoing basis rather than at periodic elections. Paine's lifelong affinity for Pennsylvania's 1776 constitution suggests that he would have found Jefferson's political vision quite congruent with his own.

Both Paine and Jefferson also recognized that a truly consensual democracy required more than just political institutions that invited participation; it also required a citizenry with the intellectual and economic independence necessary for active participation in the polity. Both Jefferson and Paine presumed that truly consensual self-government could only exist in societies marked by widespread independent proprietorship.[25] As Edward Gray shows in his essay, it was this ideal of the largely (but not solely) agrarian republic of freeholders that underlay the geopolitical vision articulated by both Jefferson and Paine during the Nootka Sound Crisis of 1790. And while Jefferson privately speculated about ways in which governments could foster economic equity,[26] Paine left behind a much more substantial body of detailed policy prescriptions that sought to ensure a degree of economic independence for every citizen. As Zuckert points out, Paine's plans for the governmental redistribution of wealth rested upon the same natural rights theory that formed the basis for his arguments in *Common Sense*. What may look like a contradiction to contemporary conservatives, thus, to Paine, felt like a natural evolution in his thinking. By the 1790s, he had come to realize that modern, commercial societies like those he observed in France and England systematically rendered large numbers of citizens so economically deprived that they were unable to participate in the processes of self-rule. Hence, it was the duty of the government to restore the natural right to property, and the attendant right to live an independent and dignified life, that had been taken away from them by historical forces beyond their control.

The implications of Paine's ideas about political economy remain contested. Some historians regard Paine as a "bourgeois liberal," someone who offered only a few incremental policy prescriptions that would tinker around the edges of the market-oriented society he, for the most part, eagerly espoused. In this sense, Paine seems like a representative of the American mainstream limned by consensus historians since the 1950s.[27] According to Gareth Stedman Jones, Harvey Kaye, and a host of other historians, however, Paine's political economy embodies an as yet unrealized third way—a non-Marxist critique of the free market that stresses the need for democratic control of the economy. This Paine is far from the anti-government thinker and market optimist depicted by Gordon Wood in this collection; rather, this Paine is an egalitarian democrat first and foremost who is sensitive to the ways the market can create unjust consolidations of power—and the ways in which ordinary citizens can use their political power to counter such consolidation and the poverty it creates.[28]

And so we return to the dispute with which this essay began—to whom does Paine belong? Is he representative of a long-standing American consensus about the beneficence of representative democracy and free-market capitalism, or is he part of a dissenting tradition that is critical of the historical inequalities and exclusions built into the nation's political and economic structures? This dispute will undoubtedly continue, for as this historiographical survey has shown, his works articulated the foundational yet contested terrain upon which America's subsequent political and economic development occurred. Like his compatriot Thomas Jefferson, Paine articulated an optimistic faith in the capacity for ordinary citizens to govern themselves, a deep-seated belief in human equality, and excitement about the social benefits that would result from granting intellectual, religious, and economic freedom to everyone. Later in his life, however, Paine became ever more attuned to the complicated ways in which forces outside of formal politics—organized religion in *The Age of Reason* and commercial capitalism in *Agrarian Justice*—made those ideals of self-rule, equality, and freedom harder to realize in practice. Paine's career thus speaks to both the conservative and the progressive strands in America's political culture. The progressives who admire the direction Paine went in the

CONCLUSION

1790s must acknowledge that most of his contemporary American readers did not follow him down those paths. The conservatives who dislike the later Paine must acknowledge that he, Jefferson, and many others regarded such ideas as logical extensions of the principles that had inspired the American Revolution. So if the question is who Paine belongs to, the answer seems to be both, and neither.

Upon Paine's return to America in 1803, William Bentley, a Congregationalist minister in Salem, Massachusetts, commented in his diary that Paine was "as great a paradox as ever appeared in human nature.... He never appears but we love and hate him."[29] Paine continues to repay our attention, and elicit both hate and love, because he offers us a uniquely articulate guide to the paradoxes inherent in America's founding principles. As with any form of "founder fundamentalism," Paine becomes less valuable when we ask him to provide straightforward solutions to our twenty-first-century problems.[30] Neither he nor we can so easily make those paradoxes go away.

NOTES

1. The most influential conservative appropriation of Paine (apart from Glenn Beck's book cited below) is a series of videos in which Bob Basso impersonates a Paine who rails against virtually every policy advocated by the Obama administration (http://www.youtube.com/user/Funbobbasso). Basso's videos have attracted 14 million views (as of April 2012), while a progressive rebuttal by Ian Ruskin (http://www.youtube.com/user/TheLife ofThomasPaine) has yet to find such a substantial audience. Although it has recently been abandoned, one of America's leading progressive websites in the first decade of the twenty-first century was TomPaine.org. The leading contemporary voice claiming Paine for contemporary progressivism is Harvey Kaye, *Thomas Paine and the Promise of America* (New York: Hill and Wang, 2006).

2. See Glenn Beck, *Glenn Beck's Common Sense: The Case against Out-of-Control Government, Inspired by Thomas Paine* (New York: Threshold Editions, 2009). Tony Benn has served as the president of the Thomas Paine Society UK and nominated Paine for a "Man of the Millennium" award (see Christopher Hitchens, *Thomas Paine's "Rights of Man": A Biography* [New York: Atlantic Monthly Press, 2007]).

3. Gordon Wood, *Revolutionary Characters: What Made the Founders Different* (New York: Penguin, 2007).

4. Eric Foner, *Tom Paine and Revolutionary America* (New York: Oxford University Press, 1976).

5. John Adams to Benjamin Waterhouse, 29 October 1805, in *Diary and Autobiography of John Adams,* ed. L. H. Butterfield et al., 4 vols. (Cambridge, Mass.: Harvard University Press, 1962), 3:333. Some of Paine's supporters regarded *The Age of Reason* as marking a

serious departure from Paine's earlier works, and they publicly rejected his theology while still embracing his political vision. Neither Paine nor his conservative detractors, however, saw a contradiction between Paine's political ideals and his thoughts about organized religion.

6. See Simon Newman, "Paine, Jefferson, and Revolutionary Radicalism in Early National America," this volume. Also in this volume, Emma Macleod's "Thomas Paine and Jeffersonian America" offers a similar assessment of Paine's intellectual consistency over the years.

7. For an excellent, sympathetic discussion of the Pennsylvania radicals behind the 1776 constitution, see Gary Nash, "Philadelphia's Radical Caucus that Propelled Pennsylvania to Independence and Democracy," in *Revolutionary Founders: Rebels, Radicals, and Reformers in the Making of the Nation,* ed. Alfred F. Young, Gary B. Nash, and Ray Raphael (New York: Random House, 2011): 67–86. On the role of Philadelphia's militia in particular, see Steven J. Rosswurm, *Arms, Country, and Class: The Philadelphia Militia and the "Lower Sort" during the American Revolution* (New Brunswick, N.J.: Rutgers University Press, 1989).

8. John Keane, *Tom Paine: A Political Life* (New York: Grove Press, 2003). The case for the influence of Paine's Quaker upbringing has been made most forcefully in Jack Fruchtman Jr., *Thomas Paine: Apostle of Freedom* (New York: Four Walls Eight Windows, 1994); and Fruchtman, *Thomas Paine and the Religion of Nature* (Baltimore: Johns Hopkins University Press, 1993). Eric Foner, in *Tom Paine and Revolutionary America,* also argues for the importance of Paine's early interactions with London's community of urban artisans.

9. Philipp Ziesche, "Thomas Paine and Benjamin Franklin's French Circle," this volume.

10. All quotes are from Thomas Paine, *Common Sense* (Philadelphia, 1776), http://www.gutenberg.org/files/147/147-h/147-h.htm.

11. E. P. Thompson, *The Making of the English Working Class* (London: Gollancz, 1963). Theodore Roosevelt dismissed Paine as a "filthy little atheist" (see Roosevelt, *Gouverneur Morris* [Boston: Houghton Mifflin, 1892], 289).

12. The list of Thompson-influenced works on Paine is far too long to include here. Some of the best works in this tradition are Foner, *Tom Paine and Revolutionary America;* Kaye, *Thomas Paine and the Promise of America;* and Gary B. Nash, *The Unknown American Revolution: The Unruly Birth of American Democracy and the Struggle to Create America* (New York: Penguin, 2006).

13. Paine's place in the broader world of British radicalism in the 1790s has been explored in several works by Gregory Claeys, most prominently, *Thomas Paine: Social and Political Thought* (London: Routledge, 1989). Anna Clark offers an important critique of the gendered limitations of 1790s radicalism in *The Struggle for the Breeches: Gender and the Making of the British Working Class* (Berkeley: University of California Press, 1997).

14. This interpretation of Morris is developed in Terry Bouton, *Taming Democracy:*

CONCLUSION

The People, the Founders, and the Troubled Ending of the American Revolution (New York: Oxford University Press, 2007).

15. Paine was hardly the only figure from his age to be portrayed in such an intentionally unpretentious manner. My sense, however, is that most viewers would be inclined to trust these Paine portraits as depicting something authentic in Paine's persona. Compare this to the healthy skepticism with which most commentators view portraits of Franklin in his coonskin cap or Jefferson in his wolf-fur collar and democratically unkempt hair. The self-fashioning behind the populist pose in the Franklin and Jefferson images strikes one immediately, whereas the Paine portraits appear at first glance to be less analytically complicated.

16. On Paine's last years in New York City, see Mark Lause, "The 'Unwashed Infidelity': Thomas Paine and Early New York City Labor History," *Labor History* 27 (Summer 1986): 386–409.

17. This approach has been taken by Hazel Burgess, who argues that Paine was essentially an opportunist and a monarchist who was working as a double agent (see Thomas Paine, *A Collection of Unknown Writings*, ed. Hazel Burgess [Houndmills, Basingstoke, Hampshire (England): Palgrave Macmillan, 2010]. The evidence for this claim is entirely circumstantial and unconvincing.

18. James V. Lynch, "The Limits of Revolutionary Radicalism: Tom Paine and Slavery," *Pennsylvania Magazine of History and Biography* 123 (July 1999): 177–99.

19. http://www.thomas-paine-friends.org/anti-defamation.html. Despite the dogmatic implications of the name, most of the commentary on this site is well informed and politically sophisticated.

20. The diary of Paine's friend John Hall from the 1780s contains several accounts of Paine's newspaper-reading habits (see John Hall Diary, Library Company of Philadelphia).

21. Trish Loughran, *The Republic in Print: Print Culture in the Age of U.S. Nation Building, 1770–1870* (New York: Columbia University Press, 2009); Sophia Rosenfeld, *Common Sense: A Political History* (Cambridge, Mass.: Harvard University Press, 2011).

22. Loughran, *Republic in Print*, 57–58.

23. Ibid., 64.

24. Rosenfeld, *Common Sense*.

25. In their essays in this collection, both Frank Cogliano and Ed Gray astutely criticize those who see profound differences between Jefferson's and Paine's political economy. The conflict between an anti-market agrarian republicanism (Jefferson) and an urban, pro-market republicanism (Paine) that shaped much scholarship in the 1970s and 1980s now appears to have been greatly overstated.

26. See Cogliano's essay in this collection, where he discusses Jefferson's plan to give fifty acres of land to every landless man in Virginia.

27. This argument has been made most forcefully in Isaac Kramnick, "Tom Paine:

Radical Liberal," in *Republicanism and Bourgeois Radicalism: Political Ideology in Late Eighteenth-Century England and America* (Ithaca, N.Y.: Cornell University Press, 1990), 133–60.

28. Gareth Stedman Jones, *An End to Poverty? A Historical Debate* (New York: Columbia University Press, 2005); Kaye, *Thomas Paine and the Promise of America*.

29. *The Diary of William Bentley, D.D., Pastor of the East Church, Salem, Massachusetts*, 4 vols. (Gloucester, Mass.: P. Smith, 1962), 3:37.

30. On Founder fundamentalism, see Jill Lepore, *The Whites of Their Eyes: The Tea Party's Revolution and the Battle over American History* (Princeton, N.J.: Princeton University Press, 2010).

CONTRIBUTORS

FRANCIS D. COGLIANO is Professor of American History at the University of Edinburgh. He is the author of *Revolutionary America, 1763–1815: A Political History* (2nd ed., 2009), and *Thomas Jefferson: Reputation and Legacy* (2006), and the editor of the *Blackwell Companion to Thomas Jefferson* (2012).

SETH COTLAR is a Professor of History at Willamette University in Salem, Oregon. He is the author of *Tom Paine's America: The Rise and Fall of Trans-Atlantic Radicalism in the Early Republic,* which won the Society for Historians of the Early American Republic's James Broussard Prize for the best first book. He is currently working on a cultural history of nostalgia in modernizing America, 1776–1860.

JACK FRUCHTMAN JR. is Professor of Political Science and Director of the Law and American Civilization Program at Maryland's Towson University. He has written, edited, or annotated ten books. His work on eighteenth-century figures includes studies of the political thought of Thomas Paine, Richard Price, Joseph Priestley, Thomas Reid, Helen Maria Williams, and Thomas Hardy, as well as the marquis de Condorcet and Jacques-Pierre Brissot. His most recent book is *The Political Philosophy of Thomas Paine* (2009). He also serves as coeditor of the Pickering & Chatto series on The Enlightenment World.

EDWARD G. GRAY is Professor of History at Florida State University. He is the author of *New World Babel: Languages and Nations in Early America* (1999) and *The Making of John Ledyard: Empire and Ambition in the Life of an Early American Traveler* (2007). He is also coeditor with Jane Kamensky of the *Oxford Handbook of the American Revolution* (2013), and is now completing a book about Thomas Paine's struggles to build one of the world's first iron bridges.

EMMA MACLEOD is a Lecturer in History at the University of Stirling. She is the author of *A War of Ideas: British Attitudes to the Wars against Revolution-*

ary France, 1792–1802 (1998), and numerous articles on British perspectives on the French and American Revolutions. Her new book, *British Visions of America, c. 1775–1820: Republican Realities*, will be published in 2013.

ARMIN MATTES received his PhD from the University of Virginia in 2011. He is the 2012–13 Gilder Lehrman Junior Research Fellow at the Robert H. Smith International Center for Jefferson Studies at Monticello, where he is working on a book manuscript on the emergence of modern concepts of democracy and nationhood in America from 1775 to 1840.

THOMAS MUNCK is Professor of Early Modern European History at the University of Glasgow. He is author of a number of books, including *Seventeenth-Century Europe* (2nd ed., 2005) and *The Enlightenment: A Comparative Social History, 1721–1794* (2000), and has published articles on a range of issues relating to public opinion, print, and the Enlightenment in Scandinavia, the German lands, and northwestern Europe up to and including the French Revolution. He is currently working on a major study of political culture and the use of print across language boundaries from 1630 to 1800.

SIMON P. NEWMAN is the Sir Denis Brogan Professor of American History at the University of Glasgow. He is the author of *Parades and the Politics of the Street: Festive Culture in the Early American Republic* (1997), *Embodied History: The Lives of the Poor in Early Philadelphia* (2003), and *A New World of Labor: The Development of Plantation Slavery in the British Atlantic* (2013).

PETER S. ONUF is Thomas Jefferson Foundation Professor Emeritus at the University of Virginia and Senior Research Fellow at the Robert H. Smith International Center for Jefferson Studies at Monticello. He is the author or editor of numerous works on the history of the early American republic, including *Jefferson's Empire: The Language of American Nationhood* (2000), and with his brother Nicholas, *Nations, Markets, War: Modern History and the American Civil War* (2006). He is currently collaborating on an intimate intellectual biography of Thomas Jefferson, *The Most Blessed of the Patriarchs*, with Annette Gordon-Reed.

MARK PHILP is Fellow and Tutor in Politics and University Lecturer at Oriel College, University of Oxford. He has written widely on the history of political thought and on Britain in the 1790s, as well as working on contemporary political theory and on political corruption. He is the author of two short books on Paine and the editor of a collection of his writings. Recent work includes *Political Conduct* (2007) and, with David O'Shaughnessy and Victoria Myers, a digital edition of the diary of William Godwin, 1788–1836 (http://godwindiary.bodleian.ox.ac.uk). A collection of his historical essays, *Reforming Ideas,* will be published in 2013.

GAYE WILSON is the Shannon Senior Historian at the Robert H. Smith International Center for Jefferson Studies, a part of the Thomas Jefferson Foundation at Monticello. Her essays and articles on Thomas Jefferson have been published in book-length compilations and journals. Much of her work focuses on Jefferson's public image, and she welcomed the opportunity offered by this volume to expand her research to include the public image of Thomas Paine.

GORDON S. WOOD is the Alva O. Way University Professor and Professor of History Emeritus at Brown University. He is the author of numerous books on the American Revolution and the early republic, including *The Creation of the American Republic, 1776–1787* (1969), which was awarded the Bancroft Prize, and *The Radicalism of the American Revolution* (1992), for which he received the Pulitzer Prize for History. In 2010 he received the National Humanities Medal.

PHILIPP ZIESCHE is Associate Editor of the Papers of Benjamin Franklin at Yale University. He is a past Gilder Lehrman Fellow at the Robert H. Smith International Center for Jefferson Studies at Monticello and the author of *Cosmopolitan Patriots: Americans in Paris in the Age of Revolution* (2010).

MICHAEL ZUCKERT is Nancy R. Dreux Professor of Political Science at the University of Notre Dame. He is the author of *Natural Rights and the New Republicanism,* among other works on early modern political philosophy. He is the founding editor of the journal *American Political Thought*

INDEX

Italicized page numbers refer to illustrations.

Adams, John: and Alien and Sedition Acts, 77; *Defence of the Constitutions of the Government of the United States,* 141; and equality, 16, 106; and mixed government, 141; and Paine, 55, 100, 203, 209, 214–16, 278–80; portrait of, 232–33; and Society of the Cincinnati, 130
Adams, Samuel, 52, 55, 58
Adams, Willi Paul, 156n11, 157n26
Address to the British Colonists in North America (Burke), 99
Age of Reason, The (Paine), 3, 87; continental European reception of, 8, 173; Dutch reviews of, 176–77; English reception of, 171; Federalists' use of, 80; in French context, 168; and Paine's reputation, 76–77, 217, 244. *See also* Paine, Thomas: religious views of
Age of the Democratic Revolution, The (Palmer), 97–98
Age of Revolution, 4, 9, 280–81, 285
Agrarian Justice (Paine), 3, 23, 171; and American progressives, 279; and Babeuf, 264–65; and distribution of wealth, 261; modern revival of, 273n2; and welfare rights, 256–57
Aitken, Robert, 29, 55
Aldridge, Owen, 150, 218
Allgemeine Deutsche Bibliothek (1765–1806), 164, 177–78
Alien and Sedition Acts (1798), 77, 81–83, 110, 215
American Citizen, 88
American Crisis, The (Paine): and American conservatives, 279; and American spirit, 3, 59, 73, 196; and Paine's early radicalism, 57; and Paine's vision of global change, 59–60
American Empire: Jefferson's vision of, 188, 201–2; Paine's vision of, 188–89, 196–97, 202, 213; Spanish fear of, 190–91. *See also* Jefferson, Thomas: and American West
American Philosophical Society, 231
American Revolution: and French Revolution, 137–38, 145–46; historiography on, 138–39; mobilization in, 100, 106–7, 112; as model for the world, 6–7, 60–62, 149, 214; and historical paintings, 232, 236; republican theory during, 26, 147–48
ancien régime, 9, 20, 62, 130, 151, 169, 171
André, John, 56, 63
Anglican Church, disestablishment of, 38, 41
Anglicans, 31
Appleby, Joyce, 141, 188
Arendt, Hannah, 154n2, 157n26, 265
aristocracy: dialectic with democracy, 96, 101–3, 106, 153; English, 282; Franklin on, 7, 126–29; in French Revolution, 100, 104–5; natural, 40; Paine on, 121, 127–31, 282
Aristotle, 102, 254
Arnold, Benedict, 56, 63
Assembly, National (France), 105–6, 137, 140–41, 176; American influence on, 143
Assembly, Pennsylvania, 31
Aurora (Philadelphia), 77–78, 88, 219, 221
Autobiography (Trumbull), 244
autonomy, colonial, 99

Babeuf, François-Noël, 265–66, 268
Bache, Benjamin Franklin, 77, 81
Bache, Richard, 121–22
Bache, Sarah, 127; and Benjamin Franklin, 239
Bailyn, Bernard, 2, 50, 203
Baker, Keith Michael, 154n2, 156n11
Bank of North America, 64

301

INDEX

Banks, Joseph, 236
Baptists, 38
Bassett, Thomas, 239
Basso, Bob, 293n1
Beard, Charles, 2; *An Economic Interpretation of the Constitution,* 2
Beard, Mary, 2
beaver, and Canadian fur trade, 185
Beck, Glenn, 278, 286–87
Benn, Tony, 278
Bentley, William, 293
Bible, 177
Bibliothèque Nationale, 172
Bill for Establishing Religious Freedom (Jefferson), 38–39
Bill for the More General Diffusion of Knowledge (Jefferson), 39–40
bill of rights, 42, 156n11, 214–15
Bonneville, Madame, 4, 247
Bonneville, Nicolas de, 69n73, 125, 150
Bonwick, Colin, 220
Boston Athenaeum, 229, 248
Bouche de fer, 150
Boudinot, Elias, 63
Bourbon imperial reforms, 190–91
Boyd, Julian P., 46n29
Brissot de Warville, Jacques-Pierre, 69n73, 126, 165
Brissotins, 166–67, 172
Broglie, Victor François, duc de, 145
Brown, Mather, 232–33
Burgess, Hazel, 158n32
Burgesses, House of, 34
Burgoyne, John, 75
Burke, Aedanus, and Society of the Cincinnati, 126
Burke, Edmund, 50; *Address to the British Colonists in North America,* 99; and American Revolution, 99; and authority of the past, 21, 262; and corporate equality, 98–99, 101; and democracy, 148; and French Revolution, 137; and Hastings trial, 193; on natural rights, 257–58; and Paine, friendship with, 193, 236, 285; on Spanish imperial weakness, 200. See also *Reflections on the Revolution in France*
Burr, Aaron, 85

Canton, as market for pelts, 189
capitalism, 18, 290

Case of the Officers of Excise, The (Paine), 28, 53–55
Cato. *See* Smith, William
Cavendish-Bentinck, William, duke of Portland, 236
celebrations, Independence Day, 83–84, 89
censorship, in Enlightenment, 162–63
Chalmers, George (pseud. Francis Oldys), 49–50
Chamfort, Nicolas, 126–27; *Considerations sur l'Ordre de Cincinnatus,* 127, 130
Charles II, 218
Chastellux, Chevalier de. *See* Chastellux, François-Jean de Beauvoir, marquis de
Chastellux, François-Jean de Beauvoir, marquis de, 13, 124; and Paine, 239–40
Cheetham, James, 221
China trade, 189–91, 200
Christianity, 76–77, 81, 88, 244; Jefferson's and Paine's criticism of, 21–22
Cincinnati, Society of the, 126, 129–30; Adams and, 130; Franklin and Paine on, 282
citizenship, 27, 42–43; Jefferson and Paine on, 5–6; rights of, in Pennsylvania, 33–34
Civil War, English, 282
Claeys, Gregory, 66n15
Clark, George Rogers, 200
Clavière, Etienne, 126
Clermont-Tonnerre, Stanislas Marie Adelaide, comte de, 144
Clymer, Daniel, 202
Cobbett, William, 23, 80–81
Cogliano, Francis, 5
College of William and Mary. *See* William and Mary, College of
Columbian Centinel, 243
Committee of Inspection, Philadelphia, 31
Committee of Public Safety (France), 167–68
Common Sense (Paine): and American conservatives, 279; and American independence, 3, 26, 53–57; composition of, 29–30, 55–56, 122–23; and equality, 99; European translations of, 173, *174;* and global revolution, 51–52, 57–58; and hereditary privilege, 36–37; and Paine's market sentimentalism, 197–98; and Paine's vision for America, 196–97, 211; publication and impact of, 287–90; and relation to *Rights of Man,* 49–51; on society and government, 16–18, 254–56

INDEX

Common Sense: A Political History (Rosenfeld), 2
conceptual change, 149–50; of democracy and nation, 95–113, 147–48, 152–53
Conditions of the Working Class in England (Engels), 147
Condorcet, Jean-Antoine-Nicolas de Caritat, marquis de, 69n73, 131, 172; and Paine, 124, 141, 144, 155n6, 164–65, 179, 218–19
confederacy, American, 26
Congress, American, 76; and Paine, 210
Connecticut Courant, 79
Considerations sur l'Ordre de Cincinnatus (Chamfort and Mirabeau), 127, 130
constitution: British, 29–30, 145; Burke on mixed, 101; mixed, 101, 103–6, 141–43, 147; Paine on U.S., 41, 126, 211–12, 214–15; Paine on French, 139, 218–19; U.S., 79, 82, 85, 140, 156n11, 209; of Virginia, 35–36. *See also* Pennsylvania constitution (1776)
constitutional convention, Pennsylvania, 31
Constitutionalists, Pennsylvania, 32–33
Continental Army, 3, 73
Continental Conference, Paine's plans for, 30–31
Continental Congress, 26, 73; Jefferson and, 34, 37; and loans from Holland, 237; Paine and, 3, 29, 60, 64
Convention, Constitutional (Philadelphia), 2, 41, 139
Convention, National (France), 20, 132, 164–67
convention, Virginia, 34–35
Cook, James, 189, 200
Cornwallis, Charles, Marquess, 57
corporate charters, Jefferson and Paine on, 21
Cotlar, Seth, 2–3, 9–10, 65n10
Crisis, Imperial, 99, 106–7
Cromwell, Oliver, 65n6

Danton, Georges Jacques, 168
Darnton, Robert, 170–71
d'Aubertueil, Hilliard, *Essais historiques et politiques sur les Anglo-Américains*, 123
da Vinci, Leonardo, 145
Declaration of Independence: and equality, 40; Jefferson's drafting of, 26, 71; and Jefferson's draft of Virginia constitution, 36–37; and natural rights, 259–60, 270–71; and Republican party, 77–79, 83–85; and Trumbull's painting, 232–35
Declaration of the Causes and Necessity of Taking up Arms (Jefferson), 34
Declaration of the Rights of Man and of the Citizen, 252
Declaratory Act (1766), 61, 99
Decline and Fall of the English System of Finance, The (Paine), 3, 171, 178
Defence of the Constitutions of the Government of the United States (Adams), 141
deference, in political writings, 128
Deism, 87, 289
DeLolme, Jean Louis, 141
Démeunier, Jean Nicholas, 103
democracy, 87; American, 277, 289–90; consensual, 291; and idea of the nation, 6, 95–96, 104–6, 112–13; Jefferson as apostle of, 16; Jefferson, Paine, and, 10, 290–91; Paine's conceptual change of, 95–103, 138, 147–49, 152; participatory, 273; representative, 7, 102–3
Democracy in America (Tocqueville), 103
Democratic Republicans. *See* Republican Party
Democratic-Republican Societies, 74
despotism, 58, 104
d'Estaing, Charles Hector, comte, 124, 131
Deutsches Magazin, 175
d'Houdetot, Elisabeth Françoise Sophie Lavile de Bellegarde, comtesse, 124
Diderot, Denis, 126, 163, 201
diplomacy, republican vs. monarchical, 19–20
Discourse on the Love of Our Country (Price), 137
Dissertation on First Principles of Government (Paine), 148, 212–13
Dissertations on Government; the Affairs of the Bank; and Paper Money (Paine), 142–43, 149–51
Doyle, William, 130
Duane, William, 77–78, 221
Dunlap, William, *History of the Rise and Progress of the Arts of Design in the United States*, 246
Duplessis, Joseph-Siffred, 231
Du Pont de Nemours, Pierre Samuel, 127, 141
Durey, Michael, 210

303

INDEX

Dyck, Ian, 50
Dylan, Bob, 2

Economic Interpretation of the Constitution, An (C. Beard), 2
election of 1800, 111
embargo: Jefferson and, 22; Hamilton on, 21
Emmet, Thomas Addis, 211
Empire, British, 99; eighteenth-century critique of, 188; Jefferson's fear of, 199–201; political economy of, 197
Encyclopédie Methodique, 103, 163
Engels, Frederick, *Conditions of the Working Class in England*, 147
English Short Title Catalogue, 171–72
Enlightenment, 4, 282; common sense philosophy of, 2; and dispersion of writings, 7–8, 162
entail, Jefferson's bill against, 37–38, 268
Eppes, Francis, 246
equality, 15, 27; Burke and Paine on, 98–102; and democracy, 6, 102, 212–13, 280; and dress styles, 241–42; Lockean, 254; through education, 40. *See also under* Jefferson, Thomas; Paine, Thomas
Essais historiques et politiques sur les Anglo-Américains (d'Aubertéuil), 123
Essay on the Theory of Painting (Richardson), 231
estate, third, 104–5
Estates General (France), 105, 140, 142–43, 186
exceptionalism, American, 112, 145, 279; Paine on, 222–23
Excise, Board of, 122
expansion. *See* American Empire
Ezran, Maurice, 50

Federalist Papers, 147, 149
Federalists, 72–74; as aristocratic counter-revolutionaries, 75–76, 82; and federal government, 110; and French Revolution, 79; and Jefferson, 83, 86–87; and Paine, 6, 79–82, 86–88; Paine's criticism of, 214–18; political economy of, 187–88; and ratification of federal constitution, 42; and Washington, 79
Ferguson, Adam, 175
First Inaugural Address (Jefferson), 111
Fitzwilliam, William, 236

Foner, Eric, 27–28, 43, 50, 214, 221, 279
Foner, Philip, 283
Forester's Letters, The (Paine), 58
Fortune, Brandon Brame, 248n4
Franco-American alliance, 62
Franklin, Benjamin, 60; and French network, 124–26; and letters of introduction for Paine, 28, 53, 121–22, 124, 139; as minister to France, 62, 103; *Model of a Letter of Recommendation of a Person You are Unacquainted With*, 122; as politician, 131–32; portrait of, 231; as radical cosmopolitan, 131. *See also under* Paine, Thomas
freedom of the press, Paine on, 213
French Revolution: and American Revolution, interpretation of, 153; and conceptual change, 95–96; cosmopolitanism and universalism of, 222–23; and fear of radicalism in U.S. and Britain, 20–21, 211; historiography on, 137–39; and link to struggles in other countries, 106; and Paine and Burke, antagonism between, 98, 100–101; Republican Party and, 74–77. *See also under* Jefferson, Thomas; Paine, Thomas
Fruchtman, Jack, Jr., 6–7
Furet, François, 154n2
fur trade, 191
Fur Trade in Canada, The (Innis), 185

Gallatin, Albert, 245
Gallois, Jean Antoine, 141
Gazette of the United States, 79, 86, 246
Gem, Richard, 144
George III, 55, 129
Girondins, 179
Glasgow Advertiser, 171
Glorious Revolution, 258
Gray, Edward, 8, 291
Greene, Nathaniel, 56, 63
Grouvelle, Philippe-Antoine, 127
guillotine, 131, 252

Haitian Revolution, 88–89
Hamilton, Alexander: and bill of rights, 156n11; and equality, 16, 107; and Jefferson, 20–21, 108; and Nootka Sound Crisis, 199, 201; and Paine, 215, 278; *Report on Manufactures*, 108; *Report on the*

304

INDEX

Public Credit, 108; Republican Party and, 73–78
Hampson, Norman, 144
Hare, Robert, 122
Hartz, Louis, 2
Hastings, Warren, 193
Hebrews, 56
Hewson, John, 122
Historische-politische Magazin, 178
Historisches Magazin, 175
History of the Rise and Progress of the Arts of Design in the United States (Dunlap), 246
Hitchens, Christopher, 278
Hogarth, William, 282
Hollis, Thomas Brand, 239
Houdon, Jean-Antoine, 231
Howe, William, 32, 57
Hume, David, 16, 201
Hutcheson, Francis, 17

ideology: Country-Whig, 17; Franklin and Paine's, 130; Jefferson and Paine's, 14
Inaugural Address, First (Jefferson), 111
Innis, Harold Adams, *The Fur Trade in Canada,* 185
iron bridge: and Morellet, 125; Paine's plan for, 3, 7, 21, 63–64, 123–24, 139, 232, 236; and Paine's political economy, 193–94; and Walker Brothers, 193

Jacobins, 166
Jacobite rising (1745), 195
Jarvis, John Wesley, and portrait of Paine, 247
Jay, John, 80, 105; and Society of the Cincinnati, 130
Jay Treaty (1795), 76, 80; Paine on, 216
Jefferson, Martha (daughter of Thomas Jefferson), 233, 235
Jefferson, Martha (wife of Thomas Jefferson), 34
Jefferson, Peter (father of Thomas Jefferson), 34
Jefferson, Thomas: and agrarian ideal, 188, 291; and American West, 186–88, 200–202; and American worthies, 8–9, 230–31, 243; background of, 13, 34; *Bill for Establishing Religious Freedom,* 38–39; *Bill for the More General Diffusion of Knowledge,* 39–40; as cosmopolitan and nationalist, 22–23; and debt, 269; *Declaration of the Causes and Necessity of Taking up Arms,* 34; and democracy, 23, 147, 277; and diplomacy, 19–20; and draft constitution for Virginia, 35–40, 46n25; election to presidency, 85; and equality, 4–5, 15, 36, 107, 146, 283; European reception of, 164; on federal constitution, 41–42; First Inaugural Address, 111; and France, expectations for, 159n47; and French Revolution, 9, 20, 103–6, 145–46, 252–53, 266, 272–73; and generational sovereignty, 144, 263, 267–71; and Hamilton, 108–9; historiography on, 4; and idea of an American nation, 96, 103–12; and imperial vision, 188, 201–2; and inaugural address, 85–86, 111; on inequality and privilege, 21, 23, 36–37, 267–68; and land reform, 36–38; as member of Continental Congress, 34; as member of House of Delegates, 36–40; and minimal government, 4–5, 16, 18; as minister to France, 103; on monarchy, 18, 104, 145–46; as natural aristocrat, 14; and Nootka Sound Crisis, 186–88, 198–202; *Notes on the State of Virginia,* 21–22, 39; optimism of, 21; Paine, comparison with, 1–2, 4–5, 8, 13–23, 43, 145, 187–88, 204, 252–53, 266–67, 277; Paine, relationship with, 4, 22, 88–89, 210, 221, 229, 244–45, 246–48; and party struggles, 96, 109–10; and political economy, 188; as politician, 22; portrait of, 233–36, *234;* and portrait of Paine, 8–9, *230,* 231–39, *234, 238, 241, 247,* 247–48; as president, 1, 22, 209; radicalism of, 4–5, 14, 22, 40–41, 272–73; on reform of education, 39–40; on religious establishment, 38–39; religious views of, 21–22, 277; as republican, 14, 17–20, 89; and republicanism, 27, 36–40, 42–43, 188, 266, 272; reputation of, contemporary and modern, 71–90; and slavery, 22, 41, 284; *The Summary View of the Rights of British America,* 34; and trust in common people, 5, 14–15, 187; and ward republicanism, 9, 252, 267, 271–73, 291
Jefferson memorial, 23
Johnson, Samuel, 216
Jones, Gareth Stedman, 292

305

INDEX

Jones, John Paul, 127, 231
Journal de la Société de 1789, 127

Kant, Immanuel, 50, 201
Kates, Gary, 114n7, 125, 150–51, 160n53, 210, 212
Kaye, Harvey, 50, 292
Keane, John, 50, 217, 282
King George's Sound Company, 191, 200
King, James, 190
Kiöbenhavnske Lærde Efterretninger (1720–1810), 164
Kosciuszko, Thaddeus, 248
Kramnick, Isaac, 50

labor unions, 54
Lafayette, Marie-Joseph Gilbert du Motier, marquis de, 20, 141, 148; in America, 63; and Jefferson, 104; letter to Washington, 150; and Paine, 7, 41, 130–31, 139, 150–51, 155n6, 194, 196, 240
Laird, Robert, 74
Lambert, Mary, 27
Lanthenas, François, 130
Larkin, Edward, 51
Laurens, Henry, 236–37, 239–40, 285
Laurens, John, 62, 123, 139, 285
Le Breton, André François, 163
Lee, Charles, 234
Lee, Richard Henry, 35
Le Roy, Jean-Baptiste, 124
Letter Addressed to the Addressers (Paine), 148
Letter to the Abbé Raynal (Paine), 5–6, 51, 57–58, 61, 123
Letters to the Citizens of the United States (Paine), 217–19
Le Veillard, Louis-Guillaume, 124
Lewis and Clark Expedition, 200
Lincoln, Benjamin, 19
literary reviews: as historical sources, 173–75; of Paine's works, 175–78
Locke, John: and natural rights, 258–59; and Paine, 253, 257, 261–64; on property, 260–65; radicalization of his ideas by Jefferson and Paine, 273; *Second Treatise of Government,* 264; and welfare rights, 264
London Corresponding Society, 285; influence on Paine, 151
Loughran, Trish, 287–90

Louis XVI, 252; and flight to Varennes, 212; Jefferson on, 20, 105; and Society of the Cincinnati, 126; trial of, 3, 20, 165, 215
Louisiana Purchase: Jefferson and, 267; Paine proposing, 219
Lynch, James V., 213, 220, 286, 290

Macleod, Emma, 8
MacNeven, William James, 211
Madison, James, 141; and Federalist Papers, 149; and Jefferson, 42, 144–45, 230, 266–67; and Paine, 278; and religious freedom, 39; and sunset laws, 269, 271; toasts to, 74; and Virginia and Kentucky Resolutions, 110
Making of the English Working Class, The (Thompson), 283
Malesherbes, Chretien-Guillaume de, 125
Malone, Dumas, 35
mammals, impact on modern world, 185
Manila Galleon trade, 190
Marat, Jean-Paul, 165–68
maritime compact, Paine's plans for, 216, 220
Marx, Karl, 268
Marxism, 14
Matthews, Richard, 268
Mason, George, 35
Mattes, Armin, 6, 284, 287
Mayhew, Jonathan, 17
Mazzei, Philip, 141
McLean, Ian, 144
Meares, John, 191–92
Methodists, 38
millennialism, religious, 28
Minerva, 177
Mirabeau, Honoré Gabriel Riqueti, comte de, 126–27, 141; *Considerations sur l'Ordre de Cincinnatus,* 127, 130
Miranda, Francisco de, 192
Mitchill, Samuel, 245
Model of a Letter of Recommendation of a Person You are Unacquainted With (Franklin), 122
monarchy: and early modern state-building, 18–20; as promoting war, 18–20. *See also under* Jefferson, Thomas; Paine, Thomas
Moniteur, 169
Monroe, James, 214, 243, 265

INDEX

Montagnards, 166
Montagu, John, Earl of Sandwich, 189
Montesquieu, Charles-Louis de Secondat, Baron de La Brède et de, 175
moral sense, Jefferson and Paine on, 14–16
Morellet, André, 124, 126–27, 128–29
Morris, Gouverneur, 77, 167, 192, 194; and correspondence with Jefferson, 199
Morris, Robert, 63, 285–87
Mowachaht, 189, 190
Munck, Thomas, 7–8
Munthe af Morgenstierne, Caspar Wilhelm von, 178

Napoleon, 213, 219
Napoleonic Wars, 220
National Emergency Civil Liberties Committee (NECLC), 2
natural rights: and civil rights, 259; Jefferson on, 270; Paine on, 140–41, 257–60
Nelson, Craig, 50
Newman, Simon, 6, 280
New Model Army, 65n6, 281
New York American Citizen, 221
New York Gazette, 219
New York Journal, 72
Nootka affair. *See* Nootka Sound Crisis
Nootka Sound, 189–90; and British presence, 190–92; and trade for pelts, 189
Nootka Sound Crisis, 8, 186, 291; and British strategy, 191–93; and Spanish claims, 191; and statecraft of Jefferson and Paine, 187
Normanism, 65n6
North, Lord, 34
Northwest Passage, 189, 200–201
Notes on the State of Virginia (Jefferson), 21–22, 39

Obama, Barack, 72
O'Brien, Conor Cruise, 159n47
Observations on Government, Including Some Animadversions on Mr. Adams's Defence of the Constitutions of Government of the United States of America: and on Mr. De Lolme's Constitution of England (Stevens), 141
Oldys, Francis. *See* Chalmers, George
Ollive, Elizabeth, 28
Ollive, Samuel, 28
Onuf, Peter, 188, 201, 217

Page, Anthony, 220
Paine, Thomas: and abolitionism, 213, 220, 285–86; and America as asylum and model for the world, 139, 213, 215–16; as American founder, 23; and American independence, promotion of, 29–31, 55–57; and American progressive tradition, 287–87; on American union, 60, 64; as America's first public intellectual, 22; and aspirations for America, 210–14; background of, 3–4, 13–14, 27–28, 52–55; and British Whigs, 140; and Burke, friendship with, 193, 236, 285; *The Case of the Officers of Excise*, 28, 53–55; constitutional thought of, 30–34, 140–43; death of, 1, 3–4, 23, 71; *The Decline and Fall of the English System of Finance*, 3, 171, 178; and democracy, 9–10, 95–103, 138, 147–49, 277, 290–91; *Dissertation on First Principles of Government*, 148, 212–13; *Dissertations on Government; the Affairs of the Bank; and Paper Money*, 142–43, 149–51; and equality, 4–5, 15–16, 98–103, 129–30, 212, 253–54, 259, 263, 280–84, 286; and federal constitution, 41; *The Forester's Letters*, 58; in France, 6–7, 123, 129–32, 164–65, 287; and Franklin, 6–7, 55, 121–32, 282; in French National Convention, 3, 20, 164–69, 252; and French Revolution, 3, 9, 20, 100–103, 145–46, 179, 212, 219, 252–53; and generational sovereignty, 144, 258–59, 263, 265–66; historiography on, 1–3, 49–51, 97–98, 125, 281–84, 287–90; and hope for revolutions in Europe, 7, 58–60, 62, 214, 258; and human nature, positive view of, 4–5, 14–16, 187; as icon for Republican Party, 6, 73–76; imperial vision of, 188–89, 196–97, 202, 213; and imprisonment in France, 3, 167–69, 210, 217, 244; on inequality and privilege, 23, 33–34, 131; as international revolutionary, 6, 22–23, 58–60, 90, 186; and Jefferson, comparison with, 1–2, 4, 8–10, 13–23, 43, 145, 179–80, 187–88, 204, 252–53, 266–67, 277–78; and Jeffersonian America, 8, 219–23; *Letter Addressed to the Addressers*, 148; *Letters to the Citizens of the United States*, 217–19; *Letter to the Abbé Raynal*, 5–6, 51, 57–58, 61, 123; and minimal

307

INDEX

Thomas Paine (*continued*)
  government, 16, 18, 253; on monarchy, 18–20, 29–30, 55–57, 69n60, 99, 145–46, 150, 283; and natural rights, 140–41, 253–56, 257–60, 291; and Nootka Sound Crisis, 186–88, 193–96; and Elizabeth Ollive (wife), separation from, 28, 139; optimistic nature of, 21, 221; on party politics, 216, 222; and Pennsylvania constitution of 1776, 32–34; and plan for a history of the American Revolution, 5–6, 60–61; and political economy, 187, 196–98, 292; and political thought, 7, 143–45, 148–54, 211–14, 253–66; and political writings, 28–29, *174;* as propagandist, 4, 32–33, 43, 139, 209–10; on property, 260–66; *Prospects on the Rubicon*, 140; and Providence, 56–57; radicalism of, 4–5, 14, 49, 52–55, 57–60, 151–52, 221, 282–83; religious views of, 21–22, 67n33, 215–16, 282; as representing core ideas of American and French Revolution, 73–76; as republican, 14, 17–19; and republicanism, 5–6, 27, 43, 194, 212–13, 263; *A Republican Manifesto,* 69n73; reputation of, contemporary, 6, 71–90, 217, 231, 239–40, 279–80, 292–93; reputation of, modern, 2, 9, 71–72, 203–4, 277–79; *A Serious Address to the People of Pennsylvania on the Present Situation of Their Affairs*, 33–34, 212; on society and government, 4–5, 16–18, 253–56; statecraft of, 8, 187, 197, 204, 216; "To the Authors of 'Le Républicain,'" 150; *To the People of England on the Invasion of England,* 222; and unicameralism, 5, 142, 215, 218–19, 281; and universal manhood suffrage, 151, 212, 218, 221; and universal peace, 19–20, 197, 213; and welfare rights, 9, 23, 252–54, 256–66. See also *Age of Reason, The; Agrarian Justice; American Crisis, The; Common Sense; Rights of Man, The*
Paine Anti-Defamation League, 286
Palmer, Robert R., *The Age of the Democratic Revolution,* 97–98
Parlements (France), 104
Parliament, British, 53–55, 61, 258; Franklin on, 129
Parton, James, 286
patronage, in monarchies, 17, 20

Peale, Charles Willson, 231; and portrait of Paine, 236–40, *238,* 243
Peale Museum, 236
Pennsylvania constitution (1776), 43, 79, 100, 280, 291; radicalism of, 31–34, 281
Pennsylvania Emancipation Act (1780), 213
Pennsylvania legislature, 202
Pennsylvania Magazine, 3, 29, 55
Pennsylvania Packet, 33
Perronet, Jean-Rodolphe, 125
Perry, James, 158n32
Philadelphia, social ferment in, 28
Philp, Mark, 7, 50, 125, 210, 214, 216, 284, 287
Piattoli, Scipione (Abbé Piattoli), 141
Pitt, William, 143, 186; as counter-revolutionary, 194; and Nootka Sound Crisis, 192, 198
Plan for Perpetual Peace (Rousseau), 58
Plumer, William, 245
Pocock, John, 51
popular sovereignty, 141; Jefferson on, 145, 148; Paine and, 145, 152, 211–12, 218, 280, 290–91
Presbyterians, 38
Price, Richard, 127, 137, 152, 220; *Discourse on the Love of Our Country,* 137
Priestley, Joseph, 220
print culture, in Enlightenment, 163–64
primogeniture: Jefferson against, 37–38; Paine against, 128
Prospects on the Rubicon (Paine), 140
Protestantism, in America, 81
Protestant Reformation, 56
Proudhon, Pierre-Joseph, 262
Providence, religious and republican, 56–57
Pufendorf, Samuel von, 262

Quakers, 31, 177
Quasi War, 76, 110

radicals, transatlantic, 8; and experience in America, 210–11, 215–16
Randolphs (Virginian family), 13
Randolph, Jane (mother of Thomas Jefferson), 34
Raynal, Guillaume Thomas François (Abbé Raynal), 5–6, 61–62; *Révolution d'Amérique,* 61

INDEX

Reading Nation in the Romantic Period, The (St. Clair), 170
Reagan, Ronald, 2, 72
Reflections on the Revolution in France (Burke), 3, 101, 140; as critique of egalitarianism, 285; and impact on British policy, 192
Reform Club (London), 1
religious toleration: Paine on, 213, 215–16. *See also* Paine, Thomas: religious views of
Report on Manufactures (Hamilton), 108
Report on the Public Credit (Hamilton), 108
representative government, Paine on, 149–50, 211–13
Republic, French, 76, 110
republican government: Jefferson's and Paine's conception of, 26–27
republicanism, 27, 186–87; as danger to Spanish crown, 190; revolutionary, 8. *See also under* Jefferson, Thomas; Paine, Thomas
Republican Manifesto, A (Paine), 69n73
Republican Party, 72–73; and Adams, 73, 84; and American and French Revolutions, 75; creation by Jefferson, 109–10; and Federalists, 110–12, 217–18; and Independence Day festivities, 80–86, 89–90; and Jefferson, 77, 81–86, 89–90; and Paine, 6, 73–79, 81–84, 89–90; Paine as supporter of, 220; and Washington, 73
Republicans (Jeffersonian). *See* Republican Party
Republican Society (Paris), 69n73, 165
republican synthesis, 2
republic of letters, Paine and, 231
republics, 27; and demands on citizenry, 17–18; and democracy, 57–58; and peace-loving diplomacy, 19–20; and virtue, 5
Révolution d'Amérique (Raynal), 61
revolution of 1800. *See* election of 1800
revolutions, American and French: historiography on, 138–39
Richardson, Jonathan, *Essay on the Theory of Painting*, 231
Rights of Man, The (Paine): and America as model for the world, 209; and American progressives, 279; British government reaction to, 170–71; and Burke's *Reflections*, 3; circulation of, 170; continental European reception of, 7–8, 173, *174;* dedication to Washington, 215; Dutch reviews of, 175–77; endorsed by Jefferson, 242; Federalists' view on, 79–80; French reception of, 171–72; German reviews of, 177–78; and natural rights, 255–60; and relation to *Common Sense*, 49–51; and Republican Party, 75–76; and welfare rights, 23, 256–57
rights of man, 14, 82; Paine on, 211–13
Rittenhouse, David, 55
Robert H. Smith International Center for Jefferson Studies, 1
Robespierre, Maximilien, 70n73, 166, 167, 168
Rochefoucauld, François Alexandre Frédéric, duc de la, 124, 131, 141
Roederer, Pierre Louis, 141
Roman Catholicism, 56
Romney, George, and portrait of Paine, 240–42, *241*
Roosevelt, Franklin, 72
Rosenfeld, Sophia, 2, 287–88, 289–91; *Common Sense: A Political History,* 2
Rousseau, Jean-Jacques, 50, 58, 201; influence on French revolutionary politics, 167; and Paine, 254; *Plan for Perpetual Peace,* 58
Royal Academy of Sciences (Paris), 64, 123
Royal Navy, 3, 195, 197, 198
Royal Society of London, 64, 122, 123, 236
Rumford, Count, 248
Rutledge, John, 198
Rush, Benjamin, 52, 57–58; asking Paine to prepare *Common Sense,* 29, 55

Sadosky, Leonard, 217
Saint-Just, Louis Antoine Léon de, 166
Salmagundi, 245
Sampson, William, 211
Sandwich, Lord. *See* Montagu, John, Earl of Sandwich
Santo Domingo, slave rebellion, 213
Saturn (Roman god), 55
Scott, George Lewis, 122
scripture, Paine's use of, 56
sea otter, 185–86; pelts of, 189
Second Treatise of Government (Locke), 264
Sedition Act (1798). *See* Alien and Sedition Acts

INDEX

sensationalism, Lockean, 15
sensibility, humanitarian, 15
Serious Address to the People of Pennsylvania on the Present Situation of Their Affairs, A (Paine), 33–34, 212
Seven Year's War, 27
Shaftesbury, Lord, 17
Sharp, William, 240–42
Short, William, and correspondence with Paine, 193–96
Sieyès, Emmanuel Joseph, 141, 148; and constituent power, 143; and Paine on forms of government, 150, 165, 175
Sizer, Theodore, 229, 248
Sloan, Herbert, 269
Smith, Adam, 17, 50, 144, 175, 268; and democracy, 147; Paine and, 187, 198; *Wealth of Nations*, 144
Smith, William (pseud. Cato), 58
socialism, 268
Société de 1789, 129
Society for Constitutional Information, 285; influence on Paine, 151
Society for Political Enquiries, Paine and Franklin as founders of, 123
Society of Twelve, 53
society: science of, 16–17; Paine on, 255–56
South America: Paine foreseeing independence of, 52
sovereignty of the people. *See* popular sovereignty
Staël-Holstein, Anne-Louise-Germaine de, 50
state of nature, 140; Locke and, 254, 262; Paine and, 254–55, 262
St. Clair, William, *The Reading Nation in the Romantic Period, The*, 170
Stevens, John, 141–44, 148; and mixed government, 141–43; *Observations on Government*, 141
Student Nonviolent Coordinating Committee, 2
Summary View of the Rights of British America, The (Jefferson), 34

Talleyrand-Périgord, Charles Maurice de, 141
Tammany Society (New York), 75, 83
taxation, progressive, 23; Paine and, 253, 267–68, 279

Tea Party, and Paine, 278
Thermidor, 168, 169
Thompson, Benjamin, Count Rumford, 248
Thompson, E. P., 283–84; *The Making of the English Working Class*, 283
Thoreau, Henry David, 253
Thornton, Edward, 243
Terror (France), 138, 168, 172; Paine during, 210
toasts: change in nature, 83–84; as expressions of political opinions, 72–73; to Jefferson, 78–79, 81–82; to Madison, 74; to Paine, 73–77; to Washington, 73–76
Tocqueville, Alexis de, 103; *Democracy in America*, 103
Tom Paine Award, 2
totalitarianism, 137
"To the Authors of 'Le Républicain'" (Paine), 150
To the People of England on the Invasion of England (Paine), 222
Trumbull, John: *Autobiography*, 244; and painting of Declaration of Independence, 232–35; and portrait of Jefferson, *235*; and portrait of Paine, 229–48, *230, 234, 235*
Turgot, Anne-Robert-Jacques, Baron de Laune, 141

United States: and American nationhood, 112–13; and conceptual change, 106; and democracy, 55, 85; and Europe, 59, 222; and independence, 59; and Nootka Sound Crisis, 185–86; Paine's opinion on, 210–11, 217; and relation with France, 76, 77; and Spanish Empire, 190–91; and Western hinterland, 8
unicameralism, 5, 140–42, 219
universal peace, 20, 209, 257
University of Pennsylvania, 58

Vaderlandsche Letter-Oefeningen, 176–77
Valmy, Battle of (1792), 75
Varennes, flight to, 212; and Paine, 146
Vaughan, Benjamin, 127
Vergennes, Charles Gravier, comte de, 141
Verri, Pietro, 50
Vincent, Bernard, 50
Virginia and Kentucky Resolutions, 110, 111
virtue: ancient vs. modern, 16; Jefferson on,

INDEX

5; Paine on, 5, 211, 255–56; revolutionary, 76; worthies and, 230–31
Voltaire (François-Marie Arouet), 50, 175

Watson, James, 237
Washington, George, 16; and Crisis papers, 59; and Nootka Sound Crisis, 199–200; and Paine, 63, 278; Paine's attack on, 22, 77, 81, 214–16, 233; portrait of, 231, 237–38; toasts to, 73–76
ward republicanism. *See under* Jefferson, Thomas
War for Independence, American, 74, 80
Wayles Skelton, Martha. *See* Jefferson, Martha
Wealth of Nations (Smith), 144
welfare state, 252–54, 273
Whatmore, Richard, 125
Whitney, Eli, 245
William and Mary, College of, 34

William of Orange, 144
Wilson, Gaye, 8–9, 285
Wilson, James, 285; on federal constitution, 140, 142
Wood, Gordon, 4–5, 50, 204, 279, 292
worthies, 448, 457–58, 479n4. *See also under* Jefferson, Thomas
Wraxall, Nathaniel William, 241–42
Wright, Joseph, 231
Wythe, George, 34, 35, 37; and correspondence with Jefferson, 146

Yale University Art Gallery, 229
Yorke, Henry Redhead, 219

XYZ affair, 76

Ziesche, Philipp, 6–7, 282, 284, 287
Zuckert, Michael, 9, 287, 291